Building a Life

By Leo Lindsay

Mon métier et mon art, c'est vivre
(My trade and my art is living)

- Michel de Montaigne

Dedicated to the loving memory of

William 'Bill' Young - master bricklayer, teacher and mentor
John P Curr - dear friend who sadly didnt live to see his plans built

ACKNOWLEDGEMENTS

First and foremost a special mention to my four wonderful children: Mark, Liz, Leo junior and Jack for being, well, my kids. and to their mother Jackie for raising them so well.

A tribute to both my wifes Jackie and Rosie for putting up with me for nearly 35 years. Also for their patient help with this book over time.

Many thanks also to Karin, Carole, Christina, Gloria, Neil and Chris.

Gary Cox – who died prematurely while helping this to be published.

Immense gratitude to my son Jack whose many finishing touches and immeasurable patience have been vital to the creation of this book.

Last but not least to Leo junior, whose inspiration has been of paramount importance in the editing of this tome. His literary nouse has its footprint on every page.

To all those souls mentioned in this book who could not look after themselves and were glad to see my mug appear; to those that were not – tough.

My thanks to everyone portrayed within this book - without you I wouldn't have been able to recount as many of these experiences.

All apsects of this collection overlap again and again; where I have not explained something in more detail I will have done so elsewhere in this book. I have used clips and articles from newspapers and magazines dated back nearly 40 years to illustrate various points.

Where an opinion is expressed it will be mine unless otherwise stated.

PREFACE

Below is an article published in 'Time Out' on January 27th 1988. Upon reading this piece of doggerel I committed myself to writing an impassioned response; here, thirty years later, is the product. Part one deals with the manifold refutation of the articles' content. Parts Two and Three elaborate on my personal experiences as a builder of fifty years.

SELLOUT

CONTENTS

108-109 FABRICS
Material world: we investigate the best shops.

109 BUYLINES Best sales and bargains in town.

110 TRAVEL
Slope off to the better resorts: snow news but good advice.

113-114 FOOD
London's trendiest new restaurants; where men's fashion designer Paul Smith eats.

EDITED BY JOANNE GLASBEY

CONSUMING VIEWS

QUICK ON THE DRAWER

The most ubiquitous symbol of the new London is The Skip. This ugly cast-iron trapezoid box is deposited by builders outside a house that is being 'done up'. Refurbished, as they call it in the trade. Gentrified, as social observers say. Into the skip goes all the detritus of the Victorian builder's trade — like old lath and plaster — plus more recent additions which the gentrifiers find detracts from authenticity. Out go the frosted glass doors, the polystyrene ceiling tiles. In come the new doors, panelled rather than flush; in come the old fireplaces, the replaced cornices and ceiling roses.

If your home possesses these 'period features' take care: the old fireplaces are worth a grate deal. It's been known for them accidently to fall off the wall. They don't get put in the skip, though. Your marble, your cast-iron original ends up in one of the burgeoning architectural salvage centres and bankrolls will have changed hands. Beware the hit and run builder. No jobs are too large for him to contemplate, and even the small will telescope into large.

It always starts off with a sharp intake of breath. This takes place simultaneously with a movement of the head to one side and a pursing of the lips. It is followed by the statement: 'Nasty, that' and ends, some time later, with an unpleasant letter from the bank. All of this is preceded by the galloping of hooves down your road and the sound of spurs jangling on the doorstep. I don't know when cowboys developed a pejorative connotation. (The emphasis there is on the *con*.) These days the word is intimately associated with the more 'flexible' end of the building trade. In the films, there was John Wayne and there was a man who was kind to women, tough to men; fearing neither man nor beast but only God and his next of kin; true to his word and fast with his gun. The high priest of a morality play where the greater good outdraws a deeper evil and rides off into the sunset bloodied but unvanquished. Up on the screen he wears a sweat-stained brown stetson, double-breasted blue flannel shirt and tan leather vest.

In your home, the cowboy resembles nothing as identifiable, except perhaps in the clothes. From horse rustling to hustling, where the covered wagon and horse has been replaced by a two-year-old Merc and the holster by a bulging wallet. Is that a gun in your pocket or have you just been paid for a previous job? And, to pinch another Mae Westism, if you ask a builder to come up and see you sometime, they'll be there quick as a flashing to give an estimate, but actually doing the work and completing it in the time they calculated is a wholly different saloon-room brawl. Ah,

yes, The Estimate. That figure, plucked from the air, with a bit added on and, by the way, excluding VAT. That figure, which has more curves on it than Rosalind Russell. Am I unfair? Why is it inevitably the case that when the invoice arrives, the estimate has been unwholesomely enlarged?

Of course, ask for an explanation and you'll get ready responses. That's because when we took up the floor boards we found . . . found what? A couple of corpses you had to bury expensively? That's because that crack we thought we could just plaster over turned out to be . . . the San Andreas fault? If you knew what was happening you would probably have been able to do the work yourself. In the land of the incompetent, the builder is dictator. And chancellor of the exchequer.

Botch. That's a jolly, onomatopoeic sort of word. And, strangely enough, with no cowboy symbolism. If Mr Botch were a person he'd have an ugly pock-marked skin, one eye larger than the other, be deaf in one ear with tinnitus in the other and hop around with the right leg shorter than the left. Why spend an extra half hour bending pipes so they follow the line of the skirting when you can just run them straight across the wall? If the customer moans, then explain we couldn't do that *because* . . .

It's basically a war of attrition. High noon. And the builders are packing all the pistols. You have little recourse, small sanction to impose, save the final payment. If you are truculent and insist on getting your way, then they'll either charge you even further over the odds for redoing the work *they* messed up in the first place or refuse to carry on, leaving you with no water, no electricity and half a floor.

For the DIY-illiterate like myself, at one with the James Thurber character who would always put plugs back in sockets for fear electricity would leak out, and for whom it takes a good half hour to put a plug on the end of something (well, at least I can do *that*), getting jobs done around the house is a slow business. Which reminds me. Guy, *my* builder (the Lone Stranger), a man of admirable energy, dexterity and a stupendous line in excuses who looks nothing like John Wayne, has been about to pay me a call for three months. Guy: you remember me pointing out that the outer wall you had so carefully damp-proofed was turning slightly green? Well, it now resembles something which has slunk off the Christmas Stilton, set up home in my wall and asked all its relatives to come and be paying guests. I think I caught it making overseas phone calls the other evening.

Hi ho Silver . . . actually, I think brass would look better, but you're the boss. And before you gallop off into the sunset, pardner . . .

The covered wagon and horse has been replaced by a two-year-old Merc and the holster by a bulging wallet. Is that a gun in your pocket or have you just been paid for a previous job?

CONTENTS

PART ONE   The Job, Memorable Sites   8

How to Find a Builder...8
The Trades 16
To Use an Architect...19
What Goes on in a Clients' Mind...22
Buying a House...23
Chimneys 29
Dampness 31
Double Glazing 32
Bricks 34
Skips 36
Using a Ladder 36
Estimating 37
Plasterer's Price...40
Not Turning up / on Time...41
Time Wasters 41
Excuses 43
Slow Progress 43
Misunderstandings...46
Getting Ripped off...49
Getting Paid on Time...51
Customers Changing...54
Extras 56
Something for Nothing...57
Archetects and Sureyors...59
Trade Organisations...67
National Federation Checklist...68
Journalists 75
Articles about Builders...78
Heroes 79
Solicitors 82
TV programmes...85
House of Horrors...86
DIY TV 87
Project Manager...92
TV Celebs 92
Insurance Companies...94
Property Developers...97
Twin Towers 98
Memorable Sites
Burnham Beeches...101
The Hautboy 101
Askgill House 103
The Barn 104
Chertsey Bog 107
Hampton Court...108
Inspired to Stitch...109
Byfleet 110
Stockbroker Belt...111
Epsom Racecourse...112
Lunchtime Exploits...112

PART TWO   Not Amusing, Sad and Funny   113

Health and Safety...113
Muddy Footings...116
Spirits 119
Near Death Experiences..119
Neighbours in Court 120
Rumpole and the Little One..121
Girl on a Bike 124
Domestic 125
Four Courses 125
Gas Men 126
Knocked Silly 127
Hurricane '87 127
Susie 128
Tables and Chairs..129
Bemoaning Babs..129
Walnut Tree 131
Car Thieves 132
Iranian Doctors 132

Sad
Vigilante Justice..133
Basement Murder...135
Dead Man in Arms...136
Bloody Mess 137
Zebra Crossing 139
Train Seats 140

Funny
Underwear 140
Sykie 141
Mick the Builder...142
Talk of the Town..146
Jack Maguire 147
Mick the Labourer..148
First and Worst Winter..149
Pants Down Chaps Out...151
Herman the German 151
Snippets on the Buildings...152
A Farce 156
Another Week 157
Short Asides 159
Bank Robbers 161
Phone Counsel 162
Pikeys 163
Signs 165
Old Building Terms...167
Houses of Parliament...167
Hard Man 167
Fire Doors 167
Barking Dog 168
Bus Stop Eavesdrop...168
Pisshead 169
Builders Bum 169

Knees and Ankles..171
Stubborn Me 174
The Lump 176
Brown Paperbag..176
Radio One 176
Building Changes..177
Dumping 180
Fly on the Wall 181
Character Traits..181
Clubs 182
Libraries 183
Inventions 183
The Batsman© 184
Ambitions 188
Charities 188
Knighthoods 189
Coal 190
As a Young Boy...190
Events at College...198
Rags to Renaissance..199
Poetry 202
Work at Home 204
John Beech 207
Brickwork Course...208
Guest Speaking..211
Floodbag 213
Mixers and Shovels..213
Modern Day 215
Self-Employment..215
A Main Burst 216
Agility 217
My Mini Cooper..218
Southall Centenary...219
Holidays 219
Blind Man 221
Space 221
Coincidences 227
My Heroes 228
Bill Young 230
Rodders 235
Unlikely Defence..238
Family 242
Mother 245
Le Chateau 246
Shocking 248
A Troublesome Loaf...248
Wasps and a Dead Cat...249
Black Face 249
Working Class 250
Fainting Jack 252
Colin and Porky...252
Uncle Tim 254

Brother In-Law John.. 256
Liz 258
Leo Junior 259
Public Schoolboy Brian..260
Mrs Priest 261
Little Helen 262
Youth of Today 263
Youth Football 264
The Wilderness 265
Old People 267
Southwood 268
Uprooted Trees 279
Problem Solving...280
The Beast 285
Sporting achievements 287
Tomato Stopped Play 288
The Sixties 289
The Modern World..294
New Beginnings..295
Epilogue 298
Weapons of Mass Deception 301

PART ONE

May I start with a question? Very well then.

Which is the heavier: a house, a blue whale, or a jumbo jet?
(You will find the answer in the section on Estimating.)

How to Find a Good Builder

In years gone by the building trade in London drew much of its talent from Parkhurst, Wandsworth and the Scrubs of Wormwood. In and around the infamous prisons that these names elicit became for generations the arbitrary breeding ground for the group of young men I was to almost become a part of. Where a portion became criminals, others become builders. Comparatively, today's tradesmen are just as likely to be educated at grammar school, where the learning process must be, one can suppose, a good deal less problematical. That is not to say that all inmates are uneducated (though this is probably quite true for first offenders), just that years ago the building fraternity was inextricably linked to uneducated felons. One reason for this might be that many prisons have a brickwork and woodwork shop in house. I have known many a bricklayer and chippie that have learnt their trade in the clink and are now making their living as builders. Nobody of moderate awareness should be surprised to find that very experienced men of the building world are often poorly educated men in the real world. Despite the comparable changes in the industry of recent years, one must still remember to tread carefully!

We may consider further the links between felons and builders. To practise the trade initially one needs no qualifications or experience; indeed at its lowest level – the labourer, most accessible to any fit young men (perhaps with little else to do?) – All that is required is strength and grunt. No surprise then why this social/professional links continues to this day.

We in England are all aware that builders have a terrible reputation for wrong- doing. Half the muggers and miscreants in the country are likely to have been builders at some point in their regrettable life. It comes to something when the two most famous builders of our modern world are Bob the Builder and Fred West! Hopefully the following information will help you to weed out the good ones from the bad.

At this early point it would be prudent not to set your expectations too high, for reliability is more often sought than perfection, and common sense equally so when sat next to rejection. Think very carefully about the sort of job you have to offer a builder. Herein I will try to categorise your requirements. Of course it goes without saying that to find the right man for the right job is easier said than done. You would not ask your butcher to lay your drains, or your milkman to build a new extension, but the difference can be much the same as say, asking a roofer to make fitted wardrobes or a glazier to plaster a ceiling.

There are numerous ways of contacting a potentially suitable builder: advertisements in the newspapers, magazines, yellow pages and, most commonly, through personal recommendations. One sure way of getting a good tradesman is to visit the building control office at your local Civic Centre, locate the building inspector for your area, and make an appointment to see him. Ask him to recommend a local builder, explain briefly what the job entails and, if he is a fairly accommodating fellow, he will match up as best he can with his knowledge of local builders. If one thinks clearly about it, the building inspector not only controls what the builders can and cannot do; he is primarily responsible for looking after your interests. If the building inspector won't commit himself directly, try presenting him with a list of local builders gathered from yellow pages, newspapers etc. Read him the list and watch his reaction to each one. Though not at all fool-proof, it does help narrow the field of people professing to practise this trade.

While on this course, one word of warning: the building inspector is not supposed to recommend anyone, but if you tell him that you have had a devil of a time trying to find a decent builder, it would only be a real 'jobsworth' who'd omit to help. Of course there has never been a shortage of these regrettable specimens within such buildings. If you have had the misfortune to be allotted one of these, don't forget that he is a public servant and it is the likes of you and I who pay his wages. It is he who sets the standard (or should do) that the builders have to abide by. The building inspector will not come straight out with a name because County Councils will not put themselves in a position to be responsible should anything untoward happen. Such is the absence of space in which they are left, by their nature, to manoeuvre.

Estate Agents can be another source for contacting a builder, although I once asked an Estate Agent if he could recommend an electrician. He said: "Sure, but I want a bung." It seems everything has a price these days.

Walk down any road where you live and I am sure you will find skips, scaffolding and other builder's materials outside houses. This is where you need to be vigilant and nosy. Do not expect a builder to be highly praised, because building work is prone to problems and people will always remember things that went wrong. Remember you are not looking for a perfect builder just a reasonably competent one. I think it is fair to say that most people work better if they are appreciated, and that includes builders.

Knock on a few doors, apologise for the intrusion, ask everything about the builders; how many days a week do they work, how many hours a day, what time do that start, what time do they finish, do they make an unholy mess, do they clean up at the end of the day?

Providing the householders don't think you are the builder's wife checking up on him they will, I am quite sure, be happy to talk to you. They might grumble about the builder's skill or attitude, or both, as the case may be (and often is). If you hit the jackpot they may want to boast about their builder being the bee's knees. All this information is like money in the bank and is a worry off the mind; this comes later when the building begins.

D.I.Y. stores hire shops, and kitchen and bathroom outlets all see the regular traipsing of builders through their premises. I'm sure these proprietors will tell you who do and who does not pay their bills. If they won't divulge anything upfront, slip them a few names you've gathered and, as with the building inspector, watch their reactions to each name.

As someone who originally thought the Internet was something to do with fishing, I have since come across many sites offering to find a builder for you online. They often conclude that their site is an accredited way of approaching builders, and warned that though their quotes were pricy, the quality was guaranteed. To draw on the analogy that because bottled water is expensive it must be better than tap water, so does it then follow that an expensive quote is better than a cheaper one? I don't think so, guaranteed or not.

One other route you might wish to take is to ask the delivery drivers at a builder's merchants. He will make his way round to all local sites at various development stages and will know which builders are getting the job done. And he might, if you are lucky and not adverse to ingratiation, introduce you to one of them. In relative point fact, the offering of a pint for the privilege will probably be sufficient.

You could also decide to take the Yellow Pages route. I am sure most people would agree that by doing so you are merely trusting to potluck on who you talk to. Most people who phone a builder from yellow pages or Thompsons will almost certainly try to contact someone who lives as near to them as possible. This is partly because of convenience and partly because the logic of the general public will infer that if the contractor has not too far to come to work, his price will be cheaper. This is of course partly true, though not nearly the most important factor. You will also notice that some adverts only give a mobile number, but no name or address. In other words, you don't know where they come from or who they are, so positively steer clear of them!

One further point about Yellow Pages and Thompsons is that the builders section is easily the largest in the book, especially if you add on the roofing and plumbing sections, not to mention the bricklayers, carpenters, plasterers, painters, glaziers, etc. All this illustrates the enormous competition across the building trades.

Another problem creeping into the trade is illustrated in the following common scenario: Joe Bloggs, having taken his redundancy money from his factory job is sitting at home doing nothing. Mrs. Anybody from next door knocks at the door and asks Joe "I know you are not busy, can you come and paint my ceiling?" She pays him cash. She then asks, "Can you repair my fence?"

Joe thinks: "This is great! I'll become a builder!" He has some leaflets printed and he joins the ranks of the building fraternity.

Of course not everyone who puts fliers out, as I myself have done for many years, comes from this background. I have never felt that advertisements in newspapers worked well for me, although it obviously does for some. I have colleagues who insist they procure work solely on recommendations and never have to advertise at all. I do not entirely believe this, because if someone wants to recommend you they have to know someone else who is having some work done straight away. You would be a very lucky man indeed to fall into work one job after another! Besides, my experience tells me that people will not wait very long in searching to find the right man for their job. If they have the money, they want the job done now, not next month or next year.

Another method of making contact with a builder is through an architect or surveyor. This method is likely to be more expensive in the long run. If the work to be done is say, over £15,000, you would be well advised to appoint a professional, or a much older and experienced tradesman to oversee the work.

If you contact someone who purports to be a specific tradesman, ask if he works for a company or is self-employed. If he works for a company the chances are high that he is used to doing just the one trade. Whereas if he works for himself, he will have over the years learned to diversity and it is quite possible that he has become competent in more than one trade. If, on the other hand, you contact someone who calls himself a builder, ask him if he has any trade qualifications and if so, which ones. Should he not have any, ask him who will be carrying out the work and will they have any relevant qualifications; also ask who will be responsible for the job. In a professional age where qualifications are almost everything, a right-minded employer cannot ignore a person who has, as in my case, half a century of practical experience to call upon.

When perusing through advertisements, look carefully at the wording, which is likely to show the advertiser's core speciality.

For example:

DAVE JONES
PLASTERING AND RENOVATION SERVICES

All aspects of plastering and rendering, dry lining, coving, cornice work, interior decorating

Kitchens and Bathrooms fitted

All Renovation and General Maintenance carried out

Telephone.............................

In this particular example the advertisers are certainly plasterers first and foremost. This is not to say that they are unable to carry out other works. What they are suggesting involves many other trades, like brickwork and carpentry, plumbing, roofing, painting, electrics, plus fitting everything in between. It is clearly advisable to deal with a person who has mastered at least one competent trade. Very few tradesmen can be competent at all these listed activities – specialisation to a practising individual in this industry, as in most if not all other industries, is a natural progression – thus when one becomes an expert in one field (e.g. bricklaying) their competence in another field (e.g. joinery) will likely wane. This is why I recommend a brickwork OR carpentry background as a core trade; these two cover the greater depth of knowledge needed, probably because most structures are made predominantly of brick/blocks and timber.

In order to do your job – supposing your job requires a range of skills, as most jobs of any size do - these spreads would have to recruit many other competent workers with the resultant extra costs. Obviously if plasterwork was required this is just the right firm. If your roof is leaking, why call in a plasterer? I am sure they will give you a quote, but now you are paying for a roofer *plus* the unwanted plasterer. Even though he has organised the roofer's visit, you can see the more people that you are involved with the dearer the price must be. In such a situation you must also question who will ultimately take responsibility for the work.

It is quite common in the building trade to find what I call <u>organisers</u>. These are simply businessmen looking for work. They are often good talkers. There is nothing wrong with engaging someone like that, except you would be adding a third party to the equation and would not be talking directly to the person who will be building your extension, or fixing your roof etc. You may be happier to talk to only one person and hold him responsible for everything. Personally I feel that, if you can stand it, it is better to communicate with the tradesman directly. In addition, by employing such an organiser one unnecessarily complicates further the natural challenges of communication between two parties with their own separate interests.

It is quite common to hear on the radio and TV, to read in surveyors' and architects' books, or be told by an executive of a large building company that the best way to find a bona fide builder is to choose one who is affiliated to a <u>trade organisation</u>, such as The Guild of Master Craftsmen, or the Federation of Master Builders. This is not so. Anyone, tradesman or not, can join the thing by paying an annual subscription and, in some cases, answering a few questions which your average first year apprentice would not find difficult. I cannot fault their good intentions, but there is absolutely no guarantee that a builder with a trade motif is any better than one without.

Lead lines in a glossy pamphlet I acquired: *'Recommended, vetted, and monitored: local trades and services'*. These are consumer protection services supported by Tesco, the Royal Mail, West Sussex County Council and the Sussex Police and Trading Standards Council. My first question is this; who on earth is doing the vetting or monitoring? The small print on the back says, *'All our listed members have agreed to serve customers with respect and politeness, to pursue honesty and integrity at all times, giving the very best attention to service and workmanship in all aspects of trading'*. The smaller print only just visible, be that with the aid of something like a telescope from Kew Garden's Observatory, says: *'Vetted Limited cannot be held responsible or liable for the quality of workmanship or service of any of the listed trades and services'*. It is not coincidental that escape clauses are written in infinitely small writing, requiring telescopic vision mixed with a learned, legal and scholarly disposition.

(For the best (or worst) example of this kind of travesty typical in the modern world, check out the small print on an insurance policy.)

Clearly this leaflet is self-regulating with an almost invisible escape clause written in. When are builders or tradesmen themselves going to be invited to take part in and help process these trade registers? It would, of course, only work if the expert involved did not have a vested interest in the individual trade personnel – like retired workers with no axe to grind. Nevertheless, they'd be paid by the trade register and not by the builders or their customers.

Letter sent to me through the post by the so called 'The Guild of Master Craftsmen':

'Dear Mr. Lindsay,

Give your business a boost!

When trading conditions become difficult, it is surprising how many companies still continue to prosper. And most of them do so for the simplest of reasons. It's not just that they are competitive and provide quality workmanship and superior service. They are also recognised for being reliable and trustworthy. They have set themselves apart from the competition.

Whatever the size of your business, you could benefit from the help and support that The Guild of Master Craftsmen offers its members. The Guild provides a wide range of benefits to over 425 different categories of business, from those in the traditional building trades through to computer consultants. These benefits include:

- sound financial advice – expert legal opinion – professional marketing advice – competitive insurances – business consultancy – low cost credit card processing fees – savings on telephone costs – discounts on vehicle purchase

To the trade and public alike, the Guild's emblem symbolises skill, integrity and professionalism, and one of the most important reasons for joining the Guild is for the prestige it brings. In fact, membership could become one of your most important assets. To build such a strong corporate identity with a comparable reputation for quality would need considerable investment in both time and money.

At one time or another you may have wondered whether you could qualify for Guild membership. As you might expect, The Guild does have stringent entry requirements. But if you genuinely share The Guild's ideals, there is no good reason why your application should not be successful. That is why we are writing to you now.

If you would like to apply to join the many thousands of other Guild members, both large and small – including famous names such as Rolls Royce, Waterford Wedgwood, Harrods and Fortnum & Mason – you can find out more by completing and returning the enclosed prepaid card. We look forward to hearing from you.

Yours sincerely,

On behalf of The Council of Management
The Guild of Master Craftsmen'

In the first paragraph they are asking us all to believe that you will survive if you are competitive, have a quality and superior service, and are also reliable and trustworthy; in essence to set themselves apart from the competition.

What The Guild is in effect saying is that these traders have our principles, but have not yet joined. Why? Because, obviously, they are doing nicely without The Guild thank you very much. To the trade and public alike, The Guild's emblem symbolises skill, integrity and professionalism. Ah bon! Really? I have been a builder for over 50 years and I have never spoken to anyone about this organisation, anyone who knows anything about this organisation, and anyone who has joined this organisation; in short, anyone who cares about this organisation.

The letter goes on about its strong corporate identity, but what sort of trader, are they looking to recruit, that would want a corporate identity? - Obviously, the companies with the most money. What I mean to say is that it is clearly a moneymaking, profit driven organisation. The letter goes on: "You may have wondered whether you could qualify for membership?" Stringent entry requirements entail the same as the National House Builders Council – give us your money and you're in! These organisations target big companies. Tradesmen like me – those of a small scale mostly unambitious for growth beyond success and improvement – cannot and should not be doing with it. Plus, having to pay for the doubtful privilege is, well, rather pointless.

I once had occasion to apply to the National House Builders' Council when I was considering building some houses. They telephoned me and made an appointment to visit my house. During the meeting I was duly asked six general building questions, five of which my wife answered instantly! Having already paid my fee I was accepted straight away.

I am sure you've read such a phrase before: "Pre-approved trade professionals, vetted local professionals, a quality screening process." The idea that these collections of words actually mean anything in the real world is misplaced. In each case they all flounder on the same basis - who is the regulatory body? Who is the best person to judge whether a brain surgeon is competent or not? Obviously – another brain surgeon. And so it is with builders and most other areas of expertise.

I could pre-approve a builder. Could you? The said regulatory body in these cases is usually a businessman trying to set up a register of builders. Well-meaning perhaps, but set up, primarily, to make money out of us tradesmen. Who vets the Vetter? Who screens the screening process? Do these companies have an advisory builder? I know they do not. It is very easy to make a living in this game, particularly if you're a good talker and can bluff with a straight face. Alas, I am no good at either, and have had to call upon other skills to make my living. The National House Building Council, far from being a regulatory body, is in effect an insurance company with a near monopoly on new homes, funded by the very builders whose work they inspect.

Governments have tried to regulate the building trade in one way or another. For example, the cowboys' working party which was dreamt up by MP Nick Rainsford, much like the ill-fated 'Quality Mark I Scheme', are doomed to fail because no-one has taken the trouble to ask a real builder for his input. **Why?!**

The multi-faceted and vast social gap between an average MP and an average builder may shed light on the absence of dialogue between these professions in such a case where dialogue is required; perhaps the difference in formal education is one root of this divide, though I dare say in days of old – picture a rural English village - this gap was not so wide. Though only a self-employed builder of many years' experience could possibly comprehend the difficulties attached to a business that is interminably and intrinsically problematical – an understanding that is without doubt beyond the capabilities of an average MP.

When I was an apprentice, many moons ago, qualifications meant serving time rather than paperwork. Nowadays it is the other way round. We need technical colleges to allow lecturers to focus on teaching skilled trades, rather than taking students through the motions to pass exams. All well-meaning articles and booklets on finding a builder will say that you must find a qualified man. How can the public find a so-called qualified man when they are being led a merry dance by companies' claims that they only use qualified workmen? Let me take two examples: double-glazing companies and companies that lay driveways. Double-glazing companies will spout "only qualified tradesman work for us".

What tosh! Any competent labourer could pick up the idea in no time at all and there are no qualifications to cover glorified labourers fixing windows. It is a myth to suggest that qualified people lay driveways; once you understand the principle of block paving the rest is, if not intellectually infantile, then only a matter of brute strength and getting on with the job. Exaggerated claims are everywhere, but I can say for sure there is no qualification that exists for block layers, who are at best bricklayers or building labourers. Sometimes you will find 6 or 7 men working on a driveway, where probably only one of them knows what he is doing; the rest are labourers.

Another way of looking at this: I know of two men who work for the council laying kerb stones along the road. They are labourers, plain and simple, and yet the men think they are stonemasons! All for a measly wage and as many kerb stones as they can eat! Qualifications, do they really matter? The best way I can qualify a tradesman is that everyone makes mistakes, but having made one, a tradesman of professional integrity will have the nous to see where he has gone wrong, and have an idea of how to put it right.

The man who makes no mistakes does not usually make anything at all.
                                                                  - **Edward John Phelps**

The Trades Themselves

There are seven main trades in the building industry. These are carpentry, bricklaying, plastering, plumbing, electrics, roofing and decorating. I will try to give you a feel for each trade, in order of importance, in order to give some idea of what each tradesman should be capable of.

Carpentry

The 'chippies' job will almost certainly criss-cross all other trades inside the house. For instance, he will have knowledge of fixing lights and sockets, plumbing, layouts, decorating, wall and floor tiling. He will also work hand in hand with the bricklayer as the structure is erected. Obviously all wood related work is his domain. Until the 1970's nearly all site agents were ex-carpenters or bricklayers.

Bricklaying

Usually all structural work, like inserting RSJ's, plus windows and doorframes, and including brickwork and block work of all kinds, are the bricklayer's field of expertise. However, a competent bricklayer (brickie) should be able to tackle concreting (having probably done a lot of this during his apprenticeship), as well as drain laying, and pointing. Also plastering is not that far removed from a brickie's everyday work, so he will likely have picked up some knowledge of this along the way (together with a bad back and knees). All building inspectors before about 1960 were bricklayers or carpenters.

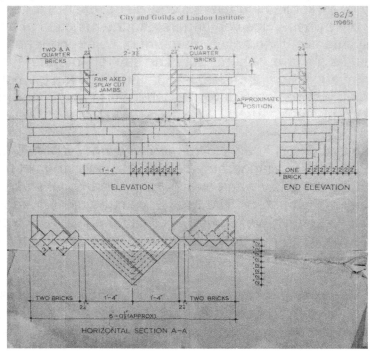

The above picture shows a City and Guilds practical exam circa 1965 if studied by an expert bricklayer, you would have to except the extreme difficulty on show here.

Electrics

Obviously it is very important to find a qualified man. 'Sparks' quite often do a small amount of plumbing because their work often overlaps, in the case of central heating for example.

Plumbing

Generally 'plums' are not so versatile in their talents, mainly because their work is not compatible with the other trades, any more than the tools of his trade are with others. However most plums have some knowledge of electrics since the work often runs in parallel, as noted above.

Roofing

Roofing is very much the sort of work that most competent tradesmen can tackle. The difference, of course, is whether you have a head for heights! And many of our species, builder or human, do not. Most roofers will only undertake to point a chimney stack because they would not stand up to close scrutiny – from the ground a rather bad job could look fine. I have never yet seen a roofer's pointing as good as that of a bricklayer's, for the obvious reason that for the latter pointing is his bread and butter, the thing he knows and does daily, whereas for the former it is an irregular doing. Often people will reason: "Since he is already on the roof, he might as well point the stacks." This is logical enough, and is partly permissible on this premise, in addition to the 'out of sight out of mind' principle noted above. Though it is a very common to see chimney stacks in desperate need of pointing.

Plastering

Plasterers are usually found with huge forearms and dirty clothes, a whirl of energy and technique. 'Spreads' usually stick to plastering only, and quite often hunt in pairs. Their brief: plastering, rendering and the laying of screed floors.

Painting

Most painters should be capable of general painting requirements, small making-good jobs, and other painting related tasks such as replacing sash cords, broken panes, or staining. As far as wallpaper hanging is concerned, my experience is that not all painters can hang wallpaper. If your wallpaper needs to be hanged, my advice is to find someone who does only this. Since you will have to pay for the wallpaper in advance it is well worth the extra time and effort involved to find the right man, rather than risking the ruin of your not inexpensive wallpaper! My father was, I am told, a very good painter. He also used to change and repair sash cords, though he could not hang wallpaper to save his life.

Stonemasonry

If an architect is the first prima donna of the building trade, then a stonemason is very close behind. Buildings built entirely of stone (very rare) certainly require the services of a stonemason, however most buildings past and present are of a brick and/or stone construction. I have been on many a job where the brickie builds the backing structure for the stonemason to face up and take, in the process, all the glory! Most bricklayers could pick up the nuances of stonemasonry without too much trouble, if they possessed the necessary patience. The same may very well be said the other way round. That buildings in the UK have evolved over centuries from mostly stone to mostly brick to mostly blocks, and the predominant professions have changed accordingly, is perhaps the chief reason why the brickie now sees the mason as a prima donna and not vice versa.

I do know of brickies and chippies that will have a go at anything and work to a good standard. It is also true to say that all self-employed workers have to diversify to stay in business. The ones you want to be looking for are those who know their limitations – a very rare breed indeed! I am sure that 95% of builders you and I know would not admit to having any particular trade limitations. For some builders 'no job too small' is a common side-of-the-van marketing theme and even the smallest jobs can become telescopic!

Nobody wants to turn down work of any sort, so work is taken on without concern about one's ability to finish the job. Of course, a builder may take on a job with the very best intentions, but somewhere along the line his circumstances may change. For example: the plumber who was going to put in the toilet has broken his arm, or just left town. That places the builder in the position where he has to decide whether to find someone else, or do the job himself. Monetary and logistic incentive indicates the latter. And then comes *the crunch.* In such a case, pay attention householder. If he is a brickie it is unlikely he will have many plumbing tools. Should he decide to install the toilet you will see him struggle, showing signs of frustration from the lack of appropriate tools. Wait until he has gone home then check the fittings on the pipe work. If he used the right tools then the fittings, particularly the brass ones, will be clean and undamaged. If they are chewed up you will know that the wrong tools were employed, and thus likely that the job done less well.
It may be as well to point out the differences between the tool bags of the various tradesmen, for possible identification and discrimination between a chap practising a trade he knows, and a chap winging it. It is also worth noting that any competent fellow always looks after his tools, for therein is his ability to do a decent job.

For instance, every carpenter I know takes great care of his toolbox. Many of his tools are very sharp, and if left lying about uncared for become blunt. It is then a devil of a job to sharpen them again which, not incidentally, he never gets paid for. Hence, his immediate incentive, to take great care of them.

Conversely, brickies' tools are not nearly as fragile and needy, nor as numerous, but contain a lot of heavy iron, some of which may be homemade for a particular job, and therefore irreplaceable. Both carpenters' tools and those of the brickies would never be left outside to get wet. If you see rusty tools steer clear of their owners!

The plumber's bag is invariably large and full of a mixture of tools and copper fittings, plus hundreds of very small items like washers and springs and such things. The very nature of the job dictates that the plums' tools are often spread all over the place, so if you cannot see a selection of fixtures and fitting lying about, the chances are that he does not do a lot of plumbing. Of course, a small job might not need all his tools in the house. As by this point he would have already started the job, you might well ask what is to be gained from this information. This aides when, if you do not feel happy with the job so far, armed with a little extra knowledge you can challenge him with some confidence.

An electrician would mostly carry his tools in a steel concertina type box; he might also have a small complement of plumbers' tools as well. A roofer's tools would all fit into a small seaside bucket, while a decorator's tools might fit into a large seaside bucket. A plasterer's tools, apart from his trowel and hawk would only be fit for throwing into the sea!

To Use an Architect, or Not

If you decide that you require an architect to supervise your project, consider this: don't let the architect pick the list of builders, on the basis that it is not in your interest to have the architect and builder on too familiar terms. It is not unknown for professionals and builders to be in collusion, and should anything go wrong on site the customer may well be made to feel in the wrong. Professionals' ethics are in my experience, no better than anyone else's.

The architect might say 'I know this builder's work is good, so let's go with him.' All very well and good you might say, and you may be right, but I would prefer the architect not knowing the builder in order that he keep a sharp lookout for problems before they arise, rather than letting complacency set in. In this capacity he is therefore working for the customer exclusively. It is not unheard of for architects to take a bung from a builder for being accepted as first choice. I believe the customer is much more likely to get the best out of their individual employees if they start out as strangers. It is as well to point out that there are no guarantees that any given project will run to a smooth conclusion either way.

It has been suggested by one and all that builders should pay compensation for bad workmanship. What a minefield this is! Who is going to decide what is and what is not good or bad work, the customer? I don't think so; for his or her expectations might be wholly unreasonable, particularly if they are holding back some of the builder's money.

The builder will have his own levels of time and working practices. Most builders like a drink, sometimes at the expense of all else! Some builders will insist on believing that the work they have completed is of a good standard whether it is or not. It is their standard, but maybe not yours. You might believe an architect or surveyor would know, but not necessarily, as their standards might be different again.

Some would say find a builder who gives you an insurance backed guarantee as compensation with your quote. I would say finding an insurance company that will pay out is harder than finding a good builder. Insurance premiums are rocketing all the time and in the case of a claim the builder, on the back foot once again, must pay out to all and sundry. Even if his work is acceptable he still has to pay the premiums.

You have now made contact with some builders. Try and make an appointment for them to call on the house, then you can arrange some support for you. The builder might turn up with a mate and you may well feel a little under pressure in your own home. I am not saying that most builders do this sort of thing on purpose, just that some of them move about in pairs, and they do tend to be large, muscular males – intimidating in themselves.

Upon arrival of the builder is really the time to engage your eyes and ears. Keep watch to see if they turn up on time and if not, listen to their reasons for not doing so. You can learn a lot about a builder, nay any man, from his excuses. If he turns up late and does not offer one, he probably does not care much anyway and is therefore one to avoid.

What happens next can depend on whether the work is fairly superficial or not. For example, if the work to be done is, say, decorating a room, it would not I think be appropriate to ask for confirmation of his qualifications. However, if the work involved some serious structural work, by all means ask for any qualifications he may have. If he baulks at this give him time to produce something. If he has no relevant papers he will not come back to you, and your diligence will have proved worthwhile.

One sure way to deter a possible dodgy character is to mention that your father-in-law or your uncle is a builder, but lives too far away to do the job. If the builder is intent on trying anything dodgy he will surely think twice about getting back to you. If he is on the level, it will not bother him at all.

Does he sound enthusiastic? Is he pleasant? Find out how long he has been a builder. Does he have a specific trade? Did he serve an apprenticeship? Don't be afraid to ask awkward questions such as; are you married? Have you any children? He is far less likely to disappear with your money without a trace if he has some deeper rooted responsibilities, and if you are aware of them. Last but not least, find out where they live and go to check out the address, the state of the place. Some of this information is quite obvious to the sensible and forthcoming among us, but judging by the amount of people who fall out with builders, evidentially not too many follow such advice.

If a friend recommends a builder don't think that is the end of your problem; if the job turns sour, whoever recommended them won't be a friend of yours for long. Furthermore, it is no guarantee at all that the recommended party is competent. I have come across the most appalling standard of work by builders who had been recommended by the customer's own family. Some have been told of a job in the next town that has been completed satisfactorily. I am not saying your friends or family are lying, merely that they are probably passing on information in good faith, but good faith is no security against bad workmanship.

Get yourself an address to visit, go and have a look, but don't be afraid to knock on a door and speak to the householders concerned. Ask them if they got on with the builders. Ask if they turned up every day. Ask if they kept to the agreed price. Ask to see the completed work and be prepared to come back if it is not convenient for them. Posing a few awkward questions at the outset could save a lot of time, money and heartache later. It is a fact that most people do not follow up these ideas and then wonder where they went wrong.

Of course it takes time to carry out these checks, but it is entirely in your own interest to do so. If the size of the job you have in mind does not warrant the effort - say a job of £300 or less - tell the builder that you will pay when the job is completed to your satisfaction.

Having completed these checks and being satisfied with the answers, ask them for an estimate, and try to get at least two more. At this point it is very important to give the same instructions and drawings to each builder; otherwise you will not be able to compare the estimates.

Now comes the crunch! At the end of the proverbial day, the price will be the biggest single reason for accepting or rejecting an estimate. Other reasons will be gut reactions to the answers given to your questions and the personalities involved. It will help, I think if you do not have any preconceived ideas or expectations of what the price might be. This is of course challenging for the budgeted home-owner. The builder's judgement is based, hopefully, on his experience of the given job. If you listen to the retired old gentleman up the road, or the old lady next door, with their good intentions and experience of the specific job, you might not get such a shock when the estimate is given. If you have the cheek to speak to another builder who was pleasant and helpful on the phone but too busy to quote, go back to him for his appraisal of your estimate, on the basis that he will not have anything to lose, and will probably say in honesty that the figure is too high or too low, or take it.

When one talks to house owners they generally agree that prevention is better than cure. Help is at hand in the form of my kind – a Building Doctor, if you will - but many of the same home owners just don't want to spend a little now to save a lot later. If I wore an architect's badge when giving a diagnosis of a building issue we could expect a quite different response.

My sometime-building-son experienced this very same disparity of treatment when visiting a house to perform a simple drainage repair, already paid for through a subcontractor. Having chatted to the owner as to the unfortunate outcome of the poor drainage – rotten floor joists and lifting of a brand new bamboo floor in three rooms – he remarked to them (as taught by me over the years) the relative in-extent of the *actual damage* to the internal floor overall; 'oh no,' said the lady of the house, 'we have had two qualified damp experts to assess the damage and they agree the whole floor must come up and all the floor joists replaced.' He poked his head under the open floor to do his own assessment. 'There are only two rotten joists though – the rest is fine,' said he, 'Once the drain is fixed you've no further issue.' She looked at him with genuine disgust. 'What,' she could not hide her thoughts, 'does this *common builder* know that our *highly paid experts* do not?' The implications, beyond the social/professional hierarchy, were straightforward – unsolicited and unpaid for advice is worth nothing; surveys done at great cost must be accurate.

She might well have said, indignant, proud, 'But I've paid an expert to rip me off!'

One of my means of advertising over the last 50 years involves distributing flyers in letter boxes and, whilst the layout and artwork has changed over the years, one line has not:

Building Problem -
Advisory Service...... First Class references.

The first headline surely speaks for itself, but not so in my experienced opinion. The public at large are quite happy to have a go at builders when things go wrong, evidenced in the fact that for 50 years I have offered customers a way out but yet not one person has ever contacted me with a concern either before or during the problem - only after - with all the resulting fury and irritations aimed at the building trade as a whole. Householders are therefore, under these conditions, deeply suspicious of builders when we house call.

The second headline about references, whether first class or not, won't mean anything to someone who has a house with a problem but doesn't know it yet. Which leads us with the conclusion that - in their mind at least - householders always know best until things go wrong?

What Goes on in The Client's Mind?

For a builder it is often difficult to fathom what a customer is thinking. For example, I have many times successfully completed a job, only to revisit six months later to find other builders in operation. Of course it is the clients' prerogative to choose whomever they want, to do whatever they want. In a case like this maybe I did not get on with the client as well as I thought. Could it be that the client did not like me and that consideration outweighed my ability as a tradesman? Quite possibly I will admit I am not the easiest person to get on with, but I am straight, upfront and honest - the attributes we builders are not supposed to have!

So you have to find a builder who smiles all the time, gets on with everybody, can count to ten and will say, "Yes" to all your demands. Someone, who can also tell the time and say, "please" and "thank you", that's it cracked then! Well, almost; you will still have to find out if this superman can cut, lay, strip, lift, glue, whack and thump his way around your house, with efficiency, skill and tidiness, no less.

To sum up what you are looking for: Find a builder who has carpentry or bricklaying background, which has at least 20 years' experience or, even better, someone who has a self-employed history. If you have completed these checks you might know whether your choice of builder is a good organiser, time keeper and is trustworthy. If your chosen man's character is in doubt, trust the information you have gleaned, after all you don't have to like the man, so long as he can do the job. Good luck!

A house is a machine for living in   - *Le Corbusier*

Buying a House

You want to buy a house. Is it to be an old house or a new one? By new I mean structures built after the 1960's.

If the house you want to buy requires, for instance, new doorways knocked out or rooms enlarging, please don't consider doing so on a building that was built after 1960. For the simple reason that most buildings constructed after this date will not stand up to the violence caused by knock-through. The structure of brickwork or block-work is built of sand and cements mortar, and therefore is hard, or harder than the bricks or blocks themselves. This is particularly true if the house is built with a cavity wall. Only a person who has carried out this operation many times will be in a position to substantiate this claim. However, whilst not impossible to achieve, the effort and cost has to be evaluated by someone experienced in this type of task.

Older structures, by comparison, are easy to renovate owing to the dead lime mortar used between the bricks, and knocking a hole through a wall is child's play. However, danger is apparent everywhere, particularly from above. Lime mortar between the brick joints is reduced by time to a dusty sawdust type-material, with no adhesion whatsoever. Brickwork above any holes knocked out will now be unstable, so considerable care must be taken to insert lintels bridging the gap.

Why then do new houses sell as well or better than older ones? I think one of the simple answers is that new houses are much easier to keep clean, due to the fact that there is considerably less dust in the structure than there used to be. If you take into account double glazing as well, which keeps out the dust, you should have a less dusty environment; heating is also a big factor, with hugely improved insulating materials now used in house building. I am not an expert in heating matters, but blocks over bricks keep out the cold particularly well, and keep the heat in, thereby lowering heating costs. If you add on new improved central heating systems as well, you can see how a new house can be an attractive proposition, particularly so now that developers spend a large proportion of cost on style and aesthetics. However the quality of new houses needs to be investigated, especially with regard to the structure.

In a marketing sort of way 'quality' is a word much overused. But where or how does quality exist in the building of a new house? Thinking about materials, let's look at some examples. Not far from where I live there is an exclusive little housing estate; being nosey during construction I asked the general foreman where he purchased the bricks used for these very nice buildings. He told me that the developers bought these white bricks from Belgium as they were so cheap - £130 a thousand. In my opinion, these bricks are of extremely poor quality, as the price would indicate. I can't imagine what these bricks will look like in fifty years' time, though one can project, given these bricks look their best now and can only deteriorate from here on in. Some bricks will look better with age, but not these.

So, quality in this instance is not in the bricks. Let's say 15,000 face bricks are required for a house of this size, which would cost approximately £2,250 per house for bricks - not much for houses sold at £650,000 each! With competition fierce, the architects constantly change the aesthetic look of a house to attract customers, deciding to use for instance soft red bricks that are everyone's favourite, but not cheap. So the developers incorporate soft reds into the structure, but in a miserly way, usually at the head of doors, windows and again at the external corners. Using soft reds mixed with white or yellow bricks lessons the cost, takes the eye aesthetically away from the cheap bricks, and provides a contrast in colour.

The quality of the bricklayer is a different matter entirely. A gang of bricklayers might start on a particular house but may not be around to finish the brickwork, and the succeeding gang of brickies might be better, or they might be worse. Look for a distinct difference on, say, a flank wall; compare the top to the bottom, is one neater than the other? Is the mortar the same colour? As a rule of thumb, if the joints between the bricks are neatly dressed and not too deep, that will show the brickies' pride in the finished job. He is more likely to have applied the same high standards in work that can't be seen or is hidden as he has with face work.

Most houses built before 1950 have a solid-wall construction: 9" thick brickwork that's plastered inside, with face bricks or pebbledash rendering outside. These structures are relatively weak due to the lime mortar between the bricks. Lime mortar has no cement content, so over a period of many years it breaks down and becomes like dusty sand. I have been asked many times, 'How does the house stay up if it is so weak?' The answer is in the sheer weight of the building and it being upright: though not on its own, this weight will be enough to hold the structure together. The arrangement of the bricks, known as the 'bond', will ensure the buildings' standing. The better the bonding, the stronger the brickwork, and the stronger the brickwork, the better the structure. The corners are obviously the strongest part of a house, therefore the more corners in a house the stronger it is. Rendering the inside walls helps when it is built, but a hundred years or more later it is often ready to fall off. As I have done many times, if you take off the roof of such a house and remove its weight, it is then possible to lift off the bricks one by one, as easy as shelling peas. This makes it possible to remove the old bricks to clean and reuse elsewhere. Such bricks have had one life - maybe 100-200 years - and now they are going to have another. Their next lifespan will in all probability be their last, due to the extreme difficulty in cleaning the stronger mortar now used from the old bricks.

Another tip: If you are looking to buy a house and you come across one surrounded by trees, and particularly if the house is a new one, look to see if the house has a proliferation of timber on the face of the house. If so the dampness surrounding the trees will eventually transfer, as likely as not, to the house timber itself. When the trees get wet the dampness hangs around much longer than it might without the trees, and being adjacent to the house its timber facia will require a long dry spell to fully dry out. Consequently you may well have to paint the exterior more often than you wish.

Another no-no to lookout for is vegetation growing out of gutters and brickwork – in fact vegetation growing anywhere else but the garden. The sight of sapling trees or bushes growing from your house or structure clearly shows something is wrong. Water will run off any surface eventually, even a flat one. If vegetation is growing on the surface of a wall that is upright, there will be an obstruction stopping the natural flow of water down the wall. It could be a crack in the joint or something sticking to the face of the wall; either way the run off is obstructed and must be removed or re-pointed, or both.

Sometimes a bush or some grass can be seen growing from and over your gutters indicating a potentially ruinous danger to your structure, and must be avoided at all costs. Simply clean out the gutters and remove all obstructions hindering the natural flow of rainwater.

Everyone assumes bricks keep out the rain because they are hard. If so, how come soft absorbent reds also keep out the rain? Bricks are a physical barrier, nothing more; if you made up a barrier of paper, albeit quite thick, it would keep the elements at bay for a time. The principle of bricks versus rain is quite simple: when it rains the water hits the upright wall and runs down, then the bricks become dry as the rain stops. This process repeats itself year after year.

The point that really matters is that the quality of the bricks will determine the longevity of their resistance to rain and damp. The porous bricks usually red in colour may, after severe and prolonged rainfall, become saturated. When a wall becomes saturated water travels through it as if there were no resistance to the ingress of moisture. A wall that is facing west will always take the brunt of rainfall, so it is incumbent on you to insure that all brickwork facing west should at least be weather pointed properly. What destroys the surface of the bricks is when brickwork is damp or saturated, and the frost then freezes moisture in the bricks and, bingo, the bricks split and crack. The pointing between the bricks, if good, will ensure the rain does not penetrate far enough into the brick to cause major damage to your wall. All flat surfaces subject to rainfall must be protected, usually by a brick on edge, or even better, by a coping stone protruding at least two inches beyond the face, to usher the rainfall away from the top of any wall and thus keep it dry. Keep the top metre of any wall dry and the pointing will take care of the rest.

Above you can see exactly what I am talking about. On the right hand side you can clearly see a coping protruding over the face of the wall keeping the top few brick courses dry. The fact that this brickwork appears clean as opposed to the rest of the wall confirms my earlier points. The rest of this wall appears dirty by comparison and is clearly damp at the top. Because there is no overhanging coping, this part of the wall will always be damp and therefore always be subjected to infestation and growth, not to mention the frost and all that that brings. The left side clearly shows the long-term effect of no top of wall protection. Some people might view this as giving the wall character; such people are not me!

I am not sure if this next tip has any merit where you live, but it sure does in my neck of the woods! Try and make it possible that all rainwater exits go to soak ways, thus relieving your water authority of any maintenance tasks. If you manage to achieve this then a reduction of at least thirty per cent should be deducted from your water bill. I did, so go and do the same!

If you are thinking of block laying your driveway there are one or two points to consider. When the driveway is finished it will never look better than it does at this moment. What I am saying is everything is downhill from here as far as the aesthetics are concerned. The blocks or pavers are reconstituted sharp sand and cement, pressed into shape under great pressure. The blocks are not burnt like bricks and will, in a short space of time, fall apart much quicker than bricks.

Because the blocks are laid dry on sand they are susceptible to slumping in areas under most pressure; under vehicle wheels for example. Any building materials on a flat surface outside at the mercy of the elements, particularly with joints, will suffer erosion very quickly. To use a comparison, if a block of concrete the size of a stone at Stonehenge was left in much the same way, it would in all probability disintegrate after about thirty years, and there would not be much concrete left at all, if any. The natural stone of Stonehenge is I think granite, which is more or less impervious to moisture. As the stones are whole with no joints to speak of, therefore no weaknesses, it is quite possible that they will still be evident and standing thousands of years from now.

You might ask why we don't build houses that will last as long today: money and thickness of walls is the primary answer. Money, because old fashioned working principles take time, these days' costs are considerably more than when those working and design practices were in operation. The thickness of walls today may be five times narrower on most buildings than it used to be. Next time you visit St. Paul's Cathedral or the Houses of Parliament, look at the thickness of the walls, particularly at the bottom. You will see the walls are at least two feet thick, possibly reducing as the walls move higher. If the walls are wide, so will the lumps of stone also be wide; although not as big as Stonehenge of course, but you can see my point about big lumps of stone lasting longer.

A friend showed me a wall in her hometown of Chichester which was supposedly built by the Romans some two thousand years ago. We had a right royal argument, because I said that the wall I was now holding onto would not last one hundred and fifty years. The flint contained in the wall certainly could, but the joints made of lime mortar most certainly could not. Maybe the oldest part of the wall is contained under this structure which was, I think, about six feet thick.

I'm sure you've all seen houses that have stone cladding on external surfaces. Not only does cladding look artificial, but the stones themselves are in effect artificial, made out of reconstituted stone dust and cement; and just like the block paving they will fall apart soon enough. But the moral here is this: don't cover up any brickwork in this way because you stop the brickwork from breathing. I can assure you that you needn't believe anything you hear to the contrary.

Council regulations have changed dramatically over the years, brought about by the need to conserve energy. One change that was not brought about by energy conservation is the depth of the foundations. When I was a young lad we used to dig down about 300mm and fill with 225 mm of concrete. The Council now insist on a minimum depth of one metre across the board, regardless of what you are building. So on occasion you can have a footing that is fifty times better than you actually need. Why? I suspect somewhere along the line a County Council has been sued for the failure of a footing, so in order to avoid such a recurrence they have doubled the depth whatever is being built, regardless of the sense and cost.

In some houses where the radiators are under the windows, and the curtains down to the floor, hot air gets trapped behind the curtains and heat goes straight out through the glass.

Glass does not retain the heat, so therefore it makes sense to shorten the curtains so that they don't cover the radiators. This is so even if your windows are double-glazed, though the salesman will, I'm sure, tell you otherwise. The fact is that the biggest benefit of double-glazing is noise reduction.

If you live in an old house and you notice during the summer months creatures flying in and out of your brickwork, these will almost certainly be mortar bees. If the mortar joints are soft and powdery, the bees will burrow in and lay their eggs, using a mixture of sand and saliva to cover their larvae. I have seen a chimney stack seriously undermined by these boring insects. I would suggest waiting until late summer before tackling the problem by raking out and repointing as appropriate. If a small creature can penetrate your brickwork via your joints, so too can rain, with possible dire consequences later.

Chimneys

One area of a house which is either not seen, ignored, or both, is the condition of your chimneys. All chimneys take the brunt of the best and worst the elements can throw their way. I have seen customers having their chimneys swept to observe the brush knocking bricks off the top! The motto seems to be "Sort out the interior first and ignore everything else!" You ignore the exterior of your chimney *at your peril*!

This picture shows a chimney stack in the last throws of its ability to repel moisture. Whilst the status of the bricks is at this point okay, the mortar joints clearly need some attention. Note that the daylight is filling gaps between the brick courses at the corners; a sure sign that re-pointing is required. If this stack is left in its present state the brickwork will always be damp, resulting in a potentially dangerous situation.

As a rule of thumb, a chimney (or part thereof) should be replaced every thirty years or so, depending on the bricks used, the strength of mortar, and prevailing weather conditions. In the Southwest and Southeast of England most of the inclement weather comes from the west, so it follows that the face of the stack looking towards the west will, in all probability, be the most affected. The very top of the stack is more important than the rest, as the flaunching (sand and cement that covers the top) holds the top area of your chimney together. A chimney without flaunching or with old and cracked cement will eventually fall apart completely. A chimney in this condition should be re-flaunched immediately, or one runs the risk of complete disintegration of the stack. I recently visited a little estate that I worked on as a boy some forty five years ago, and every single stack needs attention – some urgently. I pointed this out to some of the owners who, unsurprisingly, politely told me to piss off!

Obviously the owners did not believe what I was propounding and why should they; nobody wants to hear bad news.

Most folk don't notice the chimneys on their houses, so next time check that yours is not leaning. It is a fact that when a chimney has a tendency to gravitate, the inclination will always turn inwards towards the attendant structure. Why? I can only surmise that the greater air pressure comes from the open side, thus pushing the chimney inwards. Local atmospherics will always have their say; if the chimney leans outwards there will be a more sinister reason. If this is the case for you, you need it repaired or taken down.

I look no further to prove this point than Isaac Newton's Principia. In it he explains that if you drop a plumb line down the side of a mountain it will gravitate slightly inward toward the mass of the mountain, or, in the case of a chimney, towards the mass of the house, affected too by the gravitational mass of the earth.

When collecting rubble or hard-core, or anything that has to be shovelled up later, make sure the material is placed upon a firm surface from which to shovel. If it is dumped directly on the ground, great difficulty will arise when using the shovel to move the rubbish. This tip will save your back from the pounding it always takes when using a shovel. I'm sure I have mentioned elsewhere that a weightlifter's belt when using a shovel is a must to protect your spine from the extended leverage.

Walking along my road a thought occurred to me while watching the dustmen empty the wheelie bins. I continued on my way, and when I returned an hour later the bins had been left in a haphazard fashion outside every house. As I walked along I could clearly see which owners were at home as they had repositioned their own bins in the normal place.

Bins of the owners, who were not at home at this time, clearly in the majority, were left all over the pavement in disarray. Now, if a burglar was to walk down the road a couple of hours after the bin men had finished, it would not be difficult, as it was not for me, to establish who was currently at home, therefore making his decision as to which houses to burgle a mere formality. I'm not a burglar, but if I were, this plan would be almost fool proof as a means of establishing a trouble free criminal passage.

Dampness

May I help you to understand the term rising damp? In my opinion there is no such thing. If the affected wall is an outside wall, nine times out of ten a defective gutter and its knock-on effects is the problem. If the inside wall is damp, there is always a reason for it, you just have to find out what it is. A surveyor's damp meter will not find the reason; it will only tell you how damp the wall is. The damp-proofing companies will say look how damp this wall is, as if this wasn't the reason you called him in the first place. The damp meter will find moisture in the Sahara Desert at lunchtime! The point is moisture is present in every house in this country, but not to always its detriment.

The salesman will say: "Look at this meter reading, you need a damp proof course."

I would say at least half of all new physical or chemical damp proof courses are not warranted. But hey, we need the work! I have always told my children not to believe someone who has a vested interest in the outcome of any given thing.

One of the most frequently asked questions concerns damp and associated symptoms. Whether a house is built of a solid wall or a single skin construction (cavity wall), the damp will enter in the same way. However the cure for both types of construction could be quite different. If damp appears inside the house at a high level the cause is either a gutter problem or, unsurprisingly, a roof defect. If the ingress of moisture is detected at ground level then the problem will require greater clarification. Obviously, I cannot be specific, but as a general rule, if the external wall-face at ground level is very wet, the gutter above is usually the culprit. A garden check at the onset of rain will usually illustrate the problems root. If not, one must ask if the structure has a damp proof course of not?

All houses built around the middle of the nineteenth century had some sort of damp proof course; most were two layers of slate embedded in sand and lime mortar. Solid wall construction began thousands of years ago in the trail of the agricultural revolution, right up until the 1920s or thereabouts. Clearly, a solid wall is more prone to damp reaching the inside of your property and will require careful investigation. These days all solid external walls have a minimum thickness of nine inches, often becoming thicker the further you travel back in time. Under normal circumstances rainwater will not penetrate nine inches into the fabric unless the gutter is spewing water onto a particular point on the wall on a regular basis. As I have pointed out many times, when a patch of brickwork has become saturated the bricks' ability to repel the elements is severely compromised. Once the fault is repaired the masonry will dry out remarkably quickly.

A cavity construction is identifiable by the thickness of the external wall, its plaster twelve inches thick, (300mm). Since all houses with twin wall construction have damp proof courses, the problem could not originate from the ground. Broadly speaking the twin wall cavity system is dependent upon the wet outside skin not having any contact with the inside wall. If constructed properly the cavity is usually 50mm across, preventing the transference of moisture from outside to in. If this proves not to be the case, metal or plastic wall ties built into both walls will probably be the culprit.

During construction these wall ties should not be smothered in mortar, if they are, then they now make a bridge between the wet outside wall and the dry inside skin. Water doesn't need encouragement to run at will, even right into your front room. To solve this problem a hole or holes will have to be cut, presumably in the outside skin to save decorations. This operation requires a vast amount of expertise to conclude.

Nowadays, with the Government's incentive for energy saving, cavity walls are filled with all sorts of insulation materials, both during and after construction. Filling the cavity destroys the very essence of the original purpose of having a gap – which was to have a space between the two walls in order for air to circulate and thus keep the walls dry.

I have been asked many times: Do we put a damp proof course in a garden wall? On balance no, because, the damp proof course is a weak point in a wall, so unless there is a considerable weight on top, say twenty more courses, don't bother.

Double-Glazing

Everybody has cause for concern regarding double-glazing companies and their dubious practices; here are some of their lesser-known operations.

The first thing to remember is double-glazing companies put themselves first, second and third in order of importance. They often want full payment the very minute the job is completed, thereby denying you the chance to check the work fully. Once the double-glazing company have your money the onus is on the customer to chase up any mistakes.

One enemy of the double-glazing company is time; their fitters have a very small window of opportunity to complete your job, so the quicker your windows are replaced, even to their detriment, the happier they become. I will explain one way in which time is halved and a poor job is the result. Once the units are screwed into place, expanding foam is applied into the gap between the frame and structure thereby taking up the slack. This operation is quite simple; however the expanding foam needs three to four hours to stiffen up ready to receive a watertight mastic bead. Clearly an overnight wait is preferable, but often not given. But who cares? Expediency is the name of this particular game.

Instead of operating in the correct way double-glazing company fitters will often use a foam gun to fill only the front and back of the unit, on the basis that a very small amount of foam will harden much quicker than a full filled gap. The fact that the gap has not been fully filled is clearly to the detriment of the finished article. If the waterproof mastic beading is applied to expanding foam before it has fully cured, the two materials pushing against one another compromise the pressure needed to enforce the mastic. The result of all this for the fitters mean they can probably fit all the units in a day, while the customers are left with a job poorly done and probably very little knowledge of this, bearing in mind the finished job now hides all modus operandi.

From a commercial perspective I am sure you can see how time is everything, with fitters being squeezed to the extent that corners have to be cut in order to remain fiscally competitive. Of course a balance can ideally be struck between taking out windows and doors first thing in the morning, and waiting for the hardening process to complete before fixing the glass panels, ensuring the property's security.

If your house is to be rendered externally after fixing make sure a mastic bead is applied outside, because any form of rendered finish will not stick to a plastic surface, leaving a hairline crack for water to penetrate and eventually expand. It is best to mastic before and after rendering. The window company will be long gone by the time rendering is complete, so the onus will be on the householder to complete the finishing touch.

Also, make sure the mastic bead is sound and complete at the point of contact between render or brickwork and window or door sill. This is the most important area in the whole operation. Do not be persuaded by double-glazing personnel to the contrary, as their vested interest in not wanting to do their job completely is too strong, as will be their desire to move on to the next job asap. Beading in this area may have to be renewed every five years or so to maintain its integrity, in what is the most vulnerable spot in your house.

Something to watch out for: In most houses built before 1940 lintels were not necessarily required over windows and doors, so the frame is taking the load from above. In such houses window fitters often arrive and promptly whip out the old for the new units and hope for the best. To spot this, look to see if the brickwork or rendering has since cracked above the window or door. If so, do not pay a penny until they have rectified it by inserting a lintel above the window to take the weight.

If you choose to employ a ready mixed concrete company who purport to mix on the lorry as you lay, *beware!* I've used these companies many times with mixed results. The driver might cut down on the cement content to save himself some bags of cement, thereby reducing the mixes' strength. One way around this is to agree with the mixer/driver how many bags make up a full mix, then ask how many barrows full of concrete to a mix; at this stage, he will of course give you the right numbers. When you start barrowing write on a doorframe or wall that you are passing to keep count and signify each barrow load, this way you will know for certain how many barrow loads you should be charged for.

The driver/mixer will, in some cases venture that you've had twenty loads, when the marks on the doorframe indicate that you've had only seventeen. Show the driver your marks then tell him you will only pay for what has actually been delivered, not what he *says* he has delivered. Also if the colour of the mix is buff instead of rich grey, tell him to add more cement.

Bricks

I once had occasion to visit and take advantage of Hanson's brickworks at Capel in Surrey. This huge plant delivers nine hundred and fifty thousand bricks per week. During my apprenticeship in the early sixties I visited the London Brick Company factories in Peterborough and Bedford; what struck me now was the lack of any real technological advancement. The manager Dave Stock kindly let me roam the site, accompanied by a chap named Steve. Looking at the quarry a hundred feet down, I would say it would be possible to drop either the old or the new Wembley Stadium into this hole. Having excavated this huge gape over a period of forty odd years, Hanson will make a fortune charging waste companies to refill the crater. The rough clay, clearly blue in colour is, I'm told, three hundred and fifty million years old.

Upon asking if any dinosaurs had been found, my guide remarked, "There are a few still working here!"

The whole process, from rough clay to bricks ready to lay, was ten days. After the raw clay was placed in and then taken out of its mould, the two-day drying out began. This is to ensure that when firing begins the bricks are dry and not still damp. If bricks were not pre-dried the firing would crack the finished articles. The machinery at this plant is old, antiquated, and dirty, but highly practical and clearly functioning.

I asked Steve a question on behalf of my many clients who have queried the issue of efflorescence showing on the wall face. Saltpetre, as it is known, occurs naturally in the base material, and the best way to remove this white crystallisation from the face of your wall is to brush gently every time it appears. On no account use a wire brush, or wet the wall.

The words on a sign as I drove away were, I thought, appropriate: 'Safety is no accident'.

An interesting fact about clay in its original wet state is its ability to repel water, which is not so obvious when burnt, as the very same material becomes porous. However, both states can be used to impede the ingress of water in totally different ways. For example, the Victorians used green(wet) clay to joint salt-glazed underground sewer pipes; from about the thirties onwards neat cement was used, and nowadays, of course, plastic is king!

One money-saving tip I can share with you revolves around airbricks; this method of construction usually means a hollow floor system vented by airbricks. Normally it is taboo for the openings to be blocked, however in December and January, possibly February, when the very cold wind is whistling through the cavity under your floor boards keeping the house cold, try blocking the apertures for two months. A well-ventilated floor is a must, but for a short period of time no damage will accrue through blockage, and your house will retain most of the heat lost by that wind tunnel under your floor.

On the same theme customers have explained how their properties, when left empty for weeks or months, are showing signs of being damp or smelling musty; when I tell them to open the doors and windows thus letting air circulate through the property, they are amazed how this simple instruction works.

Bricks could be one of the most versatile manmade substances, not to mention their high marks for longevity. Did you know that in Victorian England bricks would be heated up in the oven, wrapped in newspapers, and then placed in the bed as a bed warmer! How resourceful we can be! Personally, having seen bricks all day every day, I prefer the warmth of a female body for such things.

In my working lifetime I have seen bricks made of glass, wood, concrete, terracotta and plastic. For practical purposes all have been found wanting, and nothing compares with clay bricks for aesthetics, performance, or indeed longevity. Back in the late sixties in East London a relatively new high-rise block of flats collapsed like a pack of cards. This building was constructed of solid concrete floors, as they still are today. How this block differed was because the external face was built with huge ten foot square concrete slabs measuring about four inches in thickness; these massive lumps of reinforced concrete prefabricated in a factory, were held together by copper tags built into the concrete floors on top and bottom, then grouted together.

A sound enough principle, until some movement occurred, which in this case was a gas explosion. Once the slabs moved the copper tags or toggles lost their grip and the sheets moved outwards. This sheer weight now on the move meant that one slab brought down the next and so on, like a pack of falling cards. If the walls had been constructed of brick and not concrete panels, only the brickwork appertaining to the flat receiving the blast would have been affected. Quite possibly only the windows would have been blown out with the brickwork still intact, albeit fractured and other flats in the block would have been unaffected.

This example clearly shows how brickwork, properly constructed and bonded, has huge stick-ability and strength, able to withstand just about any imposition, even earthquakes. No other building material can match this structural performance.

Skips

Another useful attribute on site is the ability to fill a skip in such a way that might result in two skip loads in the one container. Depending on what is to be put into it, think what sits best inside the skip. For example old doors should be placed on edge and upright against the sides, or used to bolster low sides of a skip. Always put the lightest rubbish in the bottom then the heavy stuff on top. If the rubbish is old brick, stack them as you would if you were actually laying them, along the sides, filling the middle as you go to keep your dry bricklaying in place. When you have completed this operation once or twice, you will see the economic benefits of carefully planning how you fill your skip.

Using a Ladder

The general public would be astonished to find how many people wish ladders to the devil, no doubt fuelled by real and imagined thoughts of impending crash landings. If the ladder is leant against a building, obviously the top of the ladder cannot go forward, but it is important to secure the base of the ladder, either by placing a sandbag against it, to restrict any movement, or by fixing a restraining strap to the ladder and say, a down pipe, or a hook in the wall. These methods are 95% safe, providing you proceed up and down the ladder without leaning extravagantly sideways. However, if you place a ladder against a gutter, then all normal principles go out of the window! To reduce movement at the top of the ladder, wedge a piece of timber about 4" or 5" x 2" into the gutter, so that the ladder is resting on a stable structure; then, most importantly, sideways movement must be addressed.

On many occasions I have secured my ladder by hammering two 4" nails into the facia board, at an angle going away from the ladder; as a rule of thumb, the nails should be placed at least 18" either side of the ladder, then I wind a thin piece of rope around each nail and tie the other ends to each side of the ladder. In the unlikely event that you decide to climb onto the roof, make sure that the ladder extends one metre higher than the gutter, which will aid balance. And don't forget the bag at the base of the ladder! Always be mindful that weight transference must travel down the length of the ladder, particularly when stepping onto the ladder from the roof.

Estimating

Ah yes, the estimate! That figure 'plucked from the air with a bit added on and, by the way, excluding V.A.T.' that figure with more curves than Marilyn Monroe.

A typical joke scenario often made out, embellishment side, to be somewhat true: "That's right, the estimate *has* changed, because that crack we thought we could plaster over turned out to be the bloody San Andreas Fault!"

Everyone knows that in the land of the incompetent the builder is both the dictator and Chancellor of the Exchequer. Stories like these are comical, and sell newspapers and magazines, but they are in no way helpful.

Estimating is obviously a huge part of business acumen, particularly if you are self-employed. You will have read elsewhere in this book about the dangers of estimating too high and getting no work as a consequence, or estimating too low and getting lots of work, but making little money. The first and last point to remember is that everyone wants the job done for, if not nothing, then as close as possible to nothing. If you always have that in the back of your mind, you won't go far wrong. Estimating can depend on the type of job to be undertaken, and on the personality of your intended client. When estimating I try to establish, early on, if there's going to be a personality clash, especially if the job looks like one that is going to take longer than about two weeks. Estimating is in itself, by definition, in probably most spheres of life, a generalisation, a guess.
I am sure everyone has heard the terms 'price work' and 'day work'. I will try to unravel their subtleties for you.

Price work can be defined in two ways: One: Price work, or 'piece work' as it was old-fashionedly known, revolved around a system whereby at the end of the week all bricks or blocks you had laid to date would be added up, then the agreed price for laying a square meter of bricks or blocks would be applied and paid each week. And two: You could also use the term price work for a job that you have priced for in its entirety, therefore no matter how long the work takes your only claim is for the agreed sum.

Day work: the same job, but a totally different way of paying for it. Essentially, a price on day work will mean an agreed price for usually a day's work. Although the two jobs involve the same business of laying bricks, etc. etc., on the one hand you are paying for a man's time and on the other, you are paying for the completed work. The benefits for price work are obvious; the more work that is completed, the more is earned. Under this system, the customer can see what he is getting for his money as the job progresses. As the customer should know how many bricks are required for his project, he will not have any nasty surprises at the end of the job.

The benefits of day work to the builder and customer could not be more different. On this rate the builder has little or no incentive to get on with the job, because he will still get paid the agreed amount, whatever he accomplishes during the day. If you employ someone on a day work basis it would normally be for a task that is uncertain in difficulty or length, or both. The benefits for the payee might be that, should some unforeseen problem occur a man is on site to deal with it. The difficulties for the employer are clear enough. You should at least know your workforce and that if you turn your back will they likely stop work? Can you trust them? And will they disappear down the pub? However, if you employ someone on a price basis and ask them to do something else from the agreed specification, even a small task, you will probably be told no, because whilst he is doing your task he is away from the paid task, and thus not earning any money.

Clearly the customer cannot have it both ways, but will always try it on. An experienced builder won't price for a job that he thinks might be problematical. What he might do is double the price to make sure of every eventuality, or offer a 'day work' price. Sometimes a builder, experienced or not, won't see possible trouble coming, and when it happens (which it does with alarming regularity) the only thing that will matter to him is, "Am I on 'price work' or 'day work'?" To sum up on price work, the customer knows exactly how much money will be going out all before the job itself starts. On 'day work' he only knows how much he is paying out on a daily basis, and thus costs do have the increased potential to run away with him.

The following story just about sums up Joe public's perception of us builders. A friend of a friend had a large building project to start and approached six builders to tender for the work, setting a deadline date to do so. They were amazed when the deadline expired and no quotes were forthcoming. My friend then had to listen to the following ranting:
"If in my business life I approached deadlines in this way I would be out of work in a month, and if I was employing these buggers myself I'd sack the lot of them!"

The key word here is 'sack'. They can't sack them because they don't employ the builders – not yet. Thus far, save for a few phone calls, the customer has not spent a penny and he is already making demands of the builders' time and resources. Why would he think that setting a deadline was going to make a difference to the builder? The customer's own business deadlines would have been set by his employers, and he is therefore, as an employee of theirs, duty bound to comply. Since the builder is often working for himself, and not the customer, not as yet, he will naturally please himself. Here you have the time honoured situation where a stranger sets a work and time deadline and expects a builder, known to him or not, to jump through hoops.

The potential employers clearly don't understand that builders don't get paid for working on or writing out estimates – often this takes a considerable amount of time. I could spend all week working on quotes and never earn any money. Obviously builders who employ Quantity Surveyors build this into the equation and will eventually be recompensed. One-man bands like me can't operate this way; what I try to do is to give a verbal estimate and leave it at that. Of course, to operate in this way there must exist, trust in some form. Should I get chosen to do the job estimated for I will write whatever the customer wants, thereby cutting out work that I don't get paid for.

Talking to a new estate agent about the last agent's pathetic attempt at selling our house, she replied: "Was it the attraction of a low commission rate? I'm afraid that cut price fees and cut price service tend to go together." - Apparently it is now a prerequisite that a wonderful job be charged at a wonderful price! In reality this is tripe.

When insurance companies are assessing a claim, they ask for three or four written estimates, then the customer phones up the builder looking for a written quote. Personally, I'd say I don't want a one in four chance of a job if I have to write out an estimate. I will, of course, give a verbal quote. When the customer has collected all the estimates and if my quote is the lowest and they contact me again, I will submit a written estimate, but charge £5 for doing so. If I get the job the £5 will be refunded. The reason for doing so is simply that customers promise you the job in return for a written estimate, and then proceed to give a crack at the work themselves, or more likely give the job to another.

Some clients have even asked to give them a blank bill head and they'd fill it in for me. Not likely! If I were to give a customer a blank bill head I would have absolutely no control over where that bill head might end up. For example the customer might decide to put thousands of pounds on that bill for which I would be liable and which could end up with the taxman, or indeed they may use it again and again. A risk that is to most of us not worth taking - would you give a stranger/customer a blank cheque?

Two further points: the insurance companies always choose the cheapest quote even if they know or think likely that the job cannot be done for the price. When you mention the mere £5, the reaction is often amazing! The time wasters put the phone down straight away. The customer who genuinely wants some help will keep talking and come to a compromise. So rather than trying to guarantee myself a job, I am saving myself the trouble of having to write out possibly four or five estimates a week for nothing, when I could be better spending my time employed and actually working!

I am sure most are aware of the term 'danger money', but what does it mean? I can tell you that to my customers it means nothing. If I were paid for being in danger after a lifetime in the building trade, I would indeed be a very rich man! I understand more people are killed on building sites than are killed down the mines (or at least were when they were in operation.) My customers won't pay me for being on the roof; only for doing their particular job. The fact that the job is on the roof is largely incidental to most people. Clients would say that it's your job to be up there so you must be comfortable with it. Danger, what danger?

The scaffold can be a most dangerous place to be, except perhaps for a war zone, though some might say worse given the builders' propensity to self-destruct. Beer and scaffold go together about as well as white shoes and dog shit! I have seen workers staggering around drunk or high up on the scaffold. And yet you don't need to be pissed to fall off; it's a one mistake and you are gone kind of place. One of the worst things you can do on the scaffold is to kick something out of your way. If you kicked a half-inch nut or bolt off the platform from, say, fifty feet, it would have a velocity comparable to that of a bullet as it hit whatever lay underneath.

I know I have digressed a little from estimating, but whilst talking about the scaffold and the danger surrounding it, it is worth noting that being high up gives one a different perspective of the surrounding area, a sense of peace and tranquillity away from the madness below. If not compensation for an accident amongst the intrinsic dangers of the job, which it is not, the change of perspective is highly pleasing, and helps the day pass in good spirits.

Plasterer's Price

Some might argue this next piece is quite perverse, given the very nature of this book. During the build at Southwood, the plasterers tried to pull a fast one, which I did in fact see coming. I agreed with the boss (plasterer) that some extra work was required; we did not talk money at that stage, because all was going well and we were only two thirds of the way through the job. I thought we could trust the plasterers' boss to be reasonable, particularly since he knew that I was also a competent plasterer. Silly me! Towards the end of the job he threw a figure at me while Leo Junior and I were half underground in the soak-away. I ignored it, but as I later found out he assumed I'd ratified the figure. The boss man wanted an extra seven hundred pounds for skimming two very small rooms, walls only, as they worked their way round the house. My belief that this was greedy was born out by the following figures:

Price of job   £7,000
Extras   £700

Meters square covered by extra work – 1/49th of total job - 49 x £700 =£34,000!!
I hope you can see the greed – almost 50 times the original price.

Nothing removes the pain of a man's toil like a whopping price for the job
-L A Lindsay

Answer to the opening question:

A house   170 tons
Blue whale   175 tons
Jumbo Jet (empty) 250 tons

Householders Perspective

Wait for that wisest of counsellors, Time   *- Pericles*

Not Turning Up / On Time

I am afraid there can be lots of reasons for not turning up. On the occasions where I did not show up it could have been one of the following reasons. When the initial enquiry by phone was made, the customer possibly said something like "Come round and give me a price for an extension. I haven't got any drawings at the moment. I just want to know a ball park figure, but I won't hold you to it." Well, I interpret that as, come round and waste my time. On other occasions the customer has been trying to tell me what they want, but are actually telling me how to do the job! This is not uncommon. Some people are too clever by half.

Sometimes, you don't turn up at all to a loose phone arrangement. When such an appointment is made, I could have said I am too busy, or I don't have time, but when confronted on the phone by stories such as these and others you will hear about later, you say "Okay, see you later." I may have said that in good faith and either changed my mind as soon as I put the phone down, or as has happened to me on lots of occasions, said to myself in the car on the way to the job, "Why am I going to help time wasters and clever buggers?", and promptly returned home.

You might well ask how I know that people are time wasters. After 50 years in the game opinion often comes down to a gut reaction to what is being said and how it is being said over the phone. Most people talk too much on the blower, and when they start to contradict themselves, I struggle not to lose interest. It is right and normal that potential clients should fill me in with what they require of me. However what is also apparent is the caller's need to inspire some sort of trustworthy response from me. Many times this is sadly not the case and therefore time and money can disappear in a hurry. In such phone calls an on the spot decision is needed, so I back my judgement, which does not often let me down. Playing the percentages I suppose, but I've lived my decision-making life on this gut instinct, perhaps in lieu of the formal education I didn't receive.

Time Wasters

Potential customers often phone up wanting a quote for extensive or small-scale works to a property. On many occasions the customer has not actually bought the property at this point, but wants to use all my experience to rebuild or renovate an intended purchase all, from my professional perspective, for nothing! I usually tell the customer to find a surveyor or pay me to do the same job as a professional would do. Why would I waste my time working out a price that will in all probability be used to carve lumps off the purchase price of the said property? A surveyor or architect would charge at least £500-£600, so why pay that when a builder looking for work will do the running around for nothing? Most of us take what we can from anyone or any given situation, depending on our temporal needs. This being so, the being taken for a ride simply because of the uneducated social stigma of builders has become over the years rather tiresome. Therefore customers automatically assume that they can take advantage of us builders. For donkey's years we have probably been the authors of our own misfortunes in putting up with this situation uncomplainingly. I suppose therein is one of the more glaring differences between the educated and uneducated.

I think customers must endeavour to understand that, although travelling to and from house visits is all part of the job, no builder gets paid for this or for the information given. If, like me, you have over half a century of experience, why should you give someone the benefit of it, of that multi-faceted education, for nothing? Ever been to see a solicitor and walked away without an invoice? Enough said!

As an example of builders not turning up, I asked half a dozen builders to come round to my house to talk about the problems we all encounter and to swap stories. I thought this might be a good way of researching my subject, though having bought all the beers, alas, only two of the blighters turned up!

I've heard customers complain: "They came round and stayed for 3 hours talking about the job, but never got back to us with a price!"

If you are in someone's house for hours you begin to build up a mental picture of the customer and it is quite possible that you hear or see something that really puts you off. For instance, they might show you some work they had done previously and comment that the brickwork wasn't straight, the corners weren't square, or the plastering wasn't smooth enough. However, when you have had a look, you find that the brickwork is perfect, the corners are very good and the plastering is as good as you will ever see! If you experienced this after 10 minutes in the house, you would only be in there 15 minutes; if, on the other hand, you heard it after three hours, you would still get out as soon as possible.

In such a case there are two reasons why you would not go back to the house. Firstly, if you felt that the last builder's work was being criticised unfairly and, having established that there was nothing wrong with it, applied some foresight as to what the customer might say about your own work; probably nothing, until it was time to pay, no doubt hoping to knock some money off the price.

Secondly, the customer in this case has no perception of what constitutes a good job. In this house you might get away with a 'so-so' job on the basis that the customer doesn't know a good job from a bad one, but I doubt it. In truth the same can be said of any job, and this is no basis outright for doing a so-so job. Do you really want to put yourself through a situation where you know you can't win? Incidentally, where do you think the customer obtained this expert knowledge of brickwork, or plastering? From the old lady next door, of course!

Another reason for not getting back with a price after a visit, which has happened many times, on leaving the house another builder crosses your path. Naturally, whether he is known to you or not, you somehow feel betrayed. Some customers will make sure you arrive and leave at the same time, so they can play one off against the other. There is nothing wrong with competition, but the thought will always be there – "Did they do that on purpose?" Therefore, can you trust them with your livelihood?

Excuses

Several excuses are always less convincing than one   - **Aldous Huxley**

All the following are builders' versions of 'the dog ate my homework' ruse. And that all have been uttered at least once I can attest to!

"My bricklayer is in custody for assault."

"My whole team of Albanian labourers were deported after the customer's little boy accidentally dialled 999."

"I took a day off work to meet the builder helping me, and stayed in all day. As night fell the moon appeared, but alas the builder did not."

My builder is an "Every night's a stag night" kind of builder.

"My wife's having a baby and I promised to attend all the anti-natal classes with her."

"I've just been offered a holiday at the last minute to Siberia, and I'm going."

"I have to attend a funeral every day next week so I won't be around for a while."

"Our van had a pile up and all my blokes are now in hospital."

"My wife's thrown me out and nicked all my tools."

Slow Progress

Builders will often underestimate how long a job will take – not on purpose, but will unconsciously tell a customer what they want to hear, namely "4 weeks madam, not 8 weeks…" and worry about it later. All of us are guilty of overstating our capabilities and timescales. If procuring a job depends on 4 weeks and not 8 weeks, then so be it. This is notwithstanding the intrinsic and specifically unknowable nature of how long any medium sized job will take. Innumerable factors can and will contribute to the time taken for any given job. Some of these factors are very much in the builders' control, and some are very much not. The following discusses such factors.

It has been suggested that builders must give customers fixed completion dates, as well as offering compensation for poor work. That is fine as far as the customer is concerned, but what guarantees has the builder to fall back on, should the customer renege on any part of the deal? On the issue of completion dates, with my wealth of experience, I find it almost impossible to put together all the components, such as: personalities and habits of customers and builders, builders' merchants and their drivers, sub-contractors, building regulations, architects, building inspectors with their vastly differing personalities and proclivities, not to mention the weather, which in this country can play a major role. All of these can be something of a nightmare to predict and coordinate. And none of this list attends to the actual material job itself! Often one does not know the specific state of a thing until it is uncovered, and thus can only guess at how long the thing will take to be adjusted / fixed / replaced; the timber under an old ceiling or floor; the ply under the felt of a flat roof; the state of the pipe-work in a drainage system (not to mention the hardness and density of the soil to be dug out!), and so the list may go on…

The idea that a customer simply has to agree to a start and finish date with a builder is fanciful. The law says work must be carried out in a reasonable time, so why not draw up a contract saying: "the work is to be completed in a reasonable time"? The customers are unlikely to wear this because, although it is the law, the clients' opinion of reasonable time will not be comparable with their builder's opinion of reasonable time. Of course, should things turn sour and the legal process is necessary to resolve differences, reasonableness of both parties will be considered, but ultimately the particulars of the job itself will wield most weight in court, given these are neutral and specific. Both parties may now be obeying the law, but world war three could be about to break out. We have now turned full circle and, as I hope you can now see, jobs in this business are interminably difficult to start and finish on a *good note*.

All these factors come into the equation when talking about time expectancy.

I suppose slow progress can mean different things to different people. For instance, the time taken for a job can depend on so many factors. If the builder has, say, a plumbing based background; it probably means he will have to call on bricklayers, carpenters and plasterers, etc., depending on what the job entails. We all know what happens when added parties and personalities are introduced – chaos! For example, in the slow doing of their job the brickies might be holding up the chippies who, in turn might be holding up the plumbers, then the plasterers, having been booked weeks ago, cannot make the rescheduled start date. It follows that the more people involved, the more can go wrong with the timing. The person you have hired might as a builder be a good tradesman, but not a good communicator, project manager or timekeeper. The builder, unless his workforce is very well known to him, is at the mercy of other tradesmen.

One of my fellow workers – a plumber, and an excellent one at that – is a classic case in point; he will be working on a job and go to lunch, not to reappear for a week!

The not uncommon fact that builders in general like a drink, reminds me of a site I worked on in Brixton. I was the bricklayer foreman when after lunch on a Friday, the entire workforce of 63 bricklayers and 22 labourers did not return from the pub, obviously having acquired an insatiable taste for the ale. Needless to say they were all sacked, but reinstated the following week.

Probably, the most common reason for slow progress is when the builder only attends the job three or four days a week. The reason for this is, in my opinion, threefold.

Firstly, I could never fathom a builder who deliberately delayed finishing the job, because if he had more than one job on the go, then presumably he had money tied up on two or more fronts, so he would have to finish all the jobs before getting paid, and thus have the incentive to do so asap. On the other hand, the builder may be taking money from one job to finance the other, which would explain why he can't pull out of, or cancel any of the work.

Secondly, and this situation has happened to me many times, where you are stuck on a four week job, then a 'nice little earner' comes along much too straightforward and profitable to turn away. It could be a one day job, or several days' work. Either way, the money is so good you just can't turn it down. I prefer to tell the client what is happening, but some builders will probably make an excuse or lie, or blame delivery problems.

Thirdly, if your builder employs more than two men he will in all probability have other sites on the go. For example, his bricklayers having done their bit cannot hang around waiting for the chippies to finish, so his workforce continues to rotate his various sites. Consequently a builder's occasional absence could be for this reason alone.

Most male clients think they are architects and their wives often purport to be interior designers. If they pretend to know more than the tradesman then the builder will surely lose interest, and time will be lost. Conversely, slow progress can sometimes be linked to the customers' own lack of knowledge. For instance, there are certain types of work where you can make it seem as though you have worked very hard, and others where you have worked hard, but there is little to show for it. The former is known as a 'big show' and often comes together in the last days of a job. The latter is mere toil, the very substance of most working days. One such job where a big show is made is plastering and rendering, where you usually cover up messy brickwork or block work in a flash, giving the impression that you have achieved far more than you actually have. Roof repairs are other examples that can be done relatively quickly, although in this case one is also paying for the danger element.

On the other hand, all work that is below ground level is usually very tough and time consuming and, of course, it always ends covered up so you cannot see the effort that has gone into it. Pushing wet concrete around is, in my opinion, the hardest task for the body to cope with, particularly if, like me, you are getting on in years!

Nowadays the proliferation of TV time afforded to builders can be summed up thus; how many programmes' projects finish on time? None, a programme on builders would not be newsworthy, if work was completed on time, and so the time-myth aspect of our work, is self-perpetuating.

One lady complained to me that her builders built a kitchen extension and loft conversion that took two months to complete. When I told her the time taken was very quick, she said, "Is it?", and then proceeded to complain about something else! The moral in the mind of these kinds of customers, these kinds of people (the worst kind) is, 'If your builder completes the job on time, complain about something else.' The less said about such regrettable perspectives, within the building or the wider world, the better.

Lest we forget, too, that slow progress may not mean the same thing to a householder as to a builder. All builders who have a price for the job must get on with it or lose money by delaying completion. So it follows that the longer the job takes to finish the less he will earn from it.

Other causes for delay could be things beyond the builder's control. For example: problems caused by unforeseen situations governed by the council building inspector, or a builder who has already drawn too much money from the job will have little incentive to return to complete it. For example on a job costing £10,000 and of some eight weeks' expectancy, there might be say four or more weeks to completion. The builder who might have asked and been given £8000 doesn't see the need to return to finish what he has started. Clearly not good, but the lesson for the customer is clear - don't pay too much up front.

To achieve continuity in time and effort, not to mention safety, I recommend insisting on no drinking on the job!

Another reason for delay could be that you, the customer, have promised to do something but have not done so. Perhaps the promised payments are slow in materialising, or, having not been offered a cup of tea on a cold day or a cold drink on a hot day, the builder feels a bit miffed. Some see no reason to go the extra mile, which of course works both ways. Obviously one should be above all that, but people and especially builders are different. Such things can often set the tone for the day, or the whole job.

Once I had a chippie working on my house that went berserk because my wife would not make him a cup of tea on the hour, every hour, and failed to accept the reasons why this would not be done! The fact that he could have made his own tea every five minutes, if he so wished, was completely lost on him! Clearly some people are just difficult, regardless of profession.

Last but not least ... you may just have a lazy builder!

Is it progress if a cannibal uses a knife and fork?   - **Stanislav Lec**

Misunderstandings

Having the builders in your house can be, I'm told, as stressful as arranging a wedding, buying a house, having a baby, or worse still, than spending two weeks with the in-laws! And so, misunderstandings can be very near the surface of everyone's emotions. Misunderstandings can be a clash of personalities and nothing more, particularly at the beginning of the job when the day starts off badly, and things get steadily worse. This can happen. Usually misunderstandings only cause trouble during and after the job. However, there is one word that when dropped into the conversation will time and again cause resentment on both sides: "I assumed you would include that in the price," or, "I assumed you would automatically do that," or, "I assumed it was part of your job to see to it," and so on, and on. On reflection it is rather a clever word to drop into a conversation because there is no defence against it. Of course like most things it's open to abuse, and if you're a customer, the subtle and timely use of it could save you a lot of money! If on the other hand you're on its receiving end, often money can be lost.

I worked on a job for a banker once, who decided to itemise and photocopy everything he wanted us to do, so that there would be no misunderstandings. Unfortunately for him he was caught reneging on the list, but do you think he would admit it? At the end of the job he proceeded to complain about everything, so on this occasion, the fool-proof plan backfired (This story is explained in further detail in 'Justice'). The moral of this tale must be that misunderstandings are always possible - and often quite likely - despite our best efforts.

If one person is hell bent on getting the better of another, particularly when the builder is owed money, all lines of communication break down and it very often seems to be the builders who get the blame.

Many booklets have been produced by building societies and insurance companies, and even newspaper articles and local councils produce literature about dodgy builders. All are well meaning, but can only see the picture from one side. After all these people work in an office, surely a disadvantageous place from which to view the realities of the building world.

All of the above often say, "don't pay money up front for materials, or anything else." So who pays for the materials required? You can't expect a builder to both fund and complete your project, only to finish the job and hope he gets paid all his money! An absurd and illogical conclusion, to a supposedly helpful initiative.

Sometimes a customer won't have the money at the beginning of the job, or sometimes won't have the money at the end. Either way, if the builder is forced to fund the project it is considerably cheaper than borrowing from a bank. Why get the bank to fund the job when the builder will do so for nothing? If the customer realises the powerful position he is now in, you can bet your bottom dollar he will use that fact to extract more from the builder. I have been in this position many times, and I can confirm that being bent over the proverbial barrel is not a nice place to be, especially with your livelihood dependent on the outcome.

I once worked on a large estate in East Horsley; the house was very old, with gardens of about 19 acres. I looked after the maintenance of the buildings for the same owner for about five years. He sold up and new owners moved in. I got on very well with the new owner, but his wife was nothing less than a cow! My first job for the new owners was a very difficult one for any builder. I worked about two weeks on that job and every time she spoke to me we had a row. Perhaps she didn't expect me to answer her back! I knew my days on the estate were numbered, and so it proved when I was asked to leave. I don't think there were any misunderstandings on my part, just a war of attrition on hers. Of course - I played my part in the drama - but I was not prepared to take her vitriol. I can only surmise there was a violent clash of personalities and, not irrelevant from my perspective, the fact that I had just finished the project to her satisfaction meant nothing.

Some fine examples of misunderstandings can be found after the great storm in the autumn of 1987. People who work on roofs as I do were in very short supply. On the Friday I organised for the weekend to visit all the people who contacted me about their damaged roofs – some forty in number. I set off early on Saturday morning with the express intention of visiting everybody, not knowing when I would be home again. The misunderstandings began on the first visit. When I had finished the roof the lady owner demanded an invoice. I'd said on the phone prior to my visit that I can't write out any invoices today, but I will get them round to everybody as soon as I can. I told her I have to get round to other people who were also in trouble. She did not understand that I had to get round to all these people before it got dark, clearly not caring a jot about anyone else. I accept the client's need for an invoice, but selfishness was to rear its ugly head more than once over the next two days; the sorry situation was repeated again and again all weekend. Good fortune then that we don't get great storms every weekend!

One day when I was talking to a lady she came up with a classic: "We hadn't paid for a first class job and we didn't get one!" Did she mean that they did not get a good job, but the price was okay? Or did she mean that they wanted a first class job, but did not get one? Or was it that they wanted a first class job, but we know it wasn't a first class price?

Cross all those with, 'We didn't want a so-so job at a first class price'. Confused? If you now throw into the mix: "If we paid for a first class job, we expect a first class job", which leads us back to square one! If she wanted a first class job knowing she wasn't paying for it, she should not have expected one – but she did.

Go back to the beginning of any given job and you can see the difficulty faced by the builder; he takes responsibility for the price before the job starts. The customer's version is always backed up by the benefit of hindsight, but still you get misunderstandings. It is at this point that I am glad I have fifty years' experience at the University of Building Psychology!

I am not sure if this next example is a case of misunderstanding, or of unrealistic expectations. An old lady asked me to build a wall at the bottom of her garden. She said, "I have a pile of assorted bricks you can use."

The bricks were very literally a heap of rubbish! She suggested I throw the wall together and make the wall look old and distressed. What she was asking me to do went against all bricklaying principles. Nevertheless I finished the project as best I could, and her first words to me were these: "I expected it to be better than that." I had done exactly as she wished, but still I got it wrong!

Criticism is something builders take on the chin over and over again. But criticism from the client is invariably with hindsight, so every customer is an expert until something goes wrong.

Once, as we had just finished fitting a new bathroom and kitchen, on the way out, the customer said: "Can you fit this new bathroom cabinet?" With the wave of my arm I replied, "Next time I'm passing I will fix it for you."

A week later she phoned up asking, "Where are you?" I replied, "I haven't passed you yet." Clearly she expected the cabinet to be fixed for nothing, and at her convenience, not mine. One can't blame her for being opportunistic, but with that approach comes the severing of certain expectations.

Another time I asked a customer to move an old mirror off the wall because it might get broken. "Put it down here," she said.
"You put it down there."
"Why, because if the mirror or the frame breaks while I'm moving it around the house you will blame me."
"Surely your insurance will cover that?"

You can now see what experience brings to the self-employed builder. The customer in this case was completely innocent, but what if the mirror or frame was originally damaged or broken, and as soon as you move it the mirror or frame falls apart, then what? Some unscrupulous customers would engineer this scenario to obtain a new mirror or frame from an unsuspecting builder. Agreed – this is rather a stinking way to live one's life, always on the alert to possible advantage taking – but decades spent in other people's houses has taught me to be highly wary of such potentialities.

At the risk of repeating myself, there are many further examples of misunderstandings in this book which are better explained and understood in the context of the particular situation. Suffice to say that misunderstandings are constant in most areas of communicative life, and often create irreversible damage to the already strained relationship between customer and builder.

Getting Ripped Off

Confusion is a word which could appear on every page of this book!

I suppose confusion can often start at the beginning of a job when the builder works out a quote for you; the customer's perception of the right price for the job might not bear any resemblance to the builder's price for the job. The builder's pricing structure is not cast in stone; the price he has quoted is his price, not the customer's. You see the customer's price cannot take into consideration the difficulties known by the builder, so not surprisingly it cannot be part of his price equation. Add on the very real fact that the client does not in real terms want to pay much at all. We as builders are only too aware of this, seeing it every working day.

Some people will never know they have been ripped off, others are only too aware of the fact, and others still think they have been ripped off because a friend round the corner thinks they have. Unsurprisingly all this is a matter of opinion – that of the customer and that of the builder.

So wary are householders of getting ripped off that the anxiety sometimes shows during the first meeting with the builder. An experienced and conscientious builder should see these signs and try not to intimidate the client.

I have at times been told, "You've ripped me off!"

And have countered, "How can you say you've been ripped off when you can see what a lovely job I have done for you, at the agreed price?"

"But it didn't take you very long," would be the reply.

At this point or just before the client will try to work out how much the builder earned out of the job, and say, "That's twice as much as I earn!"

Of course that comparison, although irrelevant on its own merit, depends entirely on what the customer does for a living – and of course the builder is not privy to that! But think how different occupations would view that last statement; A road sweeper would probably shrug his shoulders, a teacher might do the same, but a headmaster must certainly think they are worth more than a builder, self-employed or not! I don't think this attitude can be accepted or allowed for, in a quotation, as I said, the builder's price is his price based on the numerous specifics of the job, *not* the headmaster's idea of what a builder should earn. For example:

Materials – how many and how much
How long will it take?
Labour needed
Possible difficulties

Having completed a small roof repair for a wealthy girlfriend of my ex-wife, she soon began complaining about the price despite having agreed in advance.
She asked my ex-wife, "Has Leo got money?" thus implying that if I had got money, the price charged was okay, and if I hadn't, then I had ripped her off. The client was happy to pay if her money was going to someone with money, but she objected paying out to a common poor builder with basically nothing. In my opinion this is a clear case of upside-down logic which, to comprehend and transcend from, one should need some kind of degree in public and classist psychology. I can only describe her behaviour as financial subordination, or to put it another way, a snob.

No-one can make you feel inferior without your consent

- **Eleanor Roosevelt**

If the expectation level of the client is greater than that of the builder, then you can be sure that trouble is just around the corner. Naturally, neither the customer nor the builder can in any overt sense be aware of each other's expectations until the job is underway. If the customer tries to impose his expectation level on the builder beforehand, then the builder might view the customer's opinion as interfering (at best),or telling him how to do his job (at worst). I don't see how anyone can claim to be ripped off having already agreed the price beforehand! Unless of course they had reservation about the price but for one reason or another did not speak up. When a customer cries foul on these grounds, what they mean to say is that the builder's profit is more than they are prepared to accept. It is at this point that the quality of the work will be in question. As you can clearly see the customer's version, unlike the builder's, is heavily influenced by hindsight.

Headline in national newspaper: "Should the law treat cowboy builders like yobbos or ASBO's??"

If you have been ripped off could the police charge the builder with an anti-social behaviour order? What is going on when the law has to arbitrate between a builder and a client whose opinions are diametrically opposed? May I explain? Most members of the public require a price for a given job and only after the job is finished do most people complain, generally because the builder might have earned more in a shorter period of time than expected by his client. The builder's patron, being upset by what has been earned, now sets out to find fault in whatever he/she can; either way the client will think: "We've been ripped off," and will complain to whomever listens, like the Office of Fair Trading.

Take out the obvious £10,000 paid for fixing a roof tile, what numbers are we left with out of 100,000 complaints a year? I would contend about the same as those listed against lawyers, estate agents, architects and surveyors. As these professional bodies are made up of mostly educated people, can we assume it is acceptable to rip the public off legally because the practisers of such professions are better educated than most builders?

Builders Perspective

Getting Paid On Time

Certain customers or the public at large may think that we are lazy, dishonest, incompetent, etc. Wait till you hear what we builders think of our clients!

We as builders are frequently told by newspapers and mouthy television presenters we must provide references to prove we are capable of doing what we say we can. Might I suggest that clients also provide us builders with proof of a reliable and responsible attitude towards payment, and to show that they are good for the money? Turned around and on its head, the notion does seem rather absurd, doesn't it?

If you are prone as a man to self-doubt or diffidence, as a builder neither is very useful in being self-employed. I consider it crucial to be a good judge of character and not to suffer fools gladly. It is well known in the building industry that all customers want the best job possible, at the cheapest price using the cheapest materials; ideally they do not want to pay anything at all. In general this is fixed and known from the outset, and we can therefore act accordingly.

If the builder doesn't turn up regularly, or on time, then he can't expect the client to pay on time. But by the same token; if you turned up promptly and finished the job in good time and quality, then you would expect to be paid in full and on time, right? As with many things, that appear to be straightforward, they are rarely so in reality.

In theory, there's no difference between theory and practise   **- Yogi Berra**

I think it is fair to say nothing quite changes the atmosphere of any given job like its impending finish and final payment. There have been hundreds of occasions over the last fifty years of my working life where a client's mood has changed leading up to the final payday. I always tell my customers I won't give them any reason for doubting my work or my intentions, but I expect them to do likewise. I trust in all my customers until they give me reason not to, but because we are all different and looking at a situation from our own point of view, with our own standards and needs and individual pressures, problems are always likely to surface. I try hard not to give a client a reason not to pay, but of course if someone is hell bent on not paying or delaying payment, for whatever reasons, they will always find something wrong with the work to justify their behaviour.

There have been many jobs where the customer has behaved brilliantly, bringing lots of tea and coffee and patience, but as soon as the final payment is due the supplies are reduced. Or, when the customer is absent from the house or site when normally they are present, it is evidence that something is wrong. To build up a professional personality profile of a client is usually only possible on a long job, but if, like me, you live or die on a gut instinct, the essentials can be worked out much quicker. However I have been proved wrong on many occasions, when the customer has appeared with the money in hand without my having to ask for it.

Clearly, when a customer feels that something is not quite right they should say so at the time. If the alleged fault is fairly obvious they must point it out as soon as they become aware of it, although if it is that serious the decent builder must spot it first. What some devious clients do is to make a list of so called faults, wait till the end of the job then bring them all up and try to use the list as a bargaining tool to carve money off the price of the work.

People often ask who the worst kinds of customers are; the majority reply that first generation Indians (to the UK) are mostly troublesome to work for. This is not a generalisation or intended to be, just a fact of the builders' life in the generation I grew up and worked in. I will recall a few stories in later chapters, and here will offer another. I finished a small job for an Indian chap who approached me saying,
"How much do I owe you?"
"The same as we agreed at the beginning of the job."
The customer countered, "Yes, but how much do I owe you *now*?"

He wanted, of course, to change the goalposts, so I took off my coat and rolled up my sleeves. "What are you doing now?" he said.
"See this arm," I ventured, waving it about. "If you don't pay me the agreed price right now, this arm is going straight up your arse."

He was naturally offended, but could not see why I was also offended by his reluctance to stick to what was agreed before the work began. My experience with Indians as customers is that they think the price should be reduced just because the job has been completed, and then one finds oneself unfairly over a barrel. The next minute I am a racist and the lowest of the low, just because I stood up for myself.

I have been told I cannot generalise with regard to Indian customers, not PC and all that. I am not. These stories are all true, and upon asking any self-employed builder, plumber, etc. of my generation their reply will likely be the same. As a man who is so against political correctness, why would I now change a life time's rumination just to satisfy past Indian customers, who have treated me with so much contempt?

Everyone knows for a fact that customers in general want the job done for as close to nothing as possible. If you want to change the price it is only right and proper to try, but this must be before the work starts and not when the work is finished.
I once finished a job on a Friday lunchtime then approached the client for my money. She replied, "I did not think you would want it 'til Monday." The logic of that response escapes me, though I am afraid it is fairly typical, as is the next example.

On nearing the end of a large job some years ago, the client informed me that he was going abroad for about a month and that he would see me when he returned. When I enquired about some money, he said, "Can't it wait 'til I come back?"

I replied, "What are my tradesmen and their families going to eat in the meantime?"
He hadn't even given this a thought, and the property we were working on was worth at least one and half million pounds! Perhaps therein was the reason for his distinct absence of empathy.

As I touched on earlier, the last day of a job can either be something to look forward to, or something to fear. To look forward to because you have finished the job to as best a standard as you could, you have overcome the innumerable practical problems that befall almost every job, and for this you will hopefully be paid; and to fear, because maybe something went wrong, or a few words were said at some time on the job, even though the problem, fault or difference of opinion was cleared up weeks ago. Whatever was wrong then, will generally manifest itself on payday.
In nearly all cases the customer will not approach you, but will wait until you approach them, thus putting more pressure and onus on the builder with each new minute, and unfairly so at that, it seems to me; after all in most industries one does the work, sends the invoice, and soon enough gets paid. The implementation of this tactic most homeowners would not admit to, but those that practise it do so wilfully, and with intent to squeeze something out of the builder, be it favours or money, or both.

By favours I mean, "Can you just fix that for me and put that down there, and then I will pay you?"

If the builder then says, "and if I don't?" does that mean you are not going to pay me? Once you have reached that stage anything can happen, and it just might. What the customer is actually saying is this: 'I want to get as much out of you as I can while you are here, and at this moment in time I have got your money as a bargaining tool in which to manipulate the next few minutes or hours, so stop complaining and get on with it!" If you are owed thousands of pounds and the favours are not excessive you may be inclined not to argue, to do the extra work and get off the job. But if you are like me - stubborn and principled - you dig your heels in and confront the client head on. It is of course at this juncture that we builders are called the scum of the earth for standing up for ourselves.

Customers' Changing Minds

The classic situation is the husband and wife scenario, where one tells one story whilst the other tells another. Sometimes it is done in ignorance, but generally it is not. Clients quite often cannot see what effect changing their minds in the middle of a job could have on the builder and his temperament. They think that it is their right to change when and where they like, which in theory it is. But when a builder has fixed a price for the job, invariably the cost differential will not benefit the builder. Should the customer feel the need to exercise this prerogative, they must also recognise the need to reach a little deeper into their pocket.

For example, I remember one customer was asked where he wanted the light in his garage to be placed. He said: "I want six recessed lights!"

As I had only priced for one light - this he well knew - I told him to piss off and not be so greedy. A customer changing their minds before the price is given is fine if they bother to tell you, which often they don't. Sometimes the client will think that they have told you and argue the point till they are blue in the face. Invariably, given he has already allocated time and effort to the job, the builder is obliged to swallow it.

In fifty years on the job, so to speak, I have never come across someone changing his mind in a way that favours the builder. I recall one customer wanted a patio built. I had dug out the ground and was about to collect the crazy paving when I was informed that the patio was to be double the size! On completion I charged her one third of the price more, plus the cost of the extra paving slabs. She went berserk – shouting and screaming at the extra cost.
What I should have done was to charge her fifty per cent more overall. My mistake was not saying so at the point of change, but doing so I would have run the risk of the customer crying foul in the middle of the job; having got as far as halfway through the original size patio with no money yet drawn, I would have been in a very difficult position to argue my point from.

Being in this kind of compromising position is unfortunately an everyday occurrence for a builder. No wonder some of us are bullish, argumentative, obdurate, pig-headed and stubborn! It is as well to point out that in this precarious economic climate, clients see us builders in the same way as motorists would view a traffic warden or wheel clamper; a barely necessary and extortive presence.

Though this story did not involve the client changing their mind – rather it was a miscommunication that did not hinder the doing of the job - common sense should have prevailed, but it did not simply because of the increased cost to them.

I once built a very large extension for a wealthy couple, right next to the towpath beside the Thames. The clients decided to start work about a year after the estimate was given. When I re-ordered the six patio doors, I was told that the full height glass doors so desired now had new regulations attached to their use. The new rules regarding laminated or toughened glass had just been brought in so, as I was at this point three quarters of the way to completion of the job, I ordered the doors, as I must. At the end of the job the couple refused to pay the extra for the laminated glass doors, saying they didn't have the extra money. They also said I should have told them at the time, but what was I supposed to do – hold them to ransom with a job half finished?

I thought, quite wrongly as it turned out, that I could trust them to see it was not my fault that the laminated glass was dearer now than at the time of the estimate. It was also not my fault that there was a delayed starting date, which resulted in incurring the extra cost. No, I finished the job to both their satisfaction, and yet to this day I have not been paid in full. The amount of money I am owed - three hundred and fifty pounds - would not pay for the rope ladder attached to the ocean going boat moored no more than ten metres away from the extension! Was I wrong not to expect these pillars of local society to knock me? You might well say, 'It's about time you wised up on this sort of situation!' Of course you could be right, but every customer and situation is different, and to carte blanche the lot in a moody haze of distrust is no way to pass ones working days.

One trick a great many customers will try is to offer you a carrot in exchange for something which turns out to be nothing. The client might say, "I've got a small job I would like you to do for me now, but in six months' time I propose to start a complete rebuild."

By mentioning a big job in the same breath as the small one, they no doubt hope the lure of one will influence the price of the other, thereby getting the small job done cheaply with the inference of more to come. In such a case I would quote for the small job on its own merits, and ignore the client's 'wider' picture.

Extras

Extras - a word which in the mind of the builder conjures images of the devil Himself
                - L A Lindsay

This is a word guaranteed to cause trouble between builder, client or architect. The public's opinion of what constitutes an extra can be worlds apart from the builder's.

Extras don't usually make an appearance until the job is well underway. I think that at the first sign of the dreaded word some dialogue with the paymaster or architect must be made. The architect won't appreciate the situation because extras quite often mean that something unforeseen has happened, and he is being paid to make sure that nothing unforeseen occurs. It is not uncommon for builders and architects to be at each other's throats, both blaming the other with the client in the middle. Generally the client will side with the architect, not unnaturally, as they are paying him to look after the job. If the builder and architect came to an agreement about a contingency fund prior to starting the job, the architect would not be worried too much about the extra cost incurred. In reality this is uncommon.

Extras can be created in a number of ways. One is through the intervention of the building inspector. If the building inspector feels that a situation is best resolved by doing something different to that of the builder's specification, and in the process increases the cost of the job, then obviously the cost is passed on to the client. Usually a quick word from the building inspector to the client smooth's the path for the builder.

Another way extras can be incurred is when the client decides to change something for the better, rightly or wrongly. Pricing for extras can be an absolute nightmare, and potentially confusing to one and all. I will try to unravel it for you.

For example, you discover a ceiling that needs renewing, but you haven't priced for it. You tell the client that a new ceiling will cost £200. The client says: "Okay, carry on."

The client then comes back to you a couple of days later and remarks: "If you are charging me £200 for this ceiling now, why did you charge me £400 for the other ceiling you did for me last year?"

I explain that there is no comparison between last years' job and this one. On this job all my tools are here as is my scaffold and materials. On the ceiling last year, I had to bring everything to the job for the sole purpose of doing that ceiling. Therein is the price differential.

The point I am trying to make is that pricing for extras on a job already started cannot be compared to a one-off situation.

The downside of all this for the builder is that the customer thinks about the half price ceiling and gets suspicious: 'He must have overcharged me last time. Why?' Whereas for me, if I had charged £400 for the extra ceiling as I had last year, then presumably the client would not have known any different? The more devious builder would have put this forethought into action to fill his own pocket. Alas I am more transparent and, though never a stranger to stand up for myself, will invariably do my best to keep a job economical for the client, as I would want one to do for me. Alas, all this in an attempt to keep the cost down for the customer!

Suppose that the client had some other work that needed doing that I wasn't aware of, possibly in another part of the house; they might suggest that I would like to finish the rest of the house, but at the "extras" rate (half price). One cannot blame the client for simply being opportunistic, but when it directly affects the livelihood of an honest working man, when only he takes the economic brunt of the opportunism, it is just unacceptable. As I hope you can see - the whole picture has changed and turned full circle, especially if the client then says, "You could have done the whole job at the cheaper rate." Of course I could have, and then gone bust in the process!

You can see from this example that the more information you give your client, the more ammunition they have to shoot you with. Plus, if you add on a few zeros to the example figures it becomes a very serious business.

Another way that extras might be mentioned could be from the builder's side. Having started the job he may become aware that the price he has quoted is going to be a little bit too tight on his side of the bargain, and so invents ways to fashion more money out of the client in order to make himself and his pocket feel better for the mistake in quotation.

It has taken fifty years to be able to consider calling myself an expert. When people phone up looking for advice they automatically think I will do so over the phone, giving away free information. I am not saying that I wouldn't, but as I get older I have become less inclined to comply with certain requests. If you wanted advice from an architect or solicitor would you phone one up at home? What do you think the response might be? An eloquent version of 'Piss off', no doubt, or, *avec une petite surprise,* 'How much money have you got for a consultation?'

Can you imagine phoning a builder and hearing him say, "If you would like to make an appointment tomorrow, oh, and don't forget to bring your cheque book." There would be uproar in your house, and the House of Lords!

Something for Nothing

Nothing can be made from nothing   *- Lucretius*

A builder does not charge you for calling round, so don't expect him to offer solutions to all your problems without payment.

Here are some examples of a customer wanting something for nothing. Often on completing a job and diving out of the gate, the customer will halt you and say, "Before you go, can I put these bags of rubbish on your truck?"
 "Why?"
 "Because you have a truck and I don't."
 "What do you expect me to do with these bags?"
An intelligent response is rarely forthcoming. Take them down to the dump? 'I have to pay for that, but if you would like to pay me, I would be more than happy to inconvenience myself…'

On another occasion, upon starting a job, I decided against getting a skip because the skip lorry might have damaged the newly laid tarmac drive. Instead I borrowed a trailer to remove the job's waste. The lady came out and said, "Where is the skip, I've got a settee to put in it."

I am always being asked to put outgoing kitchen appliances on my truck on the basis that if they can fit in the back it's my right to take them away. I now refuse every time, because I can't afford to clutter up my truck waiting until such time as I am able to relocate them in a socially acceptable manner.

We turned up on the first day to remove a kitchen. The lady said, "My friend wants these units, could you drop them off at her house?" The job specification was to remove the units and dispose of them. The lady now wants us to take the units apart carefully, bit by bit, at least trebling the amount of time involved, and then drive ten miles to drop them off!

I said: "Okay. That will take us all morning, which will cost, say, fifty pounds." Upon hearing this, the customer dropped the whole idea. I am sure they thought we were being pedantic, but what cost does the alternative have on my time and livelihood? The fact is that most customers, given the right circumstances, will try it on. This job had just begun and already the atmosphere is strained.

I am often asked if people with money are worse payers than people without. Apart from the size of the house and cars outside, how can you tell whether someone has money or not? Especially so given the pretentious surfaces in modern society. To the builder only one thing matters; have the householders got the money to pay for the work? There are in my humble opinion only two types of customers; those who pay and those who don't.

Most customers think that by complaining they will lower the cost of the job. One way I used to deflate a customer who complained about, say, a garden wall which I had just rebuilt or renovated would be to point out to him or her that next door were happy enough with my work to compliment me on it, expressing a hope that I would rebuild their front wall to the same standard.

One situation that has always struck me as odd is that people who are cash-loaded automatically think they have a divine right to pay as little as possible. It is as if they are doing us all a favour by inviting us round to their house. It has been said before that this –

tightness, in a word - is why they are loaded, and we are not. I am not sure these people are no worse than a middle aged woman on her own, thinking builders are the scum of the earth, possibly carrying some of life's rotten baggage to thump him with when he comes around. At times I've been turned over by a little old lady shuffling along hardly able to speak. The point of course is that anyone can tell you one thing and do another. I have come to the conclusion that helping people does not enhance your prospects of getting paid or getting work. Nowadays, I will call round to a customer's house and do what I have to do, and no more. It is rather a fancy notion to think that I might become friends with the odd client. After nearly 50 years only a handful do I still keep in touch with. Outside of work situations I am a generous fellow; at work I have to temper this with the rigours of my commerce; truth is I'd be torn to shreds more often than not.

Whilst on the subject, why is a solicitor paid more than a brickie or a plumber? The fact that a so-called professional would in all probability have a better education does not alter the fact that solicitors are now two a penny and tradesmen are in short supply. This fact alone should raise the status level of manual workers, but don't hold your breath!

Money doesn't talk, it swears   - **Bob Dylan**

I remember listening to a radio phone-in about tradesmen's wages. A solicitor who had just finished his training was complaining that brickies were earning twice as much as he. The presenter, to his credit, slapped down this pompous prat's attempts to denigrate all manual workers. I suggest the solicitor write to the Jockey Club to complain!

The general public must be made to see that tradesmen of this experience are a dying breed, and must be paid accordingly to be kept alive and working.

As a man concerned about what my client is intending, I have come to the not very startling conclusion that in spite of all my experience my ability to mess-up continues to haunt more jobs than not. To be honest and straight in this commercial world sometimes feels about as much use as an ejector seat on a helicopter. The politically correct Health and Safety brigade are largely responsible for eroding the word "trust" from our everyday lives. Shame on them and us, for putting up with it.

Builder's Complaints

Architects and Surveyors

Architecture is the art of how to waste space   - **Philip Johnson**

As said in the synopsis; books have been written about buildings, not builders. Some famous names from the past - Edwin Luytens and W.G. Tarrent - are named as builders. Whilst not wanting to denigrate them or their achievements in any way, I suspect they were architects or surveyors, but they prefer to be remembered as builders – quite a change-around from today. All that they are missing is, of course, experience. Tutors like architects and surveyors are often only knowledgeable to the extent that all they have learnt is to preach from a book. Come across a problem - find the right book - problem solved.

Books are where things are explained to you, life is where things aren't.
*- **Julian Barnes***

In this most practical of professions - building - my experience leads me to believe that it is preferable to find an expert with a practical solution to all problems. Many times have I found an architect trying to impose his problem solution ideas on me; if I'm convinced that my way is best, I will take responsibility for what I suggest. Most architects and surveyors look down on us manual workers, but at the sharp end of the coalface, many architects are practically incompetent.

You would think an architect's own house, which he designed and had built, might resemble a work of art; not so in my experience and opinion, having worked on a number of these over the years. Wanting to create something different they often go too far. One that springs to mind required us bricklayers to construct a building without any plastering; therefore all walls internally were face work. Looking at bare block work in his kitchen and lounge did look choice. No plastered ceilings upstairs or downstairs. Looking through the ceiling joists one could observe the rafters and roofing felt showing. I suppose while he lived there his wife did not complain about the dust retention, although a new owner would in all probability plaster the whole house from top to bottom.

Looking through Collins Thesaurus I dallied on "A" for architect. One of many words contained therein was 'master builder'. How in heavens name could the title 'master builder' be attributed to an architect? The following tales I think prove my point.

An architect: one who drafts a plan of your house and plans a draft of your money
*- **Ambrose Bierce***

Whilst reading a newspaper one day I spotted a piece about the dismantling of an arch construction similar to Marble Arch. It was to be taken down and every brick and stone of this monument was to be numbered, boxed, and then shipped out to the United States where, I understand, it was to be rebuilt. Nothing remarkable about that you might think, except the cost! If the article was true and the cost of the operation correct, who received the money? The stated cost of demolition, boxing and transport to the docks was put at £1,500,000, (that was back in the mid-eighties). I would say that £50,000 might cover the demolition, and, say £30,000 for the transportation of the stonework, where do you suppose the other £1,420,000 disappeared to? Architects and surveyor's fees could not possibly be that much could they? You bet they could! What would these professional people do for their money? I doubt their hands would not make contact with the goods at any time in the operation, and it is highly unlikely that they would know how to dismantle the structure any better than an experienced builder, particularly a bricklayer or stonemason. How can these fees be charged and justified? Probably because someone was in the right place at the right time to capitalise on available funding. A job like that for a man like me would mean not having to work again for decades!

I know an architect I have worked closely with for many years. He is very well respected in the community. In the boom years he employed some twenty architects in a large practice taking on work up to one hundred million pounds. David kept me in work intermittently for 6 or 7 years. When he came to me with a drawing for a job, he always had a habit of telling me not only what he wanted, but also how I was to go about doing it. His practical synopsis was always laughable, and we frequently rowed.

I would say, "David I can't do it that way, I have to do it this way, surely you can see that?" "But I want it done this way," he would cry.

Almost every time this happened I ventured, "If I can't do it my way, I won't take responsibility for it."

I always got my own way, because he could not or would not take responsibility for the task in hand. I must have got it right more times than not, otherwise David would not have come back to me so many times. I think David was such a big noise in his circle that he did not like a mere bricklayer telling him what was right or wrong. I'm sure he respected me for standing up to him, but would not and could not admit it. The point about this story is that when you get down to the lowest level in the building trade, to the man that actually does the work; he surely is the one who knows best. You see the architects' pie is in the sky; mine is in my lunchbox!

What this story is leading up to is my concern about builders' Problem Pages in the daily broadsheets. The following is a letter in its entirety:

Competent or Specialist?

Question: My house has some spalling of the exterior brickwork near ground level and I would like an expert survey – for which I am quite prepared to pay. Would I need a specialist to determine the problem and the remedy, or would any competent house surveyor be good enough? I don't want a survey from one of these companies that will fill the walls with chemicals, issue a 20-year guarantee and no longer exist after five years.

Answer: I would think that any 'competent house surveyor' would be able to advise you. If he or she is baffled by the problem it is for that surveyor to call in specialist help, either from a contractor or a specialist in this type of building failure.

The expert in this article runs his own architectural practice. I will show how his answer is at odds with the building trade in general and with me in particular. The expert says a house surveyor would be able to advise you, then goes on to say "if he is baffled by the problem"… the expert has now passed the problem on to someone else and they are now baffled. The baffled ones are now asked to call in a specialist, a contractor, or another specialist in this type of failure. I think that is, including the writer, four specialists who are now on the case. I'm glad I don't have to pay all those fees! You see the original architect doesn't know how to get over this problem, so he passes the buck to another expert and so on and so on. Architects are trained to solve problems creatively.

What worries me greatly with this scenario is that the expert can presumably choose which letters to respond to, so why report on a subject he knows nothing about?

Going back to my friend David, the architect, he had the same problem when it came down to the nitty gritty. The answer to the question should have been that the only person qualified to deal with this particular problem is a bricklayer.   Ideally this is someone who has been operating as a brickie for a few decades or more, the older the man the better. Why did the newspaper's expert not go straight to the problem, because he did not know the answer? Some expert! I suppose if I don't now tell you what the problem was with the wall you will think I also don't know, so here goes.

"Ground level spalling (disintegration of brickwork) is almost certainly the result of water splashing up from a ground level path or patio when it is raining. Check the guttering when next it rains to see if there is excessive dripping at the point where the brickwork is affected."

I expect that the newspaper has to cut down the replies for print reasons, but my reply is shorter than the original and goes straight to the point – job sorted, and a reduced cost ensues. I think we have now turned full circle; the architects pass the buck as an excuse for not knowing in the first place. This very same architect was asked by his property editor to write an article on how to find a builder. Blind leading the blind comes quickly to mind. I agree he should have more idea than most, but why not consider asking a builder? Could it be that builders are not supposed to be able to write or communicate? If so, shame on everybody who thinks so!

If the blind lead the blind, both shall fall into the ditch   - **Chinese proverb**

Another newspaper, another expert, and this time supposedly a builder answering questions. Here's both the question and the answer in its entirety:

Ornate Ceilings

Question: *We have a Victorian house with ornate plaster coving and ceiling roses in two downstairs rooms. Unfortunately the ceilings are not in good repair and we have been warned that they may fall down. Is there a way of repairing them without removing the plaster or having the decorative elements removed and replaced? We are loathed to just rip them down and lose the features, so have not yet consulted a builder.*

The Expert Builder replies: *Old lath and plaster ceilings can usually be repaired and they are well worth keeping as the dense lime plaster has much better sound insulation qualities than modern plasterboard. The usual problem is that the plaster has lost its key with the lathes. If the floorboards in the room above can be lifted, the ceiling can be propped up from below and a fresh coat of plaster spread on top, which will bond it back together. If the floor above is inaccessible, then the ceiling can be screwed up to the joists from below, using expanded metal lathing to reinforce any weak areas*

I would suggest this expert has never in his life performed this task, and the way he purports to do so is downright dangerous. He suggests lifting the floor above; not telling the questioner that the whole of the floor covering must be removed for access. There is no point in just lifting one or two boards if you go down this route. Clearly, if the job is to be completed this way the mere fact of removing dozens of possibly old nails from the joists above will in all probability bring an old destabilised ceiling crashing down, assuming you have completed this task removing floor boards and nails successfully, without ruining the surface of the wood. The new plaster would not hold a very heavy ceiling. Let's say a ceiling 12ft square in size would be in the order of 10 barrow loads of lime mortar. The weight of that amount of one inch thick rendering hanging on the laths would be approximately half of a ton. This rendering is now dead, its suction long gone, the new suggested plaster would stick to the lathes all right, but would not adhere to the dry dead mortar underneath. If this job were completed in this way, nailing or screwing the floorboards back upstairs would in all probability loosen any key achieved. As for propping up the ceiling from below, the whole ceiling would need props everywhere, the room completely emptied, in addition to the disruption caused by having no floorboards. You then have, in effect – excuse the pun – rendered both the upstairs rooms and the downstairs rooms useless for a considerable amount of time, and all for a repair that in all likelihood would not work. That's one room done – now for the other one.

The rather stupid idea of screwing metal lathing into the joists from below only goes to emphasise what I said earlier, that this expert has never successfully applied his method in this way. To do so would involve holes all over the ceiling to bury the lathing into the surface of the plaster, further weakening the already unstable and dead adhesion. And re-plastering lots of holes all over the ceiling will result in a patchwork effect that will always be visible.

After all that there is another way not suggested, probably because the expert didn't know any better. The answer is to fix sheets of plasterboard with long clout nails (nails with big heads) or screws onto the ceiling, and reset this with a new plaster coat, thereby achieving a brand new ceiling with enhanced noise and heat reduction. One downside to this method is that the ceiling roses must hang down into the room by a minimum thickness of half an inch in the old ceiling. If that is so, all well and good, because the new plasterboard and skim will butt up against it. If not, the roses can be taken down and carefully stuck back on to your new ceiling.

As you can see, the newspaper expert gave the letter writer a false job prescription that would not work however much money you threw at it. Not incidentally, I approached this institution before I read their problem page and was told they already had an expert! Ha!

This same expert reviews the Joint Contracts Tribunal and offers the following:-

"A small light at the end of the tunnel appears in the shape of the new standard building contract for the home owner/occupier.

This is published by the Joint Contracts Tribunal (JCT), which normally produces documents the size of telephone directories so that architects and major contractors can spend the rest of their lives suing each other. But don't panic, this one is a little beauty, with only four pages, most of which are tick boxes, including the vital questions of whether the builder is allowed to use the toilet and/or telephone.

This is good stuff. It was written by a barrister… but the really good news is that it has also won an award from the Plain English Campaign".

Not one word of comfort for the builder from a man purporting to be one. Written by a barrister – so it must be good! Also an award from the plain English campaign – from a barrister!! Have you ever heard a barrister speak plain English? No, nor have I - and that pretty much says it all.

I did not think it fair to read this expert's column every week and then dissect his opinions, but I must take issue on a matter very close to me, since I have been present on site since the sixties.

The expert writes: *"When I started bricklaying in the 1970s there were still a few old boys who did not own a spirit level; they would gauge their work off the corners and use a line to run in between them and when they got to the top their walls would be dead level."*

When I started bricklaying in 1962 *every* bricklayer had a spirit level. In fact I don't believe you could operate on a site if you did not own one. Surely the expert must know that a tradesman working in this way would not be compatible with the traditional spirit level-owning bricklayer at the other end of the line. It would resemble something akin to a blind man working with a deaf mute on the same stage. In the early sixties my mentor Bill Young was considered on all his jobs as the last word in bricklayers, and was always the bricklayer foreman wherever we were working. He used to use a level that was only 30" long; it was originally 36" but it had cut down over a period of thirty years from so much usage. Therefore it was (in the latest) the 1940's that he, a master bricklayer even then, was using a spirit level as mandatory. This fact seems totally at odds with this expert's long-term memory.

I think this supposed authority on brickwork has got his decades mixed up, because I have at home spirit levels that are at least seventy years old (circa 2010).Are we to believe that seventy years ago bricklayers consciously ignored the use of spirit levels - albeit prototypes of today's fine models – which have since proved to be an on-site indispensable? I don't think so.

Bill Young never mentioned to me a time when he had not used a spirit level, so I can reasonably conclude that throughout his working life he had always used one.
Bill started working in about 1925. I can only assume this journalist/builder was exercising some form of artistic licence in telling this story.

I do not wish to berate this particular newspaper's expert any further so my last word is this: in such capacities as this kind of expert is permitted, how can one man be an expert on such diverse topics as brickwork, water softeners, smell of damp proof agents, central heating matters, solar panels, plastering, dehumidifiers, woodworm etc.? I think I know how – just like the architect already mentioned: find a problem, find a book to solve it. So yes, he is an expert - an expert on books!

The letter from the newspaper article in this chapter illustrates the architects' lack of ground level knowledge. So, get off our backs and out of the expert's page in newspapers, and don't flap your choppers unless you know what you're talking about! I know I'm being ever so slightly flippant, but years and years of listening to professional 'bods' telling all and sundry how to do the job wears on one, evermore so when I am in position to know what tripe most of theirs consists of. I'd rather they shut up and stick to their known areas. It seems to me that most architects and surveyors know what to do; they just don't know how to do it.

It was always said about my mentor Bill Young that he had forgotten more than most people could ever learn about brickwork and structural matters. I could not envisage Bill listening to an architect telling him how a job is to be done. More likely it would be him telling the unfortunate man to 'f**k off'! I am of the opinion that architects are the prima donnas of the building trade, so why should we builders carry the can when it is only half full?

The Sunday broadsheet is at it again, the editor asking the resident architect:

"When is it advisable to employ an architect?"

Can their readers not see the obvious conflict of interest? Not to mention an alarming vested interest. Do the editors blindly swallow every word their highly paid part-time scribes spout, not knowing or caring whether their readers get the best advice or not?

To consult: to seek another's approval of a course already decided upon.
- Ambrose Bierce

Recently I found myself in a charity shop looking for working boots, when I came across a book entitled "Concrete, Brickwork, Plastering and Tiling". A few swift glances and a pound was handed over. Some of the practices contained therein were a mystery to me. I know the manual is intended to inform beginners of the skills needed to perform the tasks named in the book's title, but how could anyone put their name to a book that is immeasurably flawed in terms of accuracy and content?

This is an amateurish attempt to portray some first-hand knowledge of a subject probably never attempted personally. Only a surveyor or architect would have the brass neck to experiment with readers' expectations. The author's pseudonym is Frank Spander – Frank Spencer would be more appropriate!

I was on my way out of my local B&Q store when I noticed a rack of leaflets purporting to be helpful. I picked up 'How to Build a Garden Wall'. Over a cup of tea when I arrived home I read with interest said leaflet. What a huge disappointment to discover that even with the massive turnover of B&Q, they could not write a more accurate account of how to build a garden wall! All they had to do was ask someone like me with decades of experience, and who teaches brickwork at several Adult Education Centres. So who do B&Q turn to? My guess is they have probably asked a resident architect or surveyor - with their vast practical knowledge of brickwork matters - to write a leaflet for their customers.

Any bricklayer with ten or more years' experience would agree that this leaflet is totally flawed. The sand and cement ratio is wrong, the phraseology is that of an amateur, and as a consequence is misleading in the extreme. The suggested example for foundations is absurd. If I or another builder were to add compacted hard-core to the bottom of our trench footings, the Building Inspector would shoot us! As for using a 'gauge stick' - here is an amateurish interpretation of a good idea, very poorly explained.

I also picked up a leaflet from The Royal Institute of Chartered Surveyors, out of which I'd like to dissect a few paragraphs:

What Type of Survey?
Outlined are the main types, all of which can be tailored to suit you.

Building Survey
This is a thorough inspection and detailed report identifying the existence of defects.

Additional specialist inspections can be arranged if necessary.

Home Buyers Report
This is a limited report on the structure together with a valuation. It is not intended to explain the causes of problems in detail or the solutions, but will show the major areas that need attention.

Valuation
An estate agent will do this for nothing!

What does it cost?
The cost will depend on the size of the property.

Then we can decide how much to charge you!

Can I sue you if you miss something? <u>Yes</u>, but only if it is something we agreed in advance to look for and most other surveyors would not have missed it. A survey is not a guarantee that there are no defects because the surveyor cannot see all parts of the property without taking it to pieces. A doctor cannot guarantee the health of a patient who will not speak, take their clothes off or allow any invasive examination.

How can you miss something you have agreed in advance to look for? How can you tell if another surveyor would or would not have missed something? If that argument were to appear in Court it would be impossible to prove. If the survey is not a guarantee, what on earth is the point of it? As far as the doctor analogy is concerned - the doctor will take the problem to the nth degree.

So the answer to the headline *'Can I sue you?'* is NO!

Surveyors are supposed to be experts but rarely are, preferring, prevarication to solving problems. In the domain of the surveyor the escape clause is more popular than Santa Claus!

What does it cost? The cost will depend on the size, etc., etc. and will be a small price to pay.

The R.I.C.S is happy to extol their virtues in this leaflet, but glaringly miss the most important aspect - the cost. Why?

One surveyor I will always remember is Tony Manners; not for his ability as a surveyor but for his eccentricity. A strange nervous sort of a chap, caught in a time warp of years gone by. Never a picture of sartorial elegance - a shade like me in fact - he used to shuffle about in a creepy sort of way, clasping his hands together with a silly grin on his face. The most obvious characteristic of this man was his ability to say hello, but never goodbye. He would greet you with hello and seemed to be happy to have a conversation of any length, but woe betides you if you hesitated or stopped talking! At the first hint of a pause he was off like a shot, not a word uttered, gone. His wife and their four children were also exceedingly odd.

Trade Associations

Trade Associations are supposed to have an awareness not seen by the general public, or so they think. The following glance through some Trade Association leaflets may help you to make up your own mind as to whether they are useful, or not.

I have in front of me a leaflet sent by The National Federation of Builders, called "Finding the Builder who's right for you". I shall pick out some helpful or not so helpful points for you to consider.

The Big Question: Price versus Quality. The price, as we all know, is everything. The quality is another issue entirely. The National Federation of Builders say: *"What's the point in having work done cheaply if it results in shoddy workmanship?"* The National Federation of Builders is implying that if you get a cheap price you will automatically receive a shoddy job. I would suggest that for a project costing less than say £2,000, the likeliness of shoddiness is much less than a project of larger proportions; a much larger job with increased timescales and increased variables will surely expand the incidents of potential shoddiness.

Does it then follow that if you accept a whopping estimate you will receive a better quality product? I would like to think the bigger the price, the better the job, but of course that's crap also.

The N.F.B say: *"What you want is a builder who will do a quality job at a sensible price. After all, you will remember the quality of your building work long after you've forgotten how much it cost."* We are now getting down to the crux of the situation. Surely what is required is a quality job with a choice of a cheap or exorbitant price; that way builders will be able to cater for all the customers' own vagaries and ideas about what is the right costing for a particular job. The point is there is no such thing as a sensible price; as a job progresses sensible goes out the window to be replaced by necessity.

Talking of quality, how can a customer with little experience of building recognise quality when they see it? Come to think of it, how would the people who run the N.F.B. recognise quality? I must get around to asking them! And the notion that a customer will soon forget how much money has been spent is fanciful to say the least. Customers always think they will recognise quality when they see it, particularly if they have paid for it. I'm sure it follows then, if you have not paid for a particular job, maybe on someone else's project, the quality is not as good as in your job. The customers' psychology about work they paid for being better than anybody else's is something to behold! The N.F.B. continue: *"We want you to get the job that's right for you, at a price that's right for you, so we have prepared this short checklist."*

To illustrate how difficult that last paragraph can be to affect in the reality of the trade; a builder working on his own house probably would not get the job he wanted at the price he wanted to pay, which leads one to the conclusion that if a builder can't get it right on his own property, with his own expertise and tools, with his own ideas and at his own pace, what better chance has he of doing so on yours?

The National Federation of Builders' checklist

1. Start with referrals (What a good idea!)

2. Ask for help from respected trade bodies

Not unnaturally, as with all trade associations, self-interest comes to the fore sooner or later. But in reality who respects these bodies? Certainly not the builders, and the customers will believe anything if it's in print. It hasn't cost them a penny, but once more the builders are the ones forking out.

3. Obtain estimates – Ask two or three builders for estimates in writing, ask them to confirm whether there is any planning permission required for the work.

I have covered estimating in another chapter. Suffice to say, builders don't get paid for writing out estimates. As far as whether planning permission is required or not, ask a surveyor and save the builder time and money. Why should a builder give out information gleaned over a number of years for nothing, when an architect or surveyor will charge heavily? Not once in fifty years has anybody suggested they pay me for information given, instead of calling in a professional. You would be amazed how many times I have given good advice for free, only for the customer to go and obtain the same advice from an architect or surveyor costing £500 or more. The moral here is quite clear; free advice is worthless because it's free. Pay a substantial fee and the advice becomes relevant and weighty, though not necessarily any better.

4. Ask for a reference

Customers are not interested in references, only the price. Twenty-five years ago I used to take with me on house visits a portfolio of photos and written references each in its own folder. I don't remember anyone taking a phone number from anything I brought with me. Sometimes I would ask if they cared to look at my completed work, and generally the customer reply, "That's all right, we believe you. How much is it going to cost?" The principle of asking for a reference is fine, but not a particularly new, practical, or useful idea.

5. Does the builder belong to a respected trade body?

As most builders don't respect the trade bodies, why should anyone else? According to the N.F.B. a builder must go through a thorough investigation of his accounts and business dealings, show membership to professional institutions and supply references from clients, suppliers and a banking institution. They seem to have covered everything except the critical fact of whether the builder can lay bricks, cut wood, lay drains, climb ladders and jump through hoops! Now, unless I am imagining it, the N.F.B. are asking the ordinary builder to work harder and harder on behalf of them – in supplying accounts and references and memberships - to then charge the builder for doing so. What can the builder expect for all this extra work, the N.F.B. logo of course (big deal)? Plus, the loss of between £300 and £500 per annum, for the doubtful privilege of belonging, to this organisation.

The N.F.B. will no doubt say that if you join up your workload will increase. Once again, for the umpteenth time, the price and only the price will determine whether you are successful in securing work on any particular occasion. I don't know the specific figures, but I would suggest that less than 5% of the entire building workforce in England is a member of a trade organisation. The N.F.B. and the other trade companies would have you believe otherwise (for their obvious self-interested reasons): "*If you join us you become one with some of the most experienced and established builders in the country.*"

6. Agree on the work and put it in writing.

As you can read elsewhere in this book - putting everything in writing will not nearly solve every problem you encounter. It might, in effect, lull the customer and maybe the builder into a false sense of security. Having put every detail on paper, contract or not, won't affect itself unless both parties are completely satisfied from beginning to end. The J.C.T. contract for homeowners – a giveaway at £9.95(but it should be free) - is loaded against the builder from start to finish. Anyone, builder or not, would be foolish to sign a contract for building work in this way. Customers don't need a document to try it on, but armed with this contract might well try to bleed us to death legally – no thanks!

7. Insurance – Ask to see the builder's public liability insurance certificate.

All builders that pay tax on an exemption certificate have to be insured. Other insurance plans for this and for that are forcibly suggested - as in most industries, evermore so in the accident prone building industry - and paid for by the builders again, the trade companies no doubt raking in commission from the insurance companies. I must move on before I start crying!

To take a moment to talk about how insurance and insurance companies can ruin a builder's existence over time. I have mentioned throughout this book how working for large building outfits is completely at odds with a self-employed at the lowest level. Is there a real need at my level for interfering with insurance? However, when it comes to big building companies with their mammoth work force, it is probably a must.

At my level can I point out how a builder's waning sense of self liability in the modern commercial world is compromised by the constant marketing of insurance companies' rhetoric? Do we as independent workers turn our bodies and or work ethics over to traders of insurance, just because that is what the modern world dictates us to do? WHY? The builder's ability to be in control of what he does is thus diminished along with his work efficiency and general sense of self-worth. Are we now breeding young men at work who find it difficult to respond to self-employed pressures in a way our forefathers did? Maybe as a self-confessed problem solver it may not be quite so troublesome. However, the young men coming up behind do not seem so willing to take responsibility for what they do. Of course the health and safety brigade create the fear and the insurance industry mop up the vacuum created. This alone emasculates workers leading to a breakdown of trust, work, health and ability issues, steering some towards breakdowns in relationships or social unrest, all because responsibility for our actions is stealthily being eroded behind the word marketing. For a self-employed builder it is in his own interest to look after himself because it is his body and his earning potential that is at risk, not because his body and soul is essentially owned by an insurance company.

Over time building workers who are employed on site clocking on and clocking off will become robots detached from all sense of responsible thinking. Can we be surprised if, working in a robotic state, our young men give in to alcohol, drugs and all manner of unsavoury pastimes? I believe workers in other businesses in the same work state will respond in like manner. To my mind, this is not a good thing.

To sum up, all self-employed people should have the skills to communicate with the rest of humanity. After all, what you do at work should mirror what you do in life.

8. Deposits and payments.

Why on earth would a builder fund an extension or some other project hoping to be paid at the end? I hope I'm not alone in the realisation that these two predicaments are as far apart as they could possibly be. A contract won't necessarily bring the two sides together, but trust surely will.

9. Beware of the 'VAT-free' deal

I don't know why the builder is hammered in this way, given that it is usually the customer who brings up the issue of a VAT-free deal. Which brings us back once more to the singularly important cost: if the customer can glean a few more pounds off the price, they are sure to go for it 100%. Sometimes the customer then can be the architect of his or her own misfortune.

All that I have written about the N.F.B. can also apply to other such trade organisations, them all making money off the backs of builders who fund their existence. One thing comes over loud and clear; the customer benefits in every way possible, while the builder has to scrap his way around all obstacles put in his way, sometimes so on purpose. Most builders would agree that working on the job is probably the easiest part of the whole operation. The hardest part is listening to your customer's moans and groans about things which are mostly utterly irrelevant to the actual physical job itself. I can't quite work out whom these trade companies are aimed at; I think the audience falls between the customers and the people who fund the whole shebang. Making money out of both sides is surely a conflict of interest. Judge and jury come to mind... or should it be Punch and Judy?

A Headline to a leaflet acquired recently:

"Avoid cowboy builders! Never employ anyone offering a cheap deal for cash, they are almost certain to be a cowboy builder and will do a shoddy job."

Is it now the prerequisite of a shoddy job, solely, to offer a cheap price? What tripe is this? Who are these scaremongers? I will tell you who. This leaflet is advertising a contract between customers and builders at various prices ranging from £9-£12 a time. You can see how these entrepreneurial parasites play the customer and the builder off against each other whilst pick pocketing from both. Upon reading this next section at the bottom of the leaflet I could barely contain myself; by way of endorsement the newspapers expert builder is praising the said contract. This expert was the very same 'man I have already raised doubts about (under 'Architects and Surveyors'). What a small world it is. I'm quite sure in the making of all these leaflets not one builder has had any input. Why not?

Having challenged many leaflet makers from B&Q to trade organisations bosses to newspaper editors, no one has the foggiest idea why a builder has not been consulted. At least that is what I have learnt from many letters and phone calls to-date. Maybe the idea that a builder should question these educated souls is an insult to their usefulness. I have found it difficult to make any headway offering my services all to no avail – a builder contributing to an article about builders – what next?!

A representative of the Guild of Master Craftsmen phoned me up and said I had been recommended as a builder who was good. I asked who recommended me; the caller was very evasive and surprised, obviously not used to awkward questions.

She said: "I can't tell you who it was".
I replied: "Of course you can't, because nobody has recommended me".

She then went on to tell me about the many benefits of the Guild, none of which had any practical or effecting relevance to me at all, plus, of course, she expected me to pay for the privilege! Such lies can be put down to a marketing ploy for; after all, this organisation and many others are just money-making machines and nothing more, really, nothing more.

The moral here is you pay your money and make your choice. The Guild implied that you join and the work will come flooding in, but I think the public well know that one only need pay a fee to the Guild to go on their register and use their logo. This is all very well, but how does the Guild know whether you are competent or not? This particular caller did not ask any relevant questions at all!

I did explain in another chapter what happened with the N.H.B.C; but briefly, our friend at Broadmoor could have answered their technical questions just as my wife did in the other chapter. I'm sorry to have to repeat myself again, but all these trade organisations want is my money, and therefore they are very little use to the public at large, despite what you are told in their advertising. The ability to conjure up work depends on one fact and one fact only – *the price*.

Having found someone who needs some work doing, as I have said, the price is always the determining factor. To get to this point involves a great deal of time, effort and ingenuity to procure the chance of quoting for a job. Many times work has accrued by just being in the right place at the right time. It is said that much business is conducted down the pub, but never has it been my fortune for it to be thus.

This was sent to me through the post: *Just a few words about "Construction News" the UK's leading weekly newspaper for the construction industry.*

Construction News (example)
From the site
Joe Bloggs (Surveyor)
To the Boardroom
Jim Bloggs (Managing Director)
Wimpy UK Limited

What in heaven's name has all this to do with builders at grass roots level? – Absolutely nothing! Joe Bloggs will no doubt be called a builder, but would not know the difference between a level and a bevel. I realise some people have to run the show, but cannot, should not, and must not at any time call themselves builders, because they are really not. Some trade association leaflets and other commercial advertisers show a Local Authority building control logo. To an ordinary punter this would appear to be an authority-based endorsement of what is being sold, a sort of kite-mark for quality. This illusion is created for the benefit of whoever is printing the leaflets, therefore to the man in the street the logo is entirely meaningless and without foundation – a bit like hiding behind the Local Authority's skirt.

The Trading Standards officers tell Joe public that under the Supply of Goods and Services Act 1982 you are entitled to expect the following standards from a contractor. Why is there not a law to protect builders from the customers' own frustrations and ridiculous expectations? The broad Contract Law and the specifics of any given case may well do this at the regrettable end of a dispute – in court. Before this last resort, some would say the J.C.T. contract protects both sides; I am afraid I would never sign this contract because it is loaded against the builder. The customer always has the upper hand and will not hesitate to screw the builder (because the handing over of their money is involved) whenever the chance comes; and you can bet that at some point in a job it will.

At the bottom of the contract advert is says: *"The building contract in this pack can only be used if a consultant is appointed to deal with the builder."* That's £10 for the contract and an arm and a leg for the consultant! The builder obviously won't pay for the consultant and if the customer pays for him, the builder clearly is at a disadvantage. I suggest the customer forget all the rubbish written about builders, and use your instincts! And don't become greedy –if you are shown no reason not to, trust the man.

Whilst reading through a tender document, which was sent to me by a good friend of my wife (admittedly a solicitor), I could not be more struck by the architect's evident determination to secure a prejudiced or jaundiced contract. The document as it applied to a builder was pure dynamite; at the conclusion of the perusal I was exhausted! Some of the P.C. requirements were simply unalterable irreverence: produce your own water, gas, electricity, provide hard hats for the architect's visits, and ascertain all site conditions **before** tendering!

One was required to provide a weekly report to the architect so that he did not have to visit too often, and point out to him any discrepancies before he did visit - who was present on the site, or not - plus give a weather report. At the bottom of the document the builder had to accept responsibility for lightning strikes, earthquakes and the architect's possible incompetence; not to mention the client's intransigence and belief that builders should be done up like a kipper as you would surely be if you signed the document! The work was duly completed, but not by me! The builder could not have made a profit with overtime damage at £450 per week, *or part thereof*!

Who are these people to demand everything from a hard working profession? And of which I suspect (based on the nature of the composition) only a very small minority are of any character. One last point about this precarious contract is revealed in the final sentence: "I/we undertake, in the event of your acceptance of this tender, to execute with you a form of contract embodying all the terms and conditions contained in this tender and any of **our** requirements." The penultimate word is the final nail in the coffin of hope for the prospective builder. After thirteen pages of "**we** want, **you** can't do," and "you are **not** allowed," this last word is issued just in case something has been missed. This damning guarantee is one that is definitely worth the paper it was written on!

Everybody knows there is no such thing as a cast-iron guarantee. As I see it, the only way you could cover a guarantee is to have one hell of a price for the job in hand; possibly treble what you would normally charge for any given work. The reason, not unnaturally, is that the customer can mess you about as much as he likes because the builder will – due to his aforementioned and forecasted estimate - make a healthy profit. I think (because I have not for obvious reasons never seen this done) and I hope so (because I do not want to see the honest and hardworking builder come up short from a job).

One very important word missing from all thirteen pages is **trust**! What is the world coming to when all forms of trust in the commercial world go out of the window? Surely we as human beings must be capable of conducting ourselves in business better than this? We certainly used to be able.

When I grew up people would work to eat and live. Companies existed to facilitate that fact. What seems to be the case now is that we still work to live and eat, but these companies' DNA forbid them to do nothing more than screw us all in the pursuit of record profits. This pervades down the ladder until everybody is on the same path, some unable to climb on and some unable to climb off. The problem with this is that the upward profit driven spiral is never ending. Unless there is change in a profit driven economy, this will only get worse. As an example, take usury - it will, mark my words, become the biggest industry on God's earth and when it does, we as human beings are doomed. This is mainly because usury produces nothing in industry, nothing to buy and sell and is therefore only of benefit to the lender, who will in all probability over time own us all. I do not believe that this affects the builder's world any more than anybody else's - just an old man recounting the bloody obvious. What has fallen by the wayside in my life is that obscure and forgotten word trust. Think how many people you can really trust with your life - I'll wager not more than the fingers on one hand.

It must be a nightmare growing up in a world where trust is only earned seemingly by a shuffle of twenty pound notes, accompanied by a roll of the eyes and a black look. It is a truly wonderful feeling (and so it should be) to trust another human being unconditionally, but too rarely do we see this.

Pay attention to your enemies - for they are the first to discover your mistakes
                                                                                    *- **Antisthenes***

We live in a world that seems to value the manic pursuit of money over patience, tolerance and kindness. Those of you that have not been self-employed won't know how much pressure is applied to both your own and your customer's conscience, to always do the right thing. Paradoxically, therein lays the biggest problem between worker and customer, both I'm sure wanting the best out of each other with our own respective proclivities in the way. As a man with a principled conscience preferring always to do the best job I can, unfortunately other factors are also at play. Not least and not believing that, everybody else is on the same page. Why?

As a small kid I usually felt somewhat different for reasons mentioned later in the chapter on pastiche of life. Even as an adult, communication with males particularly is difficult still. Part of this I think is that Bill Young drummed into me not to take or expect something for nothing. Many times when we were working at a house for say a couple of weeks, Bill would make us buy the lady of the house a box of tea bags so that it would not put a strain on her finances.

Consequently I don't gamble or even do the lottery. It is not that I disapprove, just that I'm not interested in the monetary system that breeds widespread greed and corruption.

When starting an extension on my first family home, I resolved never to borrow money from the banks, knowing that they would make even more profits out of me if I did. Instead I waited until I could afford to fund the works only when I had the money. Looking back I was not sure why the reluctance, only knowing it was best for my family. From what I have learnt as an older man, that decision was one of the very best I could have made. Simply put, had I not operated in this way the banks would have an influence in my life to this day, instead, I am free from their eternal clutches. An important decision made on a gut instinct aged about thirtyish.

I have many times as a self-employed builder been fiscally bankrupt, usually through lack of work or a banking induced recession bringing a hardworking man to his knees. This situation either turns you into a felon because of necessity – feeding four children – or strengthens your resolve further not to put up with clients' bullshit, when some of them are unemployable in the self-employed arena. On the one hand you go to work and get paid for whatever you accomplished if anything; on the other hand if we don't work we don't eat. Another way that our lives are clashing is that the very essence of trust is gone, but not forgotten, as evidenced throughout this book. Trust between all peoples has reached an all-time low, not necessarily in the building trade but everywhere. You don't have to trust somebody but you don't have to mistrust them either. Solicitors are not wholly to blame, but no win no fee culture pushes the boundary of what is truthfully decent, for a fee of course. It is not just solicitors who want to take responsibility for our actions, police and the town hall mandarins through the erosion of our civil liberties are others. We can, and we must, all be accountable to our own conscience, if not, others will fill the vacuum.

Having just finished my working life and retired it is a sad truth that bureaucracy makes everything difficult, especially for self-employed wannabees. So much so that we are unable or unwilling to think critically of people who make decisions on our behalf (politicians).

Politics – strife of interests, masquerading as a contest of principles; the conduct of public affairs, for private advantage   **- Ambrose Bierce**

Sadly there is much wrong with this world; luckily there are many good people out there, including builders.

Journalists

Journalism could be described as turning one's enemies into money
       - Craig Brown

The relentless media-focus on less than 1% of the building fraternity seems all out of proportion, and rather unfair to say the least. Such exposure reveals the scumbags and shithouses of this world that delight T.V. producers and scandal-sheet reporters alike. What newsworthy copy exists about the decent hard working souls who inhabit our world? The following is a paragraph from a newspaper, under the headline "Getting the Builders In":

One of the best ways to find a reliable firm is to ask a contractor whose work you have been satisfied with to recommend a suitable person or company, as they won't want to jeopardise their reputation.

Surely the contractor you have been satisfied with is entitled to expect you to engage them again! Instead, this journalist seems to be taking the piss out of a contractor whose opinion they value. In this way the public at large mirror the sentiment of the journalist, unless the opening paragraph is a printing error. Either way it stinks.
Another gem from the same article:

If someone should call at your door unsolicited and tell you that you need work doing, ask a reputable repairer for a second opinion.

If you are lucky enough to find a reputable repairer (whatever that is) one doesn't just use him to obtain a second opinion or a comparable price; get him in to do the job! The general public though are only too happy to play one builder off against another for their own money scrimping ends.

I have in front of me two daily broadsheet newspapers. One from April 2000 says:

"*In 1998, the most recent year for which figures are available, local Trading Standards departments received more than 100,000 complaints about builders.*"

The other quality paper dated August 1999 says, and I quote: "*In the past year Trading Standards officers have received 65,000 complaints about builders.* So between 1998 and the year 2000 the number of complaints had dropped by 35,000! The truth behind this claim is probably as impenetrable as the emotional fog that seems to obscure many of the facts about builder/client relationships. Personally, I don't believe a word any journalist writes when it comes to builders. One can't wholly expect editors to get together and universalise their facts, but surely some resemblance of truth must prevail, no?

Journalists say a thing that they know isn't true, in the hope that if they keep on saying it long enough it will be true — **Arnold Bennett**

Also from the same article:

"*Remember the cheapest doesn't necessarily mean the best. It is better to pay a little more and use a recommended, reputable builder, then save a few pounds and have a poor job to show for it*".

By the same logic, the cheapest doesn't necessarily mean the worst either. Are we to believe that a cheaper tradesman could not possibly be recommended or be reputable? Many times I have been told by intended clients that on a previous job they would have paid a bit more to have obtained a better job. Nothing wrong with that, you might say, as does this journalist. The point is, no client of mine ever said this *before* the start of a job, only after it was underway or finished, thereby reinforcing my belief that hindsight plays the biggest part in a customer's complaints strategy; that, and the fact that the price is first, second and third in order of importance to them.

This journalist, in trying to help householders, shows her ignorance of building matters by suggesting that *'an agreement should state whose responsibility it is to apply for planning permission.'* Surely even a journalist must know that you can't apply for planning permission without drawings! Without a drawing you can't expect a quote, although many clients will try (as I show elsewhere in this book). Perhaps this journalist would prefer us to guess what might be on the drawings! She goes on to say: "*If you come up against a problem, call in an expert, for example a surveyor, to give you an independent report.*" How independent can he be when you are paying him a fee? Why do journalists insist that if you are a kosher tradesman you will be booked up for months ahead? If so, how come the cowboys of this world are also fully booked? Could price have a part to play in this? What do you think?

Another example of creative scribbling: This scribe was telling her readers about her builder *"not reappearing as arranged, leaving her damp wall going green two months after damp proofing was carried out".* No wall would ordinarily go green after two months without the presence of a problem far more serious than an absence of continuation – trust me, I'm a builder.

One thread that follows all these stories is that not one builder has been consulted before opening their journalistic mouths! I was not going to mention the following because it seems petty, however, as journalists are not slow to savage us builders, I shall follow suit. I have seen articles again and again where the writers' ignorance of their subject matter shows glaringly through. When talking about a builder's labourer in whatever context it is always assumed that the man can lay bricks. Hod carriers are often mistaken for bricklayers, probably because it lends credence to an otherwise dull subject matter.

For the record, the difference between a labourer or hod carrier and a bricklayer can be about as much as the difference between a hippopotamus and a mouse.

A journalist writing about a builder who went on holiday leaving her house with no kitchen roof: did the journalist not know the builder was going away, or did the builder just decide to go when it was most inconvenient to the householder? I do not believe anybody would deliberately walk away like that, especially having already (presumably) done a good deal of work, unless there was an ulterior motive from the builder's point of view. It might be that he is owed some money. The ulterior motive from the journalist's speculative perspective might be that though the tale is fabricated, it does make a good story. Once again, we builders are just cannon fodder for journalists.

News may be true, but it is not truth, and reporters and officials seldom see it the same way
                                                                    - *James Reston*

Articles about Builders

I have in front of me articles written by famous and not so famous journalists, all of whom make a good living out of knocking us poor builders. I would not really mind if most of the contents were true. Let me give you some examples of creative scare mongering:

"Not forgetting the creative gang of criminals in Staffordshire who promised homeowners they'd lay pricey but covetable "speckled" drives of tarmac and white granite. The granite turned out to be crushed Polo Mints which dissolved at the first sprinkling of rain."
This famous journalist has failed to recognise the salient fact that to purchase the amount of these mints necessary for such a dupe would cost at least 1,000 times more than white granite itself! What would be more expensive - a bucket of granite or a bucket of Polos? I rest my case, absurd at that.

The same article gives us this gem (circa 1980):

"Then, the other friend naively agreed that her workmen should move in to the house to speed up the work's completion, only to spend the next 18 months listening to wall to wall Radio I, buying catering-size boxes of P.G. tips, and boil-washing five pairs of 'builder's buttocks' low-slung jeans!"

Exaggeration, let's take a look. She did not say what the project was, but we can assume that the house in question was not a two up, two down; five men living and working on the job for a minimum of eighteen months could probably build five loft conversions or three four bedroom detached houses. Serious money on this job! Five men at £100 per day for 18 months will come to about £160,000 plus materials, plus tea bags, plus washing powders, is it only I who can see this story as nothing short of codswallop? Is this fact or fiction? It's your call.

Literature is a luxury, fiction a necessity   *- G K Chesterton*

There is a myth doing the rounds of various publications, not to mention amongst a general public too, to the effect that a good builder will never have to advertise his services; because of the quality of his work alone he will always be in work. This is journalist-speak based on exactly nought years of experience as a self-employed builder (or a number of other self-employed professions for that matter). Surely someone who writes for a living should actually ask a builder, not the Chairman of a Master Builder's Federation, or Chief Executive of The N.H.B.C., not even the Editor of a self-build magazine. My experience leads me to believe that the sole arbiter is pricing first, everything else second. The overwhelming general attitude of those giving the work seems to be that if the price is cheap enough, we will deal with and get over everything else second.

Journalists often confuse unprofessional with common sense. As builders are not considered professional by the professionals, how then do you find journalists writing about unprofessional workmanship when all they mean is 'the cheating bastards have done this?' If you want an example of whether a builder is a professional or not, ask a loan company or a mortgage broker, ask them what status a self-employed builder has. Years ago it was easier for a postman earning £100 a week to get a mortgage than it was for a builder. Earning as we did £300 a week, insurance companies, mortgage brokers and assorted moneymen viewed us builders as 'journeymen' and not worth the risk. Clearly, times have changed. The humble builder, much in demand, has status at last, and the wage to show for it!

I would like to declare all-out war against journalists who write articles about builders that are downright lies. Journalists highlight big money scams - the bigger the scam, the bigger the headlines – and so it follows; the bigger their heads become. When journalists write especially about builders, they become masters of hindsight, and are therefore never wrong.

When a dog bites a man it's not news because it happens so often. But if a man bites a dog, that is news   *- **John B. Bogart***

As these parasitic scribes are inclined to lie about us builders, it is time for the worm to turn. Recently on the front pages there was a story about a journalist's attempt to embarrass an airport's security system by enlisting and smuggling a fake bomb into a building. Delivering a fake bomb can't possibly carry the same level of consciousness and all that it might bring to mind, not to mention the sweaty palms. Why don't the editors go the whole hog and send a journalist with a real bomb to the airport? Then and only then will we get this type of journalist earning his or her money without the benefit of hindsight!

I promised myself earlier that I would not moan or attack newspaper articles again on the basis that the incumbents can't fight back (just yet). On this occasion I can't help myself. This journalist, apparently well known to readers of all posh magazines, was listing the best architect, interior designer, and the best builder. The builder in question was an estate agent and former film producer, now masquerading as a very successful building contractor. How so? In my opinion, his moneyed connections gave him access to people with more money than sense, paying over the odds every time, and probably having the where-with-all to fund a large work force. With sufficient money it seems you can be anything you want, even a builder! This man knows as much about building as I do about flower arranging! We must watch out for the charlatans of this modern world, abound as they do.

Heroes

All my parental life I have tried to instil in my children a balanced perspective on life. Successive governments and journalists require teachers to teach kids about history's 'regrettables': Stalin, Hitler, etc. What about history's great heroes? Churchill, Drake, Nelson …? Surely these are worthy of our children's ear rather than listening to T.V. journalists fighting wars six months after the event with the blessed benefit of hindsight? This is warmongering from the side lines.

The following article from the Daily Express in 1996 turned a light on in my head which has never been extinguished, illustrating in an immeasurably fuller fashion my thoughts on this subject:

"Best of British can still inspire us to Greatness"

One of the great heroes of the Falklands War was Colonel H Jones. He along with his sergeant, died in a hail of Argentinean fire at the battle of Goose Green. He was awarded the Victoria Cross for gallantry. We learn, however, that he is about to be debunked in a channel 4 documentary. It claims that the battle should never have taken place and Jones's death was a needless waste. Well, in these absurd times, getting debunked seems to be the fate of everyone. Should we not shrug our shoulders and pass on?

No, it is time to stand up to the sneering backbiters who trade in the shock of the demeaning. Masters of hindsight, they can always fight a battle or negotiate a settlement better than the people who actually had to face the challenge. Consider what a mess the British seem to have made of their wars. We now know how in the First World War, the British were lions led by donkeys, and that in the Second the Spitfire was a notably deficient aircraft design.
As for the Boer War, or the horrors of the Crimean, they hardly bear thinking about. You would hardly gather from these memoirs of military muddle that the British have been notably successful in war. You have to go back to the American War of Independence (ending in 1783) to find a serious war the British didn't win.

This relentless media focus on the human confusion rather than heroic achievement is why we need not be surprised that the commandos of Channel 4 are now showing us how the Falklands War could have been choreographed like a Rambo movie, instead of the frail human victory it actually was. If only it had been fought by television journalists!

And since that war put Margaret Thatcher on target for a string of unforgivable election victories, many find additional reasons for debunking it. The response of Colonel Jones's widow shows that she is made of the same stern stuff as her redoubtable husband. She has commented: "There are a lot of 'if onlys' in life. With hindsight things could have been different and maybe people should not have been killed. But the answer is that they were and we should be proud of them."
What the Falklands War did prove was that, while many areas of British life had been seriously rotted by the ideological confusions of the Sixties (we are just coming to terms with the decay of the teaching profession, for example), the Army had survived intact. In a dangerous world, it retained enough old-fashioned virtue to do its duty.

The comparison with teaching is important here, because one important element in the decline of British education has been the banishing of heroes from the teaching of history. The older generation grew up thrilling to the deeds of Alfred the Great burning the cakes, Robert the Bruce inspired by a dogged spider, Thomas Cranmer putting his hand in the fire, the imaginative compassion of Florence Nightingale. History was basically a moral story.
No doubt it was rather simple history. The world is more complicated than such moral tales suggest. But, to say this, is not at all to deny that through the crimes and follies of history runs a

thread of human greatness, which we ignore at our peril. Yet just that understanding has been denied to many of our children. In the name of a vulgarised caricature of academic sophistication, many teachers, and more curricula, have banished heroes in favour of causes and victims. The key point on this question was made by the German philosopher Hegel. "No man," he said, "is a hero to his valet." He was quoting the poet Goethe, and he added: "Not because the hero is not a hero, but because the valet is a valet."

In other words, there are mean-spirited people who can only see in the world a reflection of their own limitations.

Hegel knew perfectly well that heroes and heroines have human weaknesses. They laugh when tickled, and bleed when stabbed. Like the rest of us, they often commit sins of intemperance: are lustful, or gluttonous, even mean and petty. It is revealing these aspects of the great that alone seems to delight television producers and scandal sheet reporters. When the moment of trial comes, what distinguishes heroic people is that they have a quality of steel that raises them above the generality of people. This moral recognition of the hero is something people could face was dramatised in the old-fashioned Hollywood epic. How often did James Stewart risk his neck holding a lynch mob at bay in order that the rule of law should civilise the West? The clever modern fashion is to sneer at these moral fables.

Does all of this matter? I think it does enormously, for it may lead to the destruction of our freedom. There is a famous Greek story of a new tyrant sending his servant to an established tyrant to ask for advice on how to retain power. This teacher of tyranny said nothing to the servant, except, "Let us go for a walk." As they walked through the field, the tyrant with a stick lopped off the head of every poppy that rose above the rest.

The servant did not understand the moral, but his master did. Tyrants rule by destroying heroes, and the most successful tyrants thrive by destroying the very idea of heroism.
Every hero debunked by the sneering revisionists of the media conveys a message to mankind: We're all weak, and feeble, and full of vice, and there's no point in sticking our necks out, or resisting the current fashion. It is an understanding fit for slaves.

By Kenneth Minogue
Professor of Political Science
London School of Economics

We are not attacking journalists just for the sake of it;

Just as a toothbrush is to a woodpecker, so are journalists to society
                                                        - L.A. Lindsay

I can't stop seeing propaganda all about us. Possibly the finest example is the BBC with its tentacles in technology. Driving along listening to a CD minding my own business, the music is interrupted by a weather report or announcement about traffic congestion somewhere. If I'm listening to the radio, fair enough, but it seems they (i.e. the BBC) can invade our entire world, even when we wish them not to. This leaves me to ponder what else can the powers that be use against us should the opportunity arise – AND IT WILL!

Solicitors

A lawyer with a briefcase can steal more than a hundred men with guns

- Mario Puzo

I have mentioned solicitors throughout this book dealing with problems in context. I have found most solicitors cold, blank-eyed, and ruthless, with a percentage just as corrupt as us builders. It seems you pay for two distinct services: one, for his or her experience or opinion; and two, for whatever practical work is involved, like the writing of letters, the making of phone calls, having of discussions. In this sense, much the same as a builder. I don't believe a solicitor's experience is any more saleable than a builder's experience. A better education might mean a more eloquent explanation to someone who is eloquent himself. To the rest of us, plain English will suffice.

I usually feel solicitors are talking down to me, much like one or two surgeons I have had occasion to visit. Maybe that, plus the eternal time it takes to finalise a divorce or the sale of a house, all contrives to justify the charging of exorbitant fees. How can a solicitor charge two or three hundred pounds plus per hour for imparting their knowledge and experience when a builder is offered nothing for his professional equivalent? Most solicitors work for a company, therefore they will get paid whatever is or is not accomplished that day. The builder must work all day and get paid only for what he does. Of course, his experience will be invaluable to him, but nobody will put a value on experienced advice given. When will this change?

The one great principle of English Law is to make business for itself

- Charles Dickens

Can you imagine a solicitor going shopping with a list given to him by a partner? Looking down the list he would say, "I don't want that, I only want the facts."

Back to justice and my experience of judges and the judiciary. I have had occasion to take customers to Court, from which I have made a general conclusion that if you are telling the truth you will probably win your case. Winning the case is the easier part of course; getting your money is quite another!

If I may you tell a story of taking a customer to Court back in the mid-eighties. I overwhelmingly won this particular battle of attrition. The customer had asked if he could pay me the money owed at a rate of ten pounds a month for five years. The judge asked my customer: "How much do you earn?"
"About three thousand pounds a month, Milord."
"Pay the man his money within two months!" roared the Judge.

82

Six months passed, then nine. I contacted a debt collection agency to recover my money. This is where the impossibly small print on the contract comes in; the collection agency did a deal with my customer that would ensure that I was fully paid in ten years' time because I would not pay their fee; after all, the outcome was not in my interest. The collection agency took me to Court in Romford – 50 miles from where I live no less! At this time I was having matrimonial problems and missed the Court date. In my absence, I was forced to pay. I wonder how many people have been taken to the cleaners by collection agencies, with small print claiming they are free to negotiate any sort of deal in your interests, or not. I say shame on them! The judge in this case and others since have been brilliant, but if people are hell bent on not paying, then there seems to be very little recourse open to you, even with the judge a 100% on your side! If he or she can't get it done, what chance has the rest of us?

Now post-millennium, it is possible that a County Court judgement debtor can have a charge made against his home, whereby the debtor cannot sell his house without paying up. Of course, unless the debtor is thinking of moving you will still have to wait for the monies owed. However the charge will always remain, so your hold over his assets will continue ad infinitum.

We see life through our work: to the doctor the world is a hospital; to the bricklayer the world is a scaffold; to an actor the world is a stage; to the priest the world is a church; and to the solicitor.... an open bank vault　　　　　- **L.A. Lindsay**

I found myself at a dinner party with my then fiancée; at the end of the table was a small weasel-faced woman with a voice like a goose farting in the fog; her speech resonated around the room, the rhetoric always challenging. Why do women have to prove they can talk everyone to death? I pondered. Guess her profession... a barrister! No surprise there; barristers are by necessity wordsmiths and can thus mask their failings from the world. Going out with a lawyer or solicitor one has to understand their mentality, their constant questioning and analysing and dominating the conversation. Perhaps this is one reason why the legal fraternity seem to stick with each other.

English Law is fair and just in so far as both parties are financially equal.
　　　　　　　　　　　　　　　　　　　- **L.A. Lindsay**

I must start this tale at the very beginning. A solicitor's wife contacted me with a water leak problem of some duration. It seems builders, roofers and architects were all consulted and failed to find the source. This lady wasn't interested in me finding the leak, instead wanting me to give her a price for rebuilding the roof area. I persuaded her to pay me for a day's work to find the origin of said leak. She bellowed that it was not possible, just to work out a price as wanted. I reiterated this was a particular forte of mine, and so she relented. Within two hours the problem was found, and later that afternoon the job was fixed. A job well done and thank you very much.

Now to the point of my gripe, the cost to this lady of rebuilding the roof area was approximately £3,000. I charged her £150. Five months later I needed a will written up. This lady's husband specialised in wills and probates, so it seemed a natural thing to approach his company. I went to his office and spoke to the receptionist explaining I knew the boss, and that he probably owes me one. In hindsight this was a mistake of mine; because I'd done such an efficient job for them and had – due to the wide knowledge of my trade - saved them a substantial amount of money, I *assumed* that they would appreciate this fact as much as I did. Of course, for them to do so, they'd have to be either particularly perceptive of things they know nothing about, or particularly perceptive of someone with their best interests at heart, neither abounded.

She told me what the cost was and we arranged an appointment. So far so good, so I thought at the time. Two hours later the receptionist phoned saying the solicitor would not negotiate on the price as he did not think it relevant. I said fine, let's do it. About an hour later the solicitor himself came on the line claiming, "At this time in my life I don't want any aggravation". Fair enough on its own merit, though clearly my earlier thoughtfulness towards his house and pocket had gone completely over his head. In addition, I had just spent the best part of two years at the mercy of a divorce solicitor, and so was not at my most patient and understanding with his kind.

He continued, "Maybe it would be best if you found another solicitor, as I think this could be trouble." I suggested that a guilty conscience might be getting in his way to communicate with me, and promptly told him to piss off. Clearly it is alright for me to save him a fortune, but not for him to negotiate a price with me in writing my will. True – he did not *ask* me to save him money, and so I cannot therefore ask the same of him. But how selfish and inhuman is this kind of thinking? An example of the entrenched, formulaic, and procedural behaviour of one profession ill-fittingly transferred to another with more personal scope. Despite this particular outcome, I know which one I live and die by.

This fantastic country of ours is good enough for people from all corners of the planet to set up home in, often at the expense of our children and pensioners. This is one contributory factor to Britain's gradual erosion; another is the supposed business-making strategy of solicitors. 'No win, no fee' sounds like a favour in the offing, but does in my opinion show two glaring characterisations: one looking backwards and the other looking forward. The former proves that solicitors have for years ripped people off unmercifully, taking more than their fair share of rewards. What we have now is a blame culture brought about by the fear of being sued. Solicitors everywhere are laughing at us all.
So, either we take responsibility for our own actions, or we let solicitors take it for us - for a fee of course! This clearly leads to a breakdown of our moral fibre, steering us towards vassalage. Can this be a message from the powers that be not to speak out of turn? A state of existence fit only for sheep and not, alas, fit for me.

Litigation - a machine which you go into as a pig and come out of as a sausage
                                                                                            - Ambrose Bierce

Television Programmes

Back in the 1970's when I first thought about writing this book, TV programmes about building and builders did not exist. Now there seems to be one on every night, in two distinct categories: *for the builder* and *against the builder*.
Take the first one; all good informative stuff, albeit lightweight in content and more cosmetic than structural, appealing to the lowest common denominator of knowledge, as one would expect for a show hoping to hold the attention of the masses. The second type *-against the builder* – is much more sinister in nature and intent. It is clear to see that on these (as a worst example) programmes the builder or plumber or whomever tradesman has obviously been *set up.*

Now, I have no justification or desire to suggest that all builders are angels, but the people such programmes target are known to the Standards Authorities as very bad risks and, therefore, probably pretty good TV viewing.

I contacted Surrey Trading Standards Authority on the issue of TV programmes and was put in touch with an officer who had worked on the TV programmes in question. He invited me round to his house in the evening to have a chat. I can't say I learnt much (if anything) from this chap; all he wanted to see was what I'd written about the TV programmes he was involved in. He read what I had brought with me and said, "Very interesting". The next day I found out how interesting. The pages I had written about the TV programme had been surreptitiously removed; no doubt him saving them for the programme producers to look over. So the next time you hear a Trading Standards officer talking about builders, shout 'thief!'

Customers often think that we originate from the devil's pantry, but why? Surely not because of one or two high profile cases, or these television programmes scare-mongering all and sundry? The customer has all the natural advantages of public support, including the singular variable – the price. From the builder's viewpoint the variables stretch to the horizon, including the weather, cantankerous workers and customers, indifferent builders' merchants, insufferable architects and surveyors, etc. A bookmaker would not give odds against the customer winning the day because the risks are bloody obvious and loaded against builders even before we start work.

I have tried to write this book in colour simply because most people see builders as black or white with no variables to consider, when the truth is that a customer's complaint, however trivial, may well set off a chain of events from which the builder never really recovers.

House of Horrors

One scam (or 'scrim' as the presenter likes to call them, not that I've ever heard the term before on site or otherwise) revolves around the chimney. A dodgy trader comes down from the roof holding a squirrel's nest and says:

"This is the problem."

It is not pointed out where the squirrel's nest was situated. I know the point of the thing is not to logically explain the series of events of any given 'horror', but if the programme makers would have us believe that a squirrel could enter a chimney and suspend itself while building a nest, they are surely traversing the line of viewer stupidity! But since when has reality got in the way of a programme's ability to scare people in their homes and at the same time selling advertisements. By the way, has the self-satisfied presenter ever seen a squirrel's dray before? He should have known that it was only a handful of hay or grass, but that would never be of any use to his sensationalist producers, would it?

The programme's ethos would fall apart if the presenters were as smart as they think they are. Dodgy builders will target the infirm, the aged, or those who turn a blind eye to the obvious - just like the programmes makers, in fact. Having turned full circle, who got the better of whom?

What the producers do not tell the public is how many decent builders came into their trap before they came across the most dramatic situations for the show. The programme makers knew beforehand how the set-up builders would react, because they had in their possession files on these builders from the Trading Standards Office! I can't disagree with showing these people up, but I feel the programme makers should have exercised some sort of balance; in the least to make it clear that such scoundrels are of the smallest minority, just as with any other profession. I see nothing wrong with the Trading Standards people being involved, but without them the programme would have had to stand on its own two feet. The makers would have eventually got the footage they were looking for, but on this premise it would have cost them a great deal more to make.

Surely a Broadmoor or Rampton patient could work out that it's easier to induce a fault in a heating system or roof than it is to find the fault. If nothing else, it makes the experts look very clever, the programme makers look smart, and the building traders as a whole look total idiots. The same cure is then trotted out every time; only use a builder who is a member of a trade federation. Of the actual validity of this course I have already spoken.

Some of the strokes pulled on the programme are known to most experienced builders, and can often be harder work concocting such a ruse than it is to do the job properly. One aspect of these TV programmes particularly gets up my nose, and that is (unsurprisingly) the resident experts. Who are these people? They are nearly all surveyors, architects or Standards Inspectors who have never in their lives earned a living laying bricks or repairing roofs. They might admit to working on their own houses, but that hardly qualifies them to adjudicate on numerous aspects of a build. Also, unless you have been self-employed I fail to see how you can make an informed judgement on the problems faced by those who have, such as I, and others like me on the job.

Where on earth do these people find "the right price" for any given job? I guess the pen pushers consult the Trade Union price tables and come up with a figure which can't possibly take into account overheads, tax, VAT and other unseen costs to the self-employed man. I wouldn't like to rely on the programmes' expert to pay me what I think I am worth for any job. Experts on price? No! How can somebody be qualified to put a price on a task on behalf of someone else, with no comparable experience whatsoever? Only a quasi-reality TV show of this regrettable and superfluous nature would get away with it.

Television tells a story in a way that requires no imagination
— **Witold Rybczynski**

Tuning into another disaster programme, the errant builder was again being crucified. My issue with this particular episode was the amount of money the producers deemed to put rights the done wrongs. I wrote to the producer saying so, and to her credit she phoned me wanting to know what my beef was with her show. I regaled how the outstanding work required to put right would only take me about a week to complete, so how can the show's presenters come up with a figure of £40,000? Surely the programme makers are scaremongering on a huge scale – five million viewers in fact. And then to pull the heart strings further, drawing the audience's attention to the fact that the home owners' second child has an incurable disease. Are the programme makers suggesting this builder picked out this family just to rub salt into their wounds? The morale here is a sorry tale; if you would like to appear on the telly know that your application will be helped, if a family member is extremely poorly.

An Illusion

Backdrops to TV studios increasingly show brickwork as it is aesthetically pleasing to the eye. However, only a fool like me would be studying the brickwork rather than watching a world famous celebrity spouting rubbish in front of x million watchers. What I do know is that most, if not all, studio sets are much like most TV programs, an illusion. TV companies like to look at brickwork for the reasons already stated, but brickwork effect wallpaper is a poor substitute for the real thing. Thin slivers of real bricks or briquettes as they are known are stuck on a timber backing to create the false brickwork effect. The brickwork effect could be a metaphor for TV's obvious bias towards falsification and untruth.

D.I.Y. TV

Because of D.I.Y. programmes on TV, the lure of 'doing it yourself' has reached epidemic proportions nationwide. I'm not an expert on D.I.Y. programmes; more of an expert on structural matters. I'm not sure what actual effect D.I.Y. has on us builders, but what I do know is that TV programmes about gardens and homes are at best economical with the truth. They surreptitiously suggest that the public believe what they see on the box as all there is to it, creating in the process a distortion of reality that can be a problem for us builders. Our customers expect us to compete with these programmes on time taken for the job in hand. Customers are not aware of the gangs of workers on the job, and their augmentation behind the scenes. In addition, materials materialise on cue, skips appear and disappear at will, timber so dry that they can paint it the same day. The viewers' sense of time is at the mercy of the editors.

I have on occasion been told, "A week! I saw the same job on the box that only took two days!"

It seems all these TV shows intend to demonstrate is how easy it all is. There are no warning signs of impending danger to life and limb. One sees chainsaws in the hands of someone without sufficient strength to handle the kick-back; and nothing will prepare one for the grinder that kicks like a mule in the hands of an inexperienced wielder; his limbs are in obvious danger, as are others close by.

Let me tell you a story that is both shocking and sad. A friend of a friend told me about a man who was using a grinder while working on a flat roof. I'm not sure what he was doing on this roof, but the blade of the grinder snapped in half; one half flew across the road, the other flew into his groin. The half blade that flew across the road landed in a garden close by, the occupant of which just happened to be a nurse who, alerted by the screams, went to his aid, not knowing at this point that he had in fact cut off his penis and one of his testicles. An ambulance was duly called for, but the paramedics could not get the man down from the roof, so the fire brigade was called. The only bit of luck for this man was the pair of heavy-duty corduroy trousers he had on, which helped to suck up and stem the flow of blood. The fire brigade also failed to remove the man from the roof due to the unknown extent of his injuries. A surgeon and team were called from the local hospital and the unfortunate man was treated on the roof where he had fallen in a paroxysm of shock and pain one can barely imagine. The man survived and was subsequently sewn back together, and but for a few minor checks on occasion each year all is well I am told. At the time he was 47 years old with five children!

Why the grinder blade broke in half, I don't know. What I do know is that sometimes the blade snags or sticks when cutting, and if at this point you have never used one before, you could be in trouble. Any work involving a grinder or chainsaw is best left well alone unless you are used to operating them.

Now and then there is a person born who is so unlucky that he runs into accidents which started out to happen to somebody else - **Don Marquis**

Some people building their own homes or doing large-scale works at home tell more fibs than any builder. For example, one self-builder on TV suggested that he laid all the bricks in his new house and that his wife had carried the hod! Less of a boast than a downright lie! Having carried the hod intermittently for a number of years, and doing so at six feet in height twelve stone in muscle, I found the experience very tough indeed. The mere suggestion of any woman lifting a hod full of bricks and away up the ladder is pure fantasy! (Save perhaps for the Hungarian Fridge Lifting types as seen on the 'World's Strongest' competitions, and even they might struggle with the heavy-laden ascent up the ladder.)

I am quite sure I've mentioned elsewhere that what you see on the box can either be an illusion, or the programme makers are hoodwinking us viewers into believing that what you see on the screen is factual. The following narrative clearly illustrates the point. Watching a 'D.I.Y. disasters' episode where some idiot had put up some shelves that were obviously going to fall down when tested, what did the producer do to illustrate the shabby effort? The shelves were stacked with tins of paint, the tops of which were loosened on purpose. Down they came with paints of different colours spilt all over the floor. Oh yes, very colourful! Viewers at home thus horrified at the chaotic shambles of a mess immeasurably more colourful in consequence than would in reality be. Can you see what I mean about us viewers, by simply watching this crap, that we are standing the three-card trick? Producers evidentially think we are all the very best of fools to accept such rubbish.

I was watching a building programme on cable television with a lady presenter called Meg Roughman. Surname aside she stood a tall redhead quite attractive but, alas, absolutely useless on the subject in hand. Whoever was advising the lady was making her look foolish. She tried her hand at pointing, clearly having never before attempted so before. Do the T.V. companies believe that an attractive presenter will paper over the programme's shortcomings, or are we to believe once again that (dubious) style triumphs over substance?

Another cable channel, another disaster. I watched a builder insert a lintel into a previously built house. The builder took us through the steps one by one until he arrived at transferring the weight of the flank wall onto the inserted lintel. He pushed the lintel into place and with a flippant wave of the arm said,

"All we have to do now is fill the gap on top of the lintel with cement."

As if this was to be so easy that it was barely worth filming the task! A task no less which is without doubt the most difficult part of the operation! And with this omission the programme thus fails the viewer; if the lintel does not pick up the weight that it is solely intended to do, why have a lintel at all? Why make a big show of cutting the brickwork out, shaping the lintel and putting the thing in place, not to show how the weight is transferred to the lintel?

Maybe the omission was because the presenter or director was unaware of how to accomplish the task, or oblivious to the viewer's need to see the job completed. Either way a builder or more specifically a bricklayer should have been consulted. He would never have left the viewer hanging in mid-air (excuse the pun!). I have rarely seen other builders do this operation in the way that I was taught. Many try to transfer the weight from above onto the new lintel by hammering slate into the gap. This method is likely to make a right mess and will in all likelihood only pick up 25% to 30% from above. The following undertaking requires patience aplenty and not a small amount of experience. Make up almost dry sand and cement mix with *sharp* sand and cement in a ratio of 2:1. Pack this dry mortar in the gap, using usually a thin batten that can be inserted in the small gap left. By carefully doing so you are in fact underpinning the weight above. If you try this with normal mortar, it would shrink leaving the weight still hanging. Because the mortar is almost dry very little shrinkage is evident, therefore squeezing the load from above on to the new lintel. The skill here is achieving this in such a way as to make it look like it was done when the house was built.

I find television very educational; every time someone switches it on I go into another room and read a good book - **Groucho Marx**

I have just watched a programme called 'Location, Location, Location'. A flat in Brighton was visited which had a problem with damp ceilings. The presenter said, "We will find out what the problem is later."

The ceiling collapsed and a builder was summoned to advise on cost. He walked in venturing, "£1,000 will repair the ceiling."
The buyer then used this information to knock £12,000 off the asking price. At no time did anybody on the programme ask or say why the ceiling was wet in the first place. The builder quoted to repair the ceiling, not to find and fix the source of the problem. Did nobody care why the ceiling was soaking wet? Prevention over cure was clearly far from their collective minds. The experts prattled on about the lovely kitchen, the beautiful tiles, the fantastic view of the sea, and yet without a dry roof over your head you don't technically have a residence at all. But oh no, better not dwell on such matters, we are on T.V. after all.

Having watched with interest some T.V. programmes relating to buildings and builders, I have come to the following conclusion: illusion before content and style over substance renders the essence or ethos of these programmes negligible. Viewing figures for these shows will say that the general public must like what they see.

The politically correct brigade has had a field day in respect to building or D.I.Y. programmes; every show seems to have a female bricklayer, plasterer, plumber or surveyor. I am not denigrating the fairer sex, but I have never seen so many females up front on the T.V. in such male roles. Over fifty years in the building trade only one lady bricklayer was spotted, whom I've mentioned elsewhere; no plasterers or plumbers, the occasional surveyor, and positively no female labourers have I ever seen.

Some of the politically correct aids are dangerous. For example, goggles on the scaffold are bad news owing to the restricted peripheral vision. Banging my head on site has been a normal pastime for me, so how much worse might it have been? Having said that, a helmet is also a liability when bending down; many times while lifting with both hands the helmet slips and whatever is being carried is dropped in order to catch the helmet. The P.C. brigade would say xxx amount of lives have been saved by the use of the hard hat. I am not so sure about that. One aid I wholeheartedly agree with is clear glass spectacles when using mechanised saws or grinders. There is clearly a need to protect your eyes from flying wood and metal chards.

Going back to the reason for this chapter; what have these programmes done for the builders of this world? They are now being made to show the relationships between customer and builder. Whilst the idea is good the reality is not, because human nature dictates that when the camera is turned on some will suck-up or weird-out to the lens. I don't think people behave normally when pressure of any kind is applied. However, should the characters gel then the directors will not be slow to stoke up the ire and resentment between the respective parties, after all, if everything goes smoothly the programme's effectiveness as a spectacle to the viewers is lost. I have seen programmes where the customer has picked up on a small discrepancy and in front of five million viewers has shafted the builder, much to the delight of the producers no doubt! The observations of the builder are shown in a much lower key, the producers being largely unconcerned as to whether the builder makes a profit or the customer gets what he or she requires. They only want drama, and if in doing so they have to instigate a problem - be it technical or psychological – hesitation of sinister seed sowing is unlikely to surface. Suffice to say that the building trade at both tradesman and customer end is sufficiently complicated by nature as to need no more trouble-making influences.

I particularly like and dislike some of the claims made on the D.I.Y. programmes. The presenters of property programmes often tell the householders where they went wrong *after* the job. Why not help them before they put their foot in the mire? Quite obviously if they were helped before going wrong the programme would not be much of a spectacle, though it would be of at least some educational value. Which for me raises the question, are the people taking part in these programmes set up just for the camera? You bet they are!

Surely there is a conflict of interest here: on the one hand the programme makers purport to help; on the other hand hoping against hope that the participants screw up, and invariably…. "I told you so!"

I have not watched every programme about building on T.V., but one factor seems to prevail in all shows – time! Why is time such a big issue, before during and after the programme? Is it solely to create the illusion of tension in the viewer that a, b and c must be completed in x amount of time? This is likely so. I can obviously see how a job running on and on is problematical for all concerned, but how can there be a hurry-up from the start? On any project time is the enemy, and is guaranteed to raise the hackles of everyone involved. The right-minded builder works perspicaciously from start to finish regardless. I can only imagine filming time precedes all other considerations, adding greatly to the builder's problems and customer's frustration. So who is it that sets the deadlines in each and every programme? Surely not the producers, with their vast knowledge of building or property expertise! It is not therefore difficult to see how the builder and customer are on the back foot from the outset, on purpose, in the name of entertainment.

In abject conclusion of just how sickeningly TV sucks you in only to spit you out, here is a prime example: in the GMTV studio sat a lady running a dyslexia charity, clearly upset by a member of parliament's public comments on her subject. The studio guest was satellite-linked to the said politician and promptly slaughtered him verbally. The honourable gentleman came back strongly. The lady in the studio had steam coming out of her ears and was at this point cut short, the presenter claiming 'we've run out of time'. A very promising debate shoved aside because a celebrity was waiting to talk soaps in the next studio! I shoved my cornflakes down and put my boot through the television screen.

Project Manager

On all T.V. programmes the most often heard complaint concerns project management. Those who had put themselves through this process would not do so again, but why? As I have said before this business is interminably difficult, even if you know what you are doing. In all cases on the telly the part-time project managers are educated men and/or women, more so than most builders on the programme. Their education and spirit carries them through, as does the fact that they are also the paymasters. If you make a mistake it is your own fault, but if you are a builder and make a mistake the customer will hammer you. To sum up, if you are the project manager and the paymaster combined, this is a good deal easier than being the builder.

T.V. Celebrities

How many times on the T.V. or in the media do you find celebrities moaning that ordinary people could not possibly comprehend the pressures of fame and celebrity status? What they mean to say is that they find it difficult to hold on to their money. Some of them are not very good at that, are they? Such is the distribution with us all. The reason I mention this is to put some perspective on their lives and mine. Which situation is more pressurised: trying desperately to hold on to your fortune and fame, or being a self-employed builder endeavouring to feed four kids with no work coming in?

I and many others have been there before, particularly in the recession of the mid-eighties and early nineties. Through lack of work lots of good tradesmen gave up to go mini-cabbing (amongst other surer professions) and never came back, robbing the industry of skilful labour. During the recession of the mid-eighties builders like me turned their hands to anything that would bring in a few quid. The fact that I possessed a small truck meant I could perpetrate light removals. One such task I will never forget was the delivering of thousands of Yellow Pages packed six feet high on my truck, with all four of my children running from door to door administering the yellow peril. Recompense for the operation was crap of course, but beggars can't be choosers. The recession acted like a cull of the construction industry workforce, contributing to the shortage of skilled workers which we now face. On the subject of TV in general and adverts in particular, I would like to make one or two observations, if you would kindly humour me.
Programme makers clearly think we are all fools, especially when one looks at the adverts on telly. I am spending more time than ever being at home during daytime hours, and am constantly bombarded with loan company adverts as a result. My 'favourite' is the advert

showing a goalkeeper unable to save a shot until he receives his new loan; he is then catapulted into Gordon Banks mode. Are we all so incredibly stupid to believe this crap, and then to act upon it? If you accept that business is being conducted here while we willingly watch on, what does this say about us as a nation? Scores of mooing bovine hoards come to mind.

Another gem of top notch scare-mongering from the many solicitors' compensation companies: showing a man falling from a ladder, the voice over chirps, "I was given the wrong ladder to use and I fell."
Of course the ladder was to blame, or so the advertisement would have us believe. The ladder shown in this example was a pole ladder, used primarily for scaffolding purposes, but more than adequate for any climbing situation that I know of. Solicitors again, setting the agenda for us all, and earning millions in the process. I may be wrong, but are solicitors and lawyers not the most parasitical bunch of professionals out there? Coincidentally some of the best paid too. My experience of them suggests they will be.

My late ex. father-in-law and world authority on Leishmaniasis –Professor Robert Killick-Kendrick - was asked to appear on a T.V. programme about the spread of this disease in Africa. Thirty minutes before the programme was to go live an argument developed between Bob and the T.V. people involved; the programme makers wanted Bob to make a connection between Leishmaniasis and the AIDS epidemic, to sensationalise the subject matter. Bob explained there was no possible link and that it would be foolish and irresponsible to say so. After much gnashing of teeth Bob threatened to pull out unless the idea was dropped. He got his own way and the programme went out with no further problems. I tell this story because I know it is true. What is also true is that T.V. companies invariably wish for a melodramatic conclusion, and the truth remains on the cutting room floor.

Truth can never be told so as to be understood and not believed

*- **William Blake***

In 2005 everyone heard of the failed space shuttle Columbia's demise, so why did the TV journalists react to the news that its sister ship Discovery's twenty-four hour delay in re-entering the earth's atmosphere due to bad weather was a sign of impending doom? Could it be that the newspaper hounds want a disaster because bad news sells newspapers? Is this scaremongering on a shameful scale?

Life doesn't imitate art, it imitates bad television   *- **Woody Allen***

Not T.V. but radio this time; driving down to Sussex prior to my move down south I tuned into the local radio station. The presenter was just starting his stint and was complaining vociferously about his builder's face being overdue. Apparently the delay caused the presenter to be late for a dinner date. Whether this was official business or for pleasure, he did not let on. "Call me!" He bellowed pompously, "Tell me your builder's tales of woe."

For the next forty-five minutes (the duration of my journey) he encouraged listeners to guess the identity of his dinner date, "A moderately famous woman," he trumpeted. Occasionally he interjected that his phone lines about builders were stacking up, the switchboard ablaze. I believe this part of his programme had ten minutes left to run when my journey ended, not once in the time I tuned in did he receive on air a call about the programme's theme "late or absent builders".

Insurance Companies

Insurance companies are a strong fit healthy man robbing a frail sick old lady...
legally
                                                                    - L.A. Lindsay

The police tell us that 75% of all road accidents are drink related - a staggering statistic. So with that in mind I set about procuring for myself a cheaper car insurance quote based on the fact that I have been a life-long teetotaller. Every insurance company I spoke to rubbish the very notion of a cheaper policy on these grounds. Why? What they are in fact scared of is the public at large all becoming tea-total overnight. That would not be so bad though, since prices would fall (public happy), and the insurance companies would do exactly as they do now and not pay out a penny if drink was a factor. Insurance companies would surely be happy taking money from us knowing that 75% of contracts will at the advent of a claim be null and void. The phrase 'a licence to print money' was surely conceived on the very day the first insurance company started up!

One or two facts you might not know about insurance companies. Do you know that proceeding with a car insurance policy signifies your consent to be sent rubbish marketing literature by every business under the sun? Consent of policy also entitles an insurance company to proportion your claim monies to a third party to hold on your behalf at their discretion, thereby collecting interest on *your* pay-out money! Ever wondered why it takes so long to receive money claimed? Even a fool can see an evident conflict of interests between paying out or not. No doubt your insurance company is taking a rake off in the process, but here's the worst bit; it's not against the law!

These facts are only available now due to the Freedom of Information Act, however I have long suspected this industry to be self-regulating and the ombudsman toothless. These giant legal robbers now have tentacles in all forms of business, insuring themselves against regulated sanctions. Why, for instance, are terms and conditions of a policy written in words one fifth of the normal size? The transparent and devious swine's!

I have mentioned the impact of insurance companies on our lives in other chapters of this book, but I would like to have my say again here. In my opinion insurance companies perpetuate the second biggest con of all time, after religion. How many businesses can there be where it is not in the shareholders' interests to pay out on a claim? Innumerable!

And thirty percent of these companies' profits can go into a contingency fund which tax will not be paid on. The excess payments demanded provide the pay-out for most claims called in, so who is taking the risk? Certainly not the insurance companies! I enquired about accident insurance some time ago and was told: "We pay you £100 pounds if you spend four nights in a National Health Hospital." Just think about that for a minute. Major brain surgery might require a stay of that length, or longer, but almost any other accident would result in a shorter stay. I know I am a builder, not a doctor, but you can, I hope, see my point about the insurance companies' risk being watered down so as not to be much of a risk at all. Risk assessors will say that we have to do this by law. Who makes the law?

Politicians? How many of them past and present have shares in insurance companies? How many private businesses do you have to patronise by law? None springs to mind. I once contacted a huge insurance broker for a quote for my lorry. I phoned them three times on the same day, answering the same question with the same answers. I received three quotes, all vastly different. It seems clear that as far as quotes go this industry is self-regulating in the extreme, with no tables or scales in sight. I guess that the companies work on the principle that if, say, three or four out of ten take up their offer there is money to be made. Such is the extent of their assured clientele that they can afford to spout such huge mark-ups. Why do we have to put up with brokers anyway? Tesco, the A.A - anybody with a large client base jump on the bandwagon. If fees paid out to these organisations were recouped our premiums would in all probability fall dramatically. Insurance companies have no interest in keeping premiums low, preferring to bed with their more illustrious conspirators. I think that without brokers to muddy the waters the Monopolies Commission might well sit up and take notice.

The R.A.C. sent me a renewal quote informing me how pleased they were about my renewing with them. I had in fact renewed with another company. They went bonkers, quoting their small print which I'd read. It seems as a result of doing business with them for the last year it was now *my* responsibility to inform them I will not be renewing automatically.

The R.A.C. operative told me I would have to pay for six days crossover period. They had in fact tried and failed to access my bank account. With this in mind I pointed out to a pig of a man on the phone that his company won't insure my car if the premium is not paid. "They already have," he screamed. Having changed banks six months ago I knew this was not possible – unless they had spoken to my new bank. "We will sue you for the six days we insured your car". I pointed out that if the I.C. wanted to sue me, I would simply make a claim during the six day period, knowing there was no chance of them entertaining a claim. Bang! And down went the phone. Surely the reality is either that I *was* covered during the six days or I *wasn't*; they can't have it both ways! Is it just me or is this straight robbery without violence?

One further trick perpetuated by insurance companies: you phone for a quote answering all questions asked - age, sex, address, car and breakfast preference etc. - followed by the writing of a cheque. When the cheque has cleared (and not before) they write to you with a collection of your details, saying if any of these details are incorrect contact us straight away, as this might affect your policy. A printing error or typo might have your DOB wrong, or something minor excluded. You are then obliged to contact them again pointing out *their* mistakes, whereupon you are informed that it will cost you an extra thirty odd pounds. Now, bearing in mind that you have already paid to be currently insured, you have virtually no choice but to pay up.

If you do not correct their own mistakes the insurance companies will let your policy run, knowing that in the event of a claim they have a bargaining chip triggering the escape clause. Is this done on purpose? What do you think?

The lady who bought my last house phoned me because a car had collided with her boundary wall. She told me a builder was about to repair the said wall. She was not sure that the wall was being repaired extensively enough and asked if I could go round and check, which I did. She was right - the cracks in the damaged wall went much further back than the hole in the wall. The insurance company was informed that the original quote did not cover all the damage. Incredibly, the insurance company asked the lady for an in-depth report on the state of the wall. I asked her: "Is the insurance company going to pay for this report?" Also, I was thinking, am I going to get the job of rebuilding this wall? The answer on both counts was no! The householder could not understand my reluctance to continue with this situation on behalf of the insurance company; why would I write out a report that could only benefit them alone, not to mention saving a surveyor's fee. After all this, the lady said: "I'm going to brick up the hole and leave it at that; all this is doing my head in!"

I myself once had occasion to do some consulting work for an insurance company, which looking back I'm quite ashamed. Could anyone ever have turned from poacher to gamekeeper quite so blatantly?

A further example of how insurance companies like to pass the responsibility on to you and I, came when I wanted to hire a mini excavator. The hire company saw fit to inform me that unless I took out insurance for the digger's safety, their own insurers would not approve the contract. So who do you think is taking responsibility for the machine; the hire company's insurers, or mine? The answer is neither, because if I hired the digger I would be paying both for the same job.

Your insurance documents are one big escape clause written in the smallest print only visible to those with X-ray vision. If I am reincarnated I want to come back as a female owner of an insurance and pension company; one, because of the money to be made; and two, because I'm jealous of a woman's ability to achieve multiple orgasms!

Women are really much nicer than men; no wonder we like them
- Kingsley Amis

I don't mean to labour the point about insurance companies' dubious practices, but damn it! I begrudge everything about them so I do! I recently received a new phone and contract from T-Mobile. A few weeks later I was astonished to find an insurance company's correspondence thanking me for insuring my phone with them. Why? The I.C's paperwork made it abundantly clear I had insured my new phone. In fact I did nothing of the sort. It seems T-Mobile passed on my bank details to their sister company, who in my ignorance had set up a direct debit with my bank without my knowledge. This direct debit was first paid out, and then cancelled by me just in time, more by luck than judgement. When I pointed this out to my bank they said, "What do you expect us to do about it?" A vast impenetrable web of multinationals and their minion counterparts (made of the same stuff no less), co-conspiring to surreptitiously whittle away your hard earned pennies. And all the while those who apparently exist to help you through the mire don't seem to give a damn! Incredible!

Property Developers

Throughout my life as a builder I've harboured the notion of becoming a property developer; why this has never quite materialised in the way I had hoped for will forever be an open wound. Back in the seventies, I acquired an ability to find odd parcels of land for development. I approached many developers, but for one reason or another could not quite achieve a breakthrough. Before I move on to my general failures, let me state my only success in this field - a house in Byfleet, Surrey, called Sefton. (See 'Memorable Sites')

I'd required a reputation for finding property fit for building purposes, so the following phone call came as no surprise, although the ending was. This chap asked if I could find him some building plots, to which I replied, "Of course." He went on: "I have a million pounds to spend." I asked him to send me a cheque for £10,000 to show how serious he was, not wanting him to waste my time. This complete stranger said, "Why should I send you anything? Just send me the properties you have in mind." Without further ado I put the phone down. I have often wondered whether this was the right course of action in this particular case. All subsequent dealings with greedy property developers proved I was right.

Another time I found a defunct nursery on the edge of green-belt land in a very desirable area, comprising some two acres. At this time we were working for a developer on a conversion project, so it was a natural progression to take him along. I had spent several months befriending the elderly owner who I am sure trusted me. When the developer turned up he was shocked at my find. We walked around for about an hour, then without talking to me and out of the blue, he offered the elderly old boy £70,000, take it or leave it. The old boy - obviously no fool - looked straight at me and said, "Piss off and don't come back!" I had done nothing wrong except pick another greedy property developer. That prime site was eventually sold four months later for £850,000, and now there is a plot comprising of twenty-five six-bedroom houses. My commission for this was zilch! The monetary consequences of one seemingly innocuous decision!

One other example was back in 1991 when I worked for the man who wrote the best seller "E for Additives". At the bottom of his long garden was an orchard that spread out behind both next-door neighbours' properties. I asked my client if he wanted to sell his house. His response was encouraging. I had an agreement with Berkeley Homes for a two percent commission; I also negotiated the same deal with the author/owner. Berkeley Homes agreed to purchase the house for £100,000 more than the market value, now totalling about £400,000; I was looking forward to my four per cent. Unfortunately one of his neighbours – an old man once famous pretty boy pop star of the late fifties - kicked up such a fuss that the author stayed put, much to my disappointment. Another developer eventually found an alternative route to the orchard and eleven five-bedroom houses were constructed. The same theme was repeated many, many, times over the next twenty years; I coming very close to hitting the jackpot. Alas, it was not meant to be.

Twin Towers

Having spent an inordinate amount of time during the winter of 2012-13 watching TV, rain and more rain and viewing older classics, a thought occurred to me. Listening to scripts of some forty years vintage, some real gems revealed themselves. Scriptwriters of cops and robbers programmes made various points regarding government agencies interfering with the police, the law and our civil liberties, most suggesting this would lead to the disintegration of society. Now, I know these are meant to be entertainment, but thirty years ago the underlying messages of these shows went over my head. Were these scriptwriters' psychic or old wise men repeating nefarious forms of control over the public by means of TV? Either way it is clear to me what was put in these programs in small doses has come home to roost. Diana's death, 7/7, the death of David Kelly and 9-11.

Along with everybody else my first thoughts on what occurred here were wrong, and I am ever more doubtful about the official reasons given for the towers' demise. To try and understand what transpired structurally then, we need to appreciate the relative strengths and weaknesses of the performance of concrete and steel. The reinforced concrete in this building was a non-load-bearing 4" slab resting on steel beams and used as the flooring structure throughout.

Let me remove the heat equation first. Concrete cannot dissolve on its own, but clearly, if you dipped a concrete column into the sun's core, it would vaporise. Same result if hit by an asteroid. As mentioned elsewhere in this book; if a lump of concrete is left outside at the mercy of all atmospheric conditions it would indeed dissolve over, say, thirty years or so. Yet this structure, insulated from all harmful weather extremes, fell down in thirty minutes. No concrete floor slab would stay intact once movement ensued.

My numbers taken from the many TV programmes show that burning jet fuel creates a heat of about 1500°C. The melting point of structural beams is about 2,700°C, so beams close to the impact area still had not reached failure point. Steel beams say ten or twenty floors above, and ten or twenty floors below, and still not even warm would not be affected as regards their structural integrity. Some 100 floors of structural steel columns were likely found in the same condition as they were before the plane struck, and yet down it came regardless. Now, it is quite clear that unaffected columns could not feasibly fall down of their own accord.

Many experts on demolition tell us that the building was pulled (blown up), but this is only part of the story; they also said it is not possible for a building to dissolve, when in fact it did. But *how*?

Concrete and steel on their own merits have huge structural attributes. Quite obvious to a first year structural engineer is that they too have different strengths and weaknesses. It is inconceivable for both to fail at the same time for *no* reason.

There are clearly several hundreds of thousands of bolts, plates, gusset pieces and welded joints on every floor. Add on seven different strengths of steel verified on the official plans, then failure points due to heat can only be a random event. Extreme heat would cause these weak points to fail, causing the steel to buckle in a haphazard fashion leaving a twisted heap falling to whatever side was weakened <u>first</u>, resulting in the <u>path of least resistance.</u> The towers fell into their own footprint along the <u>path of most resistance</u> (the upright steel colums). So, <u>what does this mean</u>?

We now have a situation where a structure should fall along the path of least resistance due to the heat, but in fact fell along the path of most resistance, both at the same time. That is like mixing oil and water which turns into apple pie- simply unfeasible. Isaac Newton I`m sure would say that is impossible according to his laws of motion. Gravity is always responsible for falling debris in a colapse, but here, freefall and gravity required some assistance, and they got it.

Without doubt, in order for anything to freefall there must be no resistance whatsoever, nothing, so, in order for this structure to collapse as it did the steel columns must fail at exactly the <u>same time</u> and in exactly the <u>same position</u> on <u>every floor</u>, perfectly in unision, just in the same way that demolition occurs. However, demolition is carried out in an undeniably meticulous fashion, but here we have a random act of entropy requiring an accident to effect a perfect freefall three times in one day. HOW AMAZING IS THAT!

WHAT ARE THE ODDS OF THIS ACTUALY HAPPENING?

I asked a mathematician friend to work out the odds of this scenario occurring. He said the odds were simply incalculable,so I offer you the following: THERE IS A HIGHER PROBABILITY OF TEN YEAR OLD BLIND, DEAF, AND DUMB SEXTUPLETS EACH WINNING THE LOTTERY SIX WEEKS IN A ROW. If these odds dont make you just a little suspicious, I dont know what would.Yet, down they came regardless.

In a court of law a conviction due to DNA evidence is put at about a million to one chance of being guilty, enough to send a man to the electric chair.The sextuplet odds would wear out several pencils adding on the required number of zeros to the DNA equation. So,how can the powers that be convict on a million to one chance then ignore an icomparably larger number that screams something is wrong, and not convict?
It does put rather a strain on coincidence.

Technology way beyond the remit of a humble builder was used to turn structural steel corner columns six feet X two feet thick (almost solid) to dust, as evidence by all photos and videos taken at the time.

In my opinion a greater level of skill and timing was required to demolish this building than was ever needed to construct it. Put another way; it was the cleverest engineering feat the world has ever seen, given it was hatched in secret and played out in front of the world's media live. I am not saying dont look at all the evidence but what happened in the falling of the towers should be of paramount importance, simply, because it defies the laws of physics, and my simple logic.

Professors of physics and mechanical engineering worldwide could easily come up with concrete proof (excuse the pun). Having rubbished the notion a plane was responsible, maybe Mother Nature lent a hand? She is exceedingly clever after all, but not nearly clever enough, sadly, to bring down three buildings in one day. Am I being conspiratorially naïve to suppose that one argument has incalculable coincedences, while the other just has *evidence*?

One further point to take into account: we all recognise how insurance companies' very DNA – sickeningly miserly at that - forbids them to consider a claim if a rat is smelt. The official report contains dozens and dozens of inconsistencies, coincidences, and what appear to be downright lies. Yet policies were paid out in vast numbers on property and human life. *Who on earth has the power to override the concerns of the insurance industry?* After all, if only one insurance-claim investigator got too close to the truth (that we have not been told) all hell would break loose. Better for the powers that be to reimburse the insurance industry for their kindly lack of interest (completely out of character!), and thus shutting down the need for further investigation. Do we need any more evidence of top-top level interference?

Once again we may ask ourselves, why? Alas - when money, greed, and power conspire on a colossal scale, there can only be one winner, and damn the consequences, human lives or otherwise. In conclusion, in my humble opinion, somebody richer and more successful than Guy Faulks was responsible, and I highly doubt he is of Arabic extraction either. As to the media narrative of this so called terrorism, to the bypassing of man's rational faculties in place of his negative passions, of his deepest fears... such manipulation is millennia old, and remains inexcusable.

I highly recommend reading Doctor Judy Wood's highly acclaimed and very brave book, 'Where Did the Towers go' (2005).

Nothing is more dangerous than an idea.... when you only have one idea
                                                            - Alain Propos

Memorable Sites

Burnham Beeches

At about the time I finished my apprenticeship back in 1969, I worked for a company on a massive extension to the Burnham Beeches Hotel in Buckinghamshire. The site was unremarkable but for one thing; a proliferation of rats. The kitchens were situated where the extension to the hotel met the main building. Now this hotel is right out in the countryside surrounded by fields, so the rats, no doubt driven by the smell emanating from the kitchens, were all over the site. Everyone working there had an air rifle or air pistol close by, and as soon as one of the rodents was spotted all joined in the pursuit of it. At times it was like the old Wild West; how nobody got shot is beyond me! I had always thought that rats were fairly small furry creatures, but these mutants were anything but; some were fourteen inches long with huge and heavy bellies rubbing along the ground as they ran. We must have killed dozens of the black and grey monsters. They did not seem too scared of us 'humans', and there were definitely a few rats laying bricks too! The rats came out in their droves around the lunchtime of the workers and hotel guests. The fact that the chef was really quite partial to a backhander from the builders in exchange for a T-bone steak or a string of sausages only fuelled the rats' bravery. We used to sit around the fire with our shovels poked in the flames, our T-bones or sausages sizzling away, one hand on the shovel and one hand on our chosen weapon (mine was always a pick axe handle – light, hard, wieldable), while we waited for our lunch to cook and the rats waited for an opportunity to steal the same. Tea was brewed in a new galvanised bucket that was hung over the fire.

Towards the end of that job the labourers had fire going all day long! I had just bought my first flat and needed some four-by-two and three-by-two timber; I borrowed the firm's vehicle and removed a lorry load of excess timber for my house. The last thing I remember is driving out of the site with my timber (which would have been burnt anyway) and promptly catching the bumper on a grass bank about four foot high, thus ripping it off.

Can you imagine what that site would have been like if you disliked someone? Stray shots flying everywhere – it doesn't bear thinking about. What would the current rules and regulations regarding health and safety have made of that site? Who would have been in more danger - the rats or us?

The Hautboy

Sometime in the mid-sixties I worked on a hotel site at Ockham in Surrey called the Hautboy Inn (pronounced 'hoboy'). This grand old building, with its minstrel's gallery and three-foot thick walls, dates back to 1864, built by the 1st Earl of Lovelace, who was also Lord Lieutenant of Surrey. The materials used for the original building were the famous Ockham bricks baked in the brickyards off Long Reach and for which the Earl received a medal at the Great Exhibition of 1851. Lovelace is said to have personally superintended the bending by steam of all the roof beams.

The Hautboy Inn

Ockham Lane, Ockham, Surrey GU23 6NP
Telephone 01483 225355 Fax 01483 211176

While there I was told that the disused railway carriage at the back of the car park was used as a brothel. The basement was considered to be lacking in height to the means and ends of the owner's intentions, so we had to dig out about eighteen inches of soil. No problem, you might say, but this basement was so deep, it was the lowest point for miles around. You've guessed it – it was full of water! The soil was thick clay and a pig to dig, particularly under water, and the only way in or out was via a slope at forty-five degrees, dropping about eleven feet. The shovel went into the clay all right, but removing it was entirely another skill requiring Herculean strength and not a small degree of bloody mindedness. So to dig was difficult, but to remove the waste was virtually impossible. When the clay finally, reluctantly left the shovel and fell into the barrow, it required two men at the top of the slope with a rope to pull (or should I say drag) the wheelbarrow upwards in order to empty it. I remember looking up to the ceiling and hanging there by their cables were about four or five electrical junction boxes serving the whole building. If, for whatever reason, the electrical boxes had fallen into the flooded basement, we would have all been charcoaled there and then.

The walls of the building, some three feet thick but not solid in construction, were in fact brickwork on the outside and inside face, but the middle was a mixture of rubble, broken bricks and lime. When a doorway was knocked through the rubble above the door cascaded down upon the crew in situ. Lovely! I also recall a mate getting lime in his eye; the next minute his whole face blew up like a beacon, poor chap. I understand that lime used in brickwork years ago was stronger than that of today.

We were all invited to the restaurant's opening night. I returned some ten years later with my wife, and who should we bump into but Tom Jones and son, and three lovely ladies!

Asgill House, Richmond, Surrey, after its restoration and, below, as seen from the riverside.

RCHITECTURE

One who drafts a plan of your house and plans a draft of your money

Ambrose Bierce

American meets Georgian

JOHN
ISHOLM

Drawings by
Leonora Ison

was recently reported that the American purchasers of London Bridge were er the mistaken im- sion that they were in fact ng Tower Bridge. Appar- y this peculiar trans- ntic transaction was well er way before the error realised. The agents dling the deal were, it ns, able to take some of bitterness out of their ats' disappointment with consoling thought that were " buying 2,000 years iistory."

is laughable incident pts mischievous speculation it the background to other lo-American deals involving transportation of ancient dings across the Atlantic. many haunted west wings, eted keeps and grandiose ticos, one wonders, have d themselves transplanted false pretences in the un- iliar setting of the Mid- st or Deep South.

lthough the trade in historic dings and their component s has been quietly worked some time between this ntry and the United States, e is apparently no compre- sive record of the nature quantity of goods exported. s in spite of the fact that e are any number of organi- ons in being, such as the ional Monuments Record and Society for the Protection of ient Buildings and others, se business it is to keep rds of, and protect, our inishing legacy of fine old dings.

Mixed blessing

Naturally the dealers in this profitable commodity are reluc- tant to divulge the extent of their business and although records of all exports of this type are presumably kept by H M Customs and Excise, the problems involved in obtaining information are, as might be expected, insuperable.

Nevertheless, the rate at which buildings have recently been spirited away seems to have decreased, and apart from the odd notable exception, little of importance has left this country. The most recent ex- ample was the removal, stone by stone, of Wren's Church of St Mary Aldermanbury and its reconstruction in Missouri as a memorial to Sir Winston Chur- chill.

Some, perhaps, would con- sider the present situation as a mixed blessing. Think of the civilising influence of a re-built Woburn Square on any Ameri- can university campus. Or even the enjoyment that citizens of Pittsburgh or Boston would have got from a Carlton House Mews in their city. If only it had been possible, they might say, to

snatch them in time from the jaws of the greedy demolition gangs (although readers of this column may well be beginning to tire of the repeated refer- ences to these particular acts of vandalism it is unfortunately as important as it ever was to maintain an awareness of this has not yet passed).

One building which must surely have had a menacing cloud hovering over its roof for some time is Asgill House on the bank of the Thames at Rich- mond. How easily it might have found itself today in Richmond, Virginia. Fortunately for Asgill House and Richmond, Surrey, an American family in search of a home in this country " dis- covered " it standing empty and partly derelict and were able to negotiate a tenancy with the owners, the Crown Commis- sioners. The transaction, which was dependent on the tenants' accepting the considerable re- sponsibility of carrying out major repairs, went through and several months after work started the house is now almost ready for occupation.

Days of lustre

Over 200 years ago, the then Lord Mayor of London commis- sioned Sir Robert Taylor to de- sign for him a villa at what was then, and still is, a fashion- able point on the Thames at Richmond—a part of the river which Defoe, at the time, in his " Tour through the whole Island of Great Britain," described enthusiastically as " comprised of villages so full of beautiful buildings, charming gardens and Rich Habitations for Gentlemen of Quality that nothing in the world can imitate it today," add- ing that " the whole country shines with a lustre not to be described."

Although he would hardly be dazzled by the beauty of 20th century Thameside, Defoe might well be surprised at the re- latively unspoilt nature of the lanes and buildings set back be- hind Sir Charles Asgill's stone- built villa.

However, the real significance of recent events is not that Asgill House has been saved from total deterioration, but that its new tenant, Mr Fred Hauptfuerer, had the inspired idea of restoring it to its original design. Over the years insensitive extensions had been made to this essentially sym- metrical building and Mr Haupt- fuerer was determined to re- move them. The operation thus qualified for grants from the Historic Buildings Council and the Historic Building Board of the Greater London Council.

Details of Sir Robert Taylor's original designs were obtained from museums and libraries and work on the house's restoration started. All the Victorian exten- sions were demolished and large sections of roofing removed, during which the whole building was protected by a giant um- brella of tarpaulin and scaffold- ing. The umbrella has now been removed and, with its original roofline restored, the house stands proudly, raised on a mound of grass, just as it was originally conceived; just as it must have looked to Sir George's guests as they arrived from London by barge, to be entertained in lavish style at one of his many weekend parties.

Asgill House was part of the river frontage of Richmond Royal Palace, which was first occupied by Henry I in 1125 and, I gather, Queen Elizabeth I died there on 24th March 1603.

It was a huge four hundred-year old mansion in Richmond built on the banks of the Thames, and our task was to reinstate this regal property to its former glory; its new tenant had the inspired idea of restoring it to its original design. Over the years insensitive extensions had been made to this essentially symmetrical building, and the new owner was determined to remove them; all the Victorian extensions were demolished and large sections of roofing removed, during which the whole building was protected by a giant umbrella of tarpaulin and scaffolding.

One job I got horribly wrong was in removing all fireplaces that were not covered or boxed in. I got stuck in to this particular marble surround and carried the rubble out to the skip; little did I know that what I was throwing away could have bought the entire skip company. Unbeknownst I had been breaking up a Robert Adam fireplace some 200 years old, which I was later told could have fetched some £10,000! As you can imagine the owners went mad but I was blameless (albeit ignorant of antique fireplaces) since it had not been boxed in. There were no antiques classes during my bricklaying apprenticeship...

The house had an octagonal room downstairs and one immediately above it, which was divided into two rooms. On both floors each space between the windows had canvas stretched across with the most beautiful paintings of people, landscapes and animals.

This building was also once a temporary home for the Royal Mint at the turn of the century. The story goes that on the transfer back to the Mint some money went missing; so I set about looking for it. I searched the whole building from top to bottom, and found nothing; I even crawled around the basement tapping all the flagstones for signs of an aperture, taking most of them up. And still nothing – ah well, at least I tried!

The Barn

I used to work extensively for an architect who owned a barn; taking pride and joy in the workmanship I have many pictures of this barn, and will refer to them as I go. The existing barn was only the second single-aisle barn still standing in Surrey.

As you can see the barn was on its last legs. During the demolition all manner of people came to view: the local council, parish council, the old building federation and, of course, English Heritage. I was to put aside all reusable timbers, which were to be checked by anyone who was remotely interested.

Only one piece of timber could be reused (personally, I would have put it on the fire with the rest of the timber). It was incorporated into the building as a token gesture to satisfy English Heritage. The barn now has only one weak spot – guess where?

The barn was rebuilt about a year after the hurricane in 1987. On the morning in question I could not get my vehicle out of my driveway due to the many trees that had fallen across my road. I was working on the same site as the barn, but at the architect's house some fifty yards away, and was in the process of building the bottom half of his flank wall. I had taken out all the brickwork and had rebuilt the wall, four acro props holding the wall above.

At this point my brickwork was not taking the weight because I had not started dry packing yet, so the flank wall and the roof were still resting on the props. After looking up and down the road at all the chaos I remembered my props were holding up the architect's house and I must admit I was shitting myself. I borrowed a push-bike, not knowing if the architect's house would still be standing, and sped towards the house. I needn't have worried - all was hunky dory!

The reason I mention the hurricane of 1987 at this point is that all the green oak used for the barn came from a forest in Norfolk which was devastated by the terrific storm. The architect's aunt owned the forest, so I understood. While I was digging out the new footings, the fallen oak trees were being cut to size in Norfolk. The concrete and brickwork footings were pretty standard fare.

In his wisdom the architect found two barn specialist carpenters from Wolverhampton to assist me; the two boys were about thirty, one a big lad and the other very slight, for whom I found accommodation locally and who remained on the job for about six weeks. The brummy boys were not good timekeepers, and worked, it seemed, when it suited them. Since progress was now largely dependent on the carpenters working swiftly I put my foot down, not for the first time. Batches of green oak were delivered every other day or so from Norfolk, because the oak was too heavy to bring all at once. The acid in the oak was so strong that it turned our tools black!

As soon as the basic structure was complete the brummy boys were moved on, and I organised the roof tilers and made a start on covering the sides of the barn with feather edged shiplap. I had various labourers to assist me through to the end, inside and out. My only regret regarding the barn is that I did not video the whole procedure from start to finish.

Just behind the barn was originally a corn store, propped up on stone mushrooms; I knocked that down and rebuilt it, slightly bigger than the original. I had five or six stone mushrooms made out of Portland stone, which cost £200 each then, back in 1989. It took a year to construct those two buildings, and highly pleasing it was for a brickie to build a timber structure from scratch. Needless to say I enjoyed the whole process immensely and am extremely proud of the end result.

Unfortunately about three years after the corn store had been finished, some bastards wielding a chainsaw broke through one wall of what was by then an office. The robbers took seven computers and scarpered. What puzzles me is the using of a chainsaw in the pitch-black dead of night without being heard? This always sounded fishy to me. The noise and smell grew even more when I learned that two years later the same robbery with the same M.O. on the same corn store took place; the architect's own house is no more than twenty-five metres away – was he deaf?

Chertsey Bog

As an eighteen-year-old apprentice I worked on a new housing development in Chertsey; some twenty odd units as I recall. The small road and houses should never have been built since they were built so on boggy land. When it rained the site was always flooded and workers had to move about on raised walkways from house to house. The clay in the ground was so thick that it stopped the rainwater from draining away. Consequently the footings were underwater. The gardens of the finished houses resembled a swamp. I remember building the footings to one of the garages whilst standing in two feet of water, laying the bricks two feet down and blind. How planning permission could have been obtained is anyone's guess, but let it be known that the houses are still standing. I remember being called into one of the finished houses that was now occupied; in the kitchen was a walk-in larder with an airbrick at eye level. The owner asked me, "What is that noise coming from the airbrick?"

"It sounds like rats swimming about in the flooded cavity", I thought, and said. And so it was. I left the house and walked across the newly laid lawn, to sink down to my knees in a swamp-like morass.

Recently I went back to visit the small housing estate in Chertsey which I had not seen since I worked there thirty-seven years ago. What struck me at first was that the houses were of a better quality than I remembered. The bricks were still crap, but the householders all down the road had invested heavily in new double glazed windows and new front doors, and most of the houses now have extensions to side and rear, though the ground still remains boggy and saturated. What also stands out is the condition of all the chimneys in the road - all requiring re-flaunching and re-pointing, I approached a few owners up and down the road with my story and concerns. Only one had any real interest in my observations.

Hampton Court Palace

Over the years I have worked in some truly fantastic houses. The following was one of the best. It was owned by a famous comedy scriptwriter and was situated in the grounds of ampton Court Palace, built soon after the palace as housing for its workers. While working on the roof, I remember people stuck in the palace maze directly below me, shouting "Please mister, how do we get out of here?'

The view from the roof was spectacular; I was able to see most of the palace buildings and grounds alongside the Thames. I was told that the house dates back five hundred years or so. One of its best features was the priest holes which had been built into the structure; therein priests would scramble and hide away from Cromwell's men, completely hidden in the mini rooms. There were also tunnels everywhere in the grounds leading into Bushy Park and down to the river. I remember the owner told me of a red spider indigenous to the maze of tunnels known locally as "The Cardinal".

I was rebuilding the boundary wall one day when a black furniture-type lorry stopped in the middle of the road right beside me. Two policemen appeared from nowhere, stopping the traffic either side of the large van. Both coppers were holding sub machine guns and standing guard over the van, which was by now turning right into a back entrance of the

108

palace. I wondered what was in the furniture van that warranted two armed policemen riding shotgun. Later I found out that the van was returning paintings and tapestries which had been damaged by a fire in the palace some years earlier. I remember thinking that then might not be the best time to approach the policemen for a chin-wag!

Inspired To Stitch

Whilst working on a scaffold of the house of a regular customer of mine - a lady author of a glossy book entitled "Inspired to Stitch" - she suddenly had an idea for a future project called "Men at Work". Wendy Lees positioned me ready for a set of photographs; using the best of them she constructed a picture in stitching of a man on a scaffold working. This piece of embroidery now hangs in her hallway, showing the result of her considerable talents and, I hope, a fraction of mine too!

Byfleet

My attempt at becoming a property developer started a year before the crippling recession in the late eighties. The house in question was Sefton in Byfleet, Surrey, which had a colourful history; built around 1840, the house used to be home to workers of the famous builder W.G. Tarrant. The owner of the house upon my purchasing it was Tarmac-Roadstone, which at the time was the largest house builder in the country. Tarmac also owned the surrounding five acres soon to be developed. Since the council would not allow Tarmac to demolish this historical house it was put up for sale.

The picture above shows that the house had been derelict for twenty years or so, with a roof that was unable to withstand the elements. All internal woodwork had perished or turned to powder and the staircases had disappeared completely, along with the timber floors. The second picture, by way of comparison, shows the house after it had received some tender loving care. I distinctly remember the bathroom lino floor tiles had, due to the damp conditions, lifted at the edges and curled upwards and inwards, touching at the top, every tile exactly the same. Unfortunately I can't find a photograph to show the unusual sight of every tile shaped like a round tube, all in apparent synchronisation, all still stuck to the floor, just.

Tarmac told us that we would never be able to restore the property and/or make a profit, and so they sold it to us cheaply. I worked for four months on that house, often long into the night and with mostly just one other worker for company. We achieved what Tarmac thought impossible and made the profit! We converted the house into two self-contained flats which were sold months before the recession took hold. You might consider us lucky, and you'd be right to say so, but the best thing about the project was a new friendship with the next-door neighbour John Curr, also a builder, and architect. John often marvelled at what we'd achieved with the house, and over the course of the next twenty years became a dear friend.

Stockbroker Belt

I vividly remember a residence in the Surrey stockbroker belt; the house on the hill top was quite unremarkable save for its size, and that fact that its owner was a member of a famous rock band. I understood he'd bought the mansion from the Post-Master General of that time. The main contractors for whom I worked installed a recording studio on the premises. The owner used to go to work each day in his Bentley at about four o'clock in the afternoon and return in the early hours, so I am told. His wife - a rather plain looking woman - from time to time used to flirt with all us workers. She drove a purple Lotus sports car. One day she returned by taxi and was asked by her husband, "Where is your car?"

 "I had an accident." She replied. I kid you not - two days later a brand new yellow Lotus was delivered.

The entrance hall was bigger than most people's houses, the walls beside the door were adorned with awards and photographs of the good and the great, and four platinum albums were also on display. Whilst working on a particular room the owner, who incidentally took no notice of me working close by, was telephoning Japan. Apparently the band had recently returned from the Far East where he'd bought some furniture, and he was checking up on the whereabouts of the tables and chairs. I distinctly remember thinking that the two-hour long telephone call - in the mid-eighties no less - might well have cost more than the missing furniture!

We dragged him out of bed one morning because a wasp nest was found in one of the chimneys. Two months after I left the job co-workers still on site told me the wife was having an affair with at least two of the workforce; this did not come as a surprise I have to say. To this day I have never heard the band's music, although I recognise one member's face.

Epsom Race Course

One of the best views from any house I worked on was at Epsom Race Course in Surrey, situated at Tattenham Corner looking right over The Downs. The newly married owners, whom I have stayed in touch with, threw a huge party on Derby Day, which in those days took place on a Wednesday. The daughter I remember well – a busty dark haired girl of about sixteen whom I was just about to stitch up. For a bit of fun I got a mate to phone her mum and pretend that he was from Playboy magazine, asking if she could attend an audition for a photo shoot. Since I was working all day at the house I could hear the Mum quizzing her daughter as to how Playboy came by her name. Obviously the young girl didn't know a thing. In the next room I was shaking with laughter. My mate Les phoned up six or seven times over the following week, upping the ante each time.

Eventually I had to come clean, because trying to keep a straight face was becoming more difficult after each call. Both mother and daughter forgave me, as I suspected they would, due in no small part to the mother being, for her generation, pretty hip and with it. My ex-wife and I were invited back to five Derby Day parties in a row, including the year the never to be seen again Shergar was last seen galloping up the hill to the line.

Lunchtime Exploits

Throughout my apprenticeship and in time beyond, when on site there was one part of my day I particularly always looked forward to: the lunchtime activities. It may have been an impromptu game of cricket or cards, or even swimming when possible, but the one I remember most was at a site already mentioned numerous times in this book; down by the river in Richmond. Four resident Irish labourers against four English bricklayers; the football played at lunchtimes was brutal and warlike. Some of the Irish lads used to play Gaelic football – a sport which seems to me to be a cross between rugby, American football and boxing. If the police had ventured along the towpath we'd have been up before the Beak for GBH! Going back to work was either a pleasure or a pain in the mind of those who won, or lost, and come afternoon we were always aware of the bumps and bruises inflicted on each other. In fact we took a curious pleasure to it, and the exercise itself broke up the monotony of the days' bricklaying very nicely.

During the summer months whoever you were working with and wherever your site was a swimming pool was found. I remember a pool in Feltham with a platform some six metres high. I had never dived off a podium before; it was so high I'm sure I saw snow forming on it! Streams of little kids would push me out of the way as I stood petrified on high.

"Why are you scared to jump Mister?" they'd shout. Forty-five minutes elapsed before I plucked up the courage to dive head first; it was my first and last dive of such a kind.

Occasionally a new face would appear on the site with a new game to play; a roofer once turned up with his golf clubs, and off we would troop to the driving range, all trying to out-do one another, naturally. These days such lunchtime exploits have been largely outlawed by the health and safety executive. Outlawed, but not forgotten. Never forgotten, because these were very great moments to me.

PART TWO

Not Amusing

Health and Safety

Everyone is aware of how the health and safety executive rule a portion of our lives without a hint of common sense. Indeed, their interfering causes trouble in the construction business like no other. Though this is not entirely true; they blight everybody's lives, not just us builders! Years ago the building inspector was top man, now the health and safety lot are the '*enfants terribles*' incarnate. In a world where criminality has a real corrupting influence, in certain fields of society the humble safety officer wields more power than a High Court Judge.

Do the health and safety people really save life and limb? I am not privy to the relevant statistics but I do know that backs are frequently put up in such a way as to reduce the public to anger. Surely angry people are much more dangerous than calm people? Now we have come full circle and see that common sense must dominate our lives. It seems to me one of the few areas of our lives the health and safety executive have no power over is a war zone – about the right place for them!

They have the authority of veritable experts, and indeed much of the public think they are the knowledgeable ones of the building trade. Until all goes wrong, then the cry to the builder is heard, "You're the expert, you sort it out!" Above all a practical job, surely credit must go to those able to execute practical solutions?

I have purposely omitted the horrible tales of old people being ripped off; they are unworthy of repetition here and are not in the least bit entertaining. I think that we just have to accept that these things do happen. Some of the case histories are funny, but sometimes not to the people concerned. Stories like these and many more make up the builders' public persona.

One lady phoned up in a panic and wanted me to go round immediately, she said, "I'm having a new kitchen fitted and the fitters are here now, but are scared to cut the worktop for fear of ruining it; can you come round and cut it?" What can one say to such a request without being rude?

On the theme of kitchens, another lady phoned wanting me to complete her half-finished kitchen but she wouldn't tell me why it had been left in the first place. Could it be that she was a pig to work for, or could it be that they left because they never got paid? Inferring from her narrative on the phone my guess was they never got paid. Would you risk your temporal livelihood on such a customer? I think not.

When people phone you up you have to be aware of everything that is and is not being said, and sometimes a gut reaction rises, saying, 'forget it.' The following is an occasion I got wrong!

This lady phoned up very distressed; a carpet was being delivered any day now, and her loft floor was yet to be laid. I said I was too busy, to which she cried down the phone, "I would be *ever so* grateful if you could come and have a look. I will put the kettle on, and I've just baked some scones…" So of course I go round, and what a change of atmosphere! No tea, no scones; all she wanted was a comparable price to the one she'd already accepted that morning. Needless to say; I didn't get my tea and fresh scones, and she didn't get a price. What she did get was a mouthful of a builder's frustration for her sickening performance.

I have it on good authority the following actually happened. One morning at 7:30am when bricklayers were due to start work at a house there was a knock on the door; there stood one of the workmen, who said, "Excuse me Mrs, but have you got a spare trowel?" When something like this happens as a customer, you know you're in trouble!

It is very common for people to phone up and ask you to come round when they don't have any intention of offering you work. You might well ask why they bother. What they are getting is *information* about their job; availability of materials, time scales, prices etc. and it's all for *free*! I've consistently gotten three or four calls a week of this nature, which if I were to take on face value I'd be working for nothing.

One yuppie couple I worked for complained that the fourteen locks we had fitted weren't strong enough; when we explained that the expensive door handles they'd bought were too heavy for the cheap locks they supplied us with, and despite we two tradesmen having a combined 75 years' experience in such matters, they still would not believe us and ultimately refused to pay the full price, which they still owe to this day! Sometimes the most educated people lose all common sense, especially when it saves them money. A case in point was a couple of Indian doctors. I called round on time to a very big house on a private estate. They wanted to build one two-storey extension and two single storey extensions. There were no pleasantries or formalities – straight in to the point of my being there. First they wanted me to guess the price without a drawing – when I refused; a drawing appeared out of thin air. Then the pair of them decided that they wanted the quote that night. By this time it was about nine-thirty in the evening. All this happened over a period of about two hours. What on earth made them think I could do what they were asking of me? Incidentally, a good customer of mine recommended me to these people, not mentioning (or perhaps knowing) that they'd behave so unreasonably, so detached from reality.

Should anyone be in any doubt about my beef in this case; it would have taken something like three to four hours to work out an accurate price. I am quite sure they were aware that what they were asking was not to be done properly in a moment; as such it was quite obvious all they wanted was my wealth of experience to give them a pretty accurate but rough estimate for their own musings, without dipping into their pocket or making any commitments.

I was working on my own house and under pressure to get on with the work in hand. Some lady phoned up looking to repair her roof. I told her I was too busy, but she insisted. I called round and she told me that she wanted a price for the job, for which £60 was agreed. She asked me if I could do the work on Wednesday, two days hence. Yes. I told her for me to do the job I would have to commence first thing in the morning, another yes. I turned up on Wednesday at 8:00am at the agreed time and found the back gate was left unlocked. Ladders went up and I completed the job. At 8:45am I knocked on the door, which I think I got her out of bed. She told me to get on with the job, when I pointed out that the job was completed she said, "How did you get in my back garden?"

I replied, "You left the gate open." She then went berserk, claiming I was trespassing! She then changed tack and complained that the price was excessive for the time spent on the site. When I pointed out what had been agreed, she said a roofer friend had told her £60 was a ridiculous price for the work, to which I replied, "Why then, did you not get your friend to repair your roof instead of me?"

She said, "You did not give me enough time to do so." "You have known for two days," I groaned, "how much time do you want?"

What she wanted was the time to play me off against her friend – if indeed he existed – to lower the cost. That she ran out of time is her lookout, not mine. As regards to the cost of the job, at £60 it was more trouble than it was worth, and all I earned that day. As I charged her £60 and the work only took 45 minutes many people would add up how many 45 minutes there are in a day and come to a ridiculous conclusion about my daily rate. Take into account loading and unloading ladders and tools, two visits to the site, tax and diesel etc. If I could conjure up a job like this twice a day, of course I would be happy – the reality of the profession is not so though. Moving from one site to another several times a day is unrealistic and logistically tiresome – the schedule of a garden maintenance man. In this case, as in so many others, it has taken me decades to learn how to complete a task so quickly. Customers in general cannot comprehend this, preferring instead to believe in the substance of their own fears.

A good customer of mine asked me to put up some shelves either side of a chimney-breast in the alcove, and we agreed a price. The day before I was to do the job I called round to measure up, and she showed me a page out of a magazine, saying, "I want the job to look like this." What she showed me was a picture of a Welsh dresser, and clearly she hadn't seen its price at the bottom of the page – nearly £2,000! The price of the job I had quoted for was about £400. She could not see the difference between the job that she wanted and the job I quoted for, so I walked out before a start.

Muddy Footings

Of all the projects I have worked on in the last 50 years, the following one rankles the most. I built a large extension and conservatory for a policeman and his wife, who had had some trouble finding a builder because the work was potentially problematical. I only took the job on because my girlfriend lived two doors away. The work started in January – my first mistake. The site was on a steep slope from side to side and from back to front. The site of the extension was between the policeman's house and adjacent to next door. The anticipated ground conditions did not materialise as the architect had predicted.

Not being a resident of that area I could not predict where, or if any hard chalk existed in the ground. I had anticipated some extra work in the footings, so I insisted on a contingency sum to cover us both. As the conservatory was at the top of the site I started there, where it was my job to lay a base and dwarf wall for the conservatory. Having laid the concrete trench footing, water suddenly appeared adjacent to next door on the high side. I dug away some more earth and a stream appeared which flooded my trench footings! I called the water board and they checked the quality of the stream and said it was not a broken pipe and off they went.

As I have said, the terrain was very hilly and the water could only be surface water coming down from above. We were at this time in the middle of a very wet spell; surface drainage was to plague us again and again throughout this job. Surface water can't be stopped - only channelled - and in this case I left a plastic pipe on top of the footing next to the conservatory wall before finishing the surrounding patio area. All of this work and the know-how to do it was obviously not part of the original price, but still very much down to me to complete satisfactorily. The lower end of this channel was leaking water throughout the duration of the job, sometimes a little, sometimes a torrent, but not being able to find an ultimate solution at this point in the project we managed the water as best we could, until we had completed the ground works.

The site of the ground floor extension was seven feet lower than the conservatory footings, so all surface water from the surrounding gardens arrived at the lowest point – my site! At this time on the job the weather suddenly turned very cold, and wetter.

What we had achieved up to this point was nothing short of miraculous, most of which had not been included in the price – i.e. *extras*. This turned out to be the easiest part of the job despite the biting cold. Knowing this was the lowest part of the ground works we still had to dig down for our footings to the extension, which we did. We found no hard chalk to build on so the Building Inspector requested us to dig down further to the level of the adjacent house footings – a depth of about 3 metres. I had only priced for digging down about a metre, which is why I insisted on a contingency sum of £5,000, which by this point seemed to be okay. As soon as we dug out the three metres deep by one and a half metres square hole it filled up with the surrounding surface water. We now had in effect a three metre deep treacherous swimming pool up against next door's flank wall. This hole was to be one of four dug out. Economics would normally dictate that all four holes be excavated at the same time and filled in as soon as possible with concrete.

Given the unforeseen waterfall flowing over the conservatory trench concrete footings, plus the atrocious weather conditions, you can see that some decisions had to be made immediately. The first hole, now flooded, could not be left owing to its close proximity to next door and the likelihood of water seeping into that house. We could not dig out the other three holes and risk destabilising not only the policeman's house but next door as well, so I took the decision to fill in the swimming pool which we had created. We would not be able to empty the hole ('pad' as it is called) of water quickly enough as it was filling up all the time.

To enable us to carry on we needed two pumps, one for water and one to accompany the ready-mix lorry – both expensive – neither allowed for in the original price. The contingency at this time was holding its own, I thought. I remember the water pump working full tilt, me down the hole with a shovel, scraping up the soft earth at the bottom to make a solid base for the ready-mix. The sides of the hole, although propped up, were unstable, due to the extreme weather conditions, while I'm at the bottom hoping that the sides don't collapse, that the pump keeps working, and that I get out of this hole alive.

By now it's snowing, the ready-mix lorry has arrived, but the Building Inspector has not! He has to check the bottom of the hole before we can pour the concrete into the hole. Imagine the scene – myself and my mate freezing to death, wet through – the pump's still working, the bottom of the hole is just about dry, the concrete pump lorry ready to start; by now my sense of reason was falling at the same rate as the snow! The Building Inspector's car finally appeared – he then took an age to put on his Wellington boots – I shouted at him to get a move on. He took one look and said, "Get on with it." – And so we did.

I remember looking around when holding the concrete pump; the snow at this time was very heavy, my hands wet and cold, my head and heart warm in the knowledge that the immediate crisis would soon be over. Filling the hole with ready-mix concrete by pump only took three or four minutes, yet my emotions at the start and finish of this operation could not have been more different. Once the hole was filled and the concrete covered up, I went back to my girlfriend's home to defrost my brain. I had found myself in some desperate situations before, but never with the climatic conditions playing such a major part.

The hole now filled meant that the ground between the houses was now finally stabilised. Because of the weather conditions the other three holes would have to be dug and filled separately, making nonsense of the original quote. All this and we have not yet reached the stage where my estimate for the footings kicks in. I was not at this point too concerned about the extra cost because of the contingency sum and the customer's own view of what we had been through. I had fixed up a temporary drain to run off surface water coming from beneath the conservatory – all extra work.

The Borough Council structural engineer became involved at this point and I had to negotiate the cheapest way around the rest of the pre-estimate footings.

Towards the end of the job I had a little fall, wrenching by right arm. I struggled with it for six months, and then was forced to have an operation. To this day it is still not as good as it was. (I remember trying to cut up a staircase with my arm in a sling and cutting into my left hand, just missing the tendon that works my thumb!) Nevertheless I finished the job, and was promptly staggered when the policeman said he did not have the extra money to pay me. I completed two months extra work in the footings and charged him for two extra weeks of work.

He and his wife came round to my girlfriend's house about a month later to talk about the money situation. The wife offered me half what I was asking and when I refused, went off to the toilet in a rage. In the meantime, the policeman offered me the whole amount. They agreed to pay me what they owed me in about a week. Two weeks went by and my girlfriend got fed up. The policeman told her that they had taken legal advice and were advised not to pay on the basis that they did not have to.

I wanted to take them to court, but funds at the time prevented me from doing so. <u>You might think this is an unusual occurrence – but it is not for the builder.</u> I found out nine months later that they had sold up and moved without telling their neighbours where they were going. Was this a guilty conscience on their part?

A plumber told me about a customer for whom he had fitted new kitchen taps. She called on a Saturday saying the taps were loose. The plumber duly turned up after a twenty-minute drive and checked the errant taps. "Nothing wrong with the taps, Madam," said the plumber. The woman grabbed hold of the spout, swung it across the three basins and said, "Look, its loose!" The plumber could not believe that an intelligent person would not know that the spout was meant to move sideways over the three basins! Needless to say, the woman neither apologised, thanked, nor paid the plumber for coming.

Spirits

Here's a bizarre story… I had occasion to visit a couple in Reigate. I had come highly recommended by my girlfriend, who had known and worked with the husband for many years. It is pertinent to recall what this man did for a living: a partner and director of a city-based asset management house. A very responsible position, one would think. I first met this couple in a café, and whilst chatting to the wife was informed that she had never set foot inside a Tesco store or any other food super-store. I suppose I should have expected what was to follow. Instead, I just thought she was rather lazy.

I spent three hours looking over their very large house and grounds with tennis court and swimming pool. My conclusion was that there was about thirty thousand pounds' worth of work to be done on the property. About five days later, my girlfriend received a call from this upright city gent saying, and I quote, 'I have consulted the spirits and they say that Leo is not the right man for the job.'

He never attempted to speak to me himself (thinking perhaps that the spirits might contact me direct). How can a man earning in excess of two hundred thousand pounds a year, in such a 'responsible' position, be guided by what the spirits do or do not say? What would happen if the spirits told him to sack all his staff, or give away his prized stamp collection, or go slaughter a few strangers?

I know this case is extreme, but how does anyone get to such an exalted position in society without being able to stand on his own two feet? And where were the spirits when his marriage broke down? My girlfriend told me that their relationship was doomed from the start; I suggested a full refund from the spirit world was in order. It takes all sorts I suppose.

Near Death Experiences

My first life or death experience occurred when I was about seventeen or eighteen years old – back in 1965-66. I was working with Bill Young on an office block in Watford. The basic structure was in place, that is to say, concrete columns and concrete floors, but no brickwork as yet. In the middle of the building was to be a lift, so holes in the floors were exposed. We were in the process of bricking round these openings when for no apparent reason I stepped back and fell into the opening. The only way I can explain what happened next is to say that my whole life flashed before me, both in slow motion and at a rate of knots! Something else was also working at the rate of knots – my reactions. I twisted sideways and caught my elbow momentarily on the concrete rim of the lift shaft.

My other arm quickly landed flat on the concrete rim while I dangled down the shaft. I was on my own at this time, not daring to breathe, let alone shout out for help. It seemed as though I had been hanging there for hours, whilst trying to gather my thoughts – I knew I had to get out of this predicament on my own. I managed to scramble out somehow – God only knows how. If the same situation were to occur now, I don't think I would make it, since I am not nearly as quick or as strong as I used to be.

Twenty years or so later I worked for a psychologist. I asked him for an explanation as to how or why one's mind could behave in that way. He said that he couldn't begin to explain the process, as it had never been his misfortune to be in such a situation.

The same thing happened again many years later. A different situation, the same result. I was on a ladder between two houses that were about four feet apart, and because of the close proximity of the two properties the angle of my ladder was too steep; I knew this, of course, but I had to complete the job. If I had had a mate at this point, the situation would not have occurred. However, there I was above the gutter level, ladder resting on the plastic guttering. I stretched too far to one side and the ladder slid sideways. I distinctly remember that precise moment. Brain working overtime, certain I was going to crash down, not only did my whole life flash before me in fast and slow motion but I'd managed too to pick out a patch of garden path upon which to land.

Once again, it seemed that my survival instincts worked quickest of all – thank God they did! I ended up with my legs on one roof and my torso on the other! As I struggled to straddle the gap between the two houses my brain screamed '*grab the ladder!*' So there I was thirty feet up, half of me on one roof and the other half on the other with my arm through the ladder. I managed to wedge my body across the divide and compose myself before righting the ladder and descending.

It would seem I have not had much of a life if everything I have ever done could be condensed into a split second! On the other hand I always thought that I did not possess much of a brain, but situations like this go to show that God did indeed give me one!

Neighbours in Court

At the time of writing this section I was involved in an altercation with my neighbours which showed no sign of ending.

When I decided to build an extension to my house I approached my neighbour with a view to building on the party wall. My neighbour said he also wanted to build an extension at some time in the future. I explained to him that if I built on the party wall he could also use my wall as one side of his extension thereby saving him the need to build one of four of his. I proposed that we share this wall. My neighbour agreed and my extension was duly constructed. When the whole extension was built my neighbours, in their wisdom, changed their minds. They took me to court wanting me to remove this party wall. Their reasons? Perhaps spite, jealousy, or boredom.

Judge clearly thought I was the big bad builder taking advantage of a young couple. No one could point out what advantage I had in fact gained, because there was none. I often take pictures of my work, as I did on this occasion. These show without doubt that my neighbours lied in court. And yet the Judge ignored this fact, calling it a mere 'hiccup'. Could the Judge have had a bad experience with a builder? Quite possibly. I thought that in the absence of any facts (i.e. a written agreement) common sense or simple logic would prevail.

Her honour said, "On the balance of probability, their story seems more likely." She was certainly right about a story, but there was no truth in this one! Just lies from start to finish. I don't want to bore anyone rigid with too many details but my last words on this tell their own story. The Judge twisted the knife in when the other side asked for £500 to paint over a few mortar splashes on their back wall, no further than four inches away from my new wall; quite a neat and clean job, as you would expect from a greatly experienced tradesman. So what did the Judge say? "Pay them £500." I told the Judge to read their estimate again, especially the bit about painting the whole back of the house. "You're right," said she, "I will deduct £50 off this figure. You owe them £450." Hardly natural justice!

A man who is his own lawyer has a fool for a client   - **Proverb**

Rumpole and the Little One

A few years ago I had a run in with my neighbour, who fancied himself as a bit of a gangster. He lived in a house that was at right angles with mine - mine the corner plot, his at the bottom of my garden. When he moved in ten years or so after me he used to sell cars from home and park as many as six or seven cars in front of my garage entrance, which was adjacent to his front gate. Many times I'd asked him to move his cars away from my property so that I could access my garage. He always took exception to this – quite why is beyond me.

One early evening in November as it was just getting dark I was unloading my lorry with a mate. The neighbour appeared from nowhere and started rucking, which I ignored. The next minute - a pain on the side of my head - the result of a mini-fisted right-hander swung by the midget from next door! It was cold and I had two coats on at the time; feeling restricted, I pulled one off and ran after him. I chased the midget down his garden path, and he leapt horizontally through his open front door just before I landed on the door mat. I made no effort to enter his house and walked away.

The next minute all hell broke loose. As I walked back to my garage my mate shouted, "He's got a gun!" I turned to face the midget who was standing in a Rambo-like pose with a long barrelled gun. He said, "Have some of this." I turned my back on him on the basis that if he were going to shoot me I'd rather not watch, so it would have to be in the back. I threw my arms heavenwards with frustration, my mate looking on. As quickly as the midget appeared he was gone. My mate exclaimed, "What on earth was that all about!"

I contacted the police and the farce began. My mate and I made a statement that night. I asked the police if they were going to see him, they said they'd get round to it soon enough. Well, soon enough was the next day. I watched with two of my children from my bedroom window as it overlooked his house to see two police officers knock on his front door; from our vantage point we could see the whole of his property. The next minute his back door opened and the midget flew down his garden path into his shed, his wife watching out of the window above the front door. The police having obtained no response from the occupants walked away. I thought they would come back later, and they did; four days later, to arrest him.

My next-door neighbour was about five feet four in height, hence the midget moniker. The ensuing court case was by anyone's standards a laugh a minute, a veritable circus! Our first day in court, to hear if he was to plead guilty or not, was brilliant. The Judge was a man of about sixty, and I have to say that throughout the proceedings he was fantastic – a real star. He began by asking the midget to stand up, which he did, then asked him five times what he was going to plead. He seemed very unsure. His Barrister resembled Rumpole (a real favourite TV character of mine in years gone by) in size, if not in ability. The Judge asked again, looking at Rumpole. The Barrister, clearly confused, asked if he could speak to his client. The Judge replied, "If you must, but be quick about it!"
The upshot of this was that when the Judge asked him again for the umpteenth time, "How do you plead?" the midget said, "Can I ask my wife?" (She was sitting next to me in the public gallery.) The Judge threw his hands in the air and growled, "Hurry!" Whilst the midget was having a quiet conflab with his wife, the Judge called over to Rumpole, "In my court I expect you to do your job properly *before* you come in." Now back in the dock the midget, visibly shaking, stood up. The Judge asked him, "Have you made up your mind?" To which the midget replied, "Not guilty, y're 'onor."

I could not take my eyes off Rumpole - he looked so much like him - a roly-poly sort of man. It was almost as if he was drunk as he mumbled his way through the dates being set for the trial. His apparent incompetence was truly mesmerising. Since I was a Q.C. in my past life I loved every minute of being in court. Outside the court I let slip to my mate what I thought of Rumpole. The acting barrister overheard me and shot a stare my way. About two months later we were back in court, and I was the first witness to be called; I answered all the questions put to me by the Prosecution monosyllabically – yes or no Sir.

"Please stay there, Mr, Lindsay." I'd been waiting a long time for this moment. Rumpole stood up and mumbled, "How long have you been carrying on a business from your home address?" "I haven't," I replied. "Look at these pictures of your garage," he said. "What is on your roof?" "Nothing," said I.

At this point the Judge said to Rumpole, "Get on with it man, move on!" Rumpole huffed and puffed, and proceeded to ask me the same question three more times. And three more times I gave him the same reply. By this time the Judge was clearly irritated, and turned to Rumpole, "I don't understand your reasoning." With that, I shouted at the Jury in exasperation, and no small amount of unrestrainable excitement at the apparent, impending success, "If the Judge doesn't understand the question, what chance does a builder have!" The Court at this point became alive with tension. The Judge promptly calmed them down, and turning to me uttered, "Mr Lindsay, if you don't mind, *I* will run this Court, not you." "Sorry Your Honour," I said looking away. The Judge then positively launched into Rumpole. "Where did you learn to cross examine like that? If you don't buck your ideas up, I might consider removing *you* from this Court. Now get on with it man, please."

The cross examination directed at me became more and more ridiculous, and then finished quite abruptly. I took my seat in the public gallery feeling pretty pleased with myself, eager to watch the case unfold. My mate was now in the witness box. Rumpole tried to discredit him by asking,
"How long have you been a labourer in the building trade?"
"I haven't," said my mate.
Then Rumpole, "What do you do for a living?"
"I'm retired."
"What did you do for a living?" He challenged again.
"I was a lecturer in motor mechanics at Kingston University for thirty-five years."

This knocked whatever wind was left in Rumpole good and proper. From this he never recovered. When the defence stated that a gun specialist was to be called, the Judge said, "To what ends?" Rumpole' replied, "We don't think the gun could have been fired, and we have an expert from Purdy the gun makers to explain why." Then the Judge, "I can't stop you using your witness, but if you do I will instruct the Jury to disregard everything the expert says. Rumpole insisted that he still wanted to call him. "Very well then," sighed the man, in the funny red coat. "As you've got him here - no doubt at great expense - let's hear what he has to say."

To cut a long story short, the gun expert tried to explain the fact that the gun could not possibly have been fired since its only use had been that of an ornament which hung on the wall. The Judge sent the gun expert on his way, and then turned to the Jury and said, "The fact that the gun could not have been fired is irrelevant, because there is no way Mr Lindsay could have known this at that precise moment." He told the Jury to disregard the gun expert's testimony and dismiss it from their minds.

Not long after this there occurred a situation that is almost unique in law. The Judge, still clearly irritated by Rumpole's continued incompetence, stopped the proceedings and sent the Jury away. What happened next will stay with me for the rest of my life. "Mr. O'Mally (alias Rumpole), I have never had in my court a Barrister as incompetent as yourself. Where did you learn to cross examine like this?" He then turned to the midget in the dock and said, "I do not think that you are getting a good enough defence in this case." The Judge looked over to me in the public gallery and said, "I can see that Mr Lindsay clearly agrees with me. I am going to ask the defendant if he wishes to retain his Barrister." The Judge looked straight at the dock and the midget was shaking as if he had St. Vitas Dance! When asked the question the midget looked at his even tinier wife, who motioned with her two hands to follow the learned advice.

"Mr. O'Mally," said the Judge. "Stand up when I'm talking to you! I am removing you from this Court because I have suggested to the defendant that his barrister is unworthy of continuing on his behalf."

I'm not sure how everyone became distracted – not surprising really – the tension in Court was electric. But distracted they were. The Judge asked the defendant, "Where did you find this barrister." "From the Yellow Pages," was the reply from the dock. The whole

Court was now in uproar. "Can I ask you how much you paid for this barrister?" "Seven thousand pounds, Sir. Was the reply" A big intake of breath was followed by, "Give me the name of the instructing solicitors and I will write to them." The Judge then turned to the defendant's solicitor and asked, "How many partners are there in your firm?" "One your Honour, "he replied. "Give me his name and I will recommend that he reimburse the defendant his £7,000. If there is any problem with that I would suggest to the defendant that he sue his solicitors to repay this fee. Furthermore, I will release a transcript of this case so far if it will help."

As I said earlier – distracted – we all were. The Judge spotted Rumpole sitting in his normal position and shouted with real force, "I thought I told you to leave this Court! What are you still doing here?" Rumpole stood up, fiddled with his papers for what seemed like an eternity, then waddled his way past all the other wigs much in the fashion of one leaving the cinema early; though not because they are disappointed with the film, but rather more the result of an ejection for throwing popcorn or some other uncouth misdemeanour. Embarrassing or what! He left the Court followed by the instructing solicitor, who had his Court papers in a two-wheeled shopping trolley that he dragged along behind him, rubbing his unusually long sideburns as he went.

Upon the closing of the court door the Judge remarked, "How are we going to follow that?" There was laughter all round. He set a new date for the retrial. As it happens the midget had obviously had enough and pleaded guilty the next time. He received three years suspended jail sentence for actual bodily harm. The midget's wife told me a year later that this Court case was the last straw, and after the trial she divorced him. She told me she'd believed all he said in court until my mate and I gave evidence. She knew then that he was not telling the truth and had lied throughout.

Girl on Bike

This story is as sad as it gets. Walking back to the house I was working on I passed a young girl playing on her bike; I guess she was about eight or nine years old. I said something like, "That looks like fun." She replied in the affirmative. It was then that I noticed some marks on her face and head. I asked her how she received these abrasions and was told, "I fell off my bike." It was clear someone had given her a beating. I remember thinking, 'I would like to meet the coward.' I was not kept waiting for long, as the house I was working on stood just fifty yards down the street from where I'd met this little girl. I walked on not taking my eyes off the child, who was now following me. I reached my destination just as next door's front door opened.

There stood a man of about fifty who started to scream abuse at the little girl on her bike. I turned round and she was standing behind me. "Get the f**k in here!" he ranted. The girl ran up the steps quickly and disappeared into the house. The unkempt loudmouth seemed to not notice my presence, although I was standing no more than three metres from his door. I leapt over the little wall separating one staircase from the other and held my ear against the door, straining for the slightest sound of the little girl's distress. I heard nothing and maybe a good job too; for I would have torn the door off its hinges if I had.

On reaching home some three hours later, I called the N.S.P.C.C. who didn't seem to be worried about the girl. They asked me personal questions about her that I could not answer, and finally agreed to visit the child, but only on the proviso that I did not do likewise. The N.S.P.C.C. told me not to contact them later about this case, because they would not tell me anything. I duly left them to it, but I often still think about that little girl on her bike.

There are no illegitimate children – only illegitimate parents.
- **Judge Leon R Yankwich**

It may not have escaped your attention that I become involved in all sorts of aggravation. This would occur to anyone working in hundreds of houses a year for decades. It also stems from my childhood when I had no-one to stand up for me, from which a pretty well developed sense of fair play came. Bullies are essentially cowards when confronted by people who stand up to them. I particularly dislike men who hit women and children; but who doesn't?

Domestic

On one occasion, just across the road from where I live, an argument was taking place. I looked over our six foot high wall to catch sight of a man thumping his wife. I didn't particularly want to become involved in a bust up between partners, so I watched on from a distance, the language becoming more distasteful with each passing minute. I guess it was only a matter of time before I could no longer stand by and do nothing. I approached the warring couple and asked the woman if she was all right. Looking back, that was a pretty stupid remark, since it was obvious that she was not all right. The man came towards me, not unnaturally, in a threatening manner. "What's it got to do with you?" he hollered "nothing" I replied. "Well f**k off then!" I went on, turning back to his wife and said, "I'm not going to stand here and watch you thump her again."

It was made quite clear that he should desist from his intentions. My suggestion that he leaves his wife alone or I would restrain him seemed to do the trick, and on his not so merry way he went. The wife thanked me profusely and at all subsequent meetings thereafter. I'm not sure how I manage to diffuse situations like this; I just know that it happens time and time again. Perhaps the straight-talking, clearly expressed intention in the heat of the moment does it, and the big hands. I'm sure that one day my threats won't be enough and my bluff will be called; I just hope I'm not too old or slow to cope! The lady in question divorced and remarried some years later, and called me in to administer some work on her house. And what came of it? She promptly knocked me for fifty pounds! Work that one out!

Four Courses

Working on a house in Chiswick a building inspector turned up to inspect something unconnected with what I was doing. He said on his way out: "Don't forget to make sure that you have at least five courses of bricks over that lintel." I said, "Only room for four." At this he went potty, saying that he would close down the job if I did not comply. I told him to go back to his office and send someone out who knew what he was talking about.

As he left, the building inspector made it clear that he would hand in his notice if his boss did not back him up. Two days later I'd forgotten all about this, when a smart suited chap turned up looking for me. He told me that he was the Chief Building Inspector and asked me what the problem was. I explained the different views and off he went satisfied with my explanation. I did not know at the time that the original building inspector was sitting outside in his car. He did not appear again and I learnt later that he did indeed resign.

The reason for recounting this tale is that some building inspectors, as mentioned in Part One, know only what comes out of a book. On site they have more power than the Queen and her Royal Troop, but are not always right, as in this case.

Possibly the building inspector's problem as a whole, is that they are not allowed any variation from their text book stance. We builders use all manner of variations on a daily basis to overcome whatever might be a sticking point. Building inspectors cannot do this as they have no practical experience to call upon. It is at times like this that it is quite easy to outflank them in a sometimes heated debate. Some can see the sense in what is being put to them, some will not. An impasse will only be avoided if the builder takes responsibility for what he propounded. A younger or less experienced builder might not have the confidence to take on a building inspector.

Gas Men

I once had a problem with a certain gas company. One morning at my house the flow of gas to the hob cooker was intermittent, so I phoned the service line number and an operative was sent to my home. He tried all the knobs and decided to look at the outside meter box. As we walked up to the meter box, it seemed to have fallen off the wall, and the supply pipe now had a kink clearly showing. All through the previous night the wind had howled, and a scaffold board leaning against the box knocked it off the wall. This man walked off saying a team would be out soon to fix the problem. Sure enough a man arrived and told me that the kink could not be repaired. I was told a new section of pipe would have to be inserted and the box would have to go back on the wall. I asked the man if he would like a cup of tea, and he said, "Yes please." As soon as my back was turned he ran to the back of his truck and came back with a small camera, took a shot and returned his camera to his truck. I wondered what that was all about, so I asked him. Red faced, he said the company like to have a picture of every outside breakdown to cover themselves. Okay I thought, and he began his work.

Before cutting the plastic pipe he kinked the tube further down with a kind of clamp to shut off the flow of gas, and then fixed the relocated box back onto the wall. Having jointed the box and pipe back together he produced a tool not dissimilar to a pair of pliers, specially made to un-kink the gas pipe. I remember thinking, 'that's a handy tool to have hanging around'. I asked him why he did not remove the original kink in the same way. He said that it was company policy.

I found out later why it was company policy; not only did they want to charge me for a new section of pipe and for reaffixing the box, but also for a two-man team of fixers in addition to the first man! It seems the Lord Lucan member of the repair team was doing another repair round the corner. The company wanted me to pay for the other job as well as my own, and no doubt the other customer was paying for my repair also. Nice work if you can get it! The company's advertising blurb at that time said something like, "There *are* nice people out there." People yes, companies never.

They sent me bill after bill and I sent letter after letter. They could not understand how I knew the difference between one man and two men, and they also doubled the time taken for a job that was unnecessary. Nice people indeed!

Knocked Silly

I once found myself in a position when a wall fell on my head, quite my own fault I have to say. The circumstances escape me, but I do remember that I was knocked silly for a good half an hour (some would say I never recovered!). The amazing thing was that I drove home covered in blood, and that my wife did not catch on to my state for thirty minutes or so, until I collapsed in front of her! Even then I was called a baby for complaining about a scratch on my head that needed a dozen stitches. My ex-wife was like that, only needing to stub her toe for the whole world to hear her screams!

Hurricane '87

In Part One the subject of hurricanes (1987) was discussed, in the chapter on 'Misunderstandings'.

To take you through the whole weekend of some forty telephone calls and rising. I proposed to visit all individuals spoken to, and loaded up my truck with a selection of tiles, slates and plastic sheets. I set off at first light on the Saturday, not knowing where and when the day might come to an end. I'd worked out a vague plan of action in not sticking to first come first served; otherwise I'd be criss-crossing Surrey like a demented lemming. A loose route was planned and off I went, coming across new properties and old, from folks glad to see me and those who were not.

I knocked on some doors where the inhabitants said, "Who are you?" When I explained that they had phoned me they said the work had been completed already. In many cases Joe public had called every man in the world with a ladder, and whoever came round first administered the necessary task. I did not particularly want to be there at that time, and my responsibilities to help as much as I could were receding fast!

Ten, twenty roofs I had seen, and still another dozen or so to visit. The shithouses I met along the way were offset somewhat by the joy of others, who had trusted me to appear eventually. Darkness came then food, followed by a damn good sleep. At least that was the plan. My wife woke me up at about one o'clock in the morning to inform me that a bloke was on the phone from Epsom. I distinctly remember saying to her, "I don't care if he's from Disney World, I've got to sleep." She went away and returned a few minutes later to say that he wouldn't take no for an answer. Apparently the storm had blown a hole in his roof and water was coming in, and we could now hear the rain pelting down outside.

Quite what a half-asleep man was supposed to do on a wet and dangerous roof in the middle of the night I don't know.

I fell asleep again, but was shaken awake once more. "He wants to know how much it would cost to come out now," said my wife. Whilst not wanting to rub salt into his wound, I did not want to leave my bed for a wet roof in Disney World (or was it Epsom?) "Five hundred pounds," was my half-hearted reply. "No, make that a thousand pounds," thinking he might consider five hundred pounds cheap in respect of the possible damage. I promptly fell back asleep and woke at eight to start all over again, a Sunday.

Looking back over the preceding two days I don't remember being offered a cup of tea. Of course I wasn't there to drink tea or chat, which leaves me to conclude that not many of my customers could or would see the broader picture – my frantic circumstance – in light of their own predicament. I earned well that weekend, but in hindsight it was a poor return for what I had to put up with.

Susie

This is a story right out of the scumbag's horror story book. Sue lived just around the corner from me, and has my card pinned on her notice board in the kitchen. Her next door neighbours were having their facier board and soffits renewed in plastic (the strips of material that the gutter is fixed to). The two young builders doing so asked Sue if she would like the same on her house, to which she agreed a price of £700. She was not happy with the work and asked the two builders to return and re-fix the guttering properly. Despite many phone calls the two chaps never showed. A week later, we bumped into Sue and she recounted her version of events. "Why, why, did you not call me first?" I asked. "I never thought about you until I got tucked up," said Susie.

This lady, a single parent with two small boys, didn't think that the builders would sting her because (and here comes the crunch) in her own words she 'fancied one of them"! Now I don't know if this builder had come on to her and taken advantage to procure some work, or whether she had come on to him and he was relatively innocent. Either way, something presumably frightened them off, but not before getting paid, of course! Is it a little presumptuous of me to assume that Sue did not fancy me enough to ask my opinion at the time? She did apologise for not originally asking me, and having done so I duly sorted the problem out. "I'm defenceless as to why I engaged those parasites in the first place," she kept saying.

Two months later though, I passed her house to observe a bricklayer rebuilding her front garden wall. I have yet to speak to her about this apparent and repeated snub, though in all likelihood a similar and innocuous turning of events led to her calling him and not me. It is, after all, crucial to not let ones emotions get in the way of purely work matters despite the expectations that often abound from a good customer rapport.

Tables and Chairs

I have already mentioned working at this particular house in the grounds of Hampton Court Palace, and would now like to share with you a mystery which I cannot explain. This house, owned by a famous scriptwriter, was walled in on all sides, and at the front a huge pair of wooden gates provided access to the parking area and gardens. Every time anyone went near these gates the four resident dogs went berserk, two of whom were Rottweiler's. One dark night in the summer, a group of bandits or robbers or burglars or gypsies (take your pick) crept into the property stealing a lorry full of expensive iron patio furniture.

In all the years that I've worked there on and off, not once had I been able to hide my presence from this veritable pack of hounds. How on this particular night no disturbance was observed I just do not know! I know it must have taken at least two people to remove the items because I had, with difficulty, moved them myself from time to time. The police said the patio tables and chairs were almost certainly stolen to order, and were most likely sitting pretty on somebody's patio already.

But how in Heaven's name, can a vehicle plus its occupants, appear and disappear heavily laden in the dead of night, without awaking the dogs, or anyone else? I don't know if I was at any time under suspicion, but suspicion may well be placed on the owners who would, we can assume, have received a fair wad of cash for the claiming of insurance on the furniture.

The Bemoaning Babs

One classic case showing the best and worst of our profession occurred some years after moving down to Sussex. My client, Babs, lived in a very large period mansion on the edge of a public park. She moved out of her house into an annexe to the side that she had had built years previously. The builder in question had since retired, however one of his original workers - now a painter - has been looking after Babs and the big house for decades since.

Babs was with my wife when she regaled her tales of woe. Six months after moving into the annexe, water started to appear in the basement, and then on a more and more frequent basis. It seems the method (tanking) used to keep the basement dry had failed, and the ingress of water was going up and down in unison with the underground water table. Babs complained to all in sundry and indeed anyone who would listen. When Babs found out I was a builder she begged my wife to introduce me to her, hopeful that I could help her find out what had gone wrong. I was reluctant to get involved because the resident maintenance men on site worked on the original refurbishment. It seemed to me that they should have some responsibility having been around at the time of the work years ago.

One of these maintenance men attended a poetry group we were involved with, so I had to tread carefully. Spurred on by my wife I agreed to look into the sorry mess, against my better judgement. As a stranger to West Sussex I was not familiar with this property, so I suggested a survey with a fee of £150.

The maintenance men looking after the annexe and the manor house were in attendance most of the time. I found four glaring errors all concerning rainwater removal, and considering the current problem was astonished that experienced tradesmen did not see the need to do something. Undaunted, I pointed it out to Babs, and then gave her a verbal quote for work I believed was essential. She was informed that the operation would not solve her main problem, but may well help alleviate it – time will tell. She remarked, "What you have told me seems logical, so carry on."

The price of £2,800 was agreed, to dig up a raised patio area to the rear and run a new rainwater facility to a soak-away, thereby stopping all rainwater from entering the house foundations. Three other repairs were also rainwater related, due to a design fault discovered with the conservatory roof. I was informed that the conservatory maker was a family friend.

To cut a long story short, I finished the work rather quicker than had been anticipated. The result was that Babs, now shouting and screaming, that I'd overcharged her, even though I'd stuck to my original quote. She'd scream foul to anyone within earshot, making up stories about phantom work not completed. Having worked out how much I'd earned relative to her professional point of reference – the result obviously rather upset her - she was now telling a gathered throng of friends and experts what a cowboy I was. Nobody mentioned what a good job I had done on her behalf, or that my ability to recognise the problem and relieve it quickly and efficiently comes directly from decades of priceless experience! To perceive the bigger picture is generally not a quality I have observed in people with their money on the table.

The architect who had overseen the refurbishment seven years ago was ultimately responsible for the basement leaking, as are the Council Inspectors, not to mention the retired builder on site, who kept his head firmly down throughout.
In short, all are family friends who could not possibly be responsible. I vowed to make someone accountable, to pay for the renewal of the tanking. Or so I thought.

The story does not end here. Previously, I'd asked Babs to ring the Council to ask them to meet me there, to help ascertain what happened seven years ago, and they did in fact check what was happening on site. After all this was a Grade I listed building, for which one must have documents appertaining to the work. For the same reason I fixed a meeting with the architect, but he/she (for he/she had had a sex change) did not want to know.
I asked Babs to phone the conservatory maker to meet up and explain the severe design fault. She did so, and more; a good deal of ranting and raving to him about the cost of my work, his reaction to which was to put the 'phone down and promptly ring the police (what could she possibly have told him?).

Before turning up the police contacted the Trading Standards office. I turned up purely by chance one day to be confronted by a constable and two of our Trading Standards officers, one male one female. The copper, having heard both sides, said, "I'm off." The Trading Standards officer's keen to see a resolution, asked if I would consider a reduction in the price. I remember saying, "If she is hard up she can have it all." My wife went potty and a compromise was reached.

This lady, a musician by profession, had, I am told, squandered millions of pounds in bad business ventures over the years - not that this was any concern of mine. I mention it only because of the disparity between what I earn and what I keep. The upshot of all this was that I was knocked for £800, *this* being the sole, real reason for her lies and histrionic behaviour.

A person in so much trouble cannot sell up or move out, and has to trust the one man who would have stood up in the High Court as an expert witness; against her friends, the original builder, the architect and council inspectors, plus the conservatory maker. But all Babs could see was the £800 saving, not the possibility of recovering her difficult situation by proving her friend's negligence. At the time the cost of remedial work I put at about £25,000 to £35,000.

When the Trading Standards Inspectors left they gave me six pages chock full of do's and don'ts, and yet not one sentence of these advice sheets appertained to this case or me. And what actually was the case? The inspectors were alerted by a man making faulty conservatories that I have never met or worked for. Benny Hill would be proud to have dreamt that one up!

Walnut Tree

At a site I once worked on mentioned earlier, down by the River Thames, stood a walnut tree right in the way of the proposed extension; this tree was about eighteen feet high and was documented in the deeds of the house, which showed it to be two hundred and sixty-five years old. It was suggested to me by a number of people that when uprooted and cut up it might be worth something, so I decided to investigate. I looked into who would use walnut in their business and came to the conclusion that a quality car company might well use it in their manufacture of dashboards.

I phoned Jaguar cars, still at this point made in the Midlands, who put me in touch with their veneer suppliers. I spoke to a chap who asked, "How long, how thick, how old?" He went on, "We might be interested in taking it off your hands if you could deliver it here so we can view it." If you are in any doubt about what he was asking me to do, let me summarise: cart this ancient tree, weighing possibly two whole tons, hundreds of miles up the country, with no guarantee that they would take it. And if not, what then? Clearly a compromise was not to be reached. Sadly, I ended up cutting the tree and burning it.

Car Thieves

One dark night I resolved to pick up my daughter from her friend's house just around the corner; standing in her porch waiting for Elizabeth I noticed two men both carrying what looked like champagne bottles. Walking past me and without a sideways glance, they tried every car door as they worked their way down this dark road. I phoned the police and soon enough a squad car appeared. The thieves, some two hundred yards further down the straight road, could still be seen trying all the car doors. The copper said he would take a look. "Do you want some help?" I asked. "No," He replied, and drove off. I watched on as he drove down the road and took a left, away from the crims. I assumed his bottle had gone, and two days later that was confirmed when on checking at the local Police Station he'd reported that nothing was found. Rather ironic that as he drove off, I could just about make out the thieves at work in the distance!

Iranian Doctors

A client of mine passed my details on to a pair of Iranian doctors, who were in dispute with a local builder over a new laminated floor he had laid. I went along to offer my opinion, as did a local flooring supplier; needless to say the floor fitting was of very poor quality. The consensus was to remove the said floor and refund the clients. The errant builder showed levels of prevarication rarely seen. The upshot was a letter written by me asking this builder to respond within fourteen days. He did not do so, and on behalf of these two doctors I wrote another letter pointing out that his obligation to respond to their claims had run out. I explained that a Judge would take a very dim view of not taking the opportunity offered to give his side of the story.

This modus operandi clearly had the desired effect, and he duly returned all monies. The curious thing was that Mr Doctor became furious that I'd written the second letter without his permission, even though Mrs Doctor explicitly asked me to. Despite getting caught up between Mrs Doctor wanting recompense and Mr Doctor not wanting to push for a result, when the arguing was over Mr and Mrs Doctor procrastinated over the bill -about £200 - while the amount recovered for them stood at £7,000. No solicitors, no court appearance, just an experienced builder thinking on his feet.

Procrastination is the art of keeping up with yesterday   - **Don Marquis**

In parenthesis: the professor my ex-father in law, who travelled to over one hundred countries in his long working life for the ministry of health, living in no less than 35 of them, when asked by his grandkids which place he enjoyed most unequivocally gave Iran; the culture, history, food, geography and hospitality were to him without compare.

Sad Stories

I have some stories to recount here; all sad, all true.

Over fifty years ago when I was about ten or eleven, I went late night fishing with Fred Marshal, a friend the same age as me. Teddington Lock was the venue one Friday night at 12:30 a.m., pitch black. We were fishing at the rivers' edge. Behind us about two feet away stood a six foot high grass bank, and beyond that the towpath. About a hundred yards further down the bank some older boys were camping; I could hear them shrieking and larking about.

Out of nowhere a man appeared, sitting down right behind me on the bank. Much too scared, I didn't look round. He seemed to have his hands in his pockets because he kept rattling coins, making a clinking sound. Fred did not seem too bothered by him, but I was shitting myself without knowing why. Eventually the man approached me saying, "I'll give you ten bob for a suck."

It was probably a good ten years later before I knew what he was after that night, though at the time I knew it wasn't right. I made some excuse to Fred about fetching more bait, and ran like crazy towards the tents up river, leaving Fred at the man's mercy. Later that night the older boys caught the man, and flung him in the river. Incredibly, some ten minutes later a policeman appeared on a motorbike (a coincidence for sure, since he could not have known what had happened; there were no mobile phones in those days). The reason I told this story was that - yes, you've guessed it - the man was a builder.

Vigilante Justice

I once worked on a large housing estate in Tulse Hill, South London. The site was long and narrow, flanked by the main road to Brixton and Brockwell Park. At one end was a girls' school, the name of which escapes me. One afternoon about four, in November, some thirty-five years ago, all the bricklayers and labourers heard screams coming from the park side. I sent a labourer to investigate the noise, but before he had a chance to climb over the loose chain link fence, I started sprinting across the site because the screams were now becoming more desperate and chilling.

Over the fence was a long hedge type structure that completely obscured the view. In those days I was a particularly strong, fit, athletic man, and so I leapt at the chain link fence, landing on top of it and almost decapitating the labourer who was, at my request no less, astride the fence. The poor fella must have really hurt his knackers after I smashed into the fence at full speed with him still straddled on it. About my landing I remember his language to this day! I pushed my way through the tight hedge, and was the second man through. I looked to my left, and kneeling down saw a young girl about twelve years old, with the first labourer standing at her side looking around.

I knelt down and put my arm round her as she cried her heart out; her clothes had been rearranged. I asked her what had happened - looking back rather a stupid thing to say –

133

and soon realised. I asked the girl which way her assailant had gone, and she lifted her arm and pointed in the general direction of what I now know to be Herne Hill. I looked up to see a figure running fast about half a mile away. Brockwell Park is an open space allowing one to see a very long way. By this time about ten men had gathered, looking around at nothing in particular. I shouted at the first labourer to look after the girl while the newly formed band went off to try to catch the man.

I set off with eight labourers in tow, after one hundred yards or so I looked round to see that everyone had given up. Unperturbed, I continued running down the hill across some football pitches, I think. I could make out my quarry by now; he had a donkey jacket on. He was heading for the park gates still a quarter of a mile ahead. In front of me was a tarmac road at ninety degrees from me leading to the park gates; unfortunately the road did not go directly to the exit of the park, going instead in a zigzag succession of turns. A car was coming towards me on my left, which I stopped, yanking the old lady out of the passenger seat and ordering the driver, "Get me to the gates quickly!"

The stunned lady would not drive across the grass in a direct line because of the "keep off the grass" signs. She did her best round the bends in the road and screeched to a halt. I remember trying to remove myself from this car a touch early and banged my knee; I leapt out of the car determined that he would not get away. I ran through the gates leaping over the safety barrier and across the main road, dodging the traffic as I went. About sixty or seventy yards in front of me he was running for his life. I knew he must have been running on empty because I was knackered myself. It was at this point that I was sure I had him, but as he was running past Herne Hill underground station and realised that if he disappeared down there I'd find it difficult to follow him.

By now I was only fifteen yards behind as he ran under the bridge and past the entrance to the station. I was now coasting, gathering my thoughts about what to do next. I grabbed him by the coat and said something like, "Where do you think you're going." He said: "What's up mate?" And put his hand in his pocket. I retorted: "If you don't take your hand out of your pocket I'm going to tear your arm off." I had no idea what he had in his pocket but he removed his hand promptly.

He kept saying, "Don't you like school girls?" and "Can't you let me go?" As I half-dragged him back to the park gates, about six or seven labourers appeared. "Is that him?" One stupidly shouted. I let one labourer hold each arm as we headed back to the site – by now it was getting quite dark. I waved at the two ladies in the car I had scared witless earlier, and walked after this bloke, now surrounded by labourers. I dived in to stop the bunch as they gave him a good kicking. As luck would have it I was a charge-hand on site, and so had some measure of authority over the labourers. One thing still puzzles me even now; not one of the bricklayers came over the fence in pursuit of the man, only the labourers – funny that.

By the time we reached the site it was pitch black, and there were now ten or eleven labourers at the hedge. I asked the first labourer who had been left to look after the girl. "Where is she?" "I dunno," He replied. I remember calling him all the names under the sun, because I knew that if the young girl did not go to the police we would have done this for nothing.

I was deep in thought about this poor girl, not knowing what had happened to her... I wondered if she got home okay. The next minute a scream – I turned my head to the right; once again the labourers getting stuck in, holding the man's legs apart and taking turns to kick him. I dived in once again, not because I felt sorry for him, but clearly because I did not want to be charged with murder!

It had turned ugly by now as I shouted, "Has anyone called the police!" Someone said they had been called. Two whole hours later a squad car arrived to save the man from the mob. They were late, apparently because the police were waiting at the gates of the site for us, but of course we could not know this.

The following day the police arrived on site to take statements from those involved. A detective told me that the man, a student, had attacked two little kids playing by a pond in the park earlier in the afternoon. He also told me that they had been after this man for months. The detective then told me what happened at the police station. He said, and I quote, "I took the student into an empty office to question him, where he (the student) said, "When the labourers were kicking me in the park I was coming a lot." The detective then said to the student, "You might as well come again," and promptly kicked him in the groin. I don't know if what he said was true, but I had to take his word for it.

When I asked the police about the young girl I was told that she was twelve years old and the student had indeed tried to rape her. Thank goodness the shouting of the labourers had scared him off. I asked what had happened to the girl after she left the park; apparently, she went home and told her Mum, then waited till her father, (a Docker), came home, then they all went to Brixton Police Station. When the family told the police what had happened, they must have been astonished to be told that the culprit was already in custody. I was told that the Chief Constable would write to me thanking me for my efforts. From that day, thirty-five years ago to now, I have had no such correspondence from the police. What a shame.

The C.P.S. did write to me, to say that he had pleaded guilty and so I was not required to attend court. The local labourers showed me a local paper with a report on the case; the student got two years' probation and fined £20.

Basement Murder

This sad story took place in Bollingbroke Road, Hammersmith, many moons ago. The chap we were working for owned two houses next door to each other in a long terrace. The houses were about 150 years old and four storeys high, each with a basement. Most of our work was in these basements. We decided to start and finish the left hand basement first because it was unoccupied.

As the weeks went by there seemed to be an awful lot of visitors to the house on our left, to which, other than the observation itself, we did not take too much notice. We were told that an old boy lived in the other basement, but we had not seen him at all. The owner became concerned and a few days later broke into the basement flat.

My labourer and I were outside at the time of the discovery of the old man, who had been found on his bed, dead. I rushed in to see a sight I never wish to see again; a body on the bed covered in maggots, paper money scattered everywhere. I went back outside and was promptly, violently sick. It was four weeks later before we were able to start work in that basement. Apparently it had transpired that the old man had some money in his flat. Someone broke in looking for it, and had killed him in a struggle, then, in the dark, ransacked the flat. Presumably unbeknown to the murders they'd scattered the notes all over the place, and left somewhat empty handed.

To top the story off - for better or worse I cannot quite be sure - the house to the left of us turned out to be a twenty-four hour a day brothel!

Dead Man in My Arms

This story started when I visited Bare Green Brickworks near Dorking, to collect a number of their wares. The van I had at the time was an Escort estate, and on this occasion the bricks I had collected in Dorking were, in truth, too heavy for it. Limping home along the Kingston Road towards Chessington World of Adventures, I found myself on an incline and going ever slower. I moved over lanes and a yellow BT viva van overtook me up the hill and over the top.

When I eventually arrived at the top of the incline I could see about half a mile ahead on the straight road. What in fact I saw was the yellow van in the middle of the road static, as if the driver was waiting to turn left or right. There was an articulated lorry just in front of it, on his own side of the road. As I approached, with no traffic between the van and myself, something did not look right; and so it proved to be.

I stopped directly behind the yellow van and got out, the front of the van smashed in. Looking about, the driver of the articulated lorry was nowhere to be seen. I went round the van to the driver's door and saw a leg hanging out from the bottom; the door had jammed shut, but was open about four or five inches, enough to see the leg was broken. I tried to get to the driver, who was about forty-five years old. I managed to get my shoulders into the cab and put my arm around him. He was unconscious, clearly in a bad way.

It was at this point that I became aware of other people around, and shouted for some blankets to keep the driver warm and if anyone had called an ambulance. Calming down somewhat, I had a good look at the driver; he had a spot of blood on his forehead and his eyes were closed. I could tangibly feel him getting weaker, his groans becoming faint. At that moment I remember thinking that the world had stopped moving.

I was starting to panic, still half in and half out of the van. It felt as though I'd been there for an age, although I was told afterwards it was only for ten minutes. As the driver slowly shuddered I could hear the siren, but I was losing him. I could feel everything drain out of him, ever so slowly, from the top down. The shuddering becoming less strong, time appearing to have stopped completely, both for him and myself.

When they arrived I extricated myself from the van to let the paramedics get to the driver. I helped the first medic into the vehicle, and he promptly pronounced the driver dead. Of course I knew; he had died in my arms. In rather a daze I walked over to my van and slumped myself on its bonnet. I was surprised to feel its heat -the engine was still running; in the moment, on arrival, I'd forgotten to turn it off.

The police milling about were trying to find out what had happened (at that point I had no idea that the driver of the articulated lorry was still nowhere to be seen). A policeman came up to me, and with the charm a fox might afford a rabbit, said, "Is that your van? Move it." Soon enough another copper growled at me, "Why is your van overloaded with bricks?" 'Time to go home, Leo!' I thought, and promptly did so, not a little overcome by the whole affair.

Apparently the Viva had struck the lorry head-on. I don't know why – perhaps in shock and guilt - the lorry driver got out of his cab and ran away back down the road from whence he came, where he was soon found by a local householder lying on the ground, inconsolable.

If the police wanted to find out anything about this affair, why was I not asked any questions relating to it? All they were interested in was my van overloaded with bricks and for me to get out of their way.

A Bloody Mess

This story is about a young guy called John Anderson who was, at the time, about sixteen years of age, and I must have been about twenty-three. His parents owned a cottage in Alphamstone, a small village in Suffolk. I was invited to spend the weekend with the family in return for some building work which they wanted completing.

At the bottom of the garden was a large orchard, and to one side a shed-come-caravan, with centre wheels on either of its sides. This mobile shed was in dire need of repair, was badly rusted, and the windows were broken. On this particular day John and I stepped into the rusting hulk, where we both stood by the window. As John put his arm through the broken pane, pointing at something in the orchard, I stepped away from the window momentarily. Since I was three or four stone lighter than John, the movement caused the shed to lurch forward on its axis.

The result was John's arm went up, as his weight sent the shed downwards. His arm made contact with the broken glass in the window… the scream was blood curdling. Upon regaining my own balance, the sight itself was a good deal worse; the glass had cut through the skin and bone on one side of his arm, leaving only the skin on the other side holding the thing together. John fell onto the floor of the shed trying to hold onto the almost severed arm.

His parents came rushing out to see what the commotion was about. His father took one look and promptly fainted, and his mother stood there like a dummy screaming her head off! I shouted at his sister to call an ambulance, and quick. Both John and I struggled outside, me holding his severed arm to his chest whilst John, who was obviously in a state of shock, mumbled incoherently to himself. The blood was spurting all over the both of us. I sat him down on the rear step of the family Dormobile, trying to keep him awake, whilst holding the almost severed limb upright and against the stump. I remember watching the blood run down his arm and down the length of my arms and dropping in a pool at my feet. Since we were in the middle of nowhere, the paramedics took nearly thirty minutes to reach us, by now blood covered us both, including the back of the van and the road where he sat.

Upon regaining consciousness the father had run and hid in the orchard, and the mother was still screaming as I pushed her into the ambulance with her son. I drove the Dormobile, following the ambulance to hospital, thinking that I must keep up with the medics because I didn't know where the hospital was.

When I walked into the accident and emergency unit two nurses rushed up to me gasping, "Are you hurt?" I remember thinking, 'why on earth would I be hurt?' It wasn't until I looked in the mirror that I could understand the nurses' concern – I was covered from head to toe in the crimson blood!

Needless to say it was a long drive back with John's mother, since she deemed it my fault, on top of the fact that I, as a mere and lowly bricklayer was not to be fraternised with. Till this day decades later, I don't believe she thanked me for my efforts. I understand that John still has his arm and some movement in it, and last time I heard he was working as an estate agent.

When I was taken to a very wealthy area of London to view a job, in Berkeley Square I think, by two Lebanese architects, the two chaps told me not to engage the wife of the house in chitchat. The owner was away on business and only used the flat occasionally, so it was left to his wife to open the door for us. She, also from Lebanon, was quite attractive in a Middle Eastern sort of way, but held a rather blank expression on her face.

The architects, who clearly knew her well, largely ignored her. At the conclusion of our visit I smiled at the wife and offered a few words, to which she replied without words, her eyes dead or bored, or both. Even allowing for Middle Eastern customs it comes naturally for anyone to smile when someone is being sincerely nice to them, unless they are not familiar with kindness. I found out weeks later this lady was a virtual prisoner – not being allowed out of the house - in a so called life of luxury, alone.

On one of our lunchtime sorties down by the River at Sunbury, we found ourselves swimming (in my case, drowning) in an open-air pool. Just off to my right five kids were doing back flips into the pool, and one child about nine years of age caught my eye. She jumped in five or six times, each time, her head getting closer to the pool's edge. I hurried to move closer but was too late; as I saw and heard her head thump the stonework. I bent down and grabbed the unconscious girl's arm, lifting her up out of the blooded water; placing her lifeless body down poolside, covered in blood. People were now screaming and an ambulance was duly called. Thankfully the young girl recovered consciousness before entering the paramedics' wagon, and all appeared well.

One of my mates wanted the front of his house in London re-rendered; I was not in a position to help, so he engaged a local tearaway, also known to me. Venturing uptown to play cricket, I called in to view the progress. My mate and this young lad were fretting about finishing the wall by six o'clock, to which I enquired why six o'clock so important. It seemed that this young lad had a security tag on his arm, and had therefore to be indoors by six. Running over time by fifteen minutes saw the cops arrive, to administer the tagged young chap a rollicking, even though the house the plasterer lived in was only across the road from the scaffold he was working on!

I once worked for a brickwork sub-contractor who regaled this tale one late Friday afternoon: he and two helpers (both women) were putting together our wages in his front room. A knock at the door found three hooded men each armed with pickaxe handles; an uneven scuffle resulted in the removal of our wage packets and a huge purple welt across our boss's face.

Zebra Crossing

As I've mentioned – in my younger days I could be a bit of a brute, quick to react to whatever I perceived an injustice; which, depending on the circumstances and my mood, could by a reasonable man be considered a 'loose' injustice, at best.

My eldest son recalls as a young lad returning home late from a football match with me, driving quickly and eager for bed. Approaching a zebra crossing at some speed and at the same moment as a pedestrian, I zoomed on before he'd stepped into the road. Taking umbrage to this impropriety the man shouted, "Cuuuuuuuunnnnnnnttt!" as we flew past. This did not go unnoticed.

In a moment I had screeched to a stop and was out of the car running towards the man. My son in the passenger seat watched over his shoulder in trepidation as I met the man at a jog, fist connecting with his jaw, and back around at a trot back to the car, as if in one fluid movement. Door shut I looked my son in the eyes and said, "Not a word to your mother about this." I'm glad to note this as a thing of the distant past...

Train Seats

Around the same time, again noted by my eldest son and his best friend, another altercation with, I'm pleased to say, a more moderate outcome. On the train from London to Liverpool with a dozen kids from our boys' football team, we were off to watch our beloved Everton at Goodison Park. Tickets and seat numbers in hand we boarded to find a few teenagers blithely occupying some of our seats. When asked to move they eyed the group, mostly kids, and told me to piss off. At this, so my eldest remembers, I leaned in close to quietly make clear the inevitable result of their not finding other seats, which probably involved the words 'throw', 'through', and 'window'.

They moved and another problem averted, with just the right amount of diplomacy and potential brawn. Was it down to my history as a builder - both as a self-employed man having to stand up for himself and as a grafting man with the muscles to show for it - that made me deal with this situation as I did? Without a doubt it was the building that made me so.

Funny

Humour is by far the most significant activity of the human brain
- ***Edward de Bono***

Some have had the opportunity to work with Laurence Olivier, John Wayne, or Liz Taylor. Whereas I've gotten to work with Sykie, Mick the builder, and other assorted nutters. Having said that, all the following are as much an entertaining bunch as the former or perhaps more so, when you consider the characters herein are entirely the tangible types.

Some people might see a builder like me as a surly son of a bitch, but I believe builders at work, in general, can be a very funny species indeed, as the following stories should testify. Some of these honest accounts won't please all householders, but we all have to have a laugh at work sometimes.

Underwear

I was told of an incident when roofers were working on a very large estate. The lady of the house was extremely attractive, and all watched as she hung up her beautiful underwear on the clothesline one morning. She said she was going out for the day, and the three men who were working on the roof waved her off with a smile. The labourer on the ground, thinking that the coast was clear, took off a pair of knickers from the line and put them on his head, then proceeded to prance around the back garden – a la lady of the underwear - much to the amusement of the gallery on the roof.

So amused, in fact, were all four builders that they did not see the lady of the house return to the back garden. The men on the roof, as if synchronised, buried their heads out of sight, leaving the unfortunate scarlet-faced and prancing chap to take an anticipated bollocking. Luckily, the lady saw the funny side of the joke, harmless as it was.

Sykie

The first one's name was Sykie. I only ever knew him as that; he was a charge hand to a gang of Irish labourers, and the respect they had for him was astonishing. I tentatively asked him one icy February morning: "Could you possibly dig a hole here for me?" "No problem," He said. The ground was frozen solid. Utterly undeterred, he proceeded first with a pick and then with a shovel, to dig the neatest hole in the ground that I've ever seen. Talk about mind over matter! Or was it no sense no feeling? With the point of the pick bouncing off the ground as one threw it, the man must have been made of iron to do as he did. No wonder the gang of paddies looked up to him.

The story goes that after work at about 1:00 p.m. on a Saturday, Sykie and his cronies - about nine in number - were walking home down a high street in West London. As they walked past a church hall one of the group, opened the door abutting the pavement, to discover a wedding reception laid out ready for the guests. I was told all the paddies got stuck into the food and drink like locusts. Apparently thereafter, there was very little left.

One very hot summer's day I was working with Sykie and his gang beside a high wall about nine feet high. On the other side of this boundary wall was The White Swan pub. Sykie told the youngest member to pop over the wall to get him a drink. The young lad couldn't climb over the wall, so Sykie picked him up and threw him over! As the first bottle flew back over the wall in the opposite direction from the chap who threw it, Sykie grabbed the thing, tore off the top with his teeth, and downed the contents. He struggled with the top of the next bottle, eventually ripping it off and drinking it too. Watching this, I asked him why he had trouble with the second bottle top. He said, "I wasn't as thirsty the second time around."

It was well known that he never bought a train ticket, although he used the train every day from Willesden Junction to Richmond. I have been told that on this particular day the British Rail Police, having cottoned on to his movements, were waiting for him at Willesden Junction. This station had two levels, one over the top of the other at a right angle. Sykie got off at the top and went down the stairs, where the police were duly waiting for him.

Now, Sykie really did like a drink and a punch up, best in that order, and was not afraid of anyone, least of all the police. The story goes that he broke away from their clutches at the bottom of the stairs and ran along the very long platform, turning occasionally to thump the nearest copper. In time, he was overpowered by nine policemen and taken away. I am not trying to paint a picture of a saint – in this case that would be an impossibility - merely that, the man worked hard, and damn well played hard too.

There were one or two more stories I could tell about Sykie, but I feel I can't put them in print! I would love to bump into him again sometime.

Mick the Builder

I have so many memories about Mick the builder it is difficult to know where to start. Firstly, I will say that his prowess with women was legendary, but not necessarily in the way you might think. I was present for most of these stories and the ones where I was not, I'm quite sure are true also.

We were working on a certain house, and a lady in her front garden about four houses away had over and again, over about a three-week period, hinted that she would make us a cup of tea. On this particular day she suggested that we might like a cup of tea. Mick replied, "Give us ten minutes." We then walked into her kitchen and sat down at her table. I sat opposite Mick, the lady sat at the end of the table. Suddenly Mick got up and, without a word, started to undress her. At first she did not move or say a word. I sat there fascinated, watching my mate undress this woman. The tea remained untouched.

Eventually she got cold feet and said, "I don't know you well enough." With that, Mick turned round and walked out with a pained expression on his face. I'd never seen anything like it in my life, but I suspect Mick had been there before! I have to say at this point that my mate Mick was no oil painting, not by any means, any more than I am. If Mick had had a drink, or was not very well, his fuse got shorter and shorter.

On another occasion late at night somewhere in Ladbroke Grove, Mick was on the bus; he was not feeling very good, and the bus conductor kept moaning at him, over and over again, about what I don't know. After a short while of this, Mick jumped up and chinned the conductor. The driver saw what was happening and stopped the bus, then came round to remonstrate with Mick, who duly knocked him out cold, too!

Someone had phoned the police and six officers piled on the bus to get at Mick; apparently there were helmets flying all over! One man who was sitting at the back by the entrance grabbed one of the officers and threw him off the bus - by this time no-one knew who they were fighting or why. I can only say that I wish I had been there to witness it! What I can say is that trouble follows Mick wherever he goes – the most of it, without doubt, is self-inflicted.

A builder is a man who often works with his head and heart and thinks with his feet and fists.
- **L A Lindsay**

This next recollection I was present. If Benny Hill was still alive he could not have dreamt up the following sketch.

Before Mick came up to London to become a builder, he was a manager of a boutique; he felt that any woman who came into his shop was fair game. This particular day I was visiting him at his place of work when he started chatting up a student, I think she was. I was standing by the door leaning on the doorjamb, when Mick came over and said, "Look after the shop for five minutes." I replied, "Where are you going?" "To the toilet," he answered. And so he did, with the student he had just met.

What followed was pure farce! At the time there were two other women in the shop, but not for long; Mick and the student had been in the small washroom at the back of the shop for seven or eight minutes when there was a crash – the door opened and there was Mick, trousers down by his ankles, laughing uncontrollably, with a hard on! Water was shooting from somewhere and hitting the shop ceiling, the punker fan spraying water all around like a fountain; the girl appeared from behind the water feature, holding the remains of her clothing to her as she ran from the shop!

What had happened was this; Mick had had this unfortunate girl bent over an old butler sink which, with the burden, had come off its brackets and fallen to one side, fracturing the lead rising main! The scene in front of me was, as you can imagine, hilarious – pure Benny Hill!

Prior to Mick becoming a builder, at my request incidentally, he was the manager of a boutique, or, to put it another way, a salesman. There are a lot of salesmen in the building trade these days that don't know anything about building, but seem to make a living at it, and Mick was such a one.

I remember Mick treading on a nail once. On arriving outside the hospital we were crossing the road, Mick hobbling, when a bus nearly ran us down, and certainly would have done if we hadn't taken evasive action. The bus stopped some hundred yards away at a bus stop. Mick gave chase (sort of). He opened the driver's door, yanked the poor driver clean out of his cab, and proceeded to give him a fair old pasting for nearly running us down on a zebra crossing!

Mick and I visited a house that was apparently up for sale, which had an inherent problem preventing a sale. In order to give a price we needed information, which only the estate agents could reveal. They were being difficult, but the estate agent's uncooperative attitude did not deter Mick! At lunchtime Mick returned to sweet talk the only person left in the office - a woman, naturally. Whatever he promised her, the crucial information was garnered, and a large profit was made in its subsequent buying and selling!

He was a very keen deep-sea fisherman, and was a good deal better at this than he could ever have been as a builder. When the time came we all gathered at the waters' edge looking forward to the trip out to sea. Mick was late. He finally turned up with a young girl about seventeen or eighteen years of age. He asked if we didn't mind, and we said we did, but Mick was not to be denied. He packed her into the very small cabin at the front of the boat and off we went. It was going to take two hours to reach our fishing destination. As we left Mick said, disappearing into the cabin, "See you lot later."

We fished. On the way back he once again said, "See you later," and made his way to the cabin and its contents. But before he could close the door some wag shouted, "Can we join in?" Mick, always open to this kind of suggestion, said, "I will ask her." He reappeared a few minutes later saying, "She won't wear it, but I tell you what," he went on; "if I can open the curtain a little at least you lot can watch."

And so he did. Quite how six of us were supposed to look through a very small porthole I don't know, but we tried. As the pushing and shoving soon ensued, I turned my head to the right to observe the skipper himself trying to get a glimpse. Then to the left towards the wheelhouse – empty! There we were in the middle of the busiest shipping lane in the world and nobody was steering the bloody boat!

As I've already mentioned, Mick worked in a female boutique in Brighton during the late sixties. He told me that at that time there was a proliferation of Scandinavian blonds at Brighton University, and this preponderance of blonds blowing away all males before them did not sit well with the other female students. It seems the local girls fought back in the only way possible, by dying their tresses blond! Obviously Mick continued in his way regardless, one and all.

Apart from the pursuit of women, Mick the builder had another addiction: slot machines. Once, we entered a greasy spoon for lunch, and Mick headed straight for the slot machine. I ordered two lunches and sat down wondering how a grown man could be so transfixed by a machine that was swallowing up his cash. The lunches arrived, Mick played on, and I finished mine and told Mick that he had five minutes to eat his lunch because we had to get back to work. His food untouched, me out the door, he just made it to the truck before I drove away.

Mick's delight at fronting up to women was truly amazing. If we were visiting a prospective customer and a woman came to the door, Mick would literally throw me out of the way to get to her first. He was the best salesman I have ever encountered, so I would listen to his bullshit in fascination at how he succeeded and got away with it, again and again. If Mick had been able to control and separate what he was good at from what he was clearly not - namely money and organisation - he could have gone far. Listening and taking advice were not on his agenda. A night out with Mick, especially if drink was on the menu, was certain to be an experience to behold. Seemingly without fail he could charm the knickers off any woman he'd just met. Here are a few examples.

Back in the late seventies Mick and I found ourselves on a bus travelling to Richmond. Sitting opposite us was a girl of about twenty-two. He homed in on her and started his usual bullshit. The girl stood up to get off the bus a stop before our intended destination, and he followed her as night follows day, remarking, "I'll see you later." And so he did. She happened to be an Eskimo.

Being unused to nightclubs, Mick would delight in showing me how *it* is done. On one such occasion we were in a club - Christ knows where - when two ladies came in; one was fantastic to look at, and the other very, very nice. Over the years I have convinced myself that the first was a contestant in the imminent Miss World contest; suffice it to say she was not an ordinary looking girl.

Mick was at her side instantly, grabbing her by the arm and leading her to the dance floor. I led the other lady to the floor, who I recall was very tall, slightly taller than me at six feet. After about fifteen minutes the stunning lady who Mick was monopolising ran from the floor crying. Her mate shoved me out of the way to follow. I went over to Mick and asked,

"What did you say to her?" He replied, "I asked her if she was going to drop her knickers or not." You see Mick looked at women a little like buses – another one will come along soon. Most men would have played her along for months hoping to score in the end, but not Mick!

One night in a club in Chertsey, Mick again surveyed the floor, picked out the most beautiful girl there, and homed in again. I was right behind him as he offered the following remark to her, "My name's St. George, is yours the dragon?" And I kid you not, he was snogging her within five minutes. The problem with Mick was that he became braver as the alcohol slipped down. On that occasion I was told by three strangers to remove Mick from the club, because the girl he was snogging was the local gangster's woman. I pointed this out to Mick, who said, "Tell them to f**k off!" I don't remember how, but on this occasion blood was not spilt.

My mechanic friend Richard, small statured and baby faced, once attended with me a stag night at some venue; we both sat at the front as a comic preceded the strippers. He turned to Richard and said, "Does your Mum know you're here?" My mechanic replied in the affirmative. "Just as well," the stand-up retorted, "because she's on next!"

I mention this general nature and composition of my mate Richard because it was to play a more decisive and less involved role, than that above. For, one night while sitting in my car, we were waiting for Mick to come out to the club car park. The next minute we saw Mick pinned against my driver's door, swinging and being swung at with fists. I couldn't open my door to help, so I tried to get out of the passenger's door. But Richard would not get out of the way, not wanting to get involved. "Damn you man," I cried, "Get out of the bloody car! Mick is getting a pasting!" Some pretty thick words later, he and I eventually got out. I looked for Mick, and found him upside down under a hedge. "We got them didn't we?" was all he said.

As you have probably gathered - trouble followed him around every day. Once we found ourselves in a large pub by the Thames; inside was one large room with a balcony all the way round. Now Mick could sniff a female from a hundred yards or so. Up on the balcony were three nice ladies sitting at the front, in full view of all those below; you could see all the men looking up at them and it was just a case of who was going to be the first bloke to pluck up the courage to climb the stairs in front of everyone else. Mick said to me, "Get us another drink and I'll get my arse up there." Sure enough up he went, every man watching on, wishing they had the guts. He lent across the table and spoke to all three.

The next minute he looked down to me and shouted, "Leo, three drinks up here!" One could feel a collective, but silent, three cheers for my mate.

The three girls lived in Yeading, so off to Yeading we went. Upon arrival one of them asked if we would like a cup of tea, and went to the kitchen to do so, followed by Mick. Half an hour later, thirsty, I walked into the kitchen to see Mick lying on top of the kitchen table with the tea maker underneath him. He sewed his oats but I got no tea. A late night, but with Mick, this was a quite regular occurrence.

(If you think these stories are a bit far-fetched, what about this: I decided to take a tea break from writing and switched on the telly, to spend the next thirty minutes watching Catherine Deneuve trying to seduce the late Peter Falk (Columbo) - unsuccessfully – that's what I'd call far-fetched!)

Mick the builder used to pull some awful strokes on clients; this one I swear I had nothing to do with. While we worked on a house together, tree surgeons finished cutting down several old trees, leaving the stumps still visible. The tree fellers now long gone, Mick smelt a scam coming on; he convinced the client that he could purchase very expensive material to kill the stumps over time. The liquid was theatrically poured over the said stumps. I asked Mick where he acquired this killing agent in the tin, Mick replied, "I went round the back of the house, dropped my trousers and filled the can." Knowing the crap Mick used to eat, I'm quite sure those trees are now well and truly dead!

Talk of the Town

In the early seventies I went with my ex-wife and my sister Norma and her boyfriend at the time, to the famous nightclub Talk of the Town. On stage that night was one of my favourites: Tamla Motowns' The Temptations. They were fantastic, singing and stepping their way through all the million seller hits. After the show but before we had finished our last drinks, a chap accused me of looking at his wife. Having told him to piss off he lent over the table, his face right in front of mine. This meant I was in a difficult position - sitting adjacent to the front balcony I could not move backwards or forwards. A knife appeared from somewhere and was pointed at my throat. Not daring to move, I stayed calm until the chance came to grab the man's wrist which was holding the knife. We struggled for a little while until the nightclub staff arrived.

They blamed me and threw us all out! It was clear the staff knew this man, and is likely the reason we were ejected instead of him. All through the journey home and for subsequent days I wondered why Norma's boyfriend had not helped, given he was behind the knife carrier, and that, at six foot four and fifteen stone, and supposedly a black belt in karate to boot, he might have been persuasive. But he did nothing and said nothing. As I've mentioned, Mick the builder was also going out with my sister Norma about this time. What would have transpired had Mick been present? I dread to think. Almost certainly, from behind, Mick would have dumped the knifeman over the balcony edge, to suffer whatever fate befell him! At a time like this Mick would have proven to be more than useful, if not a little wild to say the least of it.

The only time in my life I've slept on the street in London was, quite naturally, in Mick's company. Walking through Soho one night I stopped to observe a street hooker in a darkened doorway, her age or lack of it seemed to have a hold over me, not to mention the obvious. Mick had kept on walking, muttering, "You're asking for trouble." Soon enough I moved on, walking towards Mick, some sixty yards ahead of me. With providential timing, Mick turned around, shouting, "Behind you!" Looking round quickly I saw a huge black man running at me, and turned tail, soon overtaking Mick, also legging it. Quite what would have happened to me had I loitered further, heaven only knows!

As I've said elsewhere, if Mick could separate his positive skills from his negative ones he would have gone far. Unfortunately I heard just recently that he owes £250,000 to builders merchants and assorted persons unknown. He sold his house but still has money outstanding, despite many people helping him along the way. I gather he now lives in a council house with his ever-loyal wife of over thirty years. If anyone deserves a medal it is surely her. His nature was extremely selfish, but generous to a fault; I often saw him giving up his last pound to my sister. Needless to say; generosity, especially when coupled with many a wild side, will not alone get one through this life.

Jack MacGuire

I worked my first six years in the building trade for a brickwork sub-contractor by the name of Jack MacGuire. He was unintentionally very funny. I remember him turning up one day, while the foreman (Bill), the labourer (Jim) and apprentice (myself) were busy building some footings about five feet down in the ground. Now, Jack liked a drink, and was pretty much always pissed; on this day in question he tried to climb down into the trench, slipped, and knocked down the whole wall which we'd almost completed – our days labour no less! Bill the foreman went ballistic with his governor. "Jack," he screamed, "why don't you f**k off and leave it to us!" As you can imagine, Jim and I were in hysterics.

Jim the labourer, some twenty years older than me, was a strange fellow indeed; he too liked a sherbet (strictly barley wine, I recall). I caught him many times beating the shit out of the cement mixer with a short scaffold pole because it would not work properly. I was told one night he came out of The Links Hotel late at night, climbed aboard his pushbike and proceeded immediately to drive the bike straight into a garden wall, landing in the front garden, where the owners of the garden found him the next morning covered in frost, his pushbike still in the road!

Jack our governor used to pick us up every morning at Ashford train station, Bill having come from Kennington and me from Richmond. In the morning he used to drive like a lunatic to get us to the job as quickly as possible, and yet in the evening, Bill and I desperate to catch our train, he'd drive back as slowly as he could! Most evenings he was drunk, with Bill and me, sitting in the back of his van praying not to miss the train, and hoping to still be alive when we reached the station.

Despite this as a regular occurrence - him nearly killing us – one particular occasion he really did scare the shit out of us all. At the time (about 1964) he had an Austin Westminster – a beast of a car – with an enlarged and overpowered engine. It was very powerful. On this particular night we were travelling past what is now Thorpe Park, and late as usual. I looked at the Speedo - we were belting along this straight road at 120 mph!

A lorry came out of the gravel pits from the left some three hundred yards in front of us; he moved to the middle of the road, where he stayed thank goodness. Jack then had two choices - to go inside the lorry, or outside. To this day I don't know which he took, because we were all on the floor of the car at the time!

Once I had passed my driving test in 1965 Bill never again let Jack drive us anywhere, instructing the boss to, "Get in the back, Leo, you get in and drive." Jack's driving was legendary, even to the local constabulary. I do remember he had an old red Bedford van which had a bonnet about twelve inches long. He once knocked over an old lady with it, and carried her on the bonnet for a hundred yards. When the judge, asked him if he had anything to say, he said, "I never saw an old lady." Not only was he drunk and blind, he was known to go mysteriously deaf at the suggestion of a pay rise.

In the early days of my apprenticeship I used to walk down to his house from the station and wait outside. One day he backed his car out of his drive into the middle of the road and promptly put his foot on the accelerator instead of the brake. He buried the back of his car into the bay window of the house opposite. I was only about seventeen at the time and, as you can imagine, I was almost peeing myself with glee! His wife came out and blamed me, but I was to get my revenge some twelve months later.

Our gang were working close by Jack's house. I was dispatched there to collect an item, exactly what I can't remember. I let myself into the back garden without making a noise, not wanting to arouse his wife. I turned round the corner of the house to be confronted by a sight I will always remember; Jack's wife was lying down on the patio table, and on top of her was the milkman! For the subsequent four years that I worked for Jack MacGuire I could get away with anything without being told off by his wife!

And perhaps she had good reason. One day he came to fetch his men, me included, from a site in Chertsey. As I walked past him sitting in his van, pissed as usual, I observed him urinating all over his feet, because he could not remove himself from the cab!

One of the perils of working for a brickwork sub-contractor was clearly illustrated one Friday afternoon when one of the bricklayers asked our boss for his wages. The boss was a huge man by any standards: 6'3" and about seventeen stone. He told this particular brickie there was no money forthcoming, but, if he wanted to take it out on this (putting his finger on his nose), he was more than welcome. Not many did.

Mick the Labourer

Mick Connelly - one man you would not like to bump into on a dark night. Here was a labourer about 5'10" tall and possibly sixteen stone in weight, with shoulders so wide you could fit an armchair either side of his head, and a temper so fierce he'd be a worthy adversary for King Kong any day of the week. In addition, he was moody, brooding, unpredictable, unstable, and brainless. I was his boss on site, and it fell to me to tell him what to do. I once shouted at him, admittedly three floors up, to move four old three-piece suites and put them on the fire. I watched in awe from the safe vantage as he hurled these old settees around like confetti.

He was, as I have said, positively too strong and too unstable to be a free man, to be a regular builder's labourer, as he was. About three years later I learned that one night, in a drunken stupor, he'd fallen asleep in an old timber cricket pavilion. That night it burned down. I am sorry to say that Mick did not make it. Perhaps Providence itself decided he really was too dangerous to live.

First and Worst Winter

The worst winter in modern history was 1962-63, which was also my first winter on the building. During this period I did not lose any work at all due to the fact that I was working in Nestles chocolate factory in Hayes, Middlesex. In those days I rode a pushbike all the way from Ham, near Richmond, to Hayes - about fifteen miles. In the worst snow ever seen in this part of the world, I struggled to work every day. I only fell off my bike once though; looking round to get a better view of a girl, no less, I put my left foot through the front wheel, and over the top I went!

In the factory it was, as you can imagine, quite warm; when I had to fetch some bricks or cement from outside I had to put on at least two coats and a balaclava. Some of the things I saw happen in that place I could not tell you about because Nestle, as they are now called, might well sue me. Suffice to say that from those days to these, I haven't eaten one bite of a Nestlé's chocolate.

Coming home one evening about six o'clock, snow everywhere, my hands almost frozen to the handlebars I could not stand the pain in my fingers any longer, so I got off my bike, found an alleyway somewhere in Hampton Hill, removed my chap from his home and promptly peed all over my hands to warm them up! At this point I was still some five miles from home. Ah, those were the days!

Working down by the river I heard people screaming. I ran to investigate along the towpath, to find a girl of about twenty-two, screaming and crying in equal measure. She had dropped her pet puppy over the side, into the Thames. I looked over the edge to observe the puppy not yet in the water, but on a ledge just above the water line. There were chains hanging down and linked to each other all along the bank. I simply climbed down picked up the dog and climbed back up again. It was an easy thing for a strong fit and young man to do. The girl said she would do anything for me – all I had to do was ask…. I didn't say, nor shall I repeat, the nature of what I was thinking!

Once as a bricklayer I was working in Uxbridge on a huge site, along with twenty others, building a long wall in the basement. It was pitch black down there but for a long line of light bulbs connected to a looping cable fixed to a small scaffold about six feet high. I don't recall how I managed to screw up, but my trowel caught the cable nearest me and the lights went out. There were brickies and cement flying about all over the place, the scaffold having been momentarily, electrically charged. The language was fierce and fruity, everyone scheming to kill the perpetrator. When we gathered outside some brickies were covered in cement, others with white faces, and one and all wanting to know what'd happened. Of course I owned up…. the hell I did!

I worked on a vicarage in Bedfont in the early sixties where everyone knew everyone else. At lunchtime whilst playing cricket in the back garden, behind the wicket an old labourer who had very thick glasses was watching on. In those days I thought I was Wes Hall (famous fast bowler), and over keen to impress all those watching ran up and slung down a delivery. The plumber behind the stumps threw himself out of the way, and I looked on in anticipated horror.

The cricket ball was now hurtling toward the labourer with the bottle-top glasses, standing there as he was with his legs bent, and hands behind the back, oblivious to the imminent danger. "Watch out!" I shouted. But – too late – the ball went through his legs, missing his bollocks by inches, and smashed into the wall behind. Sweating buckets I ran up to him. He asked, "What were you shouting about?" He'd simply missed the whole thing!

Standing in the corner of our cricket pitch was a very tall pine tree, possibly seventy-five feet high. Being young and stupid I climbed to the top of the tree with a Union Jack, and deposited the flag on its top. The Council later told us to take it down, which of course we never did. One day a few weeks later it had vanished. The fun-sponging bastards!
Bill Young and I worked on a large site in Watford. The front of the building was constructed in such a way that four square concrete columns held up the front of the whole building. Halfway through the job after most of the structure had been built someone noticed a crack in one of the middle concrete columns. The word quickly spread, and soon enough everyone on site stood assembled at the foot of the offending column. The name of the main contractor was Streeters, and some wag shouted out aloud, "This may cause great concern to Streeters, but I don't give a f**k!" As you can imagine, the assembled crowd collapsed in laughter.

Before we started work in Watford Jack McGuire drove Bill and I to the site from Ashford. While 'driving' somewhere near Watford Jack had cut up a dustcart, just avoiding collision. A mile up the road the dustcart managed to gain revenge by cutting up our car. Static at the traffic lights Jack told me to get out and clump one of the six dustmen in the cart. Bill told Jack not to be so f**king daft and to drive off in haste, as we were almost surrounded by dustmen.

On a site in bad weather is not a happy place to be. On this site the snow was a foot deep, so the general foreman would not let us lay bricks unless the temperature on his thermometer, hanging from his office door, reached six degrees and rising. Needless to say, while hanging about none of us were earning a penny, and so while the general foreman was waylaid on the other side of the site we'd put a lighter under his thermometer to raise the temperature in order to get back to work!
When I was working on a roof at a vicarage in Lower Feltham, I noticed people stopping, looking, and then quite clearly laughing at me. I was oblivious to the reason for their mirth until a labourer came up on to the roof and told me what was so funny; apparently my balls had been hanging out of my shorts all afternoon! This was not the first, nor the last time this would happen.

Pants Down, Chaps Out

This next situation had nothing to do with building matters, but was nevertheless quite funny. My three sons and others were fishing at Hampton Court Bridge late on a Saturday night / Sunday morning, I had been out for the evening and was dressed accordingly. As I drove over the bridge at about 1:30 a.m., I turned into a little lane beside the bridge to check up on the boys; it was pitch black, no lights on anywhere. Despite this I noticed a police car at the entrance to this little lane with its lights off. I drove past and stopped at the end of the lane, some fifty yards or so further on. I climbed out of my truck and dropped my trousers intending to change my white strides for another pair I had brought with me, I didn't fancy the occasion of scrambling up and down the riverbank in white dinner trousers.

I noticed that the police car was now backing down the lane towards me. My trousers and shoes off, looking for the replacement garment, I was now aware of a policeman shining a torch at me. He said, "Could you please tell me what you are up to?" What a sight that must have been! Without looking at the policeman I proceeded to dress myself, I told him about my boys fishing. He walked slowly backwards towards the squad car. As he slowly entered the vehicle I heard his mate say, "What's going on?" He replied, "F**k knows!"

One very hot day at lunchtime I decided to shorten the shorts I was wearing; I started cutting with a Stanley knife while I still had them on, which proved quite difficult (and not a little stupid!) So I removed them and laid the shorts out on a scaffold board to cut and chop away. Job done and I put the shorts back on and continued eating my lunch. John and I were sitting on our homemade bench by a main road, and were suddenly aware of a lot of cat calls and stares aimed in our direction, which at the time we couldn't fathom. Later I realised that I'd cut the crotch out of my shorts and was now wearing a mini skirt, added to which my underpants had a rather large hole in them. The combination obviously left nothing to the imagination – yet again the crown jewels were on display!

Herman the German

I once heard about a character called Herman who, I am told, was a veritable nutter, and also a builder. One night after a drinking session Herman and a mate were walking home and passed a shop with fruit on display outside. By all accounts Herman was a certified 'tea leaf', and on this occasion he lived up to his reputation and pinched a large bunch of bananas, then walked off. He came to another corner shop and asked the proprietor for a packet of cigarettes, which in the absence of any money he wanted to swap for the bunch of bananas.
The owner told Herman to piss off or he'd call the police. After about five minutes arguing he did just that, and Herman, with his mate ran off with the bunch of fruit. Herman's mate, who clearly had more between his ears, suggested, that the police would have no trouble recognising them, if he persisted in holding on to the stolen bunch of bananas. With that, Herman hurled the big bunch over a fence. The police soon turned up, only to find a passing cyclist left prostrate on the ground, covered in the bananas Herman had lobbed over the wall!

Another tale from the Herman House of Horrors: he was working at a house where satellite T.V. was being installed. Looking up at the roof Herman decided the owner now had no need for the T.V. aerial, especially as he needed one for his own house. Later that day whilst talking to the house owner came a knock at the door. It was the neighbour, who said to Herman's client, "Have you had trouble with your T.V. reception, because mine's awful??" Herman the German had taken next door's aerial away by mistake!

I never met this Herman chap, and after this next story you will see why I'm glad I didn't. At Herman's house he had a fishpond. Or to be more exact, he had two ponds linked together by a shallow channel that fish used to travel down from one pond to the other. The next-door neighbours' cat used to lie in wait beside the shallows. On this occasion, Herman was also lying in wait, with a shovel; he walloped the cat then dug a hole in which to bury it. The neighbour came running out, shouting and screaming, "What are you doing with my cat?" Herman said, "I'm burying my goldfish." When, the neighbour asked, "Where is your goldfish?" Herman replied, "Inside your cat!"

Snippets on the Building

Looking back, some of the situations I encountered on the job seem, as memories go, like pure gold, though at the time they can be upsetting, not to mention problematical. One such job involved a research scientist working both for my father-in-law and the World Health Organisation. This was the first job I ever undertook where I was the boss and Bill Young worked for me. The owner was a pain in the neck from the beginning, unaccepting of measurements, materials, or ideas alike.

What set this man apart from others in this book, and humans in general, was that he'd only let us use his toilet for dumps, preferring us to pee in tin cans. Why? He periodically collected the urine, not only from us, but also from his wife and kids, whereupon he deposited the cans over his raspberries and blackcurrants! I'm sure I asked the chap why, and I'm sure he gave a good reason, but it escapes me.

Whilst working at my father-in-law's house in Teddington I was laying a concrete base for a big, brick built shed. As I was laying the concrete my brother-in-law Tim was wheel-barrowing it down an alley. The supplier was one of those companies that mix the concrete on the lorry while you lay. I told Tim to tell the driver that the concrete was a little weak, and for him to put more cement in the mixer. Tim came back rather sheepishly, and said most sincerely, "The driver told me to fuck off."
I stopped what I was doing and went to see the driver/mixer. He said the mix was strong enough. I said: "Put some more cement in now or I will get someone else." With that he threw the first, then the second of the wheelbarrows into the middle of the main road from atop the lorry, and drove off. Upon reflection it was very funny, but how he never killed anyone in the main road on a Saturday morning I will never know.

I once worked with a rather stupid labourer named Charlie, who'd recently bought a small decrepit little van which he said he would soon re-spray. He turned up one Monday morning with his van duly primed and painted, and when we asked, "What's with the brush marks?" he replied, "I only had a four inch brush and a tin of Dulux."

A very good friend of mine who worked for me for a few years – Les - once borrowed my black mini-van. While doing so I received a call from him, asking if I could pick him up because he'd crashed my van. When I turned up something extraordinary struck me; how on earth could he have possibly collided with a lamppost so as to leave both front headlights looking at each other? I whipped out my tape measure to confirm that the van had indeed hit the lamppost right smack in the middle of the bonnet, and turned the headlights inwards toward each other!

Talking of mini vans; having just left the builders' merchants overloaded with bags of cement, I was passing a comprehensive school when I received a puncture in the middle of the road. Because of the excess weight I could not push the van to the side of the road, and so had to change the wheel in the middle of the main road. The van's car jack would not lift the excess weight either, so I was forced to remove fifteen bags of cement and pile them up right there in the middle of the road! By this time the children were leaving school and made quite an audience for my changing the punctured tyre. Now removed, exchanged and reloaded, I was sent on my way with a chorus of insults and slow hand clapping.

I remember two brothers, both hod carriers, who were always fighting each other, both at home and at work. I was told that as soon as they'd get up in the morning they were at it, falling down the stairs, blood all up the walls, every day they'd lose claret, and turn up on the job covered in plasters and stitches. It was my job to keep them apart whilst on site, and to keep them out of the pub!

A chap in my cricket team recounted the following story: Peter, a first class cabinet-maker, was working at a large property in Surrey. The lady of the house decided to change the specification, so much so that the estimated cost of the modification totalled £50,000! The architect and customer's wife wanted to proceed with the change, but the husband said he did not want to pay the extra. The next day, as Peter sat on the throne in the bathroom, in came the wife and architect, deep in conversation. Unbeknown to them Peter heard every word uttered. At one point the wife ventured, "Don't worry about the extra cost – I'll shag his brains out every day for two weeks if necessary." The extra work was agreed to and carried out, so I imagine that she stayed true to her word. I am sure there is a word for this…

At a party one night a discussion was taking place about neighbours seeking retribution for a perceived injustice, which reminded me of the following story of a man who made a lot of money as a pop star back in the sixties. He lived in a big house in Petersham near Richmond in Surrey, and had built a long garden wall as a boundary, shielding his house from the main road. He had received planning permission then built the wall six inches too high; the local residents - up in arms – were soon to pay dearly for their intransigence. Clearly pissed off the pop star sought the advice of the builder, and then removed six inches off the offending wall. He suggested covering the entire wall with horse manure, given the reason that this was an old medieval concept of toning down or distressing the bright-looking new brickwork. So he did, claiming also that to continue this process it had to be repeated annually! Needless to say, he was the stink of the town.

One stroke I did pull – in the getting of the work, mind - happened by chance. I was employed to repoint one side of a communal chimney stack on an estate where all stacks needed pointing. Clearly it's preferable to point the whole stack as opposed to one half, little point in only doing one half (pun intended). I put a note through all letterboxes stating my intention to repair next door's chimney stack. "Would you like the same?" it read. It is amazing how many occupants assumed I meant their next door. That estate was indeed good to me!

I was called out to a job that turned out to be the weirdest house imaginable. I knocked on a front door already ajar; I pushed it open to get the shock of my life. There stood a horse in the hallway, looking straight at me! My first thought was, 'I've found Shergar!' My second was that he's too big to be a racehorse - more like a carthorse. The humans lived upstairs, the horse, the goat and chickens, downstairs – nothing unusual about that you might say (for the sixteenth century). But the funny thing about this was that the client did not see the necessity to tell me what to expect when we spoke on the phone.

April fool's Day on the site is a time to beware. On one of the fifty I have passed, I was working on a large restoration job by the river at Richmond. The toilet was situated in an old building adjacent to the main house, which was to be demolished at the end of the job. I made up a tape of myself making constipated noises and placed it in the toilet. I then cut a hole in the wall facing the back of the door, poked a lump of wood through, and thereby wedging the door shut. I then vanished up a large tree to watch the fruits of my mischief unfold. I kept all comers at bay for about two hours; some, having given up on me, walked to Richmond town centre for a dump – about three quarters of a mile away. The word went round that I was to be thrown in the Thames, but nobody on the job was fast enough to catch me!

On roughly the same theme, I once worked at a bank manager's house for about four days. The kitchen was without doubt the filthiest room I have ever seen; when you walked across the floor your feet squelched and stuck to it. The living room had a coal fire that obviously wasn't drawing properly; consequently smoke was leaving soot marks all over the ceiling. Someone had tried to clean it off with a wet rag and made it worse, leaving a smeared patch just above the fireplace – it did look choice! The bathroom was worse still! I'd say that ten years of discarded toothpaste tubes were laying around, with soap, tablet bottles, and an old bath in the middle of the room stained brown with age and neglect.

The first thing you would want to do when you leave the room is have a bath! Upstairs – you don't want to know. The bank manager treated the mess as if it was normal. Perhaps it was, to him. His wife was P.A. to a company director, used to dive out of the back door as I came in the front every morning, so I never saw her. Was she ashamed? I should hope so, for she lived in a pig sty.

I've worked in some large houses over the years, but this house - although not by any means the biggest - had a half Olympic-sized swimming pool *inside*! The inside roof covering had fallen in the empty pool, creating a right mess. Two Spanish maids lived there alone all year round. It was very cold and I remember asking in fluent Spanish, "Can we have a hot drink?" We were given two cups of viscous coffee, from which we could barely remove the spoons! Oh well.

I remember a customer telling me once that he had informed his builder that he'd be away for the weekend and the builder would be on his own. The customer changed his mind and came back unexpectedly, to find the builder in bed with his girlfriend, showing a good deal more invention with his hands than he had on the job!

Back in the early sixties I found myself at the Shepherd's Bush Empire with a group of builders and assorted degenerates. The film showing was a cowboys and Indians epic; the pony express rider flying across the desert pursued by seemingly thousands of screaming Indians. The fleeing cowboy took one, then a second arrow in the back. When he was hit for the third time, one of our group stood up and shouted, "One hundred and ayyyyy-teee! (180)" As if one the whole audience fell about laughing. I've been waiting over thirty years to repeat the quip myself.

An escort van I used to own was once full up with about ten builders, bodies all over the show. Trying to pull out and turn right into a main road I asked the nearest body to the passenger window, "Am I clear your side?" He said, "Yes," then, with me halfway through the turn, he casually added, "except for that great big truck." I spent the next few seconds in absolute panic, not knowing if we were going to be hit or not!

I heard this lovely tale about a bricklayer back in the fifties who had been knocked a few times. Every house back then required a fireplace, therefore a chimney was constructed. As an insurance policy against a reluctant payee he would build into the chimney structure a sheet of glass covering and sealing the flue. If there was any trouble about being paid he'd let the perpetrators know what he'd done and walk away, waiting, if you will excuse the expression, for the fire to commence. On reception of money owed he'd simply drop a half brick down the flue breaking the sheet of glass. This is all well and good, but what about Santa Claus? He'd be ripped to ribbons!

A builder phoned me with this tale: he was working for a rather stunning female customer, and apparently fell off the scaffold, banging the toilet window on the way down. The customer, who was sitting on the toilet, saw him fly past the window and rushed out to administer assistance. When she reached the stricken workman - who was not badly hurt - the gathered throng started laughing. "What's so funny, enquired, the stunner? The lady, in her efforts to exit the loo, had stuffed her skirt down her tights, leaving everything on show! The laugh was on her, not to mention six pairs of builders' eyes.

A plumber recalled an occasion when his customer refused to pay in full after he had completed a new central heating system. On the pretext of retightening some loose joints, the plumber inserted several lead shots (used in fishing) to the pipe work; the consequence of this action meant that the lead shot flew round the system making an unholy row, never to be quiet again, unless the entire system was dismantled and renewed – thus serving the customer right for his/her intransigence!

Andy an electrician, who at the time of the hurricane in 1987 was employed as an aerial fitter, recounted to me this tale of woe. Whilst working at a house, an old dear four doors down approached him, asking if he could improve the quality of her T.V. picture. He told her he needed to see the aerial, and she insisted that it was inside. In the middle of the lounge was, sure enough, the aerial, still attached to the chimney stack that had fallen through the roof! Looking up Andy could see blue sky and clouds. This old dear was only worried about missing EastEnders, completely overlooking the six-foot hole in her roof!

I once found myself in a pub with a group of building workers standing at the bar. In came a chap with his girlfriend. "What would you like?" he asked her. "Something long and cool," she said. Some wag in our group couldn't help himself; "What about a cucumber?" An uneasy peace was eventually restored.

This short conversation which took place in front of me whilst standing in a queue at the Builders' merchants: Paddy says, "Can I have some nails?" "How long do you want them, asked the shop assistant? "I want to keep them." said the Paddy, excitedly.

Walking home from work on a hot and sunny day, dressed only in shorts and boots, I passed two teenage school girls, one sitting astride her bike, the other standing very close by. I heard one remark, "Nice arse." I bent over and said, "Do you think so?" Upon which they both fell on the ground laughing their heads off. I walked away with them in a heap, and my fifty year-old arse feeling pretty chuffed by the compliment.

There are on the sites some very thick workers, one of whom thought "fuck all" was a stately home, another thought Sherlock Holmes was a block of flats!

A Farce

If I may recount one afternoon whilst working on this book; at about lunchtime on Friday I needed some photocopies, so after a five minute drive to the local chemist I was found pushing buttons on the copier. Having reached home, I discovered I had forgotten to duplicate my copyright document. About an hour later I walked into the chemist again and asked the lady behind the counter to switch the machine on for me. She said, "I can't, it's broken." I replied that I had used it about an hour ago. She said, "It must have been you who broke it!" "Yeah, right," I said, and turned to walk out of the shop; it was then that I caught the end of a display unit with my trouser pocket, which brought the whole row of shelves crashing down, plastic bottles of shampoo everywhere. The lady serving at the counter said, "Don't touch anything!" Another lady remarked, "Don't walk across the road, you might get run over!"

I tried other shops for a photocopier and finally found one. I pressed the start button and reached for my copy, the machine had other ideas – it went on and on until thirty or so copies had been made. Amid the confusion I went home slightly red faced and closed my front door not expecting to go out again.

I soon realised that I'd left the original document behind in the machine, so back I went to collect it, and did so without further hiccup. I spent the next four hours writing, stopping because I had a party to attend. Everything went well until I drove home after the party, soon after midnight. A squad car with two occupants flashed me to stop, which I did. One policeman said, "Do you know why we stopped you?" I said no, I did not know. He replied, "You've just jumped a red light. Have you been drinking?" "Not likely," I ventured. Then came the request, "Breathe into this."

The two policemen, both about thirty, seemed disappointed at the zero reading. Of course they could not know I was a teetotaller. I was then informed that I would be reported and would have to pay a sixty-pound fine within twenty-eight days. To cut a long story short, I believe they booked me because they could find nothing wrong with my vehicle or the breathalyser. I went home to bed pissed off, hoping to heaven that I would not try sleepwalking, for fear of a further mishap!

The next day the farce continued at my local police station. As I delivered my driving licence, insurance and M.O.T. certificate two very old ladies sitting at the desk drinking coffee - clearly volunteers - confronted me. Whilst they were extremely nice to me, they admitted never filling in the documents appertaining to this case. Together they struggled to fill in this form, eventually completing the task in about three quarters of an hour. I looked at their two cups of half-finished coffee and remarked with a touch of sarcasm, "I hope your cups of coffee are not too cold to drink." The lady replied, "Oh, that's all right, I'll make another." I walked out grinning, but shaking my head. That's what I call a calamitous twenty-four hours! On this occasion it was a happy ending to the day; I had kicked up such a fuss with the station Chief Inspector that four weeks later my cheque was returned!

Another Week to Remember

Friday started well enough with a marriage proposal from my long-standing girlfriend at the time. By Saturday late afternoon my euphoria had been reversed. While walking down at the beach with Bella and my future family's pet, Buddy. A small dog had an altercation with Buddy. He was a great lump of a dog, a bull mastiff, who took a dislike to the yappy little mutt. Bud had a history of attacking other dogs, but not when I was around.
A muzzled Buddy, however, still tried to bite the dog. Watching closely and anticipating trouble I flung myself at Buddy, grabbing him, now twisting and turning; his collar came off in my hand, as did the muzzle. The small dog's owners were screaming at me to keep Buddy away, but were not helping the situation by doing nothing themselves. Meanwhile Bella, my fiancée's dog, continually got in the way thinking that it was all a game.

The small dog broke away from its owners and did the worst thing possible by running further down the beach away from us all, with a muzzle-less Buddy in hot pursuit, and he in turn being chased by Bella and me. As the big dog turned his head occasionally I'd shout at it, knowing full well that if I could not catch him he'd eat the small dog alive. Approaching, I leapt on top of the huge dog before he could sink his molars into the terrified little nipper. Still I struggled with the beast and at the same time shouting for the two owners to disappear, fast. They seemed to not comprehend that all I had to hold on to was the loose flesh around his neck. Still they hung around fiddling with their dog's lead.

When the small dog had been removed from the beach, Bud seemed to recover his senses and peace was restored. It took me fifteen minutes to find and recover the collar and muzzle, which I found about a hundred yards from where the fight took place. To the family of the big one I gave my unequivocal opinion: the thing should be put down immediately, on the basis that this was the third incidence in a matter of months. A little dog now – maybe a small child next.

I'm not a dog psychologist (I don't even particularly like them), but when I first grabbed Buddy I thumped him hard on the rump, looked him straight in the eye – nothing. My girlfriend's family have decided to keep the dog at home letting him roam in their large garden far from others.

(Two months later whilst playing in the family's garden, Buddy attacked Rosie's sister's dog Lucy, grabbing her round the throat. And thus, eventually, the penny dropped, and the family had the vet summoned to put the beast down.)

The rest of the day we spent looking at houses, and on Sunday visiting prospective purchases. The first house we liked and viewed internally. The owner was a chap of about sixty-five with a creepy sort of son, who hung around making stupid comments about the football team I support. Whilst my girlfriend was involved in negotiations with the proprietor, his son asked me to accompany him to his room.

On the bed was a violin, and a guitar was resting up against the wardrobe, electric I think. As I picked up the violin, Vinny asked, "Can you play it?" "Sure." I said, lying and laughing at the same time. He insisted I play, but of course it was beyond me. I made the point to him: "Do you make any money out of your music I asked"? "Of course not." he replied. "What do you do for a living?" I said. "How do you earn your money?" An innocent enough question, you may well think.

At this, though, he went crackers, accusing me of insulting him. Clearly I'd hit a raw nerve. He started to swear profusely about what he was going to do to me shortly. I took a deep breath and decided not to make matters worse by reacting to what was quickly becoming an uncontrollable rage. It was at this point I realised that he must be on some kind of drugs, though whether medicative or illicit I had no idea (As with drinking and smoking, I've never been partial to either). He then put his hand on my chest and pushed me back into Bella the dog, who was right behind me. I nearly tripped over her, and fumbled to my feet with the help of the door frame.

Completely out of his tree, I thought. Reason out of the question, I figured I'd humour him for five minutes or so. Having done so, I decided I'd had enough. Then, in a split second he changed from the raging and ranting demonic state to almost charming. In talking of Bella the dog he was most complimentary, repeating over and again that she was the best looking canine he'd ever seen, and that he really would like to buy her. "Don't mind me," he announced, "I'm just a dick-head, a prat."

In a pang of conscientiousness he went on, "I hope you are not going to take this out on my Dad by not buying our house." I'm not at all knowledgeable as to what drugs have what effects on us humans, though I am certain that this particular chap was, for those twenty minutes or so, decidedly un-human.

When we left he saw us off the premises and apologised once again for his behaviour. Irrespective, we put in an offer for the house, and this was accepted forty-eight hours later. Promptly we both put our houses on the market and set a date for the wedding.

(Two days earlier, Rosie had approached her Mum suggesting we buy the family house, not realising that world war three was about to break out; both mother and sister - without reading our proposal - thought we wanted to take over their world and all its belongings. For a few days chaos reigned, some will cutting was threatened, until some resemblance of order and sense was restored.)

To sum up: an incredible five days or so; a marriage proposal, put two houses up for sale, should have put a dog to sleep, bought a house, had a war with the future in-laws, and last but not least got attacked and then apologised to by the loopy son of the house owners! Just what I like - a nice quiet week!

That week there was a toothache in most things that happened
- Charles Dickens

Short Asides

I was driving through Kingston in Surrey one Sunday when my sons and I stopped at a set of traffic lights. Walking across the road in front of us was a particularly unkempt and scruffy sort of chap about fifty. In one hand he had a bowl of what looked like apple crumble, half eaten and covered in cling film, and in the other hand was a thermos flask. We sat still and looked on in amazement as he stared back at us. Coming round to the passenger side window he remarked to my eldest son, "Would you like some?" As you can imagine - after the initial raised eyebrows - we fell about laughing and drove off, but had to stop two hundred yards further down the road because we couldn't stop laughing.

My ex-wife, who transcribed these words into the Queen's English, has at times made the odd mistake. This Freudian slip is a classic! When talking about a mate having slept with many women, he ventured: "I've had women you wouldn't want haunting your house!" Rosie blamed my writing for her version, which stated, "I've had women you wouldn't want mounting your horse!" Upon reading over the transcript I laughed, and laughed, and shall dine out on that one forever more.

A cartoon in a daily paper showed a planning application meeting; under the chairman's seat was a bomb with a wire connected to a plunger held by a man crouching beside the door. The chairman was saying the following: "Mr Richard's application to build a three storey office block on the site of his outside toilet - passed."

My ex-wife's dog Bella, who was almost human, had found a soul mate in yours truly, on account of my ability to throw stones. Years ago we kids used to try and throw stones over the Thames at Teddington Lock - a distance of one hundred and fifty yards or so. Down at the beach Bella will speed down to the sandy parts, and turn and wait for the stone throwing to begin. Up and down the beach she would fly and sprint, stopping only when either of us became too tired to continue. The stone thrower's apprentice would then lie down for the rest of the day, exhausted. Mind you - this dog, a cross between a flat coated retriever and a border collie - would not retrieve a bone if you threw it at her, wanting only to run and play.

On returning from holiday a mate gave me a sign to display in my lorry window, which read: "The more I learn about women, the more I love my truck." I retained this emblem until, while unattended, it was stolen, presumably because it struck a chord in my Ford!

Another fishy story, again, about Mick the builder. Setting out for a deep water wrecking trip we were informed by the skipper, Les Bettis - out of Newhaven in East Sussex - that the tide was in our favour to visit a not often fished wreck, some thirty miles out in the English Channel. Once there we drew a blank, the skipper left incredulous by the absence of fish. Distraught he offered us the option of returning in shore to fish a skate hole, or staying and praying. In shore now and looking for the indentation in the seabed, we came across a small uncharted wreck by mistake. We dropped anchor, and there followed three hours of madness, which made up for hundreds of fish-less trips.

On this trip eight rods were in operation, and in this spot all eight were taking fish on each cast. I managed to catch two huge cod on the same line - one of twenty-two pounds and one of twenty pounds. The skipper gaffed the lighter one then rather disgustingly stuck his fingers into the giant cod's eyes to lift him on board. It measured thirty-nine inches in length! We also caught pollock, ling and conger on that trip. Returning to harbour the fishermen only managed to gut half our catch, because only five gutting knives were available. In total our catch weighed nearly seven hundred pounds! Not a fishy tale, but fish suppers for over a year!

My son Jack's best mate Glenn mentioned an interesting incident in which he played his part, which I think deserved an airing. One day Glenn was walking along a crowded high street minding his own business, chewing gum as he went. Deciding to rid himself of the spent gum he spat it out and, as some young boys do, then tried to volley the thing into the nearest waste bin. Having got his distances slightly wrong, he overshot the bin completely and succeeded only in looping the chewing gum straight into the yawning mouth of a stranger on the other side of the bin! The unfortunate stranger immediately spat it out and gazed straight up to the heavens, looking for some guidance as to what the mystery object was or where it came from. Glenn watched for a moment, attempting to understand what just happened, while at the same time admiring his impressive feat. He managed to escape the spluttering stranger, himself struggling for breath from laughter.

Sitting in a greasy spoon somewhere in Middlesex with plumber Ron waiting to be served - the place a veritable magnet for an assortment of degenerates owned by a Greek family - it did not seem to be terribly clean. Just above the table-tops ran a dado rail, which was clearly not fixed back to the wall correctly. Apathy was to blame for my tapping the ill-fitting dado rail with a clenched fist. We leapt from our seats as half a dozen dark brown cockroaches fell onto our table. I called the proprietor over who said, and I quote, "I no understand?" Needless to say we did not touch the food, choosing the chippy next door. The following day I contacted the authorities, who sounded thoroughly interested, but contrived to do nothing. That establishment is still open to this day!

Bank Robbers

My brother-in-law at one time owned around thirty jewellery shops, dotted around the country. John used to say the insurance premiums were becoming prohibitive, so he had to devise other forms of security. One shop in Regent Street in London had its security built around air pressure inside the shop. After closing the shop for the night, and once the air inside had settled down, any movement or opening of doors or windows changing the air pressure would cause a disturbance, consequently setting off the alarm. You would think this idea fool-proof, but John didn't keep the system for long - the bandits would eventually find a way round it.

John told me of another raid at a Jeweller's shop in Hatton Garden some years ago. The security on this building was based on the principle that, as a detached property all sides were approachable, all corridors lead to the safe in the centre, the front of which could be seen from outside. Security guards patrol the perimeter, periodically looking through the windows to view the safe door. Thieves broke in with lots of scaffold and erected a screen with a picture of the safe door showing. Security personnel looking through the windows thought they were looking at the safe door, while the robbers were cutting the door open behind the screen. They left behind half a ton of scaffold, oxyacetylene equipment, and an empty safe!

John told me once about a fire at one of his shops; the Fire Brigade extinguished the fire easily enough, but some of the stock went missing. Which only goes to prove you can't trust anybody!

We have all heard stories about bodies mixed up with concrete, holding up the M4 flyover. This story, although not fatal, involved a new bank that was being built somewhere. Apparently the bank robbers paid the bricklayers to make the mortar around the night safe weak, without cement. Some two years later, a pud-lock (small length of scaffold pole) was inserted into the night safe aperture, a chain was fixed to the back of a lorry, and hey presto - the night safe disappeared into the night.

Thieves respect property; they merely wish the property to become their property so that they may then more perfectly respect it — **G K Chesterton**

Phone Counsel

The phone rang, I picked it up, and here is the following conversation, more or less in its entirety. "Hello Mr Lindsay. I would like a price for some shelving in my house." "Sure." I replied. "Give me your address and I shall give it a look." She said, "My husband is not capable of putting up fairy lights, so there's not much point in asking him." "Surely he's not that bad," I offered. I could hear her laughing. "Bad? He's not that bad - he's useless, and not just at D.I.Y!" Mischievousness got the better of me, "Please tell," said I, though I didn't really think this stranger would continue talking so. "If I ask him to do something for me, all I get is 'mañana'. Then he calls down to the pub every night before coming home."

I interjected, "What do you look like?" "Why do you ask?" she replied. "I just thought you might not be attractive enough to entice him away from the pub." Loud laughter down the phone, both of us were now, warming to each other. "What's your name?" I ventured. "Bramble," was the response. I called out, "What's your name? Not what's in your garden!" "Bramble. That's my name, honest." She went on to tell me that her family's business made paintbrushes for the trade. "What's your name?" she asked. "Leo the Lion," I replied. "Are you a Leo?" "No, I'm Pyrex," I said. "What do you mean?" "Pyrex is my birth sign... I'm a test tube baby!" I said, laughing at my own joke.

Expecting the line to go dead any second instead I heard raucous laughter. She continued, "My friends all seem to have the same problems with men that I suffer from. What can you advise us to do about it?" "Have you tried stockings and suspenders?" I suggested. "Of course I have. What do you think I am, frigid?" She retorted. "Has your husband got a white stick?" I replied. "Very funny……. you sound like just the man we women are looking for!"

I continued, "Over the phone anyone seems attractive, either you or me, especially if you are having a bad time. Don't become despondent, things may well improve." "Pigs might fly," she sighed in response. "Go and find another man then." I proffered. "Where from, Tesco's?" was the reply. "I know a few men who want a bit on the side…. A bit on the back and a bit on the front too" I suggested. She replied "I'm not sure I want to go that far, but I've sure thought about it."

How this conversation ended goodness only knows. I never did meet the lady, but I knew which house she lived in, and every time I drove past I was tempted to knock on the door. One day in a greasy spoon cafe I struck up a conversation with a builder unknown to me. He told me that he was fitting a fireplace and hearth; unfortunately, he'd broken the black marble hearth, and rather devilishly replaced it with chipboard. The 'builder' painted the chipboard with four or five coats of paint, hoping the customer wouldn't notice. The customer will surely notice when a fire is made!

Pikeys

What key opens all doors? A pikey. — **John P. Curr**

I heard of a gang of 'builders' who told a lady her chimney needed repairing. Having agreed a price of £700, the gang departed to the nearest builders' merchants to buy a roll of brickwork *effect* wallpaper, which they duly papered round the chimney. I'm sure that viewed from the ground, the stack would have looked extremely neat until, of course, it rained! Stories like this give the beleaguered builder a bad name when, not for the first time, pikeys were to blame.

I have mentioned elsewhere my thoughts about pikeys or diddikoys. This was an occasion when one got the better of us - which in all honesty they do tend to do with startling regularity. We were about two days into a project when, clearing the site, we found an old car axle half buried in the mud. Three of us tried to move it to no avail, so we waited for the digger to arrive. In the meantime a passing pikey looking for old scrap iron asked if we had any. We suggested, not without a little derision, the half-buried axle. Nobody likes pikeys, so we said, "Sure you can have it," and walked off laughing amongst ourselves.

We came back thirty minutes later and were astonished to find the pikey had dragged this old lump out of the mud to the base of his lorry, on his own. Filled with admiration for his obdurate persistence, we helped him lift the very heavy piece of iron on to his truck. No doubt he was warmed and fuelled by the thought of the few shillings he'd receive for it. The moral here: a pikey will move heaven and earth, legally or illegally, for the chance to earn a few bob.

I heard a story about four Irish labourers, all brothers, on a south coast trip with their parents. On their way back home the car spluttered to a halt, so the four brothers and their father started pushing the car homewards, no doubt hopeful of finding an open garage. No such luck! The Irishmen ended up pushing the car all the way home, some thirty miles or so! The mentality of these men, though mostly reprehensible in the extreme, is, too, when it comes to will power, truly astounding.

A hedge-bumper, as they are also known, once came into my local builders' merchants. He asked for a ton of shingle, and was informed that shingle was sold by the metre; the stuff was then loaded, the transaction duly completed. He then went to the local weighbridge to weigh his load, and came back to complain that he had been short changed. The owner, having heard the complaint as it was made, jumped in the tractor and, out of sight of Mr Pikey who was still complaining in the office, completely covered the hedge-bumpers small pick-up truck, including the cab, which was now full up with shingle. The boss came back and told the pikey where to go. I did not hear of any executed vengeance, though knowing pikies as I do, I would be surprised if they left it at that; in any confrontation, their word is invariably the last.

My eldest son Mark told me this classic pikey story. Whilst travelling down the A3 near Esher at evening rush-hour time, the traffic had slowed to a crawl. At the next junction most of the cars in Mark's lane turned off, leaving him confronted by half a dozen 4x4's, still moving but blocking all three lanes. These vehicles were stuffed full of hedge-bumpers, hanging out of the windows and moving about with vigour. What they and Mark were witnessing was a pony and trap race between two rigs of horse and rider. Only pikeys would have the brass neck to use and abuse a three-lane A-road for their own private use! What balls! The spectacle continued to Wisley Lake, some three miles or so before Mark turned off, shaking his head and fist as he went.

More pikeys, but don't read on if you easily feel sick. Picture the scene in a greasy spoon somewhere in Surrey: five gypsies order huge breakfasts and scoff the lot, all except one pikey, who put his hand down his trousers and pulled out a handful of pubic hair, then mixed it with the remainder of the remaining meal. Then, leaping in the air, he screams about dirt and filth in his breakfast, obviously refusing to pay. The proprietor, wanting nothing more than the rabble out of his café, is left little choice but to swallow the charade and send them on their way. They are little if not resourceful!

The pikeys' resounding ingenuity comes to the fore in a tale relayed to me by a relative. They broke into a house, its main doors and windows all locked, by using a very small child – presumably one of theirs, though one never knows with them – and pushing it through a tiny bathroom window left open. Once in, the child was told to open the front door. Wrong in all ways, except to the ends of burglary!

For the past twenty years or so I have owned a small open-backed truck, which is parked on my driveway right in front of my house. At the rate of four or five a week, mostly in the summer months, pikeys would roll up looking to buy my truck. The transit was a magnet for them, opportunistic as they are to turn a pound. The absence of a 'for sale' sign did not deter these rather parasitic characters, and day or night they'd knock on the door to enquire about the price I was not offering. Sometimes I'd play along, pretending that the vehicle was for sale. But I never asked for a figure, and the pikeys never ever made me an offer. Though they'd ask dozens of times, "How much do you want for it?" I' reply, "*You* have knocked on my door, so come up with a figure or piss off." As you can imagine, quite a few doorstep rows developed.

Devious as ever and not wanting to show their intentions, I remember one excuse they proffered for knocking (not that they ever needed one): "I need the truck urgently for my pregnant wife," as she climbed out of her husband's own vehicle to inspect mine.

Not far from me by the main road is a small parcel of land, commandeered at one time by gypsies. I once watched on with horror as a small boy walked down the steps of his caravan and, standing at the bottom as if in deep thought, dropped his shorts, squatted down, and proceeded to relieve himself. He got up, pulled up his shorts, and walked off without wiping a thing. It was not difficult to anticipate what was going to happen next; sure enough the mother came down the steps and trod on the steaming pile. I could just about hear her say "f**k it." She then just walked off as if nothing had happened.

Singular amongst pikey stories for its 'happy' ending, here's how to win a Pikey battle. One midday, a group of them, masquerading as builders as they like to do, approach a house and asked the woman who answered the door if she'd like her driveway tarmacked. Assuming they were not being euphemistic, and hesitant at the pressure, she insisted to them she would have to wait for her husband to return from work to consult. They persisted, she relented.

They left, only to return soon after – the owner out and unknowing – to promptly tarmac the whole drive. The Pikies then kept calling demanding payment for the job. The owners kept refusing. Soon threats came, and one evening so did a brick straight through their front room window. As a home owner, can you imagine what you'd do? We all know pikeys to be about as tenacious and unremitting as human types come. The man of the house did the only thing possible in this situation other than give in; he played them at their game.

The next day he took off work, and hired – at no small expense – the biggest bulldozer he could find. Having acquired the 'address' of these particular pikeys, he drove the thing onto their site and, as close as he could get without crushing the caravans - the inhabitants threatening hell - he called down from the cab, "If you lot don't piss off and leave my house and family alone, I shall return in this thing and flatten the lot of you!"

No further harassment occurred. In fact, so the man relayed, he sensed from them a good deal of admiration for his course of action. With the 'we won't stop – even if murder need be committed – until we have our way' mentality, I dare say anything less than a bulldozer would not have done the job, a round of applause, for that man.

I mention pikeys because we, as builders, sometimes get blamed for their nefarious activities; that many pikeys go in for a bit of building work without a modicum of standard or skill, or honesty, is a fact we professional builders have to accept. What can we do but distance ourselves from these outcasts, and provide a level of service they are unable to.

Signs

In the same way, we builders solve problems, so it follows that our company names and logos show at least some ingenuity and humour.

Grab Lorries:

Anything Goes
Away with it
Waste with haste
Lift away
Let's talk rubbish
Junk and disorderly rubbish clearance
It needn't cost the earth to move it
Grab it all
Easy Shift

165

Cart a ways
Take and tip
Quick away
Lady Muck clearance
Humpty dump waste
Get rid
Grip and tip
Dial a dump
Lift and shift
Grab and tip
Pay and away
Lump and bump
Muck and truck
All and sundry
Rapid rubbish removal

Van Logos:

John Clay (Bricklayer)
Peter Ash (Carpenter)
Joe Waters (Roofer)
Will Clear – All rubbish
Don't Plumb the Depths Try Us (Plumbers)
Don't be a drip we are legit (plumbers)
Bob a Job (jobbing builder)
The Fabrick Building Company
I Khan (You've tried the cowboys now try the Indians)

Ready Mix:

Hump it lump it dump it
Mix with the best
Mix it right
Mix it quick

And along the same lines:

In a dry cleaner's window: "If your clothes are not becoming to you, they should be coming to us."

Above the front door of a hair salon: "Come in, curl up, and dye."

A warning sign at a side gate, plus picture of a fierce dog: "I can reach the front gate in four seconds. Can you?"

The name of a garden landscaper's van: "Just-a-Mow."
Standing at a front door a gnome holds the plaque: "Welcome to our house… now piss offf!"

Old Building Terms

Noggin – A small piece of wood to separate usually vertical structural timber.
Donger – Often a bucket handle reversed to smooth out brickwork joints.
Shamfer – A rounded edge to shape the edge of a bit of timber.
Pug and Muck – Names to describe mortar.
Skewback – The angled brickwork that an arch sits on.
Joggle – A cut out of masonry commonly used in conjunction with grout.
Flaunching – The angled sand and cement mortar at the top of a chimney stack.
Haunching – Mortar tapered to hold-in raised patio.
Pardgeting – Render on the inside of a flue whilst in construction.

Houses of Parliament

Upon receiving an invitation to an MP's son's birthday bash I found myself on the terrace at the Houses of Parliament. Once there and bored silly I decided to inspect the external stonework more closely. I know this building is very old but close up it looks as rough as old boots and brought to mind another of Old Bill Young's observations – 'It'll look alright from the top of the Post Office Tower' – in other words most brick-stone structures look better from a distance, close up reveals the imperfections. Some customers I have met would reject the quality of this work I perused at the HP. As an example of my twisted sense of humour, on entering the building and being searched I remarked to the nearest policeman, holding up my invitation, "What would Guy Fawkes have given for one of these?" I saw his knuckles turning white as he gripped his machine gun tighter still, affording me the kind of look one might give a man who has just pissed in his pocket.

An ugly sight, a man who is afraid   *- Jean Anouilh*

Hard man

The following story was regaled by a chippy splashing about in a swimming pool whilst on holiday. Incidentally the carpenter had five brothers plus his father, all bricklayers. One of these brothers, an old-school brickie and real hard man, found a platform hoist falling on top of him, and lay there his head split in two. Onlookers thought him dead, but not so. He whispered "can I have a fag", it was obligingly given, and to everybody's astonishment smoke plumed out from the top of his head. He did indeed survive, a hard man for sure.

Fire doors

A fire door is a door able to withstand a fire for a period of at least half an hour, enabling an occupant time to escape the fire. One job I fitted about twenty of these, the offcuts laying around, the fitter took the offcuts home to his parents who had a log fire in their lounge. The parents piled the offcuts onto the fire but were surprised it did not catch fire immediately. They came back 35 minutes' later and just in time as the carpet and furniture went up in flames. The moral here is? Don't leave a fire unattended for long periods, know what you're putting on the fire, don't hang around in the event of a fire, and don't be late if it's already in the grate.

Barking dog

Whilst trying to recount the following story over the phone my eldest son Mark could barely get his words out, such was his anticipation of my reaction. His work colleague back in the early sixties, a BT engineer, was called out to a customer whose phone would not ring. He climbed the telegraph pole outside and found nothing wrong. From his position up the pole he called the house phone. At this point a dog started barking somewhere out back, and to his amazement the old boy living there picked up the phone.

When asked how he knew a caller was on the line he replied, "When the dog barks I pick up the phone, and there's always a caller on the line". The BT man now incredulous vowed to investigate. The large dog out back was tethered to a metal stake driven into the ground. It seems the stake was touching the underground BT cable to the house, thereby electrocuting the dog every time the phone rang. Hence the barking phone calls.

Bus stop eavesdrop

I swear this account is true. Only about five or six times in the last thirty years have I travelled by bus and this was one of those occasions, or more specifically, waiting at the bus stop. In front of me were two schoolgirls about 14 or 15 years of age. They made no attempt to keep their conversation quiet considering I was only about four feet behind them in the queue. One girl entertained the other with her weekend's house moving ramifications; she went on "David, a family friend, helped me all weekend". The other girl said, "Did you buy David a card for helping you"? "No" came the reply "I gave him a blow job".

Pisshead

While refurbishing an old cinema in Staines Middlesex I recall one old boy who used to use our site as an afternoon resting place. He used to drink seven pints of Guinness and a few malt whiskies every lunchtime, and one day we found him fast asleep lying across a pile of sand in the tool shed. It appears we had inherited the local council road sweeper who'd become accustomed to using this building ten years before we arrived. Even as a teetotaller this quantity of alcohol per day does seem rather a lot.

I arrived on the job in what I considered to be a perfect state of equilibrium; half man half alcohol
- **Eddie Condon**

Builders Bum

Early one morning in high summer I spotted the cleaner who was employed at the house I was working on. The bus stop had an endless queue of waiting travellers; traffic was backing up so I was forced to inch forward past this column of blank faces. Having decided to offer a lift to the female cleaner, my invitation to enter my truck was met with a swift turn of her back, as everybody was now staring at me and with some trepidation I moved off. Five minutes' later I realised my bollocks were hanging out of the holes in my shorts, and a tissue roll was also hanging out of my hooter due to a nosebleed ten minutes earlier. What a disgrace! The poor lady must have had nightmares.

Clearly my middle son has picked up and run with this dubious characteristic; personally I have always been satisfied to wear small shorts in summer and little else, leaving heavily browned skin head to toe, and a very, very white bottom. This son, as in other areas of life, has taken my habits one step further. When working on First Avenue, two stories up, mid-summer, while back from university and helping with the roof he decided he'd like nothing more than a perfectly brown pair of bum cheeks; and so, shamelessly, he'd roll his mini shorts until they covered nothing but the essentials, cheeks fully out. Needless to say some women walking by got quite a fright.

I have been known to accidentally cut the crotch off a pair of summer shorts, meaning I've worked the odd hot afternoon in a skirt, which is not a claim many builders could either make or own up to. I heard of a scaffolder who did the same thing, taking a Stanley knife to his garment just around the region of femoral artery - while still wearing it! - Until his more enlightened colleagues suggested a less suicidal alternative.

Indeed the demands of manual life on the building include quite serious demands on the wardrobe of the builder, so much so that there comes a time when what is left of a certain shirt or pair of shorts is so little and raggedy one must grudgingly bin the thing outright. A good gauge for the arrival of this moment is when it takes minutes more to dress for putting arms and legs through the wrong holes, or a boot leaves a full toe on show to stub, or when a baggy sleeve or trouser leg catches a rogue nail and renders the garment more open than is socially acceptable, thus when the clothing is more of a hindrance than a working aid.

Because of all this, and man's general over-attachment to material things and appearances, when working my son and I have often been mistaken for a pair of pikies or degenerates; which is, the reasonable man might ponder, good reason to change one's ways, but I think we both rather enjoy the mis-judgements, or in the least possess an immunity to the surface opinions of disturbed onlookers.

PART THREE

A Pastiche of Life's Experiences

Life can only be understood backwards; but it must be lived forwards
-Soren Kierkegaard

There can't be many builders in the world who do not drink, smoke, take drugs, or gamble. But I do have a conscience, and one or two dirty habits, not to mention the odd weakness for a shapely figure.

I have what can only be described as a contradictory nature: easy-going yet confrontational; laid back until an injustice is perceived, particularly when directed toward a party unable to defend themselves... then the red mist. For Pete's sake; an atheist with a penchant for Gospel music!

In my life I've been lucky with my choice of real mates - some four in number - three of whom are named John. Not one of them is a sporting fanatic like me, and when I need a fix they do so only to humour me. However it's clear they will be there for me and me for them. Only one is a builder, but I have worked at all their houses spread over thirty-five years or so.

Back in the year 1975, the year my first child was born, I made a promise to myself; never again will I work weekends, for the sole reason that I wanted to be around my children, for my children, as much as I could. Some thirty years later looking back, it was the best and most important decision I ever made in my life. One hears lots of dads complain, "I was too busy earning a living to see my kids." They may well be right, but theirs was choice just like mine, and that lost time with your kids can't be made up later is a fact, I felt in foresight, too precious to compromise for the sake of money only. I mean, what *exactly* are we earning it for? To cover the basic cost of living, with a few simple and choice luxuries, on the side, that has always been enough for me.

My three sons don't have aspirations of joining the ranks of the building fraternity - not quite like I did, anyhow. My eldest – perhaps in absence of any interest on my part in the field is an electrician, specifying in microelectronics, and the maintenance of central operating systems and their actual sites; my middle son studied law, before and after working as my personal labourer on numerous jobs big and small. He likes to play about with words (he has edited parts of this book), and graft with a shovel in hand; my youngest son (Who also edited this book) is into I.T. and gaming; and my only daughter likes to design and make clothes.

Is luck just being in the right place at the right time, or can luck simply be a case of whom you know? Either way judgement can only be achieved by looking back in time. Luck seems to me to be a collection of circumstances interchangeable by the minute, requiring nothing from us but to wait and see; only as adults can we start to influence proceedings.

This is a story of one such lucky break, leading to a lifelong friendship with a couple we would, under normal circumstances, likely never have met.

One spring morning my middle son Leo (junior) was picking up a friend from Gatwick Airport in my truck. In endeavouring to pass some hours until the friends connecting flight they were looking for (in his words) a place to 'chill out'. Having driven south aimlessly, chatting away and paying no attention to where they were, they found themselves a few miles off the motorway, at a village roundabout, where a small dirt track between a pub and a private house caught their attention. Down it they went. They kept driving - 400 yards, 800 yards, 1200 yards, and then, a mile and a half later at the end of this unmade road, they came upon a chocolate box cottage in the middle of nowhere.

The owner Bill came out to greet the trucking strangers, and promptly took them for tinkers on account of my truck. The thought unuttered, and after a polite chat, apologies abounding, fifteen minutes later tea was partaken in the front garden, followed by an impromptu lunch. Three weeks later and Leo was staying the night! How does he do it? He smiles all the time, invoking trust. Whether he is worthy of this trust is another matter indeed!

Their 400 hundred years old cottage and seven-acre woodland garden is visited regularly at the drop of a hat. Bill Harkin designs and constructs stages used for outdoor music concerts, past clients including Johnnie Dankworth and Cleo Lane, John Major and the Conservative Party, and The Rolling Stones, to name but a few over a career spanning fifty plus years and counting. He is a very clever, talented, and kind man. His wife Dee travelled all over the world on photo shoots in the sixties and seventies as a model, and now paints and makes pottery. They are a very sociable couple with three children equally so.

In time my middle son and I have done numerous repair jobs for them, in exchange for a hot plate of food and some fine company, in a most unique and natural paradise. Needless to say, it is a precious relationship growing out of a purely fortuitous coming together of circumstances. Or was it?

We live on the razor's edge of luck   - **Sophocles**

Knees and Ankles

As a boy growing up I remember my mother complaining that I was always bumping into chairs or table legs. When wearing boots on the site as a young man, I used to trip over or kick most things out of my way. In those days working boots had metal studs all over the soles, and when I used to run and then skid along the pavement sparks sprinkled out behind me; quite a sight in the dark!

Although it may appear that I was unsteady on my feet, this was not the case, neither in normal hours or when on a roof; or I would not have reached this age. One advantage for a young boy joining the massed ranks of the building industry, especially if like me you are into sport, is that in the years between fifteen and twenty on site, one builds up strength in the knees and ankles. The tendons and muscles holding the knees and ankles together become stronger and stronger with all the twisting and turning and tripping and walking and carrying heavy loads on uneven ground, making it possible, even at my age, to get away with the extreme movements and accidents that will inevitably befall one, in this industry.

An example of this increased durability of one's body, due in part and not without a little irony, to passing ones days on the building being physical; many times I have come flying down a ladder much too fast in complacency and confidence, and the first foot to land is planted on the side of a small recess in the ground. The ankle gives way, I collapse in a heap, the pain excruciating, the flesh turning blue and swelling up in front of my eyes. Eventually I stand up and walk around tenderly for a bit fearing the worst, knowing my body has taken far worse punishment in the past. After about an hour, although swollen and blue, no other further damage was apparent. Apply ice for an evening, and next day all is well.

As the years roll by I am less and less inclined to concern myself with the day to day fitness issues normally associated with age simply because the trust between my mentality and physicality is absolute. I see no reason to doubt that my body will hold out right to the end hopefully. This obviously means that any task coming my way is encountered without fear of my body breaking down. Quite an advantage, for a self-employed worker, who needs to be fit for work. Not only that not worrying about a thing often means it drifts off leaving me, over the years, to take it for granted.

Another clear example of the way my profession builds up the strength of joints over time is illustrated when, my labourer and I carrying a very heavy concrete lintel down some steps, my foot caught the edge of a step. My knee joint opened up and twisted, seemingly, right round. I could feel the muscles and tendons stretch almost to breaking point. The knee snapped back into place immediately with no after effects and only a little swelling.

This has happened so many times, far beyond coincidence. Being a builder, not a doctor, I can only say that I think the tendons and muscles must be stronger than normal on account of the profession's workload, and its persistent load on the body. For a young man looking forward to a lifetime of sport, he could do worse than spend a lifetime as a builder, each one complements the other.

Anyone who has worked as or for a builder will know what a dangerous business we are in. Elsewhere I have mentioned injuries sustained and life threatening situations survived. One benefit of working outdoors, other than the obvious mental and physical health benefits, is the ability for wounds to heal quickly. I recall once carrying something heavy with a colleague, then becoming unbalanced and leaning down to right myself, as my palm reached down, an upturned nail sliced right through it, appearing out the back of my hand. My hands, which were covered in soot and demolition dust at the time, were now turning red and sticky with blood and muck. Over the next week the wound was covered up as best I could, and no swelling or infection emanated from it.

On another occasion I fell off the scaffold straight down a manhole, one leg in the hole and one out, other than the bumps and cuts and scratches, not a bother. I have scars all over the top my head, plenty on the knees and shins, plenty too on the forearms, and smatterings more everywhere in between.

Once while attending Kingston Hospital Eye Unit, because there was something in my eye, the doctor pushed this huge machine right up to my face then said, "I can see the problem - it is a piece of metal sticking in your eyeball." He went on, "I can also tell you that the metal was hot when it entered your eye." That day I had used a drill on steel, and clearly some hot shards had flown off. It is astonishing to think how we ever survive our life on the building site! Clearly the human body can take a good deal more punishment than the majority of modern men put it through.

Our hands take the brunt, not unnaturally; cutting my fingers over and again, usually when using a brand new hand saw. Chisels are also incredibly dangerous tools, particularly when new. Of course we know this, but sometimes, due to the pressures of expedience - and to the fact that nothing would get done in this game if one didn't put their body about and on the line - the exact levels of danger in the doing of any given job become blurred, and one gets blasé. No excuse, though a damn good reason.

I've spent more time in Accident and Emergency Units than Dr Kildare, spilt more blood than Count Dracula, trod on more nails than a Fakir, and been stitched up more times than Henry Cooper!

All builders over the years complain about back and neck pain, particularly those of us prone to bending and stooping while lifting. I am no exception, as I get older such pains become more apparent. Many visits to rheumatologists, both state and private, could not help. My ex-wife suggested an orthopaedic pillow, and overnight the pain ceased, never to return. Not an injury as such, but a recurrent nuisance occurring directly from decades of over-exertion.

It is not often that I am laid up and unable to work, but on two or three occasions in the fifty years of my working life, this has happened. Having a cold is an everyday occurrence for some people. For me– a handful of times in a decade or so is the norm. But when it arrives, it is like an erupting volcano in my head. My natural defences fight it off most times, but on the occasions that they do not, I am in big trouble. I experience a sore throat, throbbing head, high temperature, three or four days in bed. No different from anyone else then, you might say. But not quite!

Sleepless lying in bed, I begin to hallucinate; reams of camera film come into view from right to left, small pictures dark and vague, my mind racing to make sense of the images therein. Before I can ascertain the nature of these mysterious exposures they speed up, I am unable to keep up, before starting all over again, stopping me from sleeping. At the time I am on deaths door, though two or three days later I'm asking myself what all the fuss was about. It is entirely possible that other people have the same experiences, but I'm yet to meet any.

How about this: I had occasion to visit a urologist at Kingston Hospital in Surrey, of which I am sure you know what entails; finger up the bum, possibly public weeing inspections. One does what they must. On this occasion you will not believe the consultant urologist's name: Dr J.A. Dick! As I lay on my side, the nurse pressing her bosom into my shoulder, the doctor doing that which he must - in this case shoving a television camera up my rear – and then after withdrawing (the nurse still holding me down), I remarked to her, "If I look up and the doctor is doing up his flies, there will be murder committed in this very room." I kid you not - the nurse laughed uncontrollably for four or five minutes – my tension long gone.

Stubborn Me

Argumentative, confrontational and bloody-minded? Moi? For the prime example of my bloody mindedness one needs to look no further than the existence of this very book. With a poor academic record in English, the sheer scale of writing a quarter of a million words at least twice over, due to mistakes, might equate, to extend and transfer the metaphor, to a man climbing Everest, carrying a donkey, wearing a pacemaker. Suffice to say it has been an uphill struggle, and, self-imposed, has also been highly rewarding.

I have been asked many times why I did not start up bigger building business years ago; in a word, labour. Anyone who has employed and been responsible for building workers will know what a nightmare it can be to keep control of lazy, uneducated, impolite, uncooperative, and sometimes unstable tradesmen and labourers alike. I decided years ago not to go down that route and have never regretted it. Keep it small, rely on yourself predominantly and the help of others occasionally. More responsibility is more stress.

I have two major faults in my make-up as a builder: firstly, I am argumentative, confrontational, bloody-minded and principled – oh, that's four! This tends to alienate me from my co-workers, but not as much as my second (or fifth) fault, if you can call it that. I don't drink alcohol you see, in any shape or form. Not on religious grounds, but simply because I don't like the taste. Lots of people have tried to persuade me otherwise, but as I have said I'm bloody-minded to the end. Such faults don't make it easy to make friends in this business, or indeed in life outside of work.

For example, while walking down the road and bumping into someone I may not have seen for a while, after the pleasantries I might venture, "Where have you been, somewhere nice?" He would reply, "I've been down the pub, but I only had two pints." As if I care how many they've had! Does he assume I don't approve because I don't drink? As if I know or care what people get up to! But it does make me different on that score, plus I don't make friends with men quite as easily as I do with women.

Going back to my professional beginnings, my lack of mates in the building industry led me to believe that I would have to go it alone. If my sons had shown an interest in joining me, I might have seen things differently. I have not told my sons that I'm pleased they did not decide to become builders, purely on the grounds that you rely too much on other people, for example the public's preoccupation with deceit.

I remember as a young apprentice an old boy once said to me, "After forty years on the building your body falls apart, and then you're good for nothing." He knew what he was talking about! My ex-father-in-law, a professor, once said to me, "As I get older I can command a better salary, but as you get older your earning capacity decreases." Which is true so I am trying to change that, with this book.

The very first builder I worked for as an apprentice was William Lacy and Son. I believe their specialisation was building churches, not that I ever worked on one. I did in those days however work on a number of vicarages, some of which I've already mentioned. I was assigned to a bricklayer foreman by the name of Alf Baker who lived in Heston, Middlesex. Aeroplanes to and from Heathrow used to scream overhead, seemingly missing his chimney pot by inches.

Alf was a large lump of a man, very nice, and had a rather peculiar habit: he would light a cigarette first thing in the morning, would not remove it until the fag started to burn his lips, at which point he'd replace it right away with another, repeating the process throughout the day. All day one could hear him going, "phoo, phoo," as he blew the blackened ash away with his lips, never once handling the cigarette except to put it in his mouth. Sometimes, as the thing got smaller and smaller, I'd wait in anticipation, transfixed by this curious and surely perilous habit, sure to see it burn and hear a scream; though I could barely see the fag in his mouth, I never heard him utter a thing on the matter. It did not seem to bother Alf in the slightest, and, "phoo, phoo," he went.

I worked for this company for one year. Always complaining about the lack of bricklaying practice I was subsequently offloaded to the infamous brickwork subcontractor, Jack Maguire. I do recall at that time that Jack had a contract at the offices of Billy Smart's Circus. I never worked there myself, but the practising of Billy Smart's profession could not have reached the levels of tragedy, sadness, hilarity, contempt, and sheer incompetence that my five years with Jack would subsequently reveal!
Around this time in the early sixties, whilst working on a chimney stack in Stanwell Moor near Heathrow Airport, from my position high up on the scaffold I could view the runway from one end; the planes would take off and fly overhead, the noise incredible. When passing, one particular plane, a VC-10, would make a crackling, splitting sound that used to shake the whole house; trying to use the spirit level on the brickwork was useless, because the bubble would not keep still when adjacent to the bricks.

The Lump

Back in the sixties and seventies it was fashionable to describe the building trade as "the lump" (because casual workers were paid a lump sum). At this time the Inland Revenue, in their infinite wisdom, introduced a tax exemption certificate; essentially this meant that a self-employed man could, with his 715 certificate, delay paying his income tax for a year or more. The 715 was like a chequebook, requiring weekly payments recorded on each slip, and given to the Paymaster in exchange for wages earned.

Given that they had yet to be personalised, the trouble with this system was that it created a black market in 715 books, On one site the brickwork sub-contractor had a blank book of 715's; he charged us five pounds to register on the blank slip. In total there might have been fifty men's wages going on this illegal 715. The benefit to us workers clearly was that on this particular week we did not pay any tax. The loophole was eventually closed about five years later. With a few refinements and additions, the same system still exists today.

Brown Paper Bag

My middle son tells me of one Sunday morning that has lodged in his memory, the pith of which is standard fare for most builders. As a lad of about 12, banned for the day's match, he had to watch from the side lines as I coached our team. Occupied as I was with this, I asked him to safe-keep a bulging paper bag for the duration, collected as monies owed on the way to the game from a customer. Put in his hand with no more said beyond the safety imperative, he looked inside to find a wad of several thousands, and begun to ruminate more seriously upon this mornings task. Having tried and failed to hide the bundle in various spots about the van, he decided with a gulp upon the only place he could be sure of knowing whether anyone came close to, or might interfere with, and promptly opened his waistband to place the bag alongside his own crown jewels. A lump indeed!

Radio One

Back in the early sixties the only music on daytime radio were acts like the Joe Loss Band and others of such old-fashioned ilk, not much fun for a sixteen-year old! All this changed when Radio One started playing the music that radio's Caroline and Luxembourg used to play at night time. How did this affect a young boy working on a site? I will show you.

When I was working in Chertsey building some houses; I was assigned to a house that was already built; roof on, floors down. My job was to build all the internal walls upstairs. The labourers used to appear every now and again with mortar for me to complete the slabbing. On my own for long periods of time, I'd have a radio perched on the windowsill with a length of wire about five feet long acting as an aerial, poking out of the window, endeavouring to find the best reception. I remember the first D.J. on Radio One, the first song, and the first group - The Move - Flowers in The Rain.

Looking back, how could I possibly have put up with the Joe Loss Band and his kind all those years ago? And of course I speak for the then blossoming of a generation previously incomparable. Nowadays, most sites vibrate to all manner of so called music, which is – mostly – as abhorrent to me as we were to them back then. Working with a group of old boys outside, building the flank wall of a house, I'd nestled my radio nicely on another wall. I was called away for about three hours, and on my return the much older bricklayers had built my radio, where it stood, into the wall, still playing away its pop music, which had obviously annoyed the dickens out of the older men! I removed it quickly before the mortar set hard, and learnt a lesson for the future: don't upset the old boys!

I was once asked if I had ever come across a woman bricklayer. "Only once in fifty years," was, and still is, my reply. I was not working on the small extension she was operating from, and I could see her up on the scaffold. I'm afraid curiosity got the better of me and I made some pathetic excuse to visit her up there. The girl was nineteen years of age, slightly overweight, and not the prettiest girl I had ever seen. I told her she was "very brave to consider working in the building industry, and must learn not to take any crap from anyone." She said: "I am the boss's daughter, so nobody would rubbish me." I made my excuses, wished her well, and left her smiling broadly at the interest I'd shown in her.

Building Changes

Many changes on the building site have taken place in my lifetime, some of which I have already mentioned. One such change, definitely for the better, is the use of nail guns, now to be seen in use everywhere. The prototype of the seventies required us to feed the gun with small bullets, painted according to their strength. I believe yellow was the weakest and red the strongest, with about six or seven colours in all.

The chance of someone getting killed when the thing was in use was never more obvious than when a red bullet was used on, say, a soft breezeblock wall. Instead of nailing the batten to the masonry, nearly the whole damn wall disintegrated! Woe betides someone standing behind it. I've seen half a dozen men sitting round a fire as some idiot has thrown a box of these Hilti-gun bullets on the fire. You have never seen men move so fast; for a few seconds even old men became Olympic sprinters!

Perhaps due to increased population and training, and thus increased competition, construction workers these days seem to outright specialise. For example dry liners, double glazed window fitters, block layers, etc. As little as ten years ago dry lining would have been the domain of a plasterer; it being the method of finishing the inside face of a wall, or a stud or timber partition. Instead of being plastered in the conventional way by laying a skim coat, the plasterboard joints are either filled or taped, and then rubbed smooth to a ready to paint surface. On new builds, developers like this method because the less mixing of plaster will result in less moisture contained inside the structure, therefore less shrinkage, which means less cracking on the surface of the walls, and less maintenance.

And in the past a window fitter would in all probability be an ex-carpenter. A bricklayer would, of course, best lay a block driveway, but nowadays a labourer will suffice. It is clear to me that as a consequence of this specialisation, more and more workers turn up, do their job, and then off they go. With time and the expenditure of it being of the utmost importance these days to the average worker – much more so than in days of yore - there is less time for the odd exchange of insults, the telling of a story, the practical joke.

Nowadays there is so little communication. Whereas in yesteryear, on a small site, you might have one bricklayer plus labourers, one carpenter, maybe a plasterer, and possibly a plumber; to pass the time together more tolerably banter would fly around willy-nilly, and good-natured insults were the order of the day. In those days there seemed to be more characters about: old boys with wizened features and warm hearts, telling all manner of stories…"We did this… Have you seen that?"

As a mere youngster, then, I was perpetually laughing at their antics and stories. These days' people laugh at me, with my stories and antics. Full circle? And a sign of the times, more's the pity! Nowadays I am still trying to get somewhere, but my road to riches is always under construction!

One situation that has not changed on the building site is the necessity for an early start. It remains a fact that more work is done in the hours before lunch than any hours afterwards. The exact reason for this I can't quite fathom. Possibly as lunchtime approaches other temptations appear on the horizon. Much will depend on whether you are working for yourself or for a firm; it is only natural that you will work more expeditiously for yourself.

As a consequence of this phenomenon, builders' merchants, hire shops, grab lorries, greasy spoons, and all the other effecting industries all start before seven o'clock in the morning. Some trades have no choice but to start even earlier: a flat roofer working in the mid-summer heat and long days will start at, say, six, and finish about 11a.m. The reason simply is that when the sun gets too hot he is unable to stop his feet sticking to the hot felt.

Asphalters - a dying art - have similar difficulties. For the perspicacious builder absent minded over his diet, an early breakfast at a greasy spoon is a must, about 7a.m., latest breakfast at 7:30 a.m. I am not a great lover of greasy spoons, but occasionally a fantastic chow is partaken. My favourite café in Hook makes a cracking liver and bacon with mash and cabbage with thick onion gravy, and at around a fiver - The Ritz eat your heart out! It's not a coincidence that most busy cafes open about 6 a.m.

Compared to days gone by, working practices have changed out of all proportion these days. Picture the scene on, say, The Houses of Parliament, or Westminster Abbey: A young boy might start his working life on a building of this magnitude, and stay put on the same site all his working life; then, fifty years maximum. You didn't think the Houses of Parliament were built in six months, did you? I don't know how long the Houses of Parliament took to build, but from my research it seems it took a good three hundred years to build Winchester Cathedral, and on that basis we might assume England's seat of power took at least as long, perhaps even five hundred years! Back in those days, time in the form of working practices was almost irrelevant. If a bricklayer or stonemason laid fifty bricks or 500, or one lump instead of eight lumps of stone a day, that was okay. The pace of life was markedly different. Nowadays its head down, arse up, and damn get on with it, pronto!

In centuries gone by, at the start of a project a cutting shed would be erected, where all bricks and stone and wood would be cut to size before being laid. The young boy would probably start here, and over his lifetime work his way up the ladder to become a bricklayer, stonemason or carpenter. In effect, this was a job for life. How times have changed!

The old boys I learnt from used to tell me that during the forties and fifties, when the weather was too severe for bricks to be laid, trowels would temporarily work as snow clearers. I can just see the council unions putting up with that today! You've all heard it said, "I couldn't work yesterday because it rained all day." As a builder, having spent fifty years working - outside for the overwhelming majority of that time - I can honestly say that only on about seven or eight working days has it rained all day, London's suburbs typically being drier than its northern parts.

The big difference between tradesmen and workers being employed by large construction companies as opposed to we self-employed artisans, is wages. How do you think huge builders make a profit? By paying slavish wages compared to the self-employed sector. Most building site operatives don't want the responsibility associated with finding work, preferring to turn up, clock on, do what they are told, and clock off, leaving them free to do for the rest of the day whatever takes their fancy. Self-employed workers are essentially on call night and day, but are also free – because they run their life - to attend a son's school football match or daughter's school play. It is chiefly for this reason that I chose as I did fifty years ago.

Another big change, at least on the larger sites, is the absence of muscle power, no doubt reflected in the wishes of the E.U. Cranes and forklifts now hold sway. Perhaps in the next generation bad backs will become a thing of the past – thank God!

My local builders' merchants suddenly changed hands, and I shall show how it affected my business. I had patronised a local builders' merchants for some twenty years or so, then out of the blue the whole shebang was sold off to Travis Perkins. Now I don't have anything against Travis Perkins per se, though the fact that they have 300 branches over the country is sign enough – in the predictable climate of modern day business running – that things like customer service and employer inefficiency are pretty low down on their list of priorities, regardless of the marketing blurb proffering the opposite, which one is sure to be fed. After all, shareholder profits come as the first and foremost importance.

So now I have to deal with a computer and sales staff that seems to have the right to charge whatever that particular sales person thinks I should pay. For example, two months into the changeover I asked the price of a roll of torch-on roofing felt, and was quoted fifty-two pounds! I mentioned the price of thirty-two pounds at a local roofing centre, and was promptly told they could sell the felt to me at that price also. The counter staff could not understand why, I walked away shaking my head. Am I alone in questing why as a builder I have to negotiate a different price every time I enter the place? As an account holder the last thing I need or want is to hope that the staffs are not overcharging me!

I withdrew my account shortly after I received a threatening letter stating that I owed them the princely sum of £4.24, over a total of seven days. It seems the account details were sent to the wrong address, despite me pointing this out three months earlier. You see I had been spoilt at the original builders' merchants; I could take anything I required and pay for it when the job was finished. I think Travis Perkins is now so large that it doesn't care one jot whether you stay a customer or not, preferring to spend millions on endorsing or sponsoring everything from the Federation of Master Builders to Snooker tournaments nationwide.

We've just heard that Travis Perkins have purchased, not just my local builders' merchants, but the last family run independent builders' merchants locally, forcing us builders to choose between them or Builder Centre, with a Jewson's no doubt following in due course. Different name, same bullshit. We builders have to suffer the effects of a possible materials cartel in the future… but shah, shah… in case the Monopolies Commission hears about this!

There are also Wickes, B&Q and Homebase who, along with Travis Perkins and the rest, actually sell sand by the small bag, at a relatively extortionate price. This has to be one of the biggest rip offs ever perpetrated in retail history! These household institutions would no doubt retort that the smaller bags comply with European edicts and are really quite handy, to say nothing of the five hundred per cent mark up!

For years there was a system whereby a builder could purchase goods at a reduced rate (trade price). Though by name this still exists, the reality is that now everyone pays essentially the same price. Why? Because these companies want to make the most money they can, and our customers want to pay the least money they can. We as builders are caught in the middle, squeezed by both.

Dumping

The builders' merchants where I was a regular for more than twenty-five years had a brilliant idea; for us builders, the permanent removal of rubbish is always a problem, hence the fly tipping phenomenon. It is just too easy. New government legislation required contractors to use only licensed dumps, which were disproportionately expensive. The builders' merchant placed a large container in the corner of their yard inviting us tradesmen to unload our bits of plasterboard, timber and assorted rubbish for a nominal fee. The beauty for us meant we could empty our trucks before loading up again with bricks or whatever other material. With this system everyone was happy, until the council found out; the merchants were fined and the practice was stopped.

Once we were almost caught red handed. It was the date Charles married Diana, and Mick and I had removed a large tree. Our truck overloaded with branches, the Council yard complained that our tree would clog up their machinery, and no-one would take our rubbish. At another dump we were given the same excuse. By now this particular tree removal was becoming rather expensive, on account of the time spent chasing about trying to get rid of this damn load.

At the side of this particular dump was a little lane just wide enough for our truck to pass through. To one side of the lane there was enough room to accommodate another tree, or remnants of. Halfway through emptying the lorry we noticed a man watching us at the entrance to this small one-way road; with this in mind we drove out and past the man, standing ready as he was to take and report our number plate. But he was unable to do so, as we'd wrapped a jumper and shirt around the trucks number plate, obstructing his nosey view.

Fly on the Wall

I am sure you've all heard the phrase, 'I'd like to be a fly on the wall.' But if you are easily upset, please don't try. One of the first extensions I took on when starting out as a self-employed builder taught me a lesson never to forget. On returning to my site rather earlier than anticipated, I heard my clients talking to one of my carpenters in a back room. Obviously, they were unaware of my presence and felt able to express themselves freely. I cannot remember the actual details, but the general tone was of a man (me) sometimes rude, kind, attritional, confrontational, bloody-minded, and arrogant. I swallowed hard and re-entered the room, noisily. You would be amazed what some people say about you behind your back - good, bad, or otherwise - so best not to go there.

Since that incident in about 1975 I vowed not to talk about anyone in a way I would not be capable or willing to do to their face. As a consequence, albeit thirty years later, I am not as arrogant or as bloody-minded... I think.

Character Traits (not the good kind!)

As someone who wears his head and heart on his sleeve, I feel compelled to recount some of the more unsatisfactory traits of my character. Those who know me well will recall me being banned as coach from a children's football team. I was also banned from a table tennis club and a pub based singles club.
At this point I need and want to put my point of view of these situations simply because some of the people pushing this agenda will in all probability be reading this book. This is my turn to square the circle if you will.

Clubs

Junior Football Club

I had just been responsible for procuring 17 acres of prime sports field, due almost entirely to my refusal to give up the project that I started, despite huge local misgivings about probabilities. At this time the club paid for me to attend an FA coaching course to benefit, not just my team, but the whole club. This was achieved and my kids' team went on a run of successful seasons not seen before at this quite old club. It was not a surprise that other teams/managers became jealous and my constant battles with the boys' parents (never the boys) manifested itself in some of them unseating me through a false accusation of stealing subs' money. It did not help one bit that I was head and shoulders above any player or youth coach locally, in regards of experience and/or ability. When I left half the boys came with me and the parental mafia stayed put and took over the remainder of the team. This was probably the real reason why I was shunted out. Not a good time but I was always fair and truthful and would not have survived some parents' ire without showing some arrogance.

Table Tennis Club

This was a case of one or two people who got together behind my back to lie and deceive the whole club (approximately 50 members). To cut a long and boring story down to size, the chairman, although a small man, had for years before I joined bullied his way through the player's sensibilities in a way only dictators do. Eventually after many run in's the word got round that I was to be banned, despite many innovations and suggestions by me and implemented by the committee. I was not going to put up with this crap and the trapdoor opened. Not one of said committee had the guts to face me afterwards, so why the hatred when some of them had never even spoken to me let alone knew me?

Singles Club

When I divorced, a singles club seemed a good idea and so it was at first. I kept my nose clean and went out with a local lady for about 6 months. We parted and I then found out I had been banned from this club because this lady felt uncomfortable when I was there. As she was now part of the fabric of this club, I was banned again unfairly by unknown forces behind this lady.
This is a conclusion as to what is possibly going on here by a perceptive ex-girlfriend in her own words: *Groups of people and sometimes individuals don't like the way you move around like a panther as if you own the place. They see your confidence somehow as a threat, possibly because they would like to do the same but are unable to. Because you treat everybody in an open and truthful way it scares the shit out of them.*

The truth is powerful because it is the core dynamic of solving problems; lies and false reassurances are fatal because they doom any sincere effort to fix what is broken.

The first enemy of the truth is hate   *- Albert Einstein*

Libraries

Someone asked me how much help I have had with this book. Let me put it like this: writing about builders is like dropping a four inch nail into the Grand Canyon and waiting for the echo. In other words, don't hold your breath! The following tale encapsulates all my efforts towards research. I visited my local library and asked if I could hang up on the notice board a note requesting anyone who has had trouble with his or her builders, and to share the experience - good or bad - with me. The librarian, who nearly had a heart attack at the possible responsibility she might have to take in response, rushed into the back room to consult three other people, keeping others at the desk and myself waiting. Eventually she appeared showing me a council list of do's and don'ts, within which it was pointed out to me that if this project was for commercial and not cultural or charitable reasons, they could not display my sheet on their notice board.

I replied, "Do you mean to say that I cannot do, for the very same reasons, the same as every book in this place?" She went on to say: "Leave the sheet here and we will send it to Head Office to be authorised or not. It should not take longer than about five days." I left, speechless. I revisited the same library on another matter four weeks later, and happened to remark to the librarian that I was writing a book, and this is what she said, "When the book is published bring us a copy for the library." Not, "we will buy a copy!" Thanks for your help.

According to my research, the number of books in libraries in my local area amount to more than five hundred million. I can with relative confidence say that not one of these books has been written by a self-employed builder about builders. And so it seems I am both the baker and the eater of some humble pie.

My other efforts at research were just as bad. I put up a note at my local builders' merchants. Bearing in mind I have used this place for over twenty-five years or so, the abuse written all over the poster rendered the exercise useless. I also produced question and answer survey sheets, giving them to people who had recently come into contact with a builder, some looked at me as if I had come from Mars (my ex-wife does indeed think I originate from Mars). Others agreed to take a sheet and drop it off, but no-one ever did. I called round some time later and collected a few. Most people felt the need only to answer with the odd word here and there, so most of the collected sheets were not that useful to me. Except one, which posed a question, contained in the chapter on misunderstandings?

Inventions

I am sure we have all asked and been asked what is the best invention in your opinion. My favourite invention as it applies to the building trade is the screw. Not that one, the other one; you know the little thing (careful) you drill into timber or masonry as a fixing. The screw was invented in 212BC by Archimedes of Syracuse. Screws are obviously a perfect fixing appliance. I wanted to bring to your attention the anti-gravity side of the screw thread system. You have all seen a ready mixed concrete lorry, so have you ever wondered how the concrete is expelled from the drum?

Working with gravity the filling of the drum is easy, but how it is emptied against gravity is, in my opinion, quite clever; reversing the direction of the turning drum - using the screws' upward thread inside the container - makes the operation child's play. Another priceless invention is the wedge, of wood, metal or plastic; there are problems one faces in construction where only a wedge will suffice as a remedy. On many occasions I've held up whole structures with the folding wedge procedure. This involves two wedges, usually wooden, hammered together to form a temporary lifting, which is very quick, easy and strong. Stonemasons use wedges instead of mortar to align their blocks before filling the joints with grout.

Leverage is another godsend on site, and my brain could not possibly build in the variables connected to this pre-Roman phenomenon. The building of the pyramids likely owed much to the wedge and leverage system, still used in part today.

Soon, I hope to become an inventor myself, though at present I am struggling with prototype and patent issues, naturally.

The Batsman©

(A slip catching aid for use in cricket) The Batsman was originally conceived back in 1999, followed by seven years of rumination only. Eventually I realised that I didn't want to die wondering about its potential, and decided to go for it, and find a patent agent who did not require me to raid Fort Knox. It was the intention of my ex-wife and I to present the unique characteristics of The Batsman to the world at large, never forgetting of course that a living had to be made. With the help of anyone who was interested we set about building a website.

Having borrowed a video camera, my three sons and I set about making a video demonstrating The Batsman's qualities as a slip catching aid. All of us gathered, huddled over my prototype on a very cold winter's day at Magdalen Cricket Club's ground at Kingston Grammar School's sports field in Thames Ditton, Surrey. Huddled around the prototype we set up the bowling machine, took our positions, and sent the balls flying down. Leo Jr and I catching, Mark feeding the bowling machine, and Jack on the camera. The Batsman's ability to replicate the kind of catching required in a game situation was evident, and we all agreed that the prototype was a resounding success. Perhaps a new era in the art of practising slip catching had begun.

The rather daunting task of bringing this product into the marketplace seemed huge, and proved to be so. Email addresses to anyone even remotely connected to cricket worldwide were sought and stored by my long-suffering ex-wife. My original thought was to impress the England cricket coach, and I did indeed visit the incumbent fielding coach at Loughborough University. It is pertinent to recall word for word what transpired that day, as subsequent events would back up my overall perception of the visit.

I arrived at the English Cricket Board's performance centre at Loughborough at nine o'clock in the morning and after a four-hour drive, bursting for a pee and a cuppa, in that order. While the fielding coach was making my tea, the England bowling coach approached me saying, "I'm the England bowling coach." Shaking his hand I replied, "Yes, I recognise you." Having introduced myself I ventured, "In your capacity as bowling coach you might like to see this." He asked what it was. I explained, "You will have to sign a confidentiality agreement, as agreed with the fielding coach two weeks ago." To which he threw a strop, retorting, "I'm not signing anything!" He then stormed off, never to be seen again.

Whilst drinking my tea the fielding coach signed the prepared confidentiality agreement. I was telling him about my invention whilst unloading it from my vehicle. My heart sank when he saw it and said, "Oh yes, we have something similar." We came out of the lift and walked into a room with an AstroTurf floor the size of an aeroplane hangar.   The bowling machine was already set up, so I put The Batsman in place ready for action. I positioned myself at second slip, much to the amusement of the throng that had gathered, in spite of the fact that the agreement between myself and the England coach was for only the named visitors to be present.

The coach had told me the week before on the phone that only the head coach and the performance director would be present. The fielding coach seemed oblivious to this breach of confidentiality, knowing that my invention had not been patented at that time. What could I do or say? After all I had driven for four hours to get there.

When testing started I could not believe the coach's inability to hit my device in a consistent manner. At this point I was feeling rather miffed; if the bowling machine operator can't hit my machine then I'm standing in the slips feeling slightly foolish, in front of an audience who should not be there. Finally, I had a chance to catch a ball, did so, and received a round of applause from the bystanders for my pains. After each bucketful of balls had been used, I ran around to retrieve the used balls, strewn as they were all over the place. Looking behind me I was astonished to observe that no one was moving or making any attempt to pick up a single ball, they were content just to watch an old man run about on his own showing a level of energy which they clearly did not possess.

No one had said or done a thing to help me. After two buckets of balls had been used the coach decided that my device was not as good as the one they were already using. My attempts to make it easier for the coach to hit my machine fell on deaf ears. It seemed he could not wait to show me his method, which I considered posed a very real threat to his health.

On the wicket he placed a ball throwing machine used in hockey, and the coach then knelt two feet away, in his hands a rigid plastic sheet about two feet square. The hockey machine fired the ball at eighty miles per hour into the ground, and the coach deflected the ball towards the slips using the plastic sheet. If the coach doesn't find the right angle every single time he'll surely lose a few teeth! Can you imagine a schoolboy or an adult being allowed access to this contraption? Nor can I.

What he proposed next horrified me. Moving his hockey machine adjacent to The Batsman, he bowled at eighty miles per hour from a distance of four feet into a stable structure. It hit it dead centre, which caused both the coach and his mate to jump back in a mixture of alarm and amazement. Incredulous, he then blamed me for potentially hitting a watching hero, like Ian Botham for example. Not only did he mess up The Batsman's trial, but he was trying to blame me for his own incompetence!

This once in a lifetime experience for me had been distastefully soured; firstly by the dismissive bowling coach, secondly by allowing all and sundry to wander in and out, third by missing the bloody thing with the bowling machine and thus missing the whole point of it, and finally by doing something stupid to then blame me for it! I remember asking the man questions that he could not or would not answer, choosing instead to quote the opinions of famous players. This man in the foremost position in the country seemed to know nothing about slip catching!

I drove home down the M1 with his clichés ringing in my ears. After the first ten miles or so the feeling that I'd been short-changed soon dissipated. My thoughts turned to the patent issues that had been compromised during the hour spent there; at least twenty strangers had seen my prototype who had not signed a confidentiality agreement.

Because of his complete disregard for the integrity of The Batsman, or indeed myself, I was forced to speed up the patent application before we were actually ready. The consequences of this for me were four-fold: one, November and December were not the ideal months to make a video of a summer game, not to mention the catching of a hard ball with cold fingers; two, poor daytime visibility for the video; three, two months wasted out of twelve months' grace in my patent application; and four, a manic hurry up in putting the website together before any possible third party could interfere.
Somehow Rosie managed to elicit a handbook from the English Cricket Board with not only the email addresses of all levels of county clubs, but also home and mobile numbers of those who make up the great and the good in cricket circles. We set about dissecting the handbook for the betterment of The Batsman.

Right from the word go bowling machine manufacturers seemed our best bet, simply because the usage of our product ran parallel with theirs. To every bowling machine sold The Batsman would make a perfect accessory. And the same thing in reverse for every Batsman sold: "Do you need a bowling machine?"

On the morning of 31st January came a phone call from my son Mark, which shattered my belief that all things pertaining to slip catching remained my domain. Another chap a cricket coach living, can you believe it, only forty miles away had invented something similar. Whilst my device and his differed greatly in design. The principles of both were exactly the same. His website claims seem completely at odds with the still photos on view. Consequently, I cannot wait to see for myself the cricket coach's device.

Inspecting our competitor's appliance in action on video, we came to the conclusion that our gizmo will in all probability work more efficiently throughout the speed range, up to 100m.p.h. Our apparatus stands on the pitch of its own volition needless of adjustment, whereas his seemed to require a resetting after each delivery, particularly at the faster speeds. It doesn't require a brain of Britain to work out the vast qualitative differences between the two models; one is built of steel, the other of wood.

We requested a demonstration at Sussex county cricket club, an hour's drive from us. Three of us were present, Leo Jr, Rosie and I. Mark Robinson the Sussex coach was informed that we were ready. Sussex versus Yorkshire had already started so, grateful as we were, when both teams' coaches turned up together to see our demonstration, Leo Jr and I positioned ourselves to take a few catches but the indoor school was tiny. There was not sufficient room to stand back far enough to reasonably see, let alone catch an 80 mph cricket ball. However, whilst talking specifics to our two esteemed county coaches Leo Jr took a memorable one handed catch. Both coaches looked at each other in amazement, me, I have seen him do it all before, many times. Both coaches saw the batsman's potential but complained it is inconvenient to traipse a live cable powering the bowling machine on to the pitch for practise. I pointed out that it could be used without the bowling machine also. They nodded. The upshot being there was a game going on, so both coaches left to re-join their teams. Not long after this my marriage difficulties moved into view, as she was responsible for marketing, and as I could just about turn on a computer, the batsman was put on hold.

In pursuit of sales it was always our intention to go right to the top. The following idea was probably over the top, and ultimately might prove foolish. But, after all, in for a penny, in for a pound. Early in February 2009 we wrote to Lalit Modi, commissioner of the Indian Premier League, who was soon to start the second 20-20 Cricket Competition in India. I asked him if he would consider a proposal to buy a Batsman for each of the eight cities' cricket teams in the yearly festival. The reason behind this was for him to gain some much needed goodwill from the public both in India and around the world whilst we would gain much needed publicity for The Batsman, which would carry the IPC logo on its side. I don't know why there is such bad feeling between Modi and the cricket authorities in India, but might this gesture on behalf of the cricketing cities and a fledgling inventor's business curry (excuse the pun) some favour in a cricket-mad part of the world?
Am I in cloud cuckoo land? Possibly! But if you don't ask you don't get. Will Lalit Modi fix it for me, or will he prove to be as ruthless as he's portrayed in the press, to take my invention and produce it himself? We wait with baited breath, but I am not holding mine! Meanwhile, my patent agent having viewed this other device ventured that the differences were sufficient for there to not be a conflict of design.

Ambitions

Well it is known that ambition can creep as well as soar

- Edmund Burke

One ambition of mine which has not yet materialised is to work in a jungle environment, mostly, I wager, because of my love of the sunshine. My ideal ambition would have me working on a hospital or school in the middle of nowhere, turning a sort of West Indian mahogany colour by the hour. I did approach a few charities, but no one wanted to know. The nearest I got was being on standby to rebuild Port Stanley Airport in the Falklands, after the R.A.F. had finished with it.

Charities

Charity begins at home, but should not end there   *- Thomas Burke*

On the subject of charities, how do the various charitable organisations view each other? The competition to extract our money must be as cut-throat as any other business. The large established charities looking down and pressuring the smaller ones, wishing they were not around to dilute available monies. All charities have a vested interest, which manifests itself when a television crew interviews their field agents. In a war zone for example we are told, "We are in the middle between two warring factions, so give us your money." Then complaining about both sides at war, not realising that without the fighting there would not be a charitable presence.

I am not uncharitable, but I question how much money actually seeps through to the sharp end. My own feeling is that insurance companies and charities share the same business practices: if a large pot of revenue is created, refrain from paying out for as long as possible, thereby accruing vast interest.

Why is it that charity workers abroad do not seem to appreciate that warring factions do not care two hoots who they are? History is littered with kidnappings of charity workers putting their own sides and governments in trouble. Maybe the workers think they are untouchable just because of who they work for. Above local law, perhaps!

Would it not be a better option for the international community to band together to oust the murderous dictators from their ivory towers, instead of pouring millions and millions of pounds into bottomless holes in the name of charity? Remove the warlords then pile money into areas that most need it. Surely this option must be cheaper in the long term. This is not a new idea of course, but has no chance of materialising without some kind of a worldwide collective will? And I think this is coming, but how long must we wait?

One consequence of climbing the social ladder is that we are now subjected to a non-stop barrage of garden parties. 'Save the Whale', and the 'Foundation to preserve the flop eared marmoset from Timbuktu". All well-meaning, but is there another agenda? Of course there is. Usually the hosts, mostly wealthy women, take part in these affairs because they do not have to work on a day-to-day basis; without these charitable 'do's' to enliven the dullness of their routine life I'm quite sure *rigor mortis* would not be long in making an appearance.

Look how many bands released new records after the Live Aid and Live 8 concerts, making the millionaires even more money. I am afraid, for some, charity begins at the bank.

Knighthoods

How are they earned and decided upon? I shall give a concrete example in discussion of this question. My ex-father-in-law has a better case for inclusion in this exclusive club than most of those already in it. A research scientist for over fifty years working for the British Government, specifically the World Health Organisation, he attained the status of number two in their entomology department. For thirty-five years Dr Robert Killick-Kendrick has been a world authority on Leishmaniasis, travelling to and from nearly one hundred countries worldwide, and having lived in thirty five. This disease is contracted through infected sand flies looking for blood-meal, usually in warmer climates. I think I am right in saying that Leishmaniasis dissolves the roof of the mouth leaving a gaping hole, which is open to infection. Wherever in the world an outbreak has occurred he has been despatched there, to catch more sand flies and investigate.

The Professor recounted the following tale (one of many like it) when flying to Rio de Janeiro. Apparently he left the jumbo jet for a smaller plane, and continued this downsizing a further four times until the destination was reached deep in the Amazonian jungle, astride a two-seater biplane. He told me he has a kind of diplomatic pouch carried on his person at all times, which cannot be searched. The pouch has become problematical on many occasions when passing through obscure border controls moving from country to country.

Imagine asking - or rather telling - four heavily armed border guards in the middle of some God forsaken hole not to interfere with the said pouch! No wonder his balls occasionally seem bigger than they need be. Sometimes, the pouch would be completely empty. On other occasions, it would contain disease riddled sand flies, or worse. In the event of trouble, Bob always had a direct contact number to the high powers in whatever country he found himself in. Because communications in Nowheresville are often and almost non-existent, a wait of four or five hours was not unusual. Consider his blood pressure was naturally and unusually high, for which he takes a dozen tablets a day to control, it is a wonder his head stays on. Again, no wonder he had a rather self-absorbed quality about him. Success inevitably comes with a price.

The Prof has a listing in 'Who's Who' as well as a detailed page on Wikipedia and retired to France in the nineties, though continued to work as a consultant until the end. He died of stomach cancer in October 2011, aged 82. Does it seem he was deserving of a knighthood?

As do, in my opinion, Ian Botham and Lester Piggott, both of whom have achieved more than anyone in their respective fields. Obviously trouble with the police cannot have helped their cases, but such matters did not hinder the accession of Sir Mark Thatcher or Sir Jeffrey Archer. And yet the cricket and horse racing fraternities are littered with Knighthoods. Evidentially, still, in such matters, it is not necessarily what you do or know, but who.

Now three years later "Beefy" (Botham) finally got his just reward, we are told his knighthood is for services to charity, which clearly devalues what he achieved on the pitch. This is the chicken and egg mentality gone mad.

Coal

Sometime in the late eighties or thereabouts, I once lived next door to a policeman; whilst chatting one day he remarked that the village he originated from was, at present, being taken down bit by bit; the coal pit village at Easington Colliery in County Durham. I wondered whether the bricks might be good enough to transport down south for developers to build new houses with. Old bricks usually have much better aesthetics than new ones. We decided to drive up north for the weekend and take a look. In a word, they were crap!

The village pit was almost finished as a working mine, so rows and rows of miners' cottages were being knocked down; the local bricks were made out of coal face rejects and no good to neither man nor beast. Because coal fires still burned in this part of the country the air was thick with coal dust; walking down the street you could taste it on your tongue, and to look in the mirror was to see a blackened face. I remember standing in a queue at a fish and chip shop; also in the waiting line were two miners in uniforms, both covered from head to toe in coal dust. Quite what effect this had on their health heaven knows, though, in so far as I saw it and cared, this was not the place to bring up a child.

As a Young Boy

My earliest recollection as a young boy of junior school age was as a pigeon fancier. Back then, as I understood it, my father's pal kept racing pigeons, and every time a new brood arrived I was given the odd one to keep. A coop was erected in my garden and my *piece de resistance* was to walk to school carrying one or two birds. When the bell sounded to enter school, surrounded by children they were released, and after a few circles of the school they flew home to my coop. I distinctly remember seeing one morning all my birds lying dead on the coop's floor, eaten by an infestation of ants. Strange, how one can recall so vividly an occurrence, which took place nearly sixty years ago?

Junior Football Team 1957-58, back row third from left

The junior school I attended as a small boy was situated at the edge of a vast wasteland; previous extraction of gravel long since done. There was one pit still open about half a mile away which acted like a magnet for large and small boys alike; a huge area was covered with grass some five feet high. On its open side the school had a pigsty, can you believe it, attached to our playground, separated only by a six-foot chain link fence. This was of course out of bounds, unless one had justification for being in with the pigs.

In so far as we boys were concerned, the only grounds to do so were to retrieve a football which had been kicked from the playground; the last person to touch the ball had to run the gauntlet of grunts. I climbed the fence knowing that should I be spotted, the eagle eyed teacher would not follow me. What I did not know was the nature of the pigsty floor; under a foot of swill and shit, with deep depressions and cavities used to encourage the drainage procedure.

Having succeeded on the way there, I duly threw the errant ball back into the playground, then turning round, down I went into a morass of pig shit and rainwater, up to my chest! From where I fell the other children could not see my predicament, so I waited for the bell to ring before climbing back over the fence, covered in excrement. At the tender age of nine I was given a severe bollocking, and sent home like a stinking pariah.

Apart from a paper round, my first attempt at working and getting paid was a rather curious affair. Myself and another boy, both about eleven years of age, befriended, a night watchman, who slept at night in a tent, beside a main road. Drawn as we were like a magnet to his red-hot brazier, one particular Saturday we were invited to help a tarmac gang cover a pub car park. At the end of the day, with a veritable pools win in our pockets, we ran hot foot to the local off licence. Now I know what you're thinking, but you would be wrong. We walked off home with our pockets (not to mention our stomachs) full up with Maltesers and Coca-Cola, not for the last time that month.

Way back in the late fifties I used to spend all weekend in Richmond Park. As a young boy of about eleven I could not have found a better place to play. Whilst my mates and I played our way round this wonderful park we could see in the distance tall high rise tower blocks, and coming from a two-story council estate had never before seen such buildings. These tall housing blocks situated in Roehampton became a magnet for us young boys, but not for the obvious reason.

We developed a liking for lifts, and playing in them. Having never clapped eyes on such things before, and like all boys, curiosity got the better of us; we played to our hearts' content, completely oblivious to how much misery we were inflicting on the occupants. After a few months we were chased away, but soon formed a bond of sorts with the local children of our own age.

Frequently football matches would take place in the shadowed streets surrounding the high-rise buildings, always with an air of 'them versus us'. The impromptu games might have lasted twenty minutes or two hours; only coming to an end in the same unpremeditated fashion in which they had begun, when one, two, or three little people realised they should be somewhere else. Looking back it is astonishing to think these events ever happened at all, as no appointments or meetings were ever arranged; one just needed to be in the right place at the same time, and the opposition would suffice.

As the contests spiced up, both sides used to introduce ringers - boys maybe one or two years older. At age ten or so, boys a couple of years older were almost shaving adults! If God had been looking down on us – and he may well have done - he would have marvelled at the connivance and cheating going on. You must understand that these games were not mere life or death experiences; they were, for ten year-old boys, much more important. I also recall that the high-rise boys never came over the park to our patch, for a return match – strange that.

At the weekends, if I was not in Richmond Park, I would be found at Teddington Lock on the Thames, where a cornucopia of people and water came together to provide an oasis of fun and danger, in equal measure. If you have never been to Teddington Lock, please go to take a look; the river boasts a lock, plus roller ramps for canoes and other flat-bottomed craft, and many types of water are to be found here - deep, shallow, slack, fast and tidal.

At one end is a weir spewing out white water, and at the other end are the canoe rollers, with an island in the middle. The bank on one side of this island is more like a seaside beach, and during the hot weather it is always packed. Opposite the weir on the Middlesex bank are the I.T.V. studios with their permanently moored houseboat-hosting parties. At the other end of the island, on the Surrey bank, is the lock in which I spent many an hour contemplating my next move whilst watching Mr and Mrs Admiral of the fleet, waving to all and sundry. A happy smiling place, but the danger - oh the danger - was all around for a young boy.

Access to the island from the Surrey side is via a solid, green painted, straight steel construction, whilst access to the island from the Middlesex side is via a moving swing bridge. As kids, if there were, say, four or five of us, and at that in a troublesome mood, we would stand on this bridge and make it swing noticeably, with danger. Fishing at this place was always an absolute joy on account of the different types of water to be found, not to mention the different sorts of characters hanging around at night, some of the unsavoury ones mentioned herein. A few people have been murdered on the Surrey bank over the years. Obviously not a place to be after dark, but I was!

One rather stupid game we used to play required us all to gather in a shed somewhere; then, a small pile of yellow sulphur was ignited, with the last person to leave the shed proclaimed the winner. We used to cover our faces as best we could, and then stagger from the shed covered in yellow sulphur fumes, hopefully triumphant.

One injudicious decision I made at the age of about twelve was to join the Territorial Army; not because I wanted to fight anyone, but purely because a neighbour's son of the same age was a member. The interest for me was the sporting factions, which the T.A. supported. I was informed to report to Kingston Barracks on a Sunday morning at 09.00 hours ,and invited - if I felt able - to compete in a forced march to Richmond Park carrying a full kit bag.

The commanding officer regaled to whoever was in charge, "Take it easy on Leo – he's only just joined." Although it wasn't a race, no one wanted to be last, so it was clear to me that I wasn't going to prop up the rear. What I didn't know was that as I appeared at the designated venue I had to wait fifteen minutes before the next boy turned up. The man in charge said, "Where did you learn to run like that - the Greyhound Club?" If I could bump into this man today – though in all probability he is long gone by now - I would suggest he read this book to find out!

My stay at the T.A. was short lived on account of my argumentative nature, which was beginning to manifest itself. For example, I was ordered to march across a room, bend down and kiss the skirting board, without questioning why. Well, I did question – for even I at twelve recognised it to be a stupid order - and rather more forcibly so than the commanding chap liked. The slippery slope beckoned; soon it was the trap door, and in I fell. What a relief to get away from a collection of sheep and *folie de grandeur*. My first experience of adults outside the home, and what do I get? Bloody megalomaniacs!

As a young lad of about ten I was put through a particular chore by my father, again and again. It required me, firstly, to confront the dark, and subsequently to grow up into the fittest ten year old ever seen or heard of. What my father wanted from me was either half an ounce of Golden Virginia, or a packet of Red Rizlas, or both. And so two to three nights a week I'd set off on my nightly dash to the off licence. Why on earth he could not buy these items during the day I will never know.

Since I was out playing every night it fell to me to bolt, hurry, or fly hotfoot to the said shop. Not at any old time in the evening either, but always just before closing time about ten thirty p.m. At this age I was still pretty scared of the dark, but at least I was out of the house, which was at times unbearable.

I had two running options: a shorter, darker and dangerous route, or a longer and better-lit one. The short course involved a narrowing path at the end of a garage block, beyond which stood some open ground, before reaching a proper road illuminated with street-lights. On this particular circuit I would fly through the alleyway, always fearing that someone was waiting for me at its end. I used to raise a right head of steam before entering the passage; the thinking being that, as I was running so fast, no one would see me, let alone stop me!

On through the constricted opening I flew, across the open ground, and then to the relative safety of the street-lights. Running on fear and adrenalin, I looked straight ahead neither acknowledging vehicles nor passers-by. On I flew down the middle of every road, feeling safer there than the unknown shadows of the pavement. Sometimes a person or dog, for whatever reason, would appear to challenge me; no matter, I wasn't about to stop for anyone.

I always found it easy to dodge and swerve around obstacles (after all I was steaming along), and fear had a way of moving my legs faster and faster to complement whatever predicament I found myself in at the time. That's how it seemed anyway.

On I ran, seeing in the distance the lights of the off licence in Ham Street, desperately pushing the legs to go quicker before the lights went out at ten-thirty. Then in I would charge, lungs on fire and gasping for breath. I'd buy the goods and take a big intake of air, to decide which route to pursue - long or short.

The distance, looking back, did not seem to be very far - a mile on the short journey, possibly four or five hundred yards more on the longer - however at ten years old, when I first was asked to run it, I did not consider the distance; only my father's displeasure, or the shop shutting before I arrived.

Me aged 8 years old

This lung bursting activity late at night went on for about three years, two or three nights a week. Obviously the distance did not alter, but my legs became stronger with age, and the regular race to the shop. I am quite sure that my lifelong passion for sport was conceived in no small part at this time in my adolescence, as was my ability to run long distances pretty quickly. When I was not around my two eldest sisters were shoved out of the door instead, though their attempt at the doomsday run was much more of a walk. Looking back – itself not my idea of fun – no real harm was done, and more by luck than good judgement did my father effect some kind of positivity in my young life.

Another example of how fear keeps you running when ones lungs are sore: back in the late fifties, there was a T.V. programme called "Quatermass and the Pit" which was, at that time, considered the last word in horror, and so it was for me. Most people did not have a television set, so I used to watch the serial at a friend's house along my road, about two hundred yards away from my house. After the episode my friend would open the door, and with a deep breath I was gone. As I sprinted the two hundred yards or so, at about midnight, I was quite sure I could see aliens in every doorway and spaceships hovering in the sky. This buzzing young lad's imagination helped me run all the faster. At school I was pretty useless in class, but put me on the open road – fag buying or cross-country running - and I was uncatchable!

Four years on and my first girlfriend Beverley; she lived on the other side of town, which was separated from mine by a huge area of gravel pits. At that time only one pit had water in it, the rest long filled in and its ground covered by long grass about five feet high. The conundrum remained the same as before, though later at night; do I take the short but scary way home, or the long route march round the roadway?

The short way involved a run across the pits, its path some five feet wide, with tall grass all around and no lights. Pitch black it was. Generally I took the short route, because I always left Beverley's house an hour after I should have been home, and the beating I had to look forward to was no worse than anything that had happened to me up until that time. Bigger, stronger, and faster as I was becoming, the fear was still as real.

Never happy until I reached my old primary school at the edge of the vast wasteland, where the street lights once again struck a relieved chord. I made this journey four or five nights a week for about nine months.

Aged about eleven I undertook a paper round which nobody wanted, and I soon found out why. Lugging the bulging bag around was one reason the recipients and the duration were the others. From W.H. Smith in Richmond I would climb to the top of Richmond Hill, to the Star and Garter Home for Disabled War Veterans. Over fifty years later, now, I dare say I could cope with the sights, but as a young boy the smell used to turn my stomach, with stairs, lifts, and corridors everywhere, and veterans of the war shuffling about with various parts of their bodies missing. Exiting the vast building was a genuine relief.   I was on my bike once again, descending the Star and Garter Hill, towards Petersham.

The next house belonged to Tommy Steele, where I was to work on some thirty years later. I continued on my round, delivering to approximately one house every two hundred yards, all of which were so vast that it took forever to deliver just one newspaper! The round in total took nearly two hours. I remember to this day the abuse I received from these grandiose householders, calling me all manner of names for reasons I could never quite fathom.

I remember a spat encompassing my ability to run as a young boy. We used to play cricket and football at a group of about thirty garages; at one end was a narrow pedestrian passage, at the other a vehicular access to our council estate. One disgruntled neighbour clearly pissed off at our constant incursions into his garden to retrieve our balls, once threatened to remove mine! This chap was only four or five years older than us at thirteen. Still, it was a significant age gap - he was a shaving adult. He cornered my mate on Ham Common, and chased him on a pushbike until my mate fell in a heap exhausted.

The brute then gave my pal a message for me. Suffice to say - he had plans. Eventually this animal got his chance, and positioned another thug at one end of the garage block while he came at me from the other. Thinking on my feet I realised I must run, but where? I had no choice but to run at him, and so I did, at full speed. Arriving, I first made a side step off the right foot, then a side step off the left, which left my foe grasping at thin air while I disappeared behind him. His language - possibly Swahili - was loud and precise, but he never again got as close to me as that day.

From the age of eleven to fifteen I won all the cross country runs I entered, and most of the long distance events. Unfortunately one very important quality held me back - lack of confidence. I remember a boy named Stan Lee in the year above me who also had never been beaten in a cross country race. He was competing in the annual school cross country race where everyone who could walk, including teachers, had to take part. It was his last year at school and he was a clear favourite to win. Although I was told I must too run against the whole school, I completely bottled it, suffering from kakorraphiaphobia, (fear of failure). How I wish I had taken Stan on.
On another occasion I had been selected to run for the school in the district sports competition. I had just come second in the javelin competition and was told to report to the

start of the mile race ASAP. I asked somebody, anyone, to run on my behalf. Looking back, nobody from the school ever asked me what my problem was. This is not surprising given the athletics teacher, who was a sprinter with London based Belgrave Harriers, was also, to put it mildly, a shithouse, only looking after his favourites.

I recall having a barny with him before setting off. It was to be a five mile cross country run. Remember I was only fifteen at the time, and yet he told me unequivocally that he was going to beat me back to the school. When I was the first to arrive back he complained that if he'd sprinted he would have caught me. I replied, not without a hint of sarcasm, "Yes and those pigs flying past would have beaten me too!"

Back in 1964 or 1965, whilst working in a bank at Sunningdale, a set of events transpired well worth recalling here. At about 4:30 p.m. sometime in December, quite dark outside, the bank fully operational inside, I was fixing skirting boards with very hard nails, used primarily with a Hilti nail gun. If you did not strike these nails dead square with a hammer they had a tendency to ping away very fast.

I found myself in an uncomfortable position unable to strike the nail as I would like - on the head. However strike it I did, and the nail promptly shot across the bank hitting a large light bulb and showering the bank personnel with glass. Instead of just the one light going out, the fuse tripped leaving the whole place in darkness. Normally breaking a bulb would not cause the fuse to blow, so was it a coincidence both happened at the same time? The following parallel story was also the result of my stupidity.

Whilst in Holland playing in a football competition, the whole squad of footballers roamed the streets looking for a drinking den. Me being the youngest by far and the only teetotaller, tagged along shy and bewildered by my team-mates' driving thirst for the ale. I found myself in a large bar with a skittle alley to one side. The lighting in this place was very poor, and was just about to deteriorate further. The chap I was with asked me to give him a game of skittles.

Being only about seventeen and rather stupid at that, I chose to be different, as usual. Instead of bowling underarm like anyone else, I tried bowling as if I was playing cricket. The wooden ball smashed into the rear metal wall behind the upright skittles, and as the ball made contact all the lights in the place cut out, as if by magic. We flew outside expecting to be chased by someone; instead people were pouring out into the road wondering what had happened. I can't believe that what I did would cause such commotion and chaos; was it another coincidence of timing? I've no idea.

One of the more stupid things I did in my youth was to participate in a London to Brighton charity walk way back in the late sixties. We started walking at six o'clock on Saturday morning, and I was one of sixty youngsters taking part. Speaking for myself, I was in a hurry on account of playing in a very important cup semi-final on the following Sunday morning. As a naturally quick hoofer I raced ahead down the Brighton Road from Richmond in Surrey. So much so that when I'd reached Brighton Gates, I was told the next youngster had only just passed Gatwick Airport, some twenty-five miles back!

197

All day we baked in the sun, and because I was so far ahead the cars carrying the drinks could not reach me. Undaunted but thirsty, I reached Brighton at exactly six o'clock that evening, a total journey time of exactly twelve hours. Looking back I must have been a right muppet to take on both commitments, as demanding on the body as it was. I did arrange for an immediate lift home to bed, because of my football commitments the following morning. I did indeed go straight to bed, and I did indeed get up early. And I did, if you can believe it, score two goals in a three-two win!

School is where you go between when your parents can't take you and industry can't take you
                                                            - John Updike

Events at College

Most boys in my building college class came from the same sort of background as I did – council house dwellers - with the exception of one boy by the name of Frewin, who's Christian name I can't remember. By all accounts he passed his eleven-plus exam and was withdrawn from grammar school to become a bricklayer like us all. Amongst us blockheads did his superior schooling show? What do you think? What I do know is that this boy always seemed to be one step ahead of us all as a class and light years ahead of me in particular. At the time we all thought he was just better than everyone else.

Looking back it is quite clear that his superior schooling gave him a huge advantage over us all. In addition, Frewin always seemed to have an excess of money, and owned a car of sorts. At lunchtime he would take us in turn for a ride in his three-wheeled German death trap. This vehicle - a BMW Isetta - only had one door that opened at the front, which was perfectly okay until you bumped into something because, as the door covered the whole front of the vehicle, access in the event of an accident was impossible. Still, he was popular because of it; back then in the early sixties, if you owned a push bike you were the bee's knees!

When I was at college the tutor used to arrange visits to places of interest, such as climbing all over the roof of the Houses of Parliament and Westminster Abbey. I can't imagine students being allowed to do that nowadays, which is a bloody shame really. Once, the tutor took us to see the Post Office Tower. Then in 1963 the Tower was unfinished, clad in scaffold. About ten of us idiots ran up the stairs (no lifts) to the top, some 900 feet high! Much to the apoplectic tutor's dismay we climbed out on to the scaffold, and being about sixteen years of age we started to show off, hanging upside down on the handrail, 900 feet in the air!

I must, at this juncture, tell you a story about our tutor who was upset with us all one Friday afternoon, and decided to teach us all a lesson. Instead of letting us students go home, he insisted on taking us to the college cinema to watch some crap film. By this time we should have all been on our way home. As the tutor sat in the front row, on his own, in the dark, one by one we sneaked out and off home, until he was watching the film all by himself! Served him right really for such a poor attempt at punishment.

From Rags to Renaissance

All that is valuable in human society depends upon the opportunity for development accorded the individual   *- Albert Einstein*

As a builder working at the lowest level of self-employed trading, my education is much the same as my peers, but not, it seems, as good as this next generation of tradesmen. More and more operatives are college boys who go on to become our future brickies and chippies. As a man with little formal education, in some stark respects my life changed dramatically at fifty-eight years of age, on account of my courting and marrying my long-standing girlfriend of the time, Rosie.

A woman, with an inferior education! No! A lady, with the same social standing as me! No! To put it mildly, she was a super educated, much travelled, statuesque brunette from a wealthy background and high city living, with attitude. Having spent years on and around the Mediterranean, she acquired the suntan and linguistic prowess that goes with the territory. What was that, I heard you say? You're right – on paper quite the catch for an ignorant builder.

When I first met Rosie, she came across as a lady who has fought many a battle against the male preserve, which is the City of London. As a man who can't keep his hands to himself, she would say, "I can't get used to this attention. I'm just not used to men being so nice to me." On the outside she shows how strong she is, sometimes going too far, but on the inside so insecure with her emotions, not caring or wanting to trust a man - much the same as many of her middle-aged single friends. It is a much heard story.

The Sam Cooke song, "A Change is Gonna Come," mirrored my immediate future, one that I had been adjusting too slowly, but with no little relish. Learning to eat with a knife and fork, speak like a banker (I said a banker, not wanker), work a tuxedo at dinner parties, and remodel my diction were but some of the immediate challenges faced. I'm sure you've got the message.

For these reasons and more Rosie put a hold on the development of the relationship again and again, not knowing if I had the sense or the will to conform to what she and her friends would expect of me. Rosie of course was guilty by association; at one dinner party a G.P. was heard to say, "What on earth does she see in him, for God's sake?" Like most cowardly socialites, this was regaled after we'd left.

When the wedding was announced all her female friends were ecstatic, some men friends were pleased as punch, which only goes to prove that if I can achieve a level social playing field –in theory at least - then anyone can.

Dinner parties, poetry readings, theatre visits… what's next, supper with HRH perhaps? I now count among my acquaintances company secretaries, lawyers, journalists, doctors, linguists, property developers, and the odd millionaire. If this has or hasn't changed me, I am surely not the right person to recognise.

This brings me to a charity party we once attended. The owner of the venue was a multi-millionaire, and obviously a self-made man absent of any posh-ness, and clearly as ruthless as his kind come, as indicated by what transpired at the end of the evening. I have never met or spoken to this man, but watched in horror as he spoke to his girlfriend thus. He called her over to his side, she reluctantly complied. This young girl, maybe thirty years his junior, stopped two meters away from him not daring to breathe, hands at her side. The fear etched on her face was for all to see. He seemed unaware of anyone taking any notice, particularly me. Her women friends gathered around her for moral support, the young girl's eyes fixed on her partner's, pretty face screwed up in fear. I'm not trying to sit in judgement, but I can spot a person in trouble from a mile away, and she was just a one.

I mention this little tale to illustrate how I've learnt to understand wealthy people, and how they conduct themselves socially. What might happen in this case when the lights go out heaven only knows, but it isn't likely to be pleasant. Some rich men, having spent a lifetime on the make, find it difficult to form relationships in the normal way, and so revert to type, bullying their escorts much as they might bully clients and employees, simply because they don't know any better. And besides these women live a life of luxury, so they should be damn well grateful.

Without the money, I've had to woo her in totally different ways from the manner in which she has been accustomed. The point is I rely on my instincts gained from a life of self-employed servitude, to solve a problem or two, and not my money (or lack of it).

I have mentioned earlier how affluent customers see us builders, so now it's time to change roles. Throughout my life I've been adjacent to people who have money, and what many of these individuals see as important is name dropping. Nothing makes these social snobs feel better about themselves than to mention 'we did this, and we did that, with so-and-so."

I remember my girlfriend's employment lawyer declaring over and again such loaded comments as, "I am lunching with the Prime Minister's wife for the third time this month." At a dinner party the name dropper will often be surrounded by ear-flapping, like-minded folk, then at the next gathering the recipients will say that *they* too have met the person in question themselves, and the circle continues, not exactly lying, just stretching the truth a little. To what meaningful ends, one will be searching forever more. As a man not blessed with the desired diction, not to mention a nature with absolutely no interest in the getting of fake friends to empty ends, I am often ignored at these gatherings until it becomes clear that as a builder I might be useful. To be expected really.

An example of how the other half live. Working at a private school somewhere in Surrey I befriended a teacher who said there was a pupil boarding there from one of the oil rich Gulf States. This fourteen-year-old boy had at his disposal a Rolls-Royce and a chauffeur/bodyguard twenty-four hours a day, plus the trifling matter of five thousand pounds pocket-money a week, every week. I remember asking the teacher, "This boy must have plenty of savings in the school safe, no?" The teacher coolly replied, "He spends it all every week." "What on earth on?" "We understand he visits a circle of whores on a regular basis." For goodness' sake, what else could a young boy spend this kind of money on! Good luck to him I say, without a hint of jealousy (liar)!

At this level of social standing it seems there's always someone at a gathering who possesses the social skills you might be looking for, or at least know someone who might help with whatever problem arises. For example at one party while chatting to a complete stranger about a problem with a local planning department, I was astonished to discover the lady was chairwoman of the local planning committee! As you can imagine, for me, a very positive conversation ensued.

Also at this particular party I met a gynaecologist, a journalist, a nurse, numerous businessmen and women, party caterers, a GP, and civil servants by the barrow load. Some people do make it their business to get to know such a range of possibly helpful characters, and who can blame them? One unifying fact stands out in this colourful collection of attendees, education. Of course this is something I never had, though I'm not in the least intimidated or jealous - if not a little stand-out-ish in my lack of rightful manners, and the idiosyncratic ways one develops to offset the imbalance. Consciously I prefer to embrace all and sundry, to treat everyone on the merits I see or feel. Of course this is quite the normal way to behave, though to spend too much time around brown-nosing socialites, one begins to wonder.

This is not quite a rags to riches story - more rags to redemption - born out of a shared respect for each other's achievements. For me, her talents know no bounds; for her, reverence for having brought up four children in a way that earns respect. Rarely a day goes by when I don't learn something new from her. Dressing up is a classic case in point, being largely unconcerned and unfussy with what I wear. I have never been a picture of sartorial elegance but now, due almost entirely to Rosie's dress sense; I'm told that I am the best dressed man in the place.

I've always thought of myself as an ordinary looking chap - and still do - but listening to Rosie's (albeit biased) opinion gives a warm glow inside, particularly so when I meet her mates for the first time and listen to their comments. It pays for me to listen to and trust her opinions, on anything from food to clothes to etiquette, and whilst she claims she doesn't want to change me from being a builder and proud father, she openly wants to change everything in between.

My journey from concrete to cashmere, from poetry to pomposity, starts here with the writing of this book.

Poetry is a kind of ingenious nonsense   *- Isaac Barrow*

The poetry readings we often attended were a hoot. Most members made me welcome, despite the fact that I am to poetry what King Herod was to mother care. I write the odd piece of crap now and again, damn it. Why not?

A Rose Bush

T'was a clear and sunny day when I first met Rosie-Anne,

The sun has not stopped shining and now I'm her best fan.
A weekend visit is all I get - I suppose I should be pleased,
I would prefer to spend more time with her
But will settle for being squeezed.

It is with wonder and glee that I anticipate
Walking from the road and through the gate,
To be welcomed at the door by a lady to her fella
And also by a dog with the charming name of Bella.

I live for the day when she's free from her clan;
I hope it comes quickly, at least that's the plan.

Her initials in Kensington are up in lights
At the Royal Albert Hall, I think I am right.
Respect from the city, respect from us all;
For her linguistic talents shine brightest of all.

Out of the dim and darkness I came
Had to prove that I, too, have a brain;
That I wrote this piece only disproves the latter.
Never mind; I'm sure it will get better.

Now I must be on my best behaviour,
Quiet, subdued, and reserved;
In short, display all the qualities
With which I am least endowed.

Its post-Christmas now, a new year is here;
My wish for her is to be pain free;
Not a pain in the neck, but the pain in her knee.

The moral of this story is an obvious one;
If you find the right lady, you've got to hold on!
So this lady, the one with a will of iron
Fell for the man named after a lion.

Here's another of my verses relating to the interminable toil of our new house...

Christmas on the Building Site

'T'was Christmas on the building site, the weather was set fair,
Problems with the blasted council had us pulling out our hair.
LJ left, Rosie right, the tamper now a blur,
We all knee deep in concrete, you should have heard us purr!
The job now done, the road complete:
That's thirty tons of wet concrete!
So tired now I can hardly stand,
Off home to bed, it feels quite grand.
If Christmas had come earlier, then Santa with his sack
Could have helped us with the graft, but for his bad back.

Now; Rudolph clearly is a soak, as his nose will testify,
He can't lay bricks either, but he surely can fly!
The test is to finish on time and budget, the hurry up now on;
I might well end up like Santa Claus; with the sack to chew upon!

From the Roundle out to Lapland, the weather is the same.
It's not my fault that Rudolph is unsound, and lame;
He once came across an acquaintance and a wag,
And asked, "Is Santa still hanging out with that old bag?"

So it's time to go - nuts to eat.
I'm off down the street
With a roar and a vroom,
I find myself back in Rosie's room.

Just to show I'm not all bad, here's one of my favourites:

Sir, I admit your general rule
That every poet is a fool,
But you yourself may serve to show it
That every fool is not a poet.

- Alexander Pope

Work at Home

I don't want to achieve immortality through my work - I want to achieve it through not dying   - **Woody Allen**

Having decided to divorce from my first wife in 1994 after almost twenty years of marriage, and while still living in the house which I'd converted from a three to a six bedroomed semi when we got married, I contrived to remain in the family home. At this time in our lives my youngest son Jack was about nine years old, I forty-seven.

We managed to put up with the situation for six or seven years, and when my youngest had started college I felt the time was ripe to leave. Throughout our marriage my ex-wife had never shown an affinity for money, but now, splitting the family and selling the house, she wanted the lot, or as much as she could get of it.

Uncharacteristically, my ex-wife tried manfully to remove me from our house, citing, "It's not in the children's' best interest for you to stay." All sorts of accusations about me abounded, including, rather extremely, the deliberate shitting – by me - in every bed in the house, except my own (of course).

Of course none of my kids reported anything of the kind. What happened here – during the regrettable and messy business known as divorce - was the well-known tactic of a solicitor to force out the other party. Her solicitor threatened to take me to court, to which I responded, "If you force me to attend court, I will parade my children one by one for the Beak him/herself to ascertain whether my going is in the kids' interest or not."

After my divorce I moved into a small flat-topped house in Surrey, down the road from the family home, and not far from Hampton Court Palace and the river Thames there. The circumstances in which I bought this house were by any standards bizarre.

I already knew the list of properties locally that I could possibly renovate. Since my ex-wife did not want to divide up the family home equally - 50-50 - we had to go to court. In the meantime I found a corker of a property with a much larger garden (back and side) than anyone else's in the road.

The whole garden was full of weeds and thick rose and blackberry stems, some five feet high and almost impenetrable. This pathetic little house, on the end of a block of four, seemed totally lost on the huge plot. Every time I passed the place, in my mind I was already building the extension and imagining how the finished house would look. I didn't know the owners or whether they would want to sell their house, but one evening I got my head straight and knocked on the door, and a man of about thirty answered. He lived there with his girlfriend and their little boy. I asked if they were thinking of moving, and to my surprise and joy the reply was, "Yes, possibly."

I explained my situation that I did not have the money now, but was going to court soon to divide up our family home. We talked money, haggled for a while, and eventually settled on a price for the property - £144,000 I believe. As I didn't know how long the court would take to resolve our dispute I asked the owner if he would sign a six-month contract at the end of which I would buy the property for the agreed sum. The reason I wanted to tie up the buying of the house in this way was simple; if I could see the potential of the property, then so could everyone else.

Unsurprisingly the court affairs moved on inexorably slow. Six months and two court appearances later, I returned to the desired property. I spoke to the owner's girlfriend who explained that her partner was pissed off because he had a few debts that he wanted to get rid of quickly. I asked the extent of the debts, which ordinarily I wouldn't have done, it not being my business and all. But with my opportunistic hat on, I manifested a plan. I resolved to meet him that night at his house. I suggested that if he extended the contract for a further six months I would provide the £4,000 needed to cover his debts. He thought this a good idea, only this time he insisted on retaining the £4,000 should the six months expire. I was confident of the court business sorting itself out by then, despite the fact that I had no idea what the court would apportion to me.

The judge was pretty fair, and awarded me 48% of the family house. One clear mistake the judge made was to ensure that my ex-wife must receive £160,000, irrespective of the amount actually accrued by the sale of the house. This meant she had absolutely no incentive to hold out for the best price, and in the worst case selling the house for £161,000, leaving me, in short, f**ked.

As I have said – over a period of twenty years the family house had changed from a three-bedroom semi to a six-bedroom semi. The estate agents, spurred on by my ex-wife's solicitors, would have been happy to sell at £260,000, leaving me with about £100,000 to buy a house, once all other costs were met. I found a buyer at £295,000, knowing the place was worth a lot more. By this time three months had been bitten out of my six months contract, so time was very much of the essence. My buyer pulled out leaving me in the proverbial shit. Every day a visit to my estate agent was like pulling teeth - my teeth.

In his wisdom the judge gave my ex-wife's solicitor carte blanche to dispose of the house as quickly as possible. Having easily covered the Judges award, both my ex-wife and her solicitor piled on the pressure. I was also keen to sell quickly, but was not prepared to give the house away either. Another buyer was found - a single mum with two young girls - seemingly in no hurry at that. She offered £292,500, which under the circumstances I was duty bound to accept. So far so good, not bloody likely!

At the last minute the lady buyer wanted a drain survey, knowing I could not deny her, and despite having checked the drains myself, a few years previously, I was now shuddering at what I knew was coming; I organised a drain company the very next day and watched as I was told that the drains needed lining (which they did not), and had no choice but to pay £800 to obtain a certificate before she would close the deal. At this point three weeks remained of my one year contract. I tried to remain calm, but everyone around me seemed to be moving in treacle; a sentiment which - as a self-employed man who by the nature of his living must get on with the thing if a thing is to be done - I am not unfamiliar with. The estate agents had no need to hurry - they were getting paid anyway courtesy of the Judge, as were the solicitors' costs, going up all the time. By now the owner of the house I desired was making noises about adding £30,000 on the agreed price if the contract should run out. Finally, in desperation, two days before the contract was due to expire, the thing sorted itself out with my house and we exchanged contracts, to my ragged relief. Not surprisingly the owner tried to delay further, but the money was paid in. On the day I moved in he refused to speak to me, and drove off with a downcast head. I have not seen him since. Most probably more in frustration than vengeance, before leaving a hammer was taken to the basin of the upstairs bathroom.

Although the house was passably habitable, the central heating boiler packed up three weeks later, mid-December! Three months prior to moving in I had obtained planning permission for a massive extension, doubling the size of the house. Middle son Leo had taken a gap year before going to university to help me with the work, but by the time we moved in and because of the slow moving court process, he'd already departed for the south coast to study. As I'd decided to take a year off work to complete the extension and was not earning a penny, I couldn't afford to employ my resident labourer all the time. After about a year I ran out of money and went back to work. The Court case with my neighbour, mentioned elsewhere, ensured that I wouldn't be able to finish the work until some two and a half years later.

On my extension at home I required nine double glazed windows and one back door, as well as a large patio door. I searched for quotes, the disparity of which might give you a laugh, as it did me: Everest £21,000, BAC Windows £12, 000, and Windows Direct £11,000! I eventually secured a deal with a local company for £4,000. While on the subject of double glazing companies, I once worked for a chap who said he owned the biggest double glazing company in Scotland. He also said the profit margin in double glazing windows and doors was fantastic; using the following example to illustrate this, he said that on a four or five-bedroom detached house he could afford to fit all windows and doors, then remove the lot, to replace them again, and still make a good profit!

When I rebuilt the first house I owned, somehow I found out that the building inspector for my area was partial to old bottles, the type of which are dug up in the excavation of footings and the like. If I did not want him nosing around the site, for whatever reason, I would slip him an old bottle which the digging up of our garden had so kindly supplied. Over many years of hole digging I had quite a collection at my disposal. Waving one of these old bottles in his face was, for him, orgasm time. The proverbial eating out of one's hand comes to mind.

John Beech

John Beech lived opposite me for twenty-five years. His son David was from a young age a rather clever bugger, and worked for me on and off for five years or so. John was a lecturer in Motor Mechanics at Kingston University for nearly forty years, and when he retired he came to work for me. The extent of his building knowledge was only within the boundaries of DIY. Many times I'd hear him comment with admiration on the self-employed man's desire to get the job done, come what may. He'd harp on to people of the builder's ingenuity in climbing over all obstacles to achieve the result. On occasion we'd visit a job only to realise we'd forgotten something seemingly crucial. Soon enough John came to know that we could cope with almost anything if pushed.

John was also amazed at the way customers continually berate us builders. He knows I'm not an arsehole, and that even I, after fifty years in the game, still can't get the balance right every time. John asked me once, "Have you ever refused a cup of tea?" I replied, "Not very often. In my experience, to refuse tea might lessen your chances of getting another at some later date, so you take it even if you don't want it. You can always toss it over the lawn or down a drain, and give the mug back with a smiling, 'that was lovely, thanks'." Any harm in that?

Brickwork Course

We teachers can only help the work going on, as servants wait upon a master
                                                              - Maria Montessori

I have been a brickwork tutor for a number of years now and I am always amazed to see how the classes are full up every time. Amongst other places, I have taught at Dorking Adult Education Centre and at the Henrietta Parker Centre in Molesey. I also hope to be teaching plastering very soon.

The innumerable skills that I and others have learnt from a lifetime in the building industry are slowly dying out. Dying out, not just because my generation is itself dying out, but, because legislation severely complicates anybody's ambitious intent. To become self-employed requires a skill set that opens the mind in every respect, something the authorities do not want to see happen. Ingenious, clever, skilful work forces will give way to sheep like worker bees that are easier to control and manipulate. Ambition long knocked out of the populous. Under these conditions long established skill sets will in my opinion flounder as usury and corporate considerations take over. Money laundering is the reason given for putting the noose around all ambitious intent, whilst removing the past and all the good it stands for.

Brick making goes back some 8,000 years, so we can fairly assume that bricklaying will be with us for a few years yet! An ancient documented account of brick-making exists, written by a Roman called Vitruvius, and he recalled in some detail how the application should proceed.

Bricks have been recovered from excavations in Jericho dating back to around 6,000BC!

Anyone new coming into the building business is assured of a lifelong association as a builder – as a practitioner the profession will make its mark on you. It is a tough job physically and due to the climate changing for the better, now warmer winters mean we don't have to go to work covered in two or three coats. When the summer comes people say to you, "I wish I could work outside in the sun like you." It's at this point you feel very lucky indeed.

When I was halfway through rebuilding my own house, the police turned up one day looking for the previous occupant. When they saw what I was working on they said, "You are so lucky doing your own thing. All I get is paperwork to show at the end of the day, unlike you. I wish I was a builder." Come winter - the cold and wet and short days, not to mention to aching muscles from hour upon of back breaking lifting and shifting and swinging and hitting – I am not so sure they'd feel the same way about this testing business.

All the one-day brickwork courses I tutor have different students each time, and I would like to share the memory of some of their idiosyncrasies with you. I had on one course an eighty-seven year old lady, whom I asked, "Why brickwork?" "Some years ago," she replied, "I made a list of all the things in life that I had not turned my hand to, and bricklaying was one of them." I asked the old dear, "How many tasks were left on your list?" "After today, four." I remember thinking what a wonderful attitude and approach that was. Sometime since, I was told that this inspired and wonderful old dear had died six months later. I wonder if she managed to tick off the remaining four on her bucket list. While teaching away one lady stopped me in mid flow, and said, "When do we get to hear about what kinds of mortar, are required?" I replied, "We will come to that later in the talk." About an hour later, she popped up again with, "What about the mortar?" I said, "You clearly have something to say, so off you go." Little did I realise what was to come … I don't recall her name, but I do know she was a police officer, and her story went thus.

"When I was a little girl I used to climb up on to the scaffold or wherever the bricklayers had been working that day, just to play with the mortar. I had a small trowel and would play for hours." I interrupted and ventured, "Are you sure it was not the bricklayers you wanted to play with?" "No!" she cried, and continued, "Ever since then, I have had a compulsion to play with mortar."

I told this quite serious lady of middling age, and a policewoman no less, "I've never met anyone with a mortar fetish." The other members of this particular class - two of whom were women - couldn't stop laughing, as the woman herself could not either.

After lunch it was mixing time, and guess, who was at the front, shovel at the ready? I mentioned to her that this might well be orgasm time, and I swear she was bouncing up and down with anticipation! Observing her movements it was clear she'd fiddled with bricks and mortar before; she was one of the best students I ever had. I don't think it is a coincidence that generally the best students, in terms of the quality of the work produced, are women. Every female who attends comes with a notebook and pen; some men do as well, but not nearly as many. Generally a woman will listen to what is being offered, which later manifests itself when the technique is tried for the first time. Most men forget what they have been told. Like any doing - there is an easy way and a hard way.

Here's another female tale. Two women turned up twenty minutes after I'd started the class. This mother and daughter combo were dressed to the nines, and wanting to gate-crash my class. As I wasn't expecting anyone else, I asked if the ladies had booked up with the council. They replied, "We always meant to book up but never got round to it. Can we just join in?" Dressed more for shopping than bricklaying, they were sent on their way!

As a tutor, probably the last person you want in the class is another builder, and indeed there's often someone from the building fraternity attending, usually landscape gardeners or surveyors – turning their hand to a skill on the periphery of their own abilities. Another person to be wary of is the prima donna of the building trade; the architect! I've had a few turn up, usually retired types after some practical experience. At the conclusion of my classes it is to these people I ask, "Have you learnt anything that you didn't already know?" Invariably they answer in the affirmative, and are most appreciative. Several have taken my telephone number, though I don't recall anything further transpiring. Occasionally I will run a course one evening a week for five weeks.

I remember one builder chap, on an extended course for one evening a week, for five weeks, who was not conversant with brickwork. I asked the assembly to tell me what they wanted to build over the coming weeks. This particular chap wanted to construct an elliptical soak-away out of brickwork. Not round or square, I repeat, but elliptical, as a sort of egg shaped structure. It soon became apparent that this builder had enrolled on my course solely to learn how to start and finish this specific task.

He completed his work of art in three sessions, and never turned up for the remaining two weeks of the course. Some of the students thought this quite rude, I think he showed a measure of ingenuity; after all he did pay thirty pounds to the council to attend this course, and clearly needed to build the thing for a client. For this I imagine he charged two or three hundred pounds and so likely, hopefully, a profit was made. Good on him.

Just before I left the Dorking centre for the last time before moving to Sussex, I was given a whole raft of paperwork for perusal. Having worked as a tutor with Surrey County Council for five years they now wanted me to attend courses for confidence and self-assessment training, and basic skills awareness! This might well have been a good idea had I not been self-employed for the past thirty five years. Maybe the council were trying to tell me something.

The most damning of these letters revolved around blame; mine, the council's, anyone's. Why would tutors and students not take responsibility for their own actions? Am I being naive? The last paragraph stated unequivocally that on my courses I am liable for every eventuality. This is surely as good a reason as any never to work for a county council again, not to mention the eighteen pounds an hour wage!

Should I be held accountable, if two students took a dislike to each other and, having been told to bring a shovel by the course centre, begin thumping each other with them? Could I possibly be liable for the condition of the student's heads, shovels, or both? Had I signed the form, I fear the answer would be a yes, I am indeed responsible. All this disadvantaging myself for a measly eighteen pounds an hour, and only being paid for the hours actually spent in the classroom; not for all the preparation before and after, not to mention the travelling entailed going to and fro. Never again will I become beholden to a council, when in a righteous world it is they who should be beholden to me for running the course in the first place!

Surrey County Council required the tutors to hand out course evaluation forms at the end of the day. Reading the completed forms later was interesting, the majority of which were fairly reasonable. One sticks in my mind: a small Indian man of about forty-five kept quiet all day, then completed the form, left it on my desk, and scarpered. Excellent, good, adequate, poor, and very poor were the categories to be ticked. This kind fellow had put more work into completing the form than he had into the substance of the day's activities!

He complained that I had gotten involved in my students' building problems at home! Why would students not try to take advantage of an opportunity to learn something specific and relevant and helpful to them? Most students have a project at home, and this is the chief reason they booked the course in this subject. The little Indian thought this a poor idea, so he ticked almost all of the very poor boxes. I did, however, receive two adequate nominations. I have no reason to be troubled and after all he paid his money and he made his choice.

During my first year as a brickwork tutor I had the rather fanciful idea that if we could round up unruly kids off the street, bring them to my classes and teach them the basics, then maybe - just maybe - one or two might have an affinity for the subject matter and progress with it. It could, over time, save the country millions of pounds in looking after such kids whom, for whatever reasons, can't cut it in society.

I decided to look into the possibilities and approached a lady whom I know very well. She was the top youth worker in Surrey, and put me in touch with a few numpties. The probation service said, "What a good idea, but we could not pay you as we only receive several hundred million a year from the Government. If you would consider doing this for nothing, we might talk further." Needless to say, my reply was unprintable. Having been moved this way and that, and putting up with such nonsense as above, I ran out of enthusiasm.

I know some young offenders' institutes have brickwork shops, run by schoolmasterly type tutors, likely having little in common with the young boys. As I brought up three of my own, I feel able and qualified to at least talk to young boys on their level. Being a builder, and as cantankerous as the youngsters, I know discipline would not be a problem.

Everyone who was anyone in the field in Surrey was approached, all to no avail. I did get the impression when talking with the youth workers that they saw me as an extravagance the county could not afford. I was asked by an acquaintance why I didn't consider testing legal or illegal immigrants for their suitability as builders. Immigrants over children? I think not!

Guest Speaking

To anyone who will listen I have been telling the stories from this book for years. My three boys would often bring their friends round just to hear another tale. Then it dawned on me that other people might like to hear these stories too. I approached a local women's club and offered to appear as a guest speaker, and they duly took me up on the offer.

The title of my speech was "A Builders' Tale". My first night was as nerve wracking as taking a driving test or sleeping with a woman for the first time. I arrived early, and there were some old dears already there. What struck me straight away was that the two women in charge were much younger than the audience, and very attractive fifty something's at that. At last everyone arrived, some fifty-five ladies in total. My first words to the gathered throng were: "I'm petrified. So I'll tell a joke to settle myself down, which will be one of only two I'm going to tell tonight." It went as follows.

"A mate of mine had a very large nose, so much so that he was asked to model for Concorde. One day he found himself on the top table at his daughter's wedding. He gave a stirring speech on her behalf and received a standing ovation. He was so pleased that he took a bow, and promptly cut the wedding cake in half!"
As the cake was cut in half, so the tension was swept away. Soon I was in full flow about Mick the builder, Herman the German, Rodney Blickett, and company. I was quite pleased that I resisted in swearing for the entire evening, and was thanked by everyone at the conclusion of my talk. I have more bookings arranged; maybe a change of career on the horizon?

I am told that office workers will, if given the chance, tread all over each other when a promotion is up for grabs. The building trade as a whole is less prone to hierarchical pressure than other jobs; that fanatical need to move on and up does not really apply. Can you imagine playing at backstabbing with some of the characters in this book? People would walk around with knives, bottles, maybe even trowels stuck in their backs!

No, the only pressure I recall comes as a young boy on a site; you get the blame for everything - from breaking the bricklayer's chalk-line to breaking wind. If the foreman doesn't get a grip and calm it down, the young boy will go home in tears, as I did many times despite Bill always standing up for me.

Under scrutiny, from my experience, builders tend to shrug their shoulders and move on; after all, tread over the wrong person and you could wake up dead! Our experiences as young boys on the site prepare us for the adversity of later life, or should do.

It's time for me to shoot down the myth that builders are morally no better than second hand car dealers. Firstly, builders don't try to stitch each other up, for the obvious and dangerous reasons mentioned. Conversely, a car dealer does not discriminate when it comes to selling cars; the point being that one car dealer will be happy to sell a bum vehicle to another car dealer. If he succeeds in tucking up one of his own, the word gets round and brownie points are gained. If you don't believe me, ask a dealer. This is their game, their expertise.

On the subject of cars (not my favourite topic), I periodically employed a mechanic who would use my large garage, with pit, for his own use, in exchange for looking after my truck. He searched around to purchase a car for me, and having done so I inquired about the mileage, which was dubiously low to say the least. Richard said he'd check the clock. Inside he found a note saying, "What, not again!" Clearly some joker – having wound back the mileage clock, not for the first time – thought it'd be amusing to leave a little message for next time.

One day while I was out, Richard was working in my garage and needed a screwdriver. He walked into my kitchen, where my ex-wife and a number of friends were chatting away. Richard asked her, "Where are the screwdrivers?" The reply came, "If there is any screwing to be done in this house, I'm the one doing it!"

Floodbag

In the late nineties Rosie learnt of a German who had invented a pillowcase-size bag which, when left in water, filled itself up and sealed the water inside. She inquired as to whether this bag was on sale in the U.K. Upon discovering it was not she secured the rights, and "Floodbag" was formed. Patent problems were eventually overcome and we set about trying to sell them.

Their most obvious use for this country, we thought, was in a flood situation; they could be dipped in the floodwater, and when full be used as sandbags. We also marketed them as a means of extracting water from around the bilge pump of a boat, which I understand is difficult, and tried various other uses, all of which worked a treat. We commissioned a video showing ten or twelve other uses for the bag. What we found was that the public at large is reticent to new ideas, no matter how good they are. Everyone we spoke to enthused about our Floodbag, but getting them bought was like pulling teeth.

We did sell a large consignment to Australia, and several other outlets including the Environment Agency, but never enough to encourage heavy investment in advertising. Soaking wet or waterlogged football pitches and golf courses might have been a thing of the past, but none of the clubs or courses we wrote to contacted us. We received a more insulting response from a Talksport radio show, when presenters told me to, "Come off the drink and go to bed," and then hung up. It's a good job I have a sense of humour, aside from the fact I am and always have been teetotal. Idiots!

Houses on the flood plains could have been greatly helped but the Environment Agency, despite liking the product, wanted to buy it for peanuts, naturally. We wrote to all the insurance companies in the United Kingdom in a similar vein – not one replied! The Floodbag could have saved them millions! Trying to convince the public to believe in the thing, the performance of which was consistent and highly efficient was, as I have said, like pulling teeth. Various characters bought a few bags, never to be heard of again. There is still a company trading illegally with the product, having been taken to court several times by the inventor.

Mixers and Shovels

Whilst perusing some of my old work collages in 2008, I came upon a job dated 1976. I remembered it for the fact that I purchased my first electric cement mixer on this site. Can you believe that I still own the said mixer? Having been slapped around with a shovel on a regular basis for decades, the drum at the front is now elliptical in shape, and I have only replaced the fan belt once. Mind you, I should think it will require another one soon. The working instructions and part specification are still in their sealed folder, unopened. Recalling of this story leads me to the need to convey the sometimes doubtful provenance of tools acquired. Way back in the days when Noah's ark was still afloat - about 1963/64 – I was working in a very large department store. Across the main road the same store also ran builders merchants. The building company we worked for had an account at this place, which was, unsurprisingly, abused daily!

Having mentioned throughout this book my dislike of the 'something for nothing' mentality, on this occasion I am found wanting. Rumours abounded that our builders' merchant was going skint, and our bosses were complaining that money was still in the builders' merchant's kitty. It was suggested that on our next visit we might like to acquire something useful, as collateral. On my subsequent visit with three others in tow, I wandered around the trade shop, busy fingered. I was wearing a huge, black, full-length hairy coat, because it was in a bitterly cold mid-winter, and because I needed to hide the three shovels and pickaxe underneath!

I realise that this choice might strike one as a little strange, but one must remember that hand tools - particularly shovels, and particularly clean ones - were at a premium, and still very much are today. After all one can become rather close to the tools of their trade, an extension of oneself as they are, on the job. With the whole shop to choose from we naturally went for the most useful. The quality of both my choice and the goods themselves may be observed in the fact that, fifty years hence, I still have them and they are still going strong. Sure, I still have my ill-gotten gains, still working on a daily basis.

Shovels wear out at their weakest; most exposed, and most used point - the sharp end at the corner, moving towards the middle. Over the last half century they've worn down to such an extent that I now have three rather small shovels of varying sizes, from three-quarters the norm to almost spoon size! (It is worth noting how practically helpful this differentiation of size is; depending on what is being shovelled, and what it is being shovelled off of, and given my ability and desire to hold a heavy shovel-load of anything has decreased at much the same rate as the shovels themselves, one has the right tool for the right job! Invaluable.

I'm often asked whether modern made shovels or tools will last as long as those of yesteryear. Anyone with the smallest experience in the wielding of tools old and new will instinctively know the answer. Increased mass production has ensured that the quality of manufactured goods in general, tools no exception, have suffered dreadfully, steel used as in shovels and chisels, is nowadays of poor quality, I am told because it is mixed with other materials, making it go further and in the process softer and weaker.

Although when it comes to my tools, especially these old ones of fine manufacture, their durability has been in no small part due to my loving care. After helping complete hundreds of jobs, and after thousands of hours in use, these shovels are still so clean you could eat off them, as I have indeed done many times. Why? Necessity, ease of use and no small amount of inanimately aimed affection. How? Bonfires were commonplace on sites back then, and so was the odd string of sausages or T-bone steak. And sizzle away they would, right there on my shovels. Obviously the eating irons had to be clean, but a few minutes in the fire would do the job, clean as they already were.

Modern Day

One day I found myself in a B&Q store, and decided to enquire about the possibility of doing a part-time job solving customer's building problems, in store. The manager thought it a fine idea. He said, "You'd be on call all day." I recall thinking this might suit me down to the ground, until the manager pointed out that I would be expected to serve on the shop floor all day. And, the salary for fifty years' experience? About fifty pence above the minimum wage! I watched on as a spotty teen dished out 'advice' to all and sundry.

The term 'over-qualification' comes to mind, though who could deny how helpful to the customer I'd be, in such a role? Clearly, genuine customer service is not very high on the company's priority list. Nothing new there, though this was not the case in my day. In years past builders' yards were mostly owned by whoever was working behind the counter and therefore could not do enough to assist. Nowadays half a dozen companies own most if not all builders' merchants countrywide with their impersonal touch and take it or leave it approach. It is as if they don't want your money.

Self-Employment

How many of this country's workforce is self-employed? I'd say a very small proportion, despite constantly being on the increase as people become more educated and aware, and realise that being one's own boss really does take some professional beating. By nature of the problems they face, the self-employed man/woman is forceful, bullish, hard-working, argumentative, unrelenting, problem-solving, and risk taking; in short, everything that the public servant is not.

How many days off sick are accrued by policemen and public servants alike, paid all the same whether they attend work or not? Is this not a form of robbery? Not to mention the inflated pension! Human nature dictates that a lying in bed for a few days now and then does no harm, unless your livelihood depends on whether or not you climb out of bed. Self-employed people are a different breed altogether and the backbone of this country. The difference is most obvious when dealing with council employees, known in the game as a 'Jobsworth'. Most are well-meaning, but show an absence of urgency quite staggering. It is a fact that the taking of days off owing to stress come in the main from the public service sector. Human nature again dictating that stress will appear on cue, along with the wages!

I mention policemen because, in my sporadic dealings with them over the decades, I have observed that no small portion of them are bone-idle, who would be unemployable in the self-employed arena. A copper might counter that their job is very stressful. And so it may well be, but the job was known to be stressful before they decided to join up and become stressed. I'm not picking on the police, but having read this book you will come to the conclusion that I've fallen across a number of official dipsticks in my time.

The conundrum for all self-employed workers comes down to this: do you save money in a pension plan, whereby the pension company holds all the aces and the money and the benefits – which in my game provide precious opportunity for investment and development, and therefore profit - and would not hesitate to screw you given half a chance? They can and will hide behind Government legislation always leaning their way. And then the pot created after 30 or 40 years will always be less than expected, always less than we deem is needed. Unless of course, you're a public sector worker, a council employee, or a civil servant and the like.

And so what does one do? Bricks and mortar will always be inflation proof, because this small island is saturated with people all wanting a place to live. Unless that changes, which seems highly unlikely, then neither will the value of a house. If you can, try to move house every ten years or so, making sure your next house is bigger and better than the last one. Not bigger and better than the last one, to keep up with the Jones', rather, when the time is right downsize and bingo your pension is created owing nothing to the insurance industry.

A Main Burst

Around 1990 a water main burst about sixty metres from my house. This water main was three feet wide under the road, and served the whole town. My house was situated at the highest point in our road, so the water ran right and left outside my front door. Opposite and to the right was a small open green space adjacent to the leak, and a further twenty metres behind was the River Mole. Most houses located at the lower ends of my road were flooded. The council sent various oddballs to view the scene, as did the fire service and the police. At this juncture and with many householders also present with concern, no one seemed keen to suggest what to do next.

Upon arrival the water board told us it would take about two hours to turn off the water main, but the water in the broken pipe would continue to spew out everywhere. I asked the council-workers if they could commandeer a J.C.B. digger at this hour of the night, about 8:00 p.m. My thought was to dig a trench across this grassy open space and knock a hole through a small boundary wall, thus channelling the torrent of water into the adjacent River Mole some six feet below us. This would in my opinion have stopped the flood water entering my neighbours' front rooms.

A council JCB digger and driver arrived eventually, and when my plan was put to him he shit himself, saying, "I don't have the authority to dig up this grassy patch of land." Having driven such a thing a number of times over the years, yours truly volunteered to administer the *coup de grace*, only to be told, "I don't have the authority to let you drive the digger." Although my house wasn't in the slightest danger of flooding, we were now hearing tales of two feet of water in the downstairs rooms of locals.

Myself and other concerned neighbours suggested to the council driver that he might like to take a walk; he, understanding what was not being said, informed us all that if we touched his digger he'd call the police. Meanwhile roughly eighty homes became swimming pools for the night. Ten minutes at the JCB controls would have saved the day, not to mention hundreds and thousands of pounds! But no; liability and the fear of taking responsibility for the doing of something you believe to be right – the old-fashioned courage of one's conviction – proved, in the mind of the Jobsworth, a stronger incentive to not do his job as best he could.

Agility

All people have talents; good, bad, useful, and worthless. One very useful characteristic I seem to have mustered is my very own built-in global positioning satellite. On rare occasions I become disorientated, but not often, and not for long. A preoccupied interest with maps might have something to do with it. Finding my way around, mostly without maps, amazes my family. Sometimes my children will phone up lost, quite often in central London; I ask where they are and where they are going, and am usually able to point them in the right direction without consulting a map. If I am to venture anywhere up to about three hundred miles or so away, a quick look at the map before starting the journey will suffice. Given I have been travelling to different work places in constancy for fifty

217

years; it is hardly surprising I have learnt to find my way around. That I have retained this information in detail is perhaps exceptional.

One day on leaving a local newsagent, running at full tilt as usual, aged about 43, I turned left and promptly caught my toe on a raised paving stone. Up in the air I flew. Working as a builder and being a sportsman I have learnt how to fall properly. In front of a packed bus stop, in mid-air, I twisted my shoulders round to keep my head off the ground, and landed on my back and shoulders. The momentum ensured a complete turn, and coming upright in a circular motion to my feet without pausing for breath or applause, away I sped. Though, I did glance back to the people at the bus stop, stood as they were with open mouths.

Another time when I was about 51, I flew round a corner so quickly that the four or five people gathered together there fairly scattered, expecting, I suppose, that either I had a shotgun, or someone chasing me did. Or they were just given a bloody fright by some lunatic running around street corners at full speed. Given this natural agility, it is ironic to think that I have never been able to breathe properly through both nostrils at once. Having had numerous operations on my hooter since childhood, in May 2005 another operation is imminent. I write this on the very day that splints are to be removed from said hooter.
As a boy I used to frequent Richmond Park, which I think is about six or seven miles around at the perimeter. And so it figures that as an adult I should use the park again. Which I did! This time I would wait till the traffic gates shut at dusk then, either accompanied or alone, I would run around the park as a training exercise. An abundance of trees and no cars meant a proliferation of clean oxygenated air filled the lungs. No lights and pitch black, my eyes soon becoming used to the darkness, on I would run, and looking right and left would quite often see a dozen pairs of eyes looking back at me; herds of wild deer staring on, no doubt in some confusion and fear at this intrusion of their night time and space. It is entirely possible that they were saying to each other, "He must be an Englishman, or a poacher, or just a bloody idiot!"

My Mini Cooper

Back in the early seventies I owned a racy Mini Cooper; it was bright yellow with a royal blue roof. What set this vehicle apart was its customised interior, like no other. Unhappy in traffic, on the open road a flying machine, I should have killed myself many times in that car. Apart from a few near head-on shunts, other head-shakeable memories remain.
I remember my mechanic once told me, "Fill every hole on this car with Redex upper cylinder lubricant, then fly down the nearby M3 as fast as you can, for as long as you can; that should clean out your engine nice." This I did. On returning I mentioned to him how at great speed the car became a little unstable. He looked underneath, and with a face as white as a sheet said, "The chassis is two halves bolted together. Now there are two halves completely apart!" Doing one hundred and thirty miles an hour in a car that to all intents and purposes was in two parts makes me shudder, even now!

Another time, approaching a large main road in Twickenham my brakes failed; all I could do was turn left into the main road and hope for the best. This being so, just before turning a bus crossed in front of me! Working on instinct I managed to negotiate the very busy main road without mishap. Eventually I blew up the engine; the Mini Cooper dying a death, but not taking me with it!

Southall F.C. Centennial Party, 1971

Playing football from the age of fifteen helped me to feel alive, giving me a focus to life as I knew it. Aged about twenty-three I was playing for Southall Football Club in west London. The club and stadium were taken over by a famous comedy scriptwriter - the creator of "Till death us do part", Johnny Speight. In 1971 at Christmas time we, Southall, played a charity match, after which we were invited to a party to celebrate the club's centenary, held at our patron's house in Middlesex. Quite a few famous names were present: Marty Feldman and his wife, Franklin the cartoonist, various comedians including the not to be forgotten Rita Webb, dressed up as a Christmas tree fairy all in pink. There were some people apparently famous (but not to me), plus a few named footballers, one of whom I will tell you about.

Maybe because of my knack in finding my way around, my then wife and I were the second guests to arrive at this house. It remains possibly the biggest house I've ever been in, with a huge porch area followed by a massive hallway, and a grand staircase ascending to the left and right. The food laid out to the right must have consisted of the entire contents of Harrods' delicatessen! As we marvelled at the place, near empty, a voice called out, "Cum an 'av a drink." A face, instantly recognisable to both of us, he was a Liverpool and Scotland international footballer of the time.

I hollered back, "I don't drink." "You don't drink?" he screamed. "Are you man or mouse?" Being an Everton supporter it required a will of iron not to kop him one right in the chops. Since it was not my party I didn't want to ruin it for everyone else, and it turned out a good night; the food was delicious, the company hilarious, and a good time was had by all.

One of my first girlfriends was so keen to watch me play in a cup final once that, since our coach was full up, she was happy to travel by public transport. I advised her to hop on the Number 37 bus, which she did. But she got on the bus on the wrong side of the road, and consequently went in the opposite direction. To her credit she turned up at half-time to see the rest of the match.

Holidays

As another example of my bloody-mindedness, one afternoon whilst on holiday in Fuerteventura my ex-wife wanted to retire for a siesta. I, not even considering the thought of sleeping inside while the sun was shining, looked out of the window to see a hill about three quarters of a mile away, beyond which stood a very prominent volcano. I thought to myself, yes, I'll have some of that. Already pretty much dressed for hiking in a t-shirt, shorts and trainers, I set off immediately to conquer the damn hill, maybe even the volcano.

The hill was a pushover. Looking up at the rather larger obstacle, though, was a little daunting. Nevertheless I found a starting point at an enclosed and floodlit football stadium. Just above the stadium was a plateau used by the locals as a fly tipping site, where narrow path two metres wide snaked its way upward. Walking now at an angle of forty-five degrees due to the incessant wind, I told myself, "If I don't watch out this bloody wind might blow me over the edge of the crater! Why did I not bring a large coat or a parachute?"

The wind increasing the higher I climbed, turning to look behind me was quite a sight; facing right into the football stadium, beyond which I could clearly see the offshore island of Isla de Lobos - a volcano in its entirety - and to the left Playa Blanca, a port on the island of Lanzarote. Standing –or rather leaning over - at the top, the view was incredible. "This must be the reason I decided to climb this volcano," I told myself.

The sides of the crater now only a metre away, one slip and I'd get a bird's eye view of the deck! The crater was so huge that you could put Wembley Stadium plus the Millennium Dome side by side into it. The wind blew as hard as I have ever known. A rest at the top was needed, and I sheltered behind a small pile of stones placed there for just this purpose. Naturally, I descended much quicker than it had taken me to climb. Looking back it was rather a foolish adventure, given the clothes I was wearing and the fact that I had no mobile phone with me. Still, a bloody good craic, worth it if only for the view.

Back in the late '80s with my wife and four kids, I sashayed off to Lanzarote. Timeshare personnel looking to recruit customers approached all visitors to the island. Whilst ensconced at the beach club listening to an endless round of bullshit, admittedly drinking their tea and sandwiches, carefully taking their figures into account, I worked out how much money they brought in annually, minus the cost of building the huge resort, chalet by chalet.

Back at our hotel with calculator in hand, the staggering number unfolded. If all weeks were sold, between £75 million and £100 million profit was in the offing, plus management fees ad infinitum! One needn't look far to see why the criminal classes get involved in this sorry business. Huge profit margins no doubt, but not as huge as pharmaceutical companies, not to mention insurance companies.

I am sure you are all aware of timeshare scams and the ramifications thereof, so I won't bore you with scam after scam, however I would like to open a few eyes to a type of scam I have discovered. A timeshare outfit contacts you alluding to have found a buyer for your property, then asks for a fee. When you ask what the fee is for, they will declare, "Just in case you pull out of the deal at the last minute." As if you would, having spent years trying to sell it! To this question I urge you to respond, "I will sign a contract confirming payment to you *after* the sale is completed." This would make an upfront payment unnecessary, but legally committing to the sale. I've offered this solution again and again, but company rules prohibit it. These scam outfits' rules only lean one way; once you've called their bluff they put the phone down.

Blind Man

Even with the best of intentions, a narrative misdiagnosed. Whilst waiting at the traffic lights in my village – the extended delay of which I well knew - I spotted a blind man standing at the side of the road, evidentially waiting to cross. With me sitting doing bugger all, out I jumped, asking the man with the white stick if I could help him over the traffic lights. Grumpily he said, "No, I can make out the red light still showing." I explained the slow sequence and clear road, to which he replied, "I'm in no hurry." Back in my truck I went, shoulders a shrug, it occurred to me how different both our lives were; this man had ignored the chance to save himself twenty wasted seconds hanging about. In fact, time was his only remaining faculty; for me time *is the* enemy.

Thought is the slave of life, and life is time's fool, and time, that takes survey of all the world, must have a stop
                                            - **William Shakespeare**

Space

As I have grown older I have developed a healthy interest in space in general, and specifically in UFOs. It started when I tried and failed to get my head and brain around the word 'Infinity'. Not only the numbers but the distances are quite beyond my comprehension (of course in this I am not alone). And it is this, I think, which is the fascination for me. I have no interest in astronomy, certainly not in astrology, and my belief in life after death is zero. But other worlds I think are quite possible; I mean how else are we to interpret the likelihood of life elsewhere given the sheer numbers of planets and stars in our universe? Given the extent of the known universe, it would be quite bizarre to think we're the only planet with intelligent life. Or perhaps all these planets just have builders as residents, and are therefore dead.

Space travel is particularly fascinating to me, because the shear distances involved would require mankind at the very least to reach the speed of light (seven times round the world a second), equating to three hundred and sixty million miles an hour - a few horses required, then! To reach the outer edges of our solar system would take several million light years, give or take a few weeks. In space there are millions of lumps of debris, most being inert. If only a fraction of a per cent is not inert, what are they?

Astronauts and pilots regularly see unexplained phenomena, sometimes showing up on radar, sometimes not, and it is these that I am particularly interested in. According to the laws we live by, an eyewitness in court is considered the ultimate proof of an act.
In ufology an eyewitness account is dismissed according to the persons' credibility, or lack of physical evidence, or both. How can we discount hundreds of pilot sightings logged and verified on radar? Surely something is going on. I can remember in a presidential campaign by Jimmy Carter, he said that when he gets to the White House he will tell all; the silence is deafening Jimmy!

Let us say that the unexplained flying objects are real and not mere optical aberrations; what does this mean for mankind in general, and religion in particular? Does this mean the world's religions are rendered untenable due to man's insistence that there is a superior entity looking after us? I think it might. Scientists tell us that the planet we live on is one of the youngest in the solar system; if so; anything coming from afar must technologically be millions of years in advance of us. That being the case, would it be impossible for visitors from outer space travelling at fantastic speeds to remain undetected?

Can radar detect an object moving at the speed of light? I would like to know, though it seems unlikely. Is there a worldwide cover up by governments to conceal what little we do know about extra-terrestrials? And if so, only about six or seven countries could be involved, as most countries would succumb to bribery and corruption to tell all about, what would be, the biggest story ever told in history.

Two years after writing this piece, and with three other witnesses, I observed the real thing - on 4th October 2007, on the south coast in Sussex - details of which when reported, flew around the internet. My account is as follows:

It was a very bright sunlit afternoon with a few puffy clouds in evidence. The sky in the west surrounding the sun was bright pink. I was upstairs at about 5.55 pm, when I looked out of my bedroom window to observe two perfectly round orbs gently floating above the houses and trees.

My immediate thought was of two balloons slowly moving upwards and toward me. The UFOs colour was a pinky hue, clearly reflecting the sun away to my right. At first sight the perfect circles were very close together, though moving slowly apart. I went downstairs thinking, 'I've never seen a round balloon before.' A few minutes later, while looking out of our patio door from the kitchen:

I was astonished to see that the objects had changed to silvery, pulsating, star-like objects. To the naked eye each orb, as my aunt remarked, looked like two dancing together. As my binoculars were close by I whisked them up and took a look, focusing in. I distinctly remember thinking, 'How am I ever going to draw what I am looking at?'

X marks the very spot when first spotted   Leo Lindsay ©

This shape seemed to be moving up and down in a fluttering motion, the sun catching one side then the other, giving the impression of a double act, when, on closer inspection only one object was seen. I must point out that I never observed the second UFO through the binoculars, not wanting to take my eyes away from the good visuals I had on the first. However, my wife did.

Leo Lindsay ©

(Picture one shows the object tilted towards us with the bright sun on my right lighting up the right-hand side of the craft, leaving the left-hand side in shade. And then in picture two - it levelled out to resemble a shape familiar to us all - the saucer with an upside down teacup.)

© Leo Lindsay.

The upper section revealed a random panelling effect, which my wife described as a multi-facetted diamond-like facade. The Craft was oscillating periodicaly, causing us to question whether the strong pulse was in fact light refraction from the sun when moving. Eventually it dawned upon us that this craft had a rather powerful pulse looking like a mother-of-pearl-in colour. The only contradiction I can find between my version and my wife's is that she saw the craft as upside down to mine. As I said, she was the only person to watch both UFOs through the binoculars. The drama took place against a backdrop of a translucent white puffy cloud, which had remained in a fixed position in the sky while this had all been going on. Over the six or seven minutes of concentration and amazement, we seemed to be losing focus, and realised that the UFOs, still pulsating, were moving away in a direct line from us, climbing in altitude.

Suddenly from right over our heads and heading directly for the UFOs, appeared two rapidly moving aeroplanes, directly parallel to each other. The right-hand of the two planes headed directly toward the nearest pulsing light passing right through it, not close, but *exactly* (albeit, to the human eye, from a considerable distance away.) The right-hand plane then abruptly turned sharply left then right and joined up with his companion, continuing on their flight.

I have to say that I was surprised at the height of these aircraft, presumably the same altitude as their target. They seemed to be operating at about half the maximum height of a civilian airliner (eye test best guess) say 15,000 feet. when the UFOs were at their closest to us I would guess their altitude to be about two to three hundred feet at max.

Trying to ascertain their distance from our viewing point is almost impossible, what I can say with certitude is that when using the binoculars it would have been possible to read their number plate quite easily, unfortunatly, whomever was driving the craft was doing so without informing the DVLA. Watching pulsing lights moving higher and higher there is no way to know how high they were in fact climbing, thats why I was surprised at the planes altitude. About five minutes later my heart still pounding with excitement, I first heard then noticed a plane appear from our right, clearly propeller driven at a right angle from the first two aircraft, and fly towards the puffy white cloud (our reference point) now only just visible in the sky. It flew around our reference point in front of this cloud and headed off in the direction it came from. Once again, the accuracy of where the UFOs had been viewed, was spot on, although clearly belatedly. A few minutes later I caught sight of the same plane off to my right zig zagging about presumably looking for something. This aircraft all red in colour with double pods either side of the fuselage but quite small with noticeably straight wings.

Thirty minutes later I saw a total of *six* fighter jets , only just visable as they appeared much much higher than all planes to date, flying in a line across the sky like soldiers on parade, and continuing along the same path taken by the previous aircraft over sea.

Three weeks later at a dinner party, the hostess said she saw my picture in the paper and asked me lots of questions about what we had seen. She remarked that her sibling works for the Ministry Of Defence and suggested that they phone them at their desk. She did just that, and asked them if they could confirm that planes were sent up that day. She was told that they could not access this information as they didn't have the necessary clearance to do so. I shrugged my shoulders and thought that was the end of it.

Two weeks later the lady called and told me that her sibling had been in touch and confirmed that the RAF had indeed sent up two planes that day. BINGO! The fact that the MOD contact persisted and revealed to her what they had found, and she in turn contacted me with this disclosure, shows a willingness to confirm what I had in fact seen.

A few days later I did indeed meet this helpful person and I asked them what military airbase these planes would have likely taken off from. They said "almost certainly, Brize Norton in Oxfordshire." The flying timeline from there to the south coast, lines up perfectly with all the details of this story which is now beyond coincidence. I will forever be indebted to this lady and her sibling's efforts to confirm my sightings. I feel privileged that I was part of this story as it unfolded.

My wife at the time Rosie's account:
"I had been resting my knee when my husband Leo came up with a cup of tea at about 5.50 pm. It was a lovely afternoon and he was looking out of the bedroom window, taking in the beauty of the garden, the birds he takes such an interest in, and the sky. He told me he could see 'a couple of balloon-like things' in the sky, and went downstairs to the kitchen to find his tea.

I got up and looked out of the window and saw two objects, which I didn't think looked like balloons, although it was difficult to make them out as the sun was glinting on them. I too went downstairs to have a better look at them, first with the naked eye and then through binoculars. By this time the things had changed. They were no longer round but more like multi-facetted diamonds, which were pulsating a shining light - that is the only way I can describe the two objects.

By this time Leo's aunties were also observing the phenomenon, unlike anything I had ever seen before. The sun was slowly sinking in the sky, and this made it easier to focus.

The pink hue was still present and the sky was a clear blue, apart from one fluffy white cloud. The objects then slowly started to move further away, at which point two jets appeared, seeming to fly in the same direction.

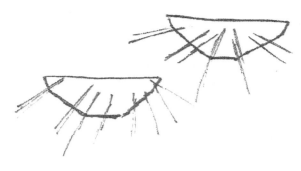

© L.lindsay

Apart from the fact that I saw the objects as upside down to how Leo saw them, I corroborate all the rest, as illustrated above."

May I offer some of my own conclusions to what we witnessed? If these flying saucers do not show up on radar as the Ministry of Defence (MOD) would have us believe, then here is our first coincidence; namely, how could the planes have found the flying saucers as precisely as they did? The first contact plane did not appear to fire on said objects, so was the pilot's intention to fly into the UFO kamikaze style? I think not. But this is exactly what would have happened had the lights not extinguished seconds earlier. Or, had the pilots some prior knowledge of likely outcomes - like moving at such extraordinary speeds as to appear to vanish into thin air? It seems unlikely a pilot would risk leaving a life or death decision until the very last second.

As I was writing this my wife poked her head round the door and asked, "What do you want for Christmas?" I replied, "That pilot's phone number will do."

Another coincidence: How could another plane arrive, albeit late, on the very same course; hit the very same target area with undeniable accuracy, to return from whence it came? A few minutes later the same aircraft was spotted zigzagging about presumably looking for something. Can it also be a coincidence that not only did I spot six fighter jets in the area thirty minutes later flying in a line like soldiers, but disappearing on exactly the same flight path out to sea that the objects had so curiously taken? It would be nice to know if flying saucers were spotted over Northern France on that early evening.

These objects were milling about at plumb centre of a very busy flight path to all points in Europe from Gatwick and Heathrow airports. This fact alone should suffice to turn a light on in the operational head of the MOD, not least because of safety considerations. Yet nothing, zilch! It makes no sense for the MOD to ignore and prevaricate, but to neglect the result of their actions is at the very hub of a story which is now beyond coincidence.

I know very little about radar, but sure as hell these UFOs must! Why would whoever is piloting them show (when we first spotted them), their largest surface area towards the radar systems of the nearby major airports? Could the occupants be testing our defence response times, as archaic as they must seem to high-advanced visitors? This begs a further question: can UFOs hide themselves from our radar screens at will?

Perhaps the answer to this lies in the fact that, in so far as we are told and know, no one yet has been able to catch one.

Some will argue that what we saw was a secret craft, either British or from another country. But if the flying discs belonged to Great Britain why send up planes to seemingly investigate our very own projects? Surely other countries would not be so foolish as to test secret craft close to our major airports? Especially so given our own air force capabilities.

As a humble builder even I know that a disc shape is aerodynamically unsound at earthly speeds. But with enough thrust even a brick could outrun the space shuttle. The point I'm coming to is this; we as humans could not possibly survive and accompany such a craft at such speeds, so who can?

Sorry, I'm not gullible enough to swallow the coincidences that transpired over this one-hour period. To project answers for these troublesome questions I prefer my own very well developed common sense, and a simple logic. I vow never to let this story be swept under the MOD's carpet. An employed source of theirs, obtained through a family friend, of their own volition reported, "Planes were indeed sent up in that area, on that afternoon." I feel quite privileged to have seen the scenario unfold, evermore so in the presence of three other people.

After all this, can we make a sound and reasoned claim for the existence of flying saucers more than black holes? On the sole premise that Professor Stephen Hawking and the world's best scientists have never seen a black hole, whereas I have *seen* two flying saucers.

We hosted a lunch party and one of our guests, a well-educated lady of eighty-six, told us that she had once worked for British Caledonian airways, and became on first name terms with all pilots. She told us, "It was a given that objects were seen very often when we ventured skywards." She continued: "The strange thing was that all pilots' log books had their encounters erased each time." An eighty-six year old British Ambassador's wife, telling porkies? WHY? I think not.

Coincidences

I was once dispatched by my cricket club to find a tour fixture in Sussex, since I was soon to move there permanently. I came across a lovely club and ground called Singleton near Goodwood. I found and then chatted to a member who turned out to be the captain and grounds-man. He said he lived up in London during the week, and spent the weekends down here where his parents lived. I asked him where in London he lived, to which he replied, "A small village you won't have heard of - called Ham, near Richmond." I informed the stranger that I was born in Ham and lived there until fifteen, then I moved to Richmond.

I owned a small open back truck for about seven years; during that time I never once washed it. So dirty was it that somebody had wiped their finger across the side, (in the dirt) writing, "I wish my wife was as dirty as this motor." Funny as that was I ventured to clean and wash the filthy thing. And the very next day the truck broke down! The moral is quite clear, or would be if it were not covered in grime.

One day in my garden an incident occurred, the likeliness of which must have been many a million to one chance in happening. I was trying to fix a freshly washed sheet on a circular washing line, the plastic pegs periodically flying off in the wind. I turned away from the line and walked towards the back door, arms at my side; as I heard another peg fly off, miraculously and with my back still turned away from the garden, the peg obviously had flown up and down, hitting the palm of my right hand. With a reflex honed by decades as a slip catcher in cricket, my palm instinctively closed around the errant peg.

I knew that I could catch anything I could see; but didn't think it possible to catch something whilst looking and walking in the opposite direction! The distance between the line and the doorway was about four metres. A mathematician friend of mine said the odds of this happening again are incalculable, and to illustrate its extreme unlikeliness he offered the following: "There is more chance of winning the lottery five weeks in a row. Or to put it another way, watching Lord Lucan ride Shergar to victory in the Derby!"
Two years after moving to West Sussex, and having just finished building my own house, I received a letter from a developer in London asking if he could visit me. Apparently my garden was clearly large enough to show up on an internet site, and so he wanted to take a look. When he arrived I asked, "Where do you live?" He replied, "Sheen, near Richmond in Surrey." Immediately I told him of my also residing in Sheen, many moons ago. When asked where exactly in Sheen, he said, "Worple Road." Having worked in Worple Road twenty-five years ago and still retaining the photographs of the job I worked on, I showed him. To a mutual astonishment the developer said, "That's my house! That's where I live!" The world is indeed shrinking.

My Heroes

A hero to me is a person who I can look up to for what he or she has accomplished. It is on this note that I would like to indulge myself here.

Not unnaturally, family first. My kids, Mark, Elizabeth, Leo and Jack all are a constant source of joy throughout my life.

And then my two wives (not at the same time): first Jackie – the mother of said children, who at twenty years of age would have paralysed a Miss World Contest.

I accept my part in the reasons for the divorce, and her integral part in bringing up our young kids wonderfully well.

Second Rosie - good at everything except dealing with stress and a tendency to panic, and so a perfect foil for me. I cannot overstate the part she played in the typing of the original manuscript, which would not have been possible without her.

Sam Cooke. For those of you who don't know the man's music – a singer from the fifties and early sixties with a strong, smooth, raspy soulful voice of exquisite range. For over forty five years I've marvelled at a voice beyond compare. Jerry Wexler, famous for being the founder of Stax Records, is quoted as saying, "Sam Cooke has the best voice that ever lived, bar none!" I quite agree.

Muhammed Ali. Quite by chance he was a buddy of Sam Cooke. Over fifty books have been written about Ali, thirty-two of which my middle son and I have read. There is nothing I can add here that has not already been written about a man whom I have never met, but feel I know so well. His accomplishments and belief have carried me along on a wave of euphoria ever since I was twelve years old, and will only stop when I die. If you accept my sentiments about this man, I can tell you we are not alone; millions of people around the world feel just the same. To us all he will always be the greatest!

George Best. He has recently passed away while writing this section, and although not a life hero to me, he was quite simply the best footballer I have ever seen. Pele, Maradona, Cryff, Platini, I have seen them all. Now here's a thought to back up the claim: firstly, he was born with the biggest footballing handicap in being Irish; secondly, he played in an era when pitches were often waterlogged and of shocking quality, making it infinitely more difficult to be skilful. This poses the question: What would Besty have achieved had he been born Brazilian, playing on flat, mud-free pitches with the sun on his back? I contend he would have outshone all others to date, as he very nearly did when the circumstances permitted him.

Trying to compare sporting greats from the past and present is the primary conversation in most public bars when talking about sport. Would Joe Louis have beaten Ali? Would Jessie Owens have beaten Carl Lewis? Would Rod Laver have beaten Pete Sampras? We will never know. I can't think of a better explanation of this point than the following quote:

A sound inclination is to preserve great triumphs from the vandalism of the shortened attention span; only by looking back do we achieve an accurate measure of today's' achievements
                                                                        - Ed Smith

Sport is a perfect metaphor for the human spirit mirrored in our everyday lives: passion, despair, elation, courage, even cheating and the like are all present. In our house my ex-wife is the antithesis of a sport-loving gal; she could never work out the neurotic compulsion needed to follow a particular sport or team.

A team of any sport finding themselves behind in goals or points, and then to come back from the dead to equalise or win - these players hitherto dead and buried are now fighting as if their lives depended on what happened next. A psychologist could not possibly work out these kinds of mental dynamics associated in human behaviour, in the same way my ex-wife could not work it out. This behaviour is not only confined to players; the relevant supporters also go nuts. Many wives flinch at the weaker sex's conception of our sporting heritage, asking, with two minutes left in the game, in the matter of fact way only females possess, "Could you put the bins out?" In my opinion women would be better off riding with this inveterate behaviour rather than fighting it – they can't win.

Bill Young

As he knew not what to say, he swore   **- Lord Byron**

In this book I have referred to Bill Young many times. This is to let you know who he was, and of his lasting and crucial importance to my youth and subsequent adulthood. He was the second mentor I had through my five year apprenticeship. During this time, and for decades after, he was to teach me innumerable tricks about the building trade, and about life itself.

Bill was by any standards a small man with a huge heart, who liked a few drinks - Double Diamonds, a type of pale ale - but *never* during work.

I remember one painful lesson he taught me while we were building a house up on the first floor. I was constructing a brickwork corner, and so was he. I'd built the wall to about 5'6" high; standing back to reflect on my days labour, not without a little admiration, Bill appeared. Without looking at it, though of course he already had, he put a forceful boot against the corner of my masterpiece, and down it came. My protestations were useless, and I had to rebuild it. At the time I could have killed him, but on looking back it didn't do me any harm, and his point was quite clear; this is crap, so do it again.

Bill once told me a story about trouble on a large housing estate in East London just after the war. It seems that the public footpath which led across the site had been closed by the general foreman, which meant the local school kids had to walk around the huge area that was the site in its entirety. Bill warned the foreman that he was asking for trouble, and so it proved to be.

The foreman returned from a bank holiday weekend to find the local kids had started up the cement mixers, and built a wall right across the footpath! Characteristically astute in his observations on all matters concerning building, Bill pointed out to the foreman that the wall was out of upright, and not at all level. I was not told of the general foreman's response, but I can quite imagine it!

If there is one discipline he drummed into me over and again, much more by example than explanation, and one that will stay with me forever, is the freedom and ability to have a row with someone. And from this, to never hold a grudge, to never keep going with your anger, to express the thing and walk away, and to forget it. He managed it with me many times; having given me a fearful bollocking in the moment, once over he'd just as soon act as if he'd forgotten all about it.

Some of Bill's stories from the war deserve an airing. Like the day he woke up with the ceiling all over himself in bed. He got up and went to the window to look at what had happened; all he could see were the piles of bricks where last night a street of houses had been bombed. He'd slept through the whole air raid!

Another time while he was rebuilding a house, a bomb dropped a few streets away, throwing everyone off the scaffold and knocking half the house down. Talk about demoralizing!

One story I must recall was when Bill was working at Winston Churchill's H.Q. in Whitehall. Bill was the foreman bricklayer, so it fell to him to show any visitors around. On this site a long wall was in the course of being constructed with some dozen bricklayers working on it. The great man Winston himself turned up to view the progress. It is well known that Winston Churchill was an avid bricklayer in his spare time, supposedly having helped build a wall in the gardens at Chartwell, and so he took a keen interest in the work and the workers.

He proceeded along the line of bricklayers all standing attentively to meet the great man, with Bill in tow. He stopped halfway along the line to speak to the only brickie not standing to attention. At this point Bill said he cringed at the great man's choice of worker to talk to, because this chap was a communist! Winston asked the trowel, "What are you doing my man?" The man replied, "Minding my own f**king business. What are you doing?" Bill told me that he had no choice but to remove the man from the site, pronto!

I remember Bill telling me about being on site after the war, with long columns of men wanting work, waiting for someone to get the sack. When the next man was offered a job, he was first asked if he smoked. If the answer was yes, the second question would be, 'Do you roll your own?' If the reply was yes again, he was told to piss off. The reason simply was that rolling your own fags took longer, therefore less production.

Bill always said that you must respect everyone on site, because one never knows what an individual might be capable of. The following story illustrates his point. On a site somewhere in London just after the war, a problem developed between the architect's surveyors and the builders. This apparently went on for days without solution, when out of the blue the site alcoholic - a bricklayer's labourer - found himself in the hut housing the site plans. By all accounts he took one look and suggested to all that he may have found the answer. The drunk had come close enough to solving the problem that a debate soon became the gathered throng and the problem was duly resolved. This story sounds like one of those carling drink adverts, only fifty years earlier.

Bill Young was an unintentionally funny man given to profanities, but never in front of women or children. Here are just some of his ubiquitous phrases that I've adopted myself. So many more have been forgotten…

"That wall is so far from level - "it's up and down like a whore's drawers."

If an aperture were too big: "It's like pushing your prick up a shirt sleeve."

I used to sing a lot at work (well, sort of), to which Bill would critique, "If you were singing for shit you wouldn't get a lick."

If something happened that was absolutely a waste of time: "That's like pissing up your own prick!"

Or if you'd produced a poor piece of work he'd point out, "That's too rough for a dog to fuck."

For a show of apparent incapability: "You couldn't organise a blind duck going for a shit."

On the subject of being in debt: "Big debts we can't pay, little debts we can't be fucked about with."

Bricklayers are particularly good at angles, levels and straight lines, or at least should be. To a working chap producing the contrary Bill would scream, "That's about as straight as a donkey pissing in the snow!"
And if one day was chillier than another: "its two coats colder than yesterday."

As a bricklayer looking for work one might ask the foreman, Bill, "What's the rate?" To which he liked to reply, "As fast as you can go."

A saying I have adopted over the years was one that Bill used if he thought someone was incompetent: "He should be working in a laundry washing out socks."
If Bill thought someone was very tight he'd say, "That man wouldn't give you the drippings from his nose."

And on a more philosophical note: "If it's got tits or wheels, its aggravation."

When taking us through the learning process: "If you can't build the wall upright, line it up with that tree, because it's a plumb tree!"

And if he thought something ought to be hurried up he'd holler, "For Christ's sake, put a shovel of coal on!"

Pulling my leg, Bill would tell me, "There is an old Chinese proverb that says if things don't change around here, they will stay the same."

In the movement of something by the smallest amount: "Just a bit more, about the width of a gnat's cock."

While awaiting his turn outside a toilet, "Hurry up for Christ's sake, I'm touching cloth!"
If I was making a mountain out of a molehill: "Don't make troubles out of trifles."

On the subject of remuneration: "I'll see you alright, when I get my glasses."

There is a modern film called "Eyes Wide Shut". Fifty years ago Bill would scream, "Have you got your eyes wide shut?"

He often used to mix up his metaphors, deliberately I think, claiming, "Are you blind in one ear or deaf in one eye?" When used in context on the job such sayings made everyone laugh, and clearly had a lasting and humorous effect on me, as I'm still repeating his little quips fifty years later. Mostly vulgar of course, but that's the building trade for you!

(On the subject of crude and colourful aphorisms, here are a few memorable others from my mate Johnno. After spotting a stunning lady: "I bet she's had enough hickory to make a handrail from here to Reading!" When talking about the number of women he'd slept with: "I've been with women you wouldn't want haunting your house." If you were perpetrating something improbable: "You've got more chance of handcuffing a ghost.")

Bill once recalled to me the situation before and after the war when it became fashionable for workers to strike. He recounted his version of events of the various trade unions all putting their wants and requests to the government of the day: The miner's union, going for broke, asked for an extra six pence an hour; the post office workers asked for four and a half pence; the public transport union claimed four; and the building trade union (of which Bill was an active member) asked for one and three-half pence an hour more.

All the trade unions got what they asked for except the builder's union, who were completely refused. I asked Bill why this was, to which he replied, "Builders have no status whatsoever, and so who gives a shit if builders strike? If the other unions did strike the country would come to a standstill, that's why they got their raise and we didn't."

In my opinion unions have had their day, and are no longer appropriate; nowadays everyone is able to compete on a more or less level playing field in terms of pay, and if you are prepared to work hard in whatever field you operate in, you can succeed. If council house tenants can advance to Oxford, then people from humble backgrounds - union or not - can travel to the moon. It brings a warm glow to think that anyone can achieve status in their lives – even we builders!

When talking about a labourer's incompetence: "His head is like old Mother Hubbard's cupboard: there's nothing in it."

If I mentioned a girl on my scene that needed impressing, Bill would proffer, "Tell her you're a burnt clay artist."

Halfway through a job in Virginia Water, Bill's wife Dolly phoned up early morning to say that Bill would not be coming to work that day, because on leaving his block of flats at half six that morning a milk bottle had fallen (or been dropped) on his head, and this had knocked him out. Sadly Bill Young never really recovered from the effects of this incident – deliberate or not – and only went on to work a few more days before retiring for good. The end of a long and illustrious, if not glamorous career. I can only hope that the offending milk bottle was a gold top as the great man deserved the very best!!
I'm sure Bill would take this line in the best way possible. He was after all, the cream of the crop (pun fully intended).

Bill's life took a considerable turn for the worse two or three years later when on holiday in Cornwall he suffered a stroke. This left him almost entirely unable to speak, only able to utter the words, "fuck, fuck," over and over again, which I am told is quite common for stroke sufferers. As a prolific book reader all his life you would think this a saving grace, but the stroke rendered him unable to concentrate long enough to even read a newspaper. His life pretty much ended there, with Dolly looking after my stricken mentor 24/7. Bill used to tell me such wonderful stories, some of which I have already shared with you. Unfortunately the stroke put paid to the many, many more I have long since forgotten.

Bill died in his early seventies in the spring of 1982; my middle son Leo was born in October of that same year – hence his name Leo William Lindsay. By all accounts Bill was no saint; he liked a drink and a smoke, and gambled moderately on the horses. I'm sure he wasn't the same man to his family as he was to me, however as a young man I was privileged to have been under his wing and in his care, god bless him.
In the desire to find out more information about Bill Young, some time ago I decided to contact his only son, John. Not having seen or spoken to John for twenty-three years, it turned out to be quite a performance! Routing through telephone directories and visiting West Wickham in Kent where I last met him ended fruitlessly. The skipper of my cricket team who lives in Beckenham, adjacent to the area in question, told me of a local newspaper with a section on missing persons.

After a few phone calls a reporter called me and spent forty-five minutes grilling me on John Young, and then very soon the conversation turned towards my upbringing and early life. He wanted to know why it had been Bill and not my own father who had had the greatest influence on me. I ended up telling this journalist about my father's links to the IRA, and a number of other personal facts. Now, bearing in mind my objective of this exercise, I reveal the journalist's piece:

Bricks and mortars

AN IRA sympathiser's son is looking for information about the builder who gave him a career.

Leo Lindsay, 58, was William Young's bricklaying apprentice in the 1960s.

Now he wants to include stories about him in a book he is planning on the building trade.

Mr Lindsay said: "Mr Young taught me how to have a row with somebody and then completely forget it."

He says this advice helped growing up with a father who made him sing IRA songs.

Mr Young died in 1983 but his son John and widow Dolly may still be in the area.

After the headline and four or five words the whole exercise is not only insulting to me but almost useless, the writer homing in on facts irrelevant to finding John Young, or indeed presenting a side of me that would not likely appeal to a potentially helpful reader. Clearly, the so-called journalist was only sensationalising a topic, and doing so in an insulting manner. The editor didn't send a draft, only the article after it had been printed. I called him to say what a disgrace it was, and he agreed to rewrite his piece. We await the outcome of this, and despite a number of phone calls, any kind of useful information about Bill or his son.

Rodders

To know where to begin in talking about this man I've known for about 30 years is rather difficult. In almost all the ways one might immediately observe him, Rodney is an utter disgrace. He is the archetypal village idiot, a shambles. However he ran an insurance brokers for some twenty years, and being a keen cricketer for many clubs at once had most of his team's car insurance policies on his books. He played all over the south of England, recruiting cricketers and policies wherever he went. In short, not short of a brain.

Thus far you may have come to the conclusion that he sounds like a normal kind of chap, but this would be doing him a disservice. The truth is he is quite extraordinary, in all the wrong ways. To observe him is to look at everyone's idea of a pervert, and a dishevelled one at that. His clothes are never worn as they should, and in them he shuffles about at a snail's pace. He wears an unkempt and droopy moustache, and has been known to adorn his bald head with toupee creations absurd in the extreme. He is a picture of incompetence. In addition, all his life he has mumbled to the point of incoherence, and now after a number of strokes he can barely put two words together. A conversation with him is a testing thing. And yet despite the completely regrettable nature of his appearance, movements, and communication, he is in fact harmless. Moreover, if one can look beyond the surface (a real challenge!), it is quite apparent he's rather a nice man, without a proverbial bad bone in his body. I've come to the conclusion that he latches on to me because I tell him to piss off less regularly than everyone else.

More than once I have seen him playing cricket, padded up and going into bat, when someone watching has shouted, "Rodders, look at your car!" All doors open, the boot too, engine running, his work papers flying everywhere. To call him forgetful would be inaccurate, but does he give a stuff? Na!

I lived on a corner plot, and one day while driving past he decided to call in. After about ten minutes I made a cup of tea, and an hour later when leaving I followed him out to his car. He'd parked it right across the corner, almost stopping the traffic. The rear door was open, the driver's door was too, and the engine was still running!

Of course nobody ever got in the car in case they caught something from the interior! Suffice to say his cars were never stolen. He was always getting picked up by the police though, and always for nothing. Looking as he did – shifty and improper - was more than enough to convince any copper worth his salt that something was up, and that this creature needs to be investigated further.

Like the time his ex-wife would not let him have access to his children, so in his innocence he went down to the school gates to take a peek. He was promptly arrested (can we really blame them?) as a suspected pervert, not for the first time; but as I said, everything happens to Rodney.

One story unfolded at teatime in the middle of a cricket match. Our wicket-keeper on that day Alan Hughes - just back from a holiday in deepest France - was sitting opposite me in the middle of a long table as both teams ate their tea. The wicket-keeper was recounting the events of his holiday; his car had broken down in the middle of nowhere and was duly towed into a garage. The attendant asked him who his insurance broker was, to which Alan replied, "Rodney Blickett." The Frenchman threw up his hands and screamed, "Rodney Blickett! Non, Non, Non!" I was at this point halfway through a mouthful of tea and cake, and promptly, involuntarily, proceeded to pebbledash the surrounding walls. People were falling off chairs uncontrollably, the hilarity of the quip with us all for a good five minutes. Sitting at the end of the table Rod was laughing too, but I don't think he knew why. I will never forget the joy, shock and laughter of that moment as long as I live.

This conversation did actually happen, though it is hard to believe. Rodney phoned a member of his team and spoke to the player's wife, asking, "Can Peter play tomorrow?" To which the wife replied, "I'm sorry Rod, Peter died two days ago." "Sod it, "he burst out without thinking, "we're two short for tomorrow." Rodney wasn't being nasty or disrespectful; he was just being himself – wrapped up in his cricket. I know Rod was upset at the news, but his immediate emotion got the better of him, and it just came out that way.

I was told of a story that speaks volumes about the fortunes of Rodney Blickett. He was asked by a rich widow to come round to insure her much pampered cat. The house was huge with a long driveway; on leaving the house in his banged up Ford Fiesta, and having wrapped up the adequate insurance policy with the lady, he promptly ran over the newly insured cat!

On another occasion Rod rang me up, to explain, "I've been mugged by a woman in Soho." "What do you want me to do about it?" I said "I would like you to come with me here tomorrow," said he, "to look for her." It did not occur to him that there are ten million people in London, but that's Rod for you; he lives in a rather small world.

In light of the facts - Rodders has the mind of a child, is the antithesis of a village idiot, and has the style of a man fifty years past his sell-by date – it is ironic to note that he is also hung like a horse. I remember standing on the boundary's edge on match day talking to Rod when he decided to take a pee up against a tree. An older woman walked past, sneaked a peak, and promptly fainted. When she came round, the look on her face was as if she'd been soundly beaten in a cake-baking competition by the village whore.

I'm sure you can work out which one of these gents the great man is...

It has for decades been agreed upon around the amateur cricket grounds in Surrey that were it possible to put Rod on the stage, he would make a fortune. I was sitting in my front room with my three sons when in came Rodders. Nowadays he doesn't have a lot of hair of top of his head, and with a kind of misguided naivety sometimes attempts to mask over this most obvious fact by donning a toupee, as was the case, on this occasion.

Observing this, I suggested, "Why don't you take that dead cat off your head?" My three sons fell about laughing. If you think I was extracting the Michael you would be right, but the unfortunate truth is that Rod has had to put up with much worse from others over the years. He knows I laugh at his expense, but he also knows, as I will now show, that I am unchangeably on his side. The picture I am painting is 100% Rodney Blickett, and also 100% true.

An Unlikely Defence

About two weeks after the event, Rodney told me that his dog Ben had bitten a child, and that the parents had informed the police. I asked Rod to tell me the story from the beginning, which he duly did. I told him to send the police round to me if they should get in touch. Rodney had had a stroke a year earlier and his speech, which was never that good, was now mostly incomprehensible. I felt it incumbent upon me to assist my friend as best I could; the fact that I don't even like dogs didn't come into it.

Ben always seemed a dopey and docile sort of animal, pretty much like his owner I suppose. I understood that Ben was a cross between a retriever and a collie, which I think that qualifies him to be called a mongrel. As such, he even looked like his owner – dishevelled, unkempt, old and doddery.

Obviously I was not present on this occasion or the subsequent days, when further trouble between Rod and the angry dad ensued. I read the statements from all concerned and came to the conclusion that Rod had done as much as he could, and Ben the dog was entirely blameless. One thing that ought to be made clear is that Rod with dog in tow became an easy target for adults and kids alike, because he is so eccentric and shambolic, and slow moving. Ben was frequently attacked simply for being with Rodders.

Approximately two months elapsed when out of the blue Rodney was informed that he was to go to Court to face a charge of being the owner of a dog that was dangerously out of control in a public place. As soon as I read this charge sheet, it seemed to me to be out of all proportion to the story I had heard, and my experience of Ben the dog. I arrived at the local police station in quite an angry mood and asked to see the highest-ranking officer in the station. I spoke to the station sergeant who tried to fob me off. I asked him if the officer whose name was at the bottom of the charge sheet was in the station, and I was told he was not. I made an official complaint there and then.

I was told the Chief of the police station would contact me, which he did, but not until I'd phoned the police station a further three times. An appointment was made and he duly arrived at my house. He was full of contrition, assuring me that the policeman at the centre of the nonsense was a good officer. No surprise there, I thought. I explained that the officer had not even spoken to my friend prior to involving the Crown Prosecution Service. "Why?" I asked, and went on, "How can he be deemed to be guilty when you haven't given him a chance to reply to the charge?". He told me that the officer had called round to Rodney's house several times and had got no answer. I promised to give the situation some thought and get back to him.

I visited the police station again, and for the umpteenth time asked to see the errant officer, which eventually I did, accompanied by his sergeant. I asked the officer why he could not contact my friend, to which he said, "I tried the door three or four times, then gave up." I suggested that he might have left a note. He said, "I did!" At this point I called him a liar, and soon left. If all this wasn't bad enough, it became much worse when we arrived at court. I explained to the Magistrate that I was there to look after Rodney's interests. She treated Rod, and then me particularly, with extreme indifference, to put it mildly. The chairwoman, clearly irked by my presence in her court, told me to keep quiet. She tried to communicate with Rodney, who turned to me for guidance. The Magistrate asked me what he was pleading, I said, "Not Guilty." To then the chairwoman replied, "Leave this court and I urge you to see the duty solicitor, then return!"

The duty solicitor was very nice. He said, "The CPS was willing to accept a lesser charge thereby saving the dog from being put down." I told him, "If we accept the lesser charge we will be deemed guilty in the eyes of the law." I put it to the duty solicitor, "What happens if Ben bites someone else at a later date? With a previous conviction the dog's case would be indefensible." I decided to call the CPS's bluff. "You're a better man than me," he said, "Go for it." We went back into court and the Magistrate asked again, "What do you plead? "Not guilty, madam." By this time she was well pissed off at my insistence not to be tried here and now. She adjourned the case and told us to come back a month later. By this time I was convinced of the dog's innocence, having read all the statements pertaining to this case. There were more than a few contradictions that I'd picked up on, so I felt I was more than justified in calling their bluff and going for it.

Back in court the same Magistrate, probably mortified to see me again, flanked by a white-haired woman on her right and an unmemorable man to her left, said: "Now Mr. Blickett, where is your solicitor?" Rod lifted his arms towards me and mumbled something towards her. She then turned to me and said, "Mr Lindsay, I hope you have taken legal advice for your friend?" "No," said I. "I will do whatever it takes to get this charge thrown out." "I suppose you are pleading not guilty then," she said. "Correct." I told the Chairwoman, "The CPS doesn't have a case, or they would not have wanted to lessen the charge. So on that basis; we want to go to the Crown Court in front of a jury." Clearly irritated, she said, "You can't do that!" I said, "I believe I can, and will!" She consulted the court representative and said, "That is your prerogative." I said, "Yes, I know it is." At this point the white-haired lady on the bench threw her hands in the air and laughed out loud. I knew it was a sign of disapproval, because serial criminals often opt to go before the jury to gain valuable time to regroup. Her actions clearly indicated to me that she already thought Rod was guilty. What price a fair trial, had we given in?

The Magistrate said, "If you go before the jury you must find a solicitor." I told her, "I will defend him in court as a MacKenzie Friend, with the judge's permission." She looked daggers at me, as if someone had just shit in her handbag. She did not wish us well, and dismissed us from the court.

We were met outside by the duty solicitor, who said to me, "Can I ask you what you do for a living?" I told him, and he said,"That figures, I just had to know, because I could not have done what you did." He wished us well and walked off smiling, shaking his head. The CPS's barrister approached us and gave me the telephone number of her boss, the Head of the Crown Prosecution Service in Surrey. I called him as soon as I reached home, and incredibly he knew all about the case. I told him in no uncertain terms to drop this case before a miscarriage of justice took place. He suggested I visit Mr. Blickett's doctor to find out exactly what his condition was and to send him the doctor's report.

Unbelievably, he then went on to suggest that maybe it's not in the public's interest to pursue an invalid in this way. This top man in Surrey was already looking for a way out and, as yet, nobody – not the police, the CPS or the court – had heard our defence. This was not really surprising since I hadn't formulated it yet!

About a month later I received a letter informing us that the case was to be dropped forthwith. Insufficient evidence was the reason given. I thought this strange since the evidence was the only consistent theme throughout the case. In summary, because Rodney was denied his right to answer the charge, due to the police's incompetence, the CPS naturally thought that the case was cut and dried. And the officer who was responsible for wasting thousands of taxpayers' pounds gets a slap on the wrist. I'd like to give him a slap myself.

I'm afraid my efforts on Rodney's behalf didn't end there. I complained about our treatment in court by the Magistrate. The white-haired lady on the bench upset Mr. Blicket and me, as did the Chairwoman, who showed no concern for Rodney's feelings, confused as he was. The court authorities spoke to the Magistrate who remembered the case, but, alas, not their indiscretions. What a pity their memories failed them this time. I checked with the court representative who also remembered the case, but not the bench's transgressions, which was not surprising since he sat in front of the Magistrate's bench and would have needed eyes up his arse to see what happened behind him! So I wrote back to the court saying:"Two out of three Magistrates are liars, and if I had proof, which I haven't, I would make them pay." I also suggested the white-haired lady be sacked for what she did.

To this day we still have not put this issue to bed. We are trying to sue the police for incompetence, but it is proving difficult. Since we were not given the chance to answer the charge, our defence to this day has still not been told. I will endeavour to do so here.

Rod left his dog tied to railings outside a pub while he went in to ask if any lunches were still available – they were not. While he was gone, three children about seven or eight years old started bothering Ben the dog. It seems that the kids started kicking the helpless creature, and it promptly turned round and bit one of them. The kids' parents, who had been drinking in the pub, rushed out on hearing the kids' cries, and the father started kicking the dog as well. The irate father knew Rod and he swung him a right-hander. The child was treated in hospital for his/her injuries. Witnesses were found and statements taken.

The police's part in this drama is nothing short of scandalous. Nearly all officers I spoke to lied to me, covering their backs in a way only cowards will do. The police have still not spoken to Rod, years after the child was bitten. In my opinion the police have failed totally to exercise any sort of control over a case that should never have been brought in the first place. Who are the winners and losers here? Rod and the dog are clearly winners, and so am I, albeit out of pocket! I did try to claim my out of pocket expenses, initially from the CPS, then from the court, but I was told that since I was not a barrister I could not make a claim.

I was written the following by the head of legal services. *"The Court has discretion to grant rights of audience to any person in the proceedings, you were not granted such rights and Mr. Blickett saw the Duty Solicitor on the advice of the Court. Under the circumstances, I can find no authority that allows your fees and expenses to be paid from central funds as you were not required to attend Court and attended only as a friend."*

Subsequently I spoke with the chairman, who said:
"Whilst clearly the defendant had difficulty in speaking, the disability was not such as to require the services of an interpreter; if, however, you did charge Mr. Blicket for your services, then it is for Mr. Blickett to apply for his costs to be paid from Central Funds; the application must come from himself and be placed before the Court for authorisation. Before such sums are paid, the Court must determine whether those costs were actually and reasonably incurred. With regard to your complaints concerning the bench and legal advisor, I have spoken with the Chairman who sat on both occasions, and she does not accept that the bench or legal advisor acted improperly in any way."

These people are so educated they can't see the wood for the trees! Can you imagine what the chairwoman would say – I having called her a liar – about my application for costs? If I wasn't considered necessary in court, how come we walked out scot free? Who called the CPS's bluff? Who stopped a miscarriage of justice taking place? I have of course all documents appertaining to this ridiculous story.

This story as a genuine case is incomplete without the input of the Metropolitan Police, the Crown Prosecution Service or the Court Authorities – who all had their part. The parents and children's side of the story has yet to be told and that of the witnesses' part in the drama needs to be explored too. Clearly, as the primary instigator in this case, I am not party to the above; therefore I can't offer an opinion.

And sadly a most unfortunate end to the tale. One day about a year later, Rod went up to London with Ben. Whilst on Vauxhall railway station he somehow managed to knock Ben on to the track. The frightened dog took off, his lead still attached, never to be seen again. What happened to the dog is anyone's guess, but live railway tracks and metal dog leads don't match. Rod told me later that he'd had Ben for about ten years.

Family

The best way to give advice to your children is to find out what they want and advise them to do it.
                                    - Harry S. Truman

This picture is taken in 1983/4, my three children at the time and I standing in the newly laid foundations of a large extension of the family house for the next 18 years.

Every family must have some amusing tales to tell, and mine is no different. Here are a few chronicles.

My sister Norma, not the most proficient cook you will encounter, once decided to make a jelly; she read the instructions then placed the completed sweet on the toilet windowsill. Back in the late fifties we didn't own a fridge, so the bathroom was the coldest room in the house. Every day the jelly was visited by all and sundry waiting for the thing to set. A week went by and still it hadn't set. I asked Norma to take me through the process of making a jelly; it seemed she misread the manufacturer's instructions, mixing only one square to the portion of water; the errant jelly being so weak it wouldn't have set six months later!

Another sister, Helen, whose daughter Rebecca was responsible for one of the best Freudian slips I've ever heard. A real handful when starting her teens, knew she was to soon receive an injection for Rubella. The unfamiliar word got mixed up with another, resulting in, "When do I have to have this jab for *rebellion*?" As every parent will know - what an asset an antidote for rebellion would be! Imagine bending your kid over the kitchen sink to administer the knockout drop!

My youngest son Jack carries with him a comical air which has been evident from the youngest age. On this occasion in junior school his teacher was going off on one for the umpteenth time because Jack had failed to bring a slip of paper from his parents, of which time was apparently the essence. On and on she ranted, Jack not listening to a word began fiddling in his school bag in the forlorn hope of finding something more interesting therein. Suddenly he came across the errant slip of paper, then promptly whipped it out, and with a triumphant roar yelled, "A-ha! Think again!" Other pupils present in the class have spoken of the scene that followed, every child laughing uncontrollably. I only wish I could have been present myself.

A never ending source of comic observation, Jack once hit the spot in our front room. On this particular day were my other two sons, Mark and Leo, and their mother, with Elizabeth and her friend playing upstairs; the friend's mother expected any minute to pick her up. A car stopped outside and the friend's mother, who had given birth late in life, sat waiting for her daughter. Jack looked at the vehicle and said, "Who is the old goat in the car outside?" Jack was about ten years old at the time. We all fell about laughing, Jack was also laughing, but not sure why.

Way back in the early sixties my sister Norma was the antithesis of a sixties child. She absorbed everything popular and connected with that period, including at one point working for Biba in Kensington High Street. One day a man walked in to tell her he'd come to repair the till, one of those big old antique cash register numbers. He thought it easier to remove the lump and repair it in his van parked down the road. The man and till disappeared, never to be seen again! A cunning ruse!

The reason Mick the builder - whom you've heard about liberally in this book - came into my life was because he was my sister Norma's boyfriend for about four years. They used to live in various bed-sits all over West London, where I was often recruited to help them 'move' in midnight flits. In the world of bed-sitting the properties were easy to manipulate to one's own cause. I once watched Mick wire up his electric fire to next door's meter, milking it for a whole winter!

Once, in a very large house at one o'clock in the morning, with the three of us carrying everything she owned down a grand staircase, Mick tripped over me, and down we went. As you can imagine, the noise woke the landlord; we ran out of the front door into the night chased by the landlord, and others who thought we were burglars!

As a child Norma would try my father's patience time and time again. One Sunday lunchtime, she was still in bed, having danced the night away with her old boyfriend Mick the builder. Dad told her four or five times to get out of bed, and having gotten no reply he threatened to throw a bucket of water over her. Norma took no notice of him, and if she heard him filling the bucket, she did not say so. He stood over the bed and asked her one more time to shake a leg, and again she ignored him, assuming a bluff I suppose. I watched on as he grabbed the bedclothes, ripped them away, and tipped the bucket-full all over her, defiantly she stood her ground horizontally. Norma went berserk, but she never called his bluff again!

Most of my time as a wee boy was not very happy, my father careless to my needs or wants. I remember once I asked him on a Saturday if he could take me to a football match; he walked outside, looked up at the almost clear blue sky but for a few puffy white clouds, and said, "No, it's going to rain." I was possibly seven or eight at the time. Unsurprisingly, sadly, we never ever made it to a football match. The only time I remember going anywhere with him was greyhound racing at Catford dog track in the late fifties. One other memory was staying up late listening to boxing live from America. The bout was Don Cockell's attempt to win the heavyweight championship of the world from Rocky Marciano. I distinctly remember Eamon Andrews' excited voice, and from this point on I was hooked on boxing. This was a primer for a more specific sporting love affair with the man who was to follow a few years later – Muhammed Ali.

Once, there we were sitting in our living room watching none other than the World Cup Final in 1966, on our first television. At one point during the match my father, not a football fan, put his hand towards the back of our television and said, "It's getting hot. I must turn it off." And so he did! We all jumped out of our chairs threatening to kill him if he didn't turn it back on immediately. He obliged, and the rest, as they say, is history.

My Dad had a very thick Irish accent, which he used for his own amusement when our friends came to visit. He would deliberately say something very quickly, knowing full well that no one would understand. His audience would smile politely, unknowingly, which he found highly amusing. He was also very good at cocking a deafen when it suited him. Hence the reason I can speak two languages: Irish and rubbish.

My father used to suffer dreadfully from migraines that would last between one day and two weeks at a time. When in pain the slightest noise would send him into a rage. He would tie a scarf round his head as tight as he could, looking quite the Red Indian chief, while nearly always wearing full length nightwear – what a sight he looked! Washing up, or more specifically drying up the cutlery, was a no-no at times like these since he couldn't stand the noise of knives and forks landing on the draining board.

He once told me a story about being in the RAF during a migraine attack; sitting on his own feeling very poorly, three men started to wind him up. My Dad jumped up with his gun threatening to shoot them if they didn't shut it. He appeared at his own Court Marshal and was exonerated because the RAF doctor said in his defence that he was not responsible for his actions while under a migraine attack.

Once a year, every year, on 24th December my father and I would travel to Smithfield meat market by train, at the ungodly hour of 10:30p.m. The object was to purchase a cheap turkey or two, and there we would stand shoulder to shoulder haggling for the best deal on offer. My job was to lug the chosen bird or birds home in a carrier bag.

Being out at night on my own was not unusual given my father's penchant for Golden Virginia at the end of a day, but being out with him so late was strange to say the least. Once home my mother would pluck the birds, then it was my turn to truss the following day's table guest ready for the oven.

Some seven years later when I was nearly seventeen, my mother was diagnosed with cancer. Not unsurprisingly my father took it badly. He found it hard to sleep while she was in the hospice, preferring to drive all night, anywhere. One evening my father asked if I would like to drive him around and since I was nearly seventeen the timing for practise was perfect. We drove for hours, mostly up in town around Marble Arch, Piccadilly, and through the West End and beyond.

Learning to drive round Marble Arch to Oxford Street was quite an experience, pushed this way and that by uncaring taxi drivers. It shouldn't come as a surprise to know that I learnt rather quickly to handle everything the Queen's highway threw at me, and in the process memorising my way round the streets of London. Despite the regular evening practice I failed my first driving test, for the sole reason that I failed to look both ways during a three-point turn; the examiner clearly ignoring the fact that I had two ears to assist me! The second test started amidst heavy snowfall. Fifteen minutes in, the examiner got out of the car and told me he was cancelling the test. I asked why and he said "it's too dangerous to continue". I then did a U-turn, on passing him I asked if he wanted a lift back to the test centre, he replied "not likely", not surprising really as I was now driving on my own illegally. So due to the six inches of snow, it was third time lucky for me.

During the war my dad served in the RAF on ground security, at airports dotted around the country. One day a bomber plane came back and crash landed, and my dad was called upon to clear up the debris. Whilst doing so he picked up a stray helmet only to find half the airman's head still inside it!

Mother

Talking to my elderly aunt (my mother's sister) about this book, she enquired as to what I'd written about my mother. Having put pencil to paper extensively on behalf of my father, I now feel ashamed to say that so far I've barely written a word about my mother. What I do know is that my mother and father never married. This was due, I thought, to the fact that my father already had a family in Northern Ireland. Not so. Apparently it was my mother who was already married, and left her husband to move in with my father. She was, I recall, almost as tall as my father at about five feet nine inches; quite an Amazon for that wartime period. I guess it's true to say that she was dominated by her partner, working all the hours god sends as well as looking after us all – six in number - while my father himself frequently didn't work.

A tale about my mother's derring-do, around winter of 1946/47. They lived in a flat opposite the entrance to the botanical gardens at Kew. The snow fall at this juncture was the worst ever seen in this part of the world. Bags of coal were available at your nearest power station as long as you collected it. My mother pushed an empty pram from Kew near Richmond all the way to Kingston-upon-Thames and back with a pram full of coal, a round trip of about fifteen miles. Not only did she have the severe snow fall to contend with, she was also carrying moi, aged minus two months. I guess this kind of spirit was one of the reasons why Hitler failed to destroy the English psyche.

Le Chateau

Back in the early nineties my father-in-law and I travelled to the South of France. He, for research work in the region, (soon after he retired). I, to suss out the possibilities of buying some properties to renovate. Bob Killick-Kendrick was a world authority on Leishmaniasis. Bob spent the second half of his life trying to find a cure for a disease prevalent in hot climates that eats away at the roof of the mouth leaving a gaping hole. The disease is carried by parasitically infected sand flies which bite in search of blood meals. When you look around to view what some people have managed to achieve to procure a knighthood, the question has to be asked, "Why not him?"

Despite my divorce from his daughter we still got on quite well whenever we met up. Bob can speak French fluently, or so he thought, until he met my girlfriend of the time. She's English, although she does not look it. Damn it, when she was younger she used to teach French children French, how competent is that? My contribution to French conversation is, 'vive la France,' and 'a bon!' Bob always said that when spoken to in French, if you didn't know what they asked, reply 'a bon' with feeling. It's French for 'REALLY'?

The region we visited deep in the south of France was an hour's drive north of Montpellier, at the beginning of the Cevennes Mountains. Once out the plane the wall of heat was almost suffocating, the landscape burnt and brown. Into a car heading north following the Herault River, the terrain changed from brown to green; higher and higher the road climbs until we reached the nearest town to our destination, Ganges. The twice-weekly market in this small provincial town took my breath away: I flitted from fishmonger's stall, where whole bass, swordfish and shark were on parade; to the outrageous display of cheeses, maybe sixty varieties on show; and then the bread counter, after all we were in baguette country, not to mention the weighty whole-wheat breads in innumerable shapes and sizes; and the vegetable stall was a cornucopia of dark green with red splashes.
I must stop now, I'm feeling hungry! Now half way up Mont Agual in the Cevennes, it was still very warm, I'm told that towards the end of the year, when conducive weather prevails, it is possible to venture to the beach on the Mediterranean (an hour and a half away), to come back later and on the same day travel in the opposite direction to the top of Mont Agual to go ski walking. Not a bad day funning - sunning and eating yourself silly, then ski walking in the snow - not forgetting the dodging of a wild boar or two, and the twitching of the golden eagles overhead!

My guide and I visited a number of chateaux, the details of which I'd like to share with you. We turned off the small road into a driveway about a hundred yards or so long, flanked by vineyards. We parked beside the open garage, and when I looked inside it was quite clear this part of the structure was hewn from the local landscape. The garage was, in effect, a cave, the rest of the structure built on and around the surrounding natural rock. We climbed the stairs to the entrance and on through to the main room, some sixty feet in length, its width about twenty-five feet. I distinctly remember thinking that all I need to divide this cathedral sized room into a dozen units was a lorry full of blocks.

The ceiling was so high that I could have built a minstrel's gallery all the way round! There were various other outbuildings to the rear, and a hedge bordered on one side which I forced my way through to take a look. If I could have jumped over this hedge at five feet high (and in days gone by I might indeed have tried), I would have killed myself! No more than four feet behind was a sheer drop. At the bottom some fifty feet down was a river, or at least there should have been; instead a small shallow stream. I stood there trying to picture how the scene would look in severe rainfall.

Anyone thinking of buying this church-like building would have to discount the possibility of children being present. The vineyards were leased to the locals of the village, maybe ten dwellings in all. I suppose all the village families could have lived in this one property. The strangest business lay five hundred yards further up the road; bearing in mind that we were in the back of beyond, civilisation at least twenty minutes' drive away, we found a restaurant; not French, not Moroccan, not even English – have a guess – and I kid you not – Yugoslavian!

Of the chateau I was informed by the agent of the price – £14,000 English pounds! The agent could not wait to inform me that the owners would take an offer of £10,000 – a bargain, or a folly? What do you think? We visited six or seven more properties and I built up a more than useful collage of photos and facts of what was on offer. Like so many endeavours in life nothing came of it beyond the negative affirmation to put ones energies into other areas of possibility.

I would like to mention some of the work related tasks my father-in-law asked me to help him with. His business, as you can imagine, was catching sand flies, and then dissecting them. Tonight I was a guinea pig; some would say quite a good choice, given what I look like! This involved yours truly doing nothing more than sitting in a tent at about midnight attracting sand flies; with the use of a tube via a vent axia at one end - to draw air into the tent -and the other into the night sky. In the middle of this tube was a wall of fine electrified wires. The sand flies would smell me sitting in the tent and think *blood*, and down the tube they would be drawn, colliding into the wires, sparks flying all round; quite a sight in the dark. The shock stunned the flies, which were then collected and tested for Leishmaniosis.

The Prof had set up a temporary laboratory in a local school to dissect the unfortunate sand flies. Needing to know at what atmospheric level the infected sand flies were flying at, and being a clever bugger, he came up with the idea of commandeering two model plane enthusiasts from Weybridge. The planes, now modified with pouches at the front, flew around, hopefully, picking up infected sand flies.

My last word on this trip; approaching Gatwick and flying at forty-five degrees for about twenty minutes through thick cloud, some people were shouting and screaming as the clouds tossed the plane backwards and forwards. At last the plane burst through the clouds just above the runway to land safely. A few years later upon thinking it over, the question struck me: how thick or deep was the cloud that day flying at 200 mph, at forty-five degrees, descending for approximately twenty minutes? All I know is the cloud was so dense and dark it seemed as though we were moving at one thousand miles an hour! I never want to experience it again.

Shocking

The following story is one where my son Mark managed to avoid a serious injury. Halfway through an extension to the rear of my house the roof was already on, inside and dry. I'd spent all day building honeycombed dwarf walls, bedding 4" x 2" wall plates levelled to receive floor joists. The little girl next door was in and out all day playing with Mark, about six then. At least four times throughout the day she managed to knock or push these levelled and bedded wall plates out of level. My shouts of, "are you coming in or out," fell on deaf ears.

By now the extension-lead light hung on the wall shining brightly, but not for long. Scrambling over the small walls she caught her foot on the loose cable and the light and holder fell down. The light went out, but the bulb did not break, so I picked up the little girl and deposited her over the fence. The extension now in semi-darkness, I picked up the lead light and extracted the bulb, dashing the useless article at the party wall in anger. In the meantime Mark had been nosing around, had picked up the bulb holder minus the bulb, and proceeded to poke a curious thumb into the bulb fixture. The result was, inevitably, a loud scream. I rushed to his aid, the bulb holder now stuck to his thumb. One of the two pins inside the bulb holder had fused into Mark's thumb. I pulled the two apart, and realised that Mark's rubber wellies had saved him and me from a tragedy for which I would not have forgiven myself. The little girl's antics had taken my eye off the ball. A lesson and story I will never forget.

A Troublesome Loaf

In the middle eighties my family departed to Greece on holiday. Being inundated with work meant I couldn't join them. Driving home in my escort van about six o'clock in the evening I was stopped by a squad car, and told to remove myself from the vehicle. Many questions later I was informed that the police computer showed I was not the owner of the van! I told the officer that I'd been the owner of the van for eight whole years, but they remained adamant and disbelieving, checking the thing out.

I looked at my watch - the shops were about to shut – and I required a loaf of bread, pronto. To the coppers I mentioned I'd be back in a jiffy, and then I turned and sprinted to a shop, a mere sixty yards away. On leaving the shop with the loaf tucked under my arm I was surprised to see one of the officers standing outside waiting for me. It seems both coppers had chased after me, believing me to be a guilty car thieving crim, making a run for it!

Back at the van and still not happy, nay, distinctly less happy than they had been, the officers followed me back to my house, insisting on entering my property. Whilst talking to one policeman I noticed the other nosing about. On entering the kitchen I found the copper going through some drawers; I flew at him, and told them both to piss off sharpish or I'd throw them out. And depart they did. To this day I still don't know what that was all about.

(Incidentally, the shop Londis where I purchased that loaf must have a telephone number similar to mine, because folk are forever phoning up asking "Is that Londis?" I tell them we've had this number for the last twenty-five years.)

My father told me a tale when he was a boy during the twenties in Belfast, Northern Ireland; he and a mate had changed clothes, piling them neatly at the foot of the ladder. When they returned their garments had disappeared. Looking around they spotted a wild goat that just happened to be chewing a shoe; the consensus of opinion was that this animal had eaten their outfits!

Wasps and a Dead Cat

During my time in the building trade I've tried to combine the things I've seen and learnt with the eye-opening experiences of my children. If I happened upon something interesting on the job I'd keep it to show my children. Inevitably I'd find old newspapers - some from a century ago - under floors or in roofs, and would spend hours with my kids' reading out aloud some interesting facts of the day. I've also carefully removed the odd wasp nest with a palette knife and taken it to my children's school for all the kids to observe. If you have never seen a wasp nest close up, take any opportunity you can get to do so, because it knocks into a cocked hat most other wonders of this world, especially the manmade structures. The engineering is more precise than anything man could achieve, the 'workmanship' as good as to be breath-taking. The humble wasp; can sting you with its rear end and also captivate you with its ingenuity and architecture.

I once found under the floor a dead kitten, or to be more precise the skeleton of a kitten. What was unusual about this find was that as the animal lay on its side the flesh underneath had disappeared, leaving a perfectly preserved skeleton, while on the top side the fur was intact, showing the animal as the kids would recognise it. The effect was to show both the inside and outside of this kitten as if in 3-D or x-ray mode. The kitten still had a leather collar round its neck. This skeleton was on show in a glass case at my children's old junior school, along with various wasp nests.

Black Face

No one has ever called me a racist, but if they should I would recount this short tale involving all my children. On this particular day both we parents were absent from the house, the brood left in the hands of my eldest Mark, aged about fifteen. A knock at the front door sent the kids scurrying to the window adjacent to the door; the visitor was informed that I was not at home, whilst the front door stayed closed. My wife and I spent the next three days quizzing our children trying to ascertain who the visitor was, how tall, short, fat or thin, etc. Running out of options I ventured, "Was the man black?" "Of course," they shouted in unison. These kids, as they tend to be, had not seen the fact that the black face of this chap was a distinguishing feature; as far as they were concerned he looked the same as anyone else.

Working Class

Throughout my working life the phrase "working class" has cropped up time and time again. What does it mean to a self-employed man doing his own thing?

As a young man I was led to believe this applied to people who were wealthy, or at least rich. If that's true then most of this country is in this particular category, right? When I was a boy my elder sister started going out with a man whose father was by any standards very wealthy. My sister married this man John, and the set of circumstances that preceded this union played a large part in my formative years as an apprentice.

The point is this: although John's dad had three jewellery shops, John, having joined the family business, was working day and night, and at weekends. No one would have called John working class in those days, but he worked harder than anyone I knew. Clearly the phrase 'working classes cannot be taken literally to mean someone who works hard. More likely it means a person who did not have the advantages that John had in his earlier years. In my humble opinion, a person who has had an expensive education cannot be categorised as working class. These days' people reach very high office from relatively modest educational beginnings, and long may this continue.

As an unhappy chappy I feel I couldn't be included in this or any other group as a child, and my education suffered as a result of my father's allegiance to the Irish Republican Army. He would say to me, "Don't trust anyone, you are better off on your own." So I grew up thinking I should be a loner, with my father showing the way and ignoring his only son. He doted on my three sisters, although I later found out that all was not well with their relationship either. My mother died when I was seventeen. At forty-eight years old, she'd had a tough time looking after four children and my father.

I don't think my father was inherently lazy, but what laziness he had become more prevalent with age. Taking this as historical fact, the credit for me becoming a grafter came from my association with Bill Young, not my father. My father used to keep a gun in the house. Quite why, I don't know. On the occasions that I saw it, the gun seemed to me to look as if it belonged to a bygone age. As a young boy of about seven I used to listen to daring, if not rather improbable tales from Northern Ireland; like women digging up cobbles on the streets of Belfast, heaping them up ready for IRA sympathisers to stone any unwary policemen. I don't want to turn this book into a religious divide, so I won't, particularly given what I said about religion in a previous chapter – namely, that I couldn't give a monkey's about it.

Back in the winters of the late fifties my father used to delight in helping traffic, during the infamous 'pea soup fog'. I remember we'd walk three-quarters of a mile to the nearest parade of shops in Ham - between Richmond and Kingston, in Surrey - at the end of which was a crossroads and on one corner an exit road from a British Aerospace Factory.

The main road was quite wide, and consequently when the fog descended and the factory workers poured out into the main drag, the kerbstones seemed to disappear, the visibility at times no more than the length of your arm.

My father used to take great pleasure in standing in the middle of the crossroads with a torch, directing vehicles away from the factory towards Kingston or Richmond. We might spend two hours untangling dozens of cars sat bumper to door, looking for the kerb. In searching for the roadside some cars had turned full circle not knowing where the hell they were. All you could see were headlights trying to break through the fog, and the exhaust fumes eventually drove us home. My dad would talk about his night's entertainment to anyone we bumped into on our way home, or on subsequent days.

I only recall this helping side of his character manifesting itself on such occasions; mind you this pea soup fog was a common occurrence in those days. Sometimes it would freeze heavily, making the journey hazardous, but no less fun. Towards the late fifties, and seemingly overnight, the Clean Air Act was introduced putting an end to my father's singularly charitable activity.

As a kid growing up I needed, as all kids do, a father who I could look up to as a good role model. My father rejected me for good at about the age of fourteen, by which time my own senses told me how to behave. I didn't understand why the other children shunned me at school, just thinking that I must be an arsehole like they used to say I was. A school playground is not the place to be if you are a loner. I probably survived secondary school because my elder sister was, for my first two years there, head girl.

For the decade between fifteen and twenty-five I was a mess; going through my apprenticeship, losing my mum, leaving home and fighting my dad. About two months prior to leaving school at fifteen my dad said, "What job are you going to do when you leave school?" I replied, "I don't know." My father suggested, "Why don't you become a bricklayer?" And that was it - the rest is history.

I was blundering along in my mid-twenties when I learnt, seemingly overnight, to stand up for myself in a way I hadn't been able to before. I will admit that I went too far and became arrogant. It was not until I reached the age of about forty-one when I realised the effect I was having on those around me. Dogmatic, argumentative, bloody minded; I must have been a nightmare to have been around, and I must apologise to all who were on the wrong end of my tongue during those years. Despite this, with my ex-wife I brought up four children who share broadly the same values, and have grown up knowing the practical difference between right and wrong, between good and bad.

The years after this period - from the early forties to the present day seventies – have been the best days of my life, easily. Knowing my children have a better education than I had is deeply satisfying. Now, I really enjoy when my boys bring their mates round and I tell them a few stories about the characters in this book. As a consequence of having some sort of rapport with my children's mates strengthens my relationship with my own boys. All three have told me at various times that their girlfriends and mates like to visit me because of the warmth generated in my house, something it seems not all kids experience in their own homes. To me this is clear proof that I made it as a dad. A typical example of the rapport between my kids and me; dressed up and venturing out of the door, my boys might say, "Going to a fancy dress party again Dad?" To which I reply, "If you boys want to borrow my clothes, you only have to ask."

You might ask what about my daughter Elizabeth; I always get on well with her on the rare occasions we get to meet up. Unfortunately this is not often enough for me. She lived with her mother after the split in 2001, and within a few years I moved out of London for the south coast. Now in her thirties I take Liz to dinner occasionally. She's old enough to make up her own mind about who is or is not at fault in the break-up of the family home. I'm hopeful one day she'll see that the split was not one person's fault; she has only ever heard one side of the story to date. I have no wish to discuss my relationship with her mother to Elizabeth; me and time have moved on.

Fainting Jack

Coming home from work one day approaching my house, about a hundred yards away I could see an ambulance outside. As I drew up alongside a paramedic appeared in a hurry, carrying my youngest son Jack, five months old. I shouted to my wife, now following the paramedics, "What's happened?" She said, "Jack's stopped breathing." It turned out that his temperature had climbed too high and he'd blacked out. What a shock that was. We were told later that this is quite common. Before Jack was to reach five years old he had another four such fits.

One of these involved his older brother Leo. Jack was strapped in the back seat of his mother's car, Leo seated beside him, while their mother nipped into a pharmacy. Leo, about four or five years old at the time, could see Jack turning blue and struggling to breathe. He removed himself from the car and ran along the main road and into the shop.

The poor kid had to make a judgement to brave the main road and his mother's possible admonishment for having left the safety of the vehicle. He reasoned quite rightly that his brother's predicament was more pressing. His mother returned in haste to administer due care, as she had done for all our children, by loosening the clothing particularly around his neck. We'd been told that Jack would grow out of this, and thankfully he has. Why are parents not told about this common affliction? My wife along with a few mothers approached our GP, where collaboration resulted in a pamphlet for parents, taken as we were by surprise.

Colin and Porky

Way back in the mid-eighties my four children would encourage me to make up stories on the hoof, or in this case, in bed. One story I can still recall goes as follows. And whether you laugh at my efforts or not, year after year they loved them!

"Colin the cow and Porky the pig were cycling down the road, porky complaining that he was hungry, as usual. As they came upon a school which was closed for the day, Colin suggested breaking into it to look for food. Porky thought this a great idea. Colin climbed up the drainpipe and through the window. Now in the school kitchen, Colin rummaged through the fridge, periodically dropping food through the window to the waiting Porky pig below. The fridge now empty, Colin made his way back through the window and down the drainpipe to re-join Porky, but once down he could not find his friend. "Porky, Porky," he shouted. Eventually Colin spotted Porky sitting in a heap up against a hedge. "Where is our food?" cried Colin. "What have you done with it?" "I was rather hungry," said Porky. "Do you mean that all that food is in your stomach?" exclaimed Colin. "You greedy pig!" With that Colin picked up the gluttonous pig and promptly threw him in the little duck pond nearby. The pig's bicycle soon followed, and Colin stormed off, still hungry."

I told you not to laugh! But when first heard in about 1985 this story went down a treat, and was henceforth requested almost nightly for the next decade! What I remember most is the fact that sometimes when in a hurry I'd try to skip little bits of the story, to which they would all shout in unison, "You've forgotten a bit! Go back to the beginning and start again!" I receive as much pleasure looking back on these times as I did regaling this story and many other stories back then. I don't think my wife was privy to any of these bedtime story-telling sessions with my gang; she never mentioned that the kids had told her about the stories, which is rather a shame.

My eldest son Mark was looking forward to joining the big boys at middle school. When the big day arrived, and passed, that evening I ventured to him, "How did it go?" "Quite good," he replied, "but when do I go to the next school?" He was under the impression that this was it - one day at school and on to secondary education! I then asked him what he liked most about his first day; his response cracked up the PTA committee when I recalled it a month later. "I liked school dinner the best, particularly the mashed potatoes." "Why?" I asked. "Because it had nuts in it." Not lumps, just nuts! We never did put him right on that.

I once found myself and four attendant kids tobogganing in Richmond Park. The eldest Mark at the front, then Elizabeth followed by Leo, as I stood upright on the runners holding Jack in my arms. Down we sped, until the hitting of a large bump at the bottom resulted in cartwheels for us all! Still holding onto Jack I landed quite heavily, and expecting tears all round I was astonished to hear a collective, 'gain, 'gain!" (Again).

Memories like these are unforgettable, as is a story recalled by my eldest. When he was about fifteen years old he went on a school skiing holiday to Italy; his first journey down the piste resulted rapidly in a visit to the bushes. Shaking his face clear of snow, not to mention a little reddened with embarrassment, he came to see that the trees were full of unfortunate souls like him!

Tim

I am not sure where to place this very sad story, so here it is under families.
When I first met Tim, my ex-wife's only brother, I couldn't help but notice how handsome he was. At school he was a part time actor, sometimes getting picked up from school by a Rolls-Royce, and chauffeur driven to the studios. Tim once had a fairly large part opposite the well-known French actor Louis Jourdan in the film "Walk a Crooked Mile", and also played a small role in "Chitty Chitty Bang Bang".

As much as I don't like what I am about to reveal, it is relevant in my opinion to Tim's current plight. Tim's father, mentioned earlier in this book, was a world renowned professor in the field of entomology at the London School of Tropical Medicine and Hygiene. As you can imagine, Tim's Dad was never at home, often spending weeks and months away from home, mostly in the jungle somewhere. Incidentally, the number of countries he has visited so far amount to seventy-five, quite a traveller. When he did come home all he wanted to do was relax, and to do anything other than talk about what he'd been up to was considered by him a bore. Whilst he and I never had much in common he tolerated me and I endured - along with his family - the selfishness.

Despite this, Bob and I always respected each other; for me, anyone who couldn't afford to attend university, instead learning at night school and working his way up the ladder to the top deserves all our respect. Tim's mother was an extremely capable secretary, but found it difficult bringing up three children virtually on her own, despite money not being a problem.

An incident I recall back in the early seventies did, it seems looking back, sow the seeds of Tim's misfortune. Having been invited reluctantly to Sunday lunch, and having almost finished, Tim left the table to answer a knock on the door. He returned to tell his mother that a friend was now waiting in the next room for him to finish lunch. His mother, in her infinite wisdom, kept Tim waiting for a full hour before letting him go. At the time I considered this rather cruel, unnecessary, and ultimately foolish. Tim's resentment towards such behaviour was beginning to manifest itself. His mother was clearly fed up with her lot and was liberally taking out her frustrations on all those around her; not only her two older daughters and me too, but especially the young and impressionable Tim.

Fifteen years or more later, Tim was sectioned under the mental health act. At this point I was quite close to him, and insisted to the police and doctors present that I would take Tim to the hospital myself; they refused saying that Tim had to be arrested first and then taken by the authorities to the hospital. Tim locking himself in his bedroom made the dreadful situation worse, and the police wanting to knock the door down to get at him seemed to me to be overly aggressive considering the boy I knew was no danger to anyone.

However with no option left I asked the policeman in charge if I could break in for them, because Tim would at least first see a familiar face, and might not react badly. I stood at the top of the stairs; sledgehammer in hand, the police - about five in number - right behind me. At this point Tim was threatening to jump out of the window if we came into the room, so it was imperative the door be opened quickly, to stop any mishaps. My emotions and adrenalin were now at full tilt, and it was because of this that, as I swung the sledgehammer, I missed the door stile, only hitting the glass in the door. Knowing that speed was of the essence I tried again; this time the door positively flew open, and there was Tim was sitting on his bed.

The first copper to enter the room roughly grabbed Tim round the head, so I in turn threw him out of the way to give Tim a cuddle; and there we sat on the bed quietly while the police and two doctors filled in the paperwork. I escorted Tim out to the waiting ambulance, and off to the hospital we went. I hung about for hours waiting for the doctors to finally usher me away. While waiting I managed to collar a doctor and asked the question, "How can you tell if anyone is schizophrenic?" His reply was entirely logical. He said, "If you were brought here and locked up against your will, how would you react?" I recall responding, "I'd pull the windows and doors off their hinges to escape, if necessary." "Exactly," replied the doctor.

All that I've learnt, seen, and heard since leads me to believe that his relationship with his parents and in particular with his mother is responsible for this shocking unfolding of circumstances. Tim told me many times that he could not handle his mother's relentlessness assault on his senses that she refused to listen or take in anything he had to say. Many times, he said, he'd called his mother some disgusting names, and of the things he'd like to do to her to shut her up. Tim was looking for a reaction, but mother always knew best, voraciously about her task of telling him what he need do and be.

In a mad moment many years after his sectioning I relayed my thoughts to his mother, who proceeded to blame anyone but herself. The sorry mother-son relationship was clearly made worse by the constant absence of the father, who, when Tim was a teen, walked out one day, never to return, leaving him at the mercy of his own mother's frustration, her man-hating tendencies coming to the fore and pointed directly, solely, at Tim. It is all too easy looking back and with the benefit of hindsight to say who was responsible. Could we all involved have done more? Regrettably, the answer to such a question is so obvious as to be completely irrelevant.

For me the most upsetting part of the drama apart from Tim's demise would be that as a young man observing from an outside perspective the miscommunication and abuse, I could see the seeds growing. Many times I tried to speak out – at least as I remember it I did - but was considered an uneducated idiot whose opinion was not required, desired, or listened to. If anyone has lived a wasted life it is surely Tim, now hanging around waiting for his time in this life to run out. I fondly remember the fun times Tim and I had while he worked for me on site, albeit intermittently. Maybe some of what I saw and disapproved of made me realise what I had to achieve as a parent.

Perhaps not surprisingly, as with many people when they get older, Tim's mother has mellowed considerably nowadays and at recent family gatherings she's been happy to stop and chat to me.

Brother In-Law John

The late sixties and before the technological revolution really became accessible to all, my prosperous brother-in-law used to spend his money on all manner of gadgets; wristwatches and TV's and hi-tech kitchen appliances like motorised carving knives, and all that crap. I remember first laying eyes on my first home video recorder, a Betamax, which was about the size of a wardrobe; the blank video tapes the size and shape of a suitcase. The blank tapes, I'm told, cost twenty pounds back then. Of course John, like anyone else, is entitled to spend his own money when and how he likes.

I have been told many times, and I suspect it to be true, that the hungriest person on god's earth is a first time millionaire; having made his or her first million, is now positively bursting to make their next one.

Back to John. At his huge house in Richmond one afternoon Harrods delivered five pounds of potatoes and two pounds of carrots. Goodness knows how much that cost! I spent a lot of time in this house in the sixties and seventies, and very grateful I was to do so. One Christmas I turned up without my wife who was ill, the four children in tow, the youngest Jack about six months old. At some point in the evening I laid him down on the floor to change his nappy. Later I was collared outside the toilet by a man unknown to me.

He turned out to be a solicitor, also with four kids. To me he mused, "I could never have done what you did earlier, changing your child's nappy, particularly in front of an audience." With heaps of money and status, but incapable of changing his child's nappy! When will fathers wise up to the fact that the clock ticks faster with time, and that to spend it with your kids is to receive the kind of benefit that cannot be bought back at a later date.

One summer while my sister and brother-in-law were away on holiday, an ex-girlfriend of mine was looking after their house. One evening going home from work I passed 131, there was a small furniture van parked in the driveway. Driving home I wondered what my ex, Helen, was doing with a large van, four days later I found out burglars had cleaned out my sister's house in broad daylight and the only person to see them was me!

In the late sixties my sister employed a succession of au pairs from France, Spain and Portugal. Did I make the most of the company of these girls? What do you think? What would you do as a late teen lording it up in a house beyond your wildest means?

One Christmas night at least fifteen of us were watching the film about man-eating plants, "The Day of the Triffids." John's garden was huge, with a vast illuminated lawn. John sneaked out and grabbed a white sheet and a previously cut branch, and appeared into the floodlit portion of the garden sending most of the women apoplectic. Without such amusing interludes at this house, at such a very difficult time in my formative years, life could have been a good deal nastier.

Back in 1973 when it became certain I was getting married, my prosperous brother-in-law suggested that he buy a house which I would then turn into two flats, and he would sell one of the flats to me for whatever it cost him. He was as good as his word and I spent every night after work doing another day's work on this flat, which entailed brickwork, plastering, painting, concreting and labouring night after night for four months. I purchased the top flat at a price I could afford, and John, as far as I know, still owns the bottom one in South West London.

Author working on the flat above.

At a time when my children were aged between thirteen and three, periodically I used to manufacture a sort of fire drill, since not all of our double glazed windows upstairs could be exited quickly, safely, or at all. This concerned me, hence the drill. I used to assemble all four kids and move from room to room explaining which rooms to proceed to in the event of a fire. I would explain that if the stairs could not be used they should move quickly to a room where it was possible to open the window wide enough either to escape or for an adult to enter. For whatever reason I recall my ex-wife was singularly unimpressed with my safety modus operandi.

Liz

This is my only daughter and I on my (second) wedding day in 2005

I write this on the very day of hearing that the Conquest Hospital in Hastings, East Sussex announced a new surgery technique. This prompted me to recount my daughter's own experience at the same hospital, and with the very same surgeon I have just read about. Way back in 1980 Elizabeth was born with dislocated hips, and fortunately this was diagnosed early; her first six months were spent entirely encased in a metal and plastic-coated frame. This frame, solid in construction, came over her shoulders and round her waist, tucking under her pelvic area, forcing her little legs apart, the idea being that the ball joints would stay in their sockets and grow at the same rate.

Unfortunately this was not entirely successful; the ball joints being bigger than the sockets meant that the hip came apart and dislocated on a regular basis. Having been born at Roehampton Hospital in West London, she was referred to Westminster Children's Hospital where she was monitored until the age of fifteen. What happened from here on in is a little sketchy to me, because of my enforced non-involvement in my daughter's welfare;as my ex-wife was not forthcoming with information. An appointment was made to see Professor Acroth. After six months had gone by I enquired to my ex-wife, "Why the delay?" She said, "Mind your own business." As if it was not mine!

At this time all six of us were living in the same house, all with our own bedrooms. Again I asked the question. "I don't know," came the curt reply. I resolved to find out why the appointment had not been confirmed or acknowledged. To cut a long story short, the professor in question had retired. We were now up the creek without a paddle. Further investigation revealed that the pioneering reconstructive surgery professor had two assistants now working elsewhere. It transpired that one was working in Bristol whilst the other was in Australia on a break, but soon to take up a post at an orthopaedic hospital in Hastings. Since we did not know either surgeon, we plumped for the nearest one to us, which was Hastings.

An appointment was eventually made and the day arrived. Ten minutes before leaving I was informed that my attendance was not wanted or required. To say I was upset is an understatement given my efforts to arrange the appointment. My wife had put her irritation and frustration with me to effect, and made a quite evil last minute change. Only now can I say that she wasted more than six months by not wanting to push the London hospital administrator around. One thing I have learned throughout my life is that nobody is exempt from a gentle push or a forceful shove, not a doctor or a hospital. I know for a fact that my ex-wife dislikes my proclivity to force an issue; she finds it embarrassing.

Reconstructive surgery, as I understand, required building up the hip socket around the ball with a graft from the thigh, enabling the ball to stay engaged in the socket. Clearly Liz needed a new hip, but unfortunately at sixteen years old she was thirty years too young. I believe hips currently only last ten to fifteen years each, so buying time was the order of the day for her. Maybe a new joint that lasts longer will be invented soon. I hope so.The surgeon who operated on Liz is the very same consultant named in the newspaper as pioneering this new treatment. Coming up to date, Elizabeth's hip is still wobbly, but stable and due for further treatment in the coming years.

Leo Junior

My middle son seems to have inherited most of our family's brains put together. On leaving school he asked me, "What should I study at university?" (Does this son asking father what to do in his next phase of life sound familiar? It is lovely to note that where my choices were surely limited, his were really not.) As the world was his oyster I narrowed the options down to two, as I saw it. First, I asked him, "What do you want out of life?" He replied, "I want a job where money would not be a problem, and a car and a family of my own."

I suggested law, on the basis that with this as his educational background, any employer would take him on, no matter what he eventually decided upon as a career. The other option in my mind was accountancy, because the number crunchers hold the world's money in the palms of their hands. The example I gave Leo at the time was as follows. An accountant might say to a client, "I can save you two hundred thousand pounds this year, and for this I will charge you twenty grand." No client would argue about that suggestion, and of course you would know he had the funds to pay you. Another benefit of these two professions is that when qualified you can set up yourself and become self-employed. Leo now has a Law degree under his belt. (Not that he uses it mind you)

Brian the Public Schoolboy

My sister-in-law was married to Brian, a well-educated public schoolboy who possessed the rather curious trait of making appalling decisions. This meant he often made the same mistakes over and over again. He worked briefly for me when one of his many business ventures collapsed, soon claiming, "This is an easy way to make a living." What in fact he could see was me making it look like an easy way to make a living, on account of my time spent – the small matter of twenty five years - on the job.

An educated brain clearly thought his better schooling would bridge the gap; this too was to prove a duff idea. Before becoming a builder his first business venture that I am aware of was to me a damn good one. (All this information comes, albeit thirty years ago, courtesy of his long suffering wife Anne and her sister, my ex-wife Jackie.) He decided to make those pear-shaped cushion seats filled with polystyrene balls, which one sat down on and wiggled one's backside around in, so the seat took the shape of your rear end. A consumer novelty come and gone nowadays, but back then in the mid-seventies this would have been novel indeed. He found an old warehouse in London and recruited some old dears for stitching purposes, and set to work making the said bag seats. We had one in our house for twenty years or so.

Brian placed an advert in a Sunday supplement, which cost him one thousand pounds. The response was very positive indeed, and lots of orders ensued. I was informed at the time that Habitat became interested and ordered a substantial number of chairs. Unfortunately Brian and his partners didn't see this coming and fell between two stools; feeding Habitat, or making the chairs in small quantities. Apparently they did neither and paid the price. A shame really.

After this he upped and left for South Africa. Selfishly alone, Anne followed a year later. Brian started a driveway block-laying company, which I understand was building nicely. Then the South African police appeared one night, took him away, and deported him over night. To this day I don't know why! It was left to Anne to sell up and ship home all they owned.

Fast forward to the late eighties. Brian believed he could operate as a builder in organising both work and tradesmen alike. The problems started when one of his tradesmen walked out leaving him on his own. With no practical experience to fall back on, he struggled to maintain his momentum. He worked as a builder for many years then went bankrupt, owing many a thousand to many an individual. Their house in west London was sold, and the sequestrator who was appointed royally ripped them off, leaving Brian and Anne with just one thousand pounds each. Everyone told Anne to hold on to her half of the monies, but he grabbed it in the end. Not for the first time, then, Brian walked out of Anne's life. Good riddance I say. I am told he is now a ceramic tiler; the only craft he would admit to learning after what must be nearly twenty years!

Mrs Priest

Looking for a place to live away from home I answered an ad in a local post office in Teddington, and called round to view. Mrs Priest met me at the door, an old lady who was very obviously not used to strangers popping in. I found out years later that Mrs P was horrified at seeing this brawny and scruffy chap standing there. As an early twenty-something and Mrs P pushing seventy, we clearly had nothing in common. Despite this and possibly against her better judgement she asked me to become her lodger. Eva Priest had lost her husband ten months earlier, and wanted a male presence in her house; what she ended up with goodness only knows! I lodged with her for four years until I married my first wife; during my stay with her all hell broke loose on many an occasion!

Eva was married to a bank manager for forty years, so money was never a problem to her, whereas my only problem was the lack of it! I remember her pointing out that the old lady next door had inherited a whisky company fortune and was drowning in money. Eva always insisted that she had had the same upbringing as everyone else, telling me once, "We never had much money, though I do remember venturing out in my father's car in about 1912…"Can you believe that! Her father was the grocer's boy to Mr Budgen who died leaving mrs P's father in charge of numerous Budgens' stores. When Eva's dad died he was as I understand owner of some three hundred Budgens shops. Sadly for those losing out, he divorced Eva's mother and remarried, leaving the bulk of his wealth to his new wife of two years' standing. Mrs P never seemed bitter, but could never understand how I never had any money despite working all day long and hard. We had many rows, some of them heated; but for my part I always wanted to look out for my very old landlady, and in truth, as I was a kind of surrogate son to her, so she was a surrogate mother to me.

She had a thing about not going into my bedroom under any circumstances, never illustrated better than when I specifically asked her to wake me up at twelve midnight, because I had a precious ticket for a Muhammad Ali fight in London. I missed the fight because, according to her, having apparently knocked furiously on my door she could not wake me! She knew how much I wanted to see that fight, but would not and could not enter my room. You see Mrs P came from a different era, spending all her young life at the tennis club before getting married. I don't think Mrs P ever had a job, apart from attending charity do's; this fact alone rendered her incapable of focusing on any part of my life, but oh how hard she tried!

I owe her a debt I can't possibly repay for her kindness towards me, never more evident than in a bequest to me in her will. I have photographs of her at my wedding to remind me of a time long gone, but not forgotten. When I left her house my best mate at the time, Les, took over my room and continued to watch over her until he left a few years later. One postscript to her death; while I lived there I bought Mrs P a kitten, and later it fell to me to take the pussy home with me, since at the end Mrs P was going blind and the cat was being fed mostly on prawns and such like, and its claws were so long that they were growing in circles, poor thing. At home with my family and two well established cats, this new addition found it hard; dodging my whirlwind kids after only being used to a slow moving old lady. Eva's cat managed to escape from our house somehow, and never returned.

Little Helen

Whilst true, this tale is one I wish never to repeat again. My elder sister Patsy lived in a large house, while I lived in a grotty one room hovel up the road. My second sister Norma lived nearby. The youngest member of our family was Helen, some ten years our junior, and she lived with our father in Basildon, in Essex, a two hour drive away. We siblings knew that Helen, about eleven at the time, was not at all happy there with him. All of us had been arguing whether it was in Helen's best interests to leave our Dad and come to live with Patsy, who could well afford to feed another mouth. Dad naturally saw it another way and wished us to the devil. Eventually we all decided that we would snatch Helen from Essex come what may.

With my fiancée at that time I set off to abduct the young sibling, little knowing of the trouble our actions would bring. Helen had been briefed of our intentions and was happy to see us arrive. Dad barricaded the door, which I promptly removed, and Jackie ushered Helen into the car whilst Dad screamed obscenities at anyone who moved. I dived into my car and he dived into his, obstructing me with his car at every opportunity; finally a route round his car was found. We were expecting police sirens all the way home, but none materialised. Half an hour after arriving at my sister's the cavalry appeared at the door. Five officers trooped in, three of whom were women, and over a cup of tea the ramifications began. Halfway through the drama five were reduced to two, presumably because the minor was clearly in no danger. The next day social workers arrived to give an evaluation of her well-being.

To cut a long story short Helen stayed with her sister until she was old enough to make up her own mind where she wanted to be. My Dad naturally blamed me for the sorry state of affairs, particularly because he could no longer knock my block off. Ironically, years later when my father became terminally ill, he too moved into Patsy's.

Youth of Today

The media, and the generic moaning old goats knocking about, are continually lambasting the youth of today; unfairly so, in my opinion. Are we to believe that if war broke out now, as it did generations ago, today's youth would not take up the fight? You bet they would! A rugby crowd is so different on account of the quality of people who attend the game. Many times I've sat next to families of opposing sides, themselves sitting next to each other, and observed the passionate banter they throw about between them. This is much less common in football matches, though we do now have the family areas at stadiums comprising of supports of both teams. I've never seen a rugby crowd get out of hand. In a football crowd two different and passionate supporters close by one another might start a riot, so why does this not turn ugly with rugby? As a man brought up on football the reason is quite obvious: education! The football crowds argue with their fists because they have never learnt to argue any other way, whilst the rugby fraternity can argue with their tongues, beating their opposition up verbally.

It is quite stimulating listening to one supporter trying to berate another and vice versa, in evermore clever and underhand ways. Such a situation is almost unheard of in football, although to compensate, football crowds are extremely funny in isolation. The rugby people are made up of doctors, dentists and other professionals, positively educated souls as players and supporters alike. There you have it; in my opinion education wins the day. This is not to say there aren't educated people playing or watching football, because of course there are, but compared to rugby it will always remain the poor man's game.

My son Mark told me he was in a pub when a fight started; the next minute all hell broke loose, and Mark became embroiled in a good old fashioned fisticuffs. All of a sudden, as the fellow was in the act of clumping him shouted, "You're an Everton fan aren't you?" "Yes," crowed Mark holding a fist back, waiting to see where this chap was going with his questioning. "So am I!" boasted his adversary. Allegiances now agreed they made their apologies, dusted each other off, and off they went for a drink together. This would not be a one off occurrence, nor confined to one team. All the weight of the police force and judicial system this country has to strike down upon one could not possibly control an individual in this way. It is, so to say, far beyond the point of reason. On the other hand two people fighting from different clubs would surely intensify the argument. A last word on this topic; players, managers and chairmen sooner or later move on, while the supporters stick with their club forever.

Youth Football

Over about 5 years I coached these boys to dozens of trophies. (1992) Leo Jnr bottom row third from left

I am concerned, as a number of well-meaning folk are, about the selling off of school playing fields. Governments, concerned as they are with seemingly more pressing issues like healthcare, education and corruption, tend to be blind to the effect sport plays in some people's lives, particularly as children. Not all children have a scholastic aptitude or outlook, and the self-confidence gained from being competent in other aspects of everyday life is often overlooked in favour of the purely academic. So is it to be grass or concrete? As a builder concrete sounds about right for me, but of course it is not. I understand governments accept five billion pounds a year from sport or sport related businesses - that's £5,000,000,000 - where does that money go? Grass roots they cry, not so, as I have first-hand knowledge not only of concrete, but of youth football in particular, and sport in general, in society.

I was a qualified football coach for ten years, and no one ever approached me with their hands out. Huge companies jump on the bandwagon purporting to offer deals for kids, when the reality is the deals don't stand up to close scrutiny. The following promotion tells its own story. In the store one day a display caught my eye, 'Buy as many Mars bars as you can, to help your local football team.' The chairman of our junior football team was approached by the nation's favourite grocer, and asked to participate in a local promotion to sell Mars bars; if the local store sold more Mars bars than half a dozen other stores in

Surrey, we, the children's junior football team, would receive a free team kit. The chairman, a useless lump of lard, did not see the necessity to check what was involved first or ask anyone else.

The store manager was asked by me to explain how this promotion worked (bearing in mind this particular store must be the smallest shop in their armoury); for the six month term of this promotion, the number of bars sold are added up, and if this shop sold the most the kit was handed over. One store in the group of shops taking part in this promotion was the biggest in the country at the time! How could a tiny shop in suburban Molesey compete with a much larger store, and all the other competing stores? In short this great public company in my considered opinion was ripping off our local kids by putting them in a competition with only the illusion of winning the prize.

When I put this to the manager, he shrugged his shoulders and admitted they stood no chance. I withdrew the promotion immediately. The consequence of my actions was that the chairman made sure that I was thrown out of the club at a later date. I was to get my own back on the idiot in a big way, but I don't want to rub it in here, in order to protect the innocent.

Why is it, that sport has become so big in this country? Big enough for it to become Sky's flagship programme, big enough for insurance companies and banks sponsorship (where the real money lies in this land of ours), but not big enough for Great Britain to catch up with Australia, or France's sports budgets! Shame on them!

The Wilderness

Back in the early nineties I was a coach to my son Leo's football team, where we played our matches at a local school sports field. This junior boys' club paid for me to attend a football association-coaching course. My first coaching course was an unmitigated disaster, mainly because the head coach and I couldn't get on. There were about fourteen of us in total, aged from twenty-five to thirty-five, one of which was female, and me at forty-six years old. Three weekends in a row were spent chasing around after these young kids. The head coach seemed to dislike the fact that I was far and away the best player, and also the fittest.

During one session I took it upon myself to usher this rather obese girl through the game, as the other coaches' ambivalent attitude towards the girl was clearly upsetting her. She could not run, jump, kick, or head the ball. In fact I'm not sure that it was a good idea for her to attend this course at all. But the outcome of the course just goes to show what I know; she passed and I did not! Undaunted, I tried again. This time the head coach was some twenty years older than me and much more on my wave length. Having explained to him my bad experience last time, he assured me that he would take a close look at my efforts.

After the first hour-long session he took me to one side to explain that he was awarding me my badge already saying, "Don't tell anyone else. But you will have to finish the whole course." At the end of this first day of six, he explained his decision, "I don't care what happened last time, but football needs characters that can play; I bet the kids in your team love the fact that you can show them what and how to proceed, indeed I would put my grandson in your care. Most coaches don't have the age, and all *that* brings to the party."

To say I went home with my tail wagging would be an understatement! My team was at this time the most successful in the club's long history, and this success proved to be my biggest mistake, for jealousy was never far away. The club consisted of about a dozen teams; some managers of which asked for my help, but most just talked about me behind my back.

The chairman and I never really got on, fighting tooth and nail endlessly. I had lots of ideas, most of which were implemented one way or another. One idea I was responsible for was looking into the possibility of acquiring a permanent home ground for the whole club. In my road stood a patch of ground which was used as a public convenience for dogs; the size of three football pitches, the space had been left to local children by a rich man whose family were now living in the West Country. We, meaning club secretary Linda and myself contacted this gentleman's family in Cornwall and, encouraged by their undoubted interest, I pushed on.

The local Council contacted us and suggested we hold fire for a few weeks becausey another situation was accruing. Two weeks later I was let in on the possible acquisition of a better field next door; there, developers of a new housing estate were only allowed to build along the roadside. At the back of this development was the best private sports ground I have ever seen; having played football and cricket at the Standard Chartered Bank sports ground many times over the years, I could barely contain myself at the new development opportunity for my club.

The prize grounds were creating a lot of interest, not just locally. Pre-Abramamovich Chelsea F.C. showed an interest and a top private school in Shepperton too. The nineteen acre sports field, separated from the development site by the River Mole, had no vehicular access. We set up a meeting with all the ward counsellors in the local youth club, and all were right behind what we were trying to accomplish on behalf of our local kids. At this meeting at least two other managers of our club said I was wasting my time, as the school, which was also interested in the field, had more money and would win in the end. I retorted, "Sit down and watch developments unfold."

The private school concerned did indeed put up a bounty of one million pounds to the Council. As a builder, I was only too aware that if all ward counsellors backed me I'd be home and dry, and so it proved to be. One of the ward counsellors warned me that this was just the start, and others would soon look to procure a slice of the action sooner or later. How right he was! You see most committee members and managers were sheep, inertly working for employers, having no perception of the business end of business matters. This was never more evident than when formulating a business plan to apply to the fledgling National Lottery. I could not possibly do so either, but I was adamant of finding someone who could! I realised that a father of one of my team was a teacher at the London School of Economics. Bingo, I thought. Whereas, to illustrate the kind of people I was making all this effort on behalf of, the wife of the chairman remarked to me, "We don't want him. I don't like his pony tail." How Idiotic!

Notwithstanding, I contacted the ponytailed economics man, he put together the application, and we put in a proposal to Camelot, who at this point had not quite embarked on The Lottery. The Lottery people required us to produce like for like; as we were asking for £150,000, this required a small children's football club to produce out of thin air 150 grand! The whole process was now rendered useless.

We approached Camelot asking if the value of our nineteen acres, some £200,000 could be offset against our obligation to them; we, courtesy of the developer Cala Homes, had also been given a free bridge and roadway over the River Mole costing £150,000. Camelot said, "This is a grey area which we are looking at." I ventured that we could act as a test case that in the event of success could act as a promotional tool for the Lottery. Still no joy – what more, need we do, to satisfy Camelot's ridiculous expectations? After this I rowed with a few parents, who soon got together behind my back to unseat me from my team using, with the chairman's approval, a trumped up charge of fiddling expenses! What they did not know was the fact that my wife looked after my team's money, not me, and she was most certainly not fiddling!

When I was kicked out of this club, most of the boys and parents came with me. To this day these parents and boys cannot understand why I was shunted out; leaving a deep division that is still raw, even today!

On a lighter note; whilst coaching this club one rather stupid dad I had to contend with – a local gangster no less - I gave him a progress report on his son's footballing. I mentioned that he, his son, could do with an extra yard of pace, to which, I kid you not, he replied, "Where can I buy this yard of pace?" Incredible!

Old People

Age appears to be best in four things; Old wood best to burn, Old wine to drink, Old friends to trust, Old authors to read - **Francis Bacon**

As a man with an affinity for very young and very old people, a question I ask elderly folk on a regular basis is, "In your life time, what have been the biggest changes to your world?" The majority of people I've asked this to, born around the turn of the century, have replied, "Man on the moon." One can only marvel at living or surviving two world wars then witnessing a man walking on the moon. Others would recall how the world has shrunk due to the jet engine and telecommunications. Oddly, many also favoured how the world had fared before progress raced ahead of expectations. Almost without exception a dig was made at the youth of today, to this I cannot concur, as the kids of today are just different, no better or worse. A selection of old people believes that a war would soon sort out the kids of today, but I believe a war would have the same effect on our youth today as in yesterdays.

Old age is the most unexpected of all the things that happen to a man
- **Leon Trotsky**

(Other than an ice-pick fatally striking the back of your head?)

Southwood

In June 2005 my wife of the time and I purchased Southwood; it was a small, unimpressive bungalow set in a three quarters of an acre plot, right in the middle of a private estate. Apparently this site was originally designated as community tennis courts, but for some reason the idea was shelved. The tiny albeit serviceable property was to change dramatically over the ensuing two years. This is my account of what transpired before, during, and after this huge project was taken on.

I asked Rosie to draw up some sketches of the kind of place she would like us to build, but little did I know the scale of her intentions: a kitchen seven metres square; a formal dining room measuring seven metres by five; and a drawing room seven metres by six! As a builder there are only two problems to overcome with such a plan; space to build and money to pay. As I've intimated the plot was so huge that we could have built four houses, so room was not a problem. Money, as it tends to be, was an altogether different proposition.

I approached a very good friend of mine John Curr, also a builder, but who was more suited to architectural drawings than building, and asked him to draw up some plans for us; on seeing the size and scale of Rosie's plans, John remarked: "What are you building here, a Sussex version of Hampton Court Palace?" We toyed with the idea of knocking down the whole building and starting again, but the increased cost of doing so soon became apparent. A kit house manufacturer was contacted with a view to building a timber framed structure, but the price of £280,000 made this option untenable. We did approach a TV company to see if they might like to film the build, but without even looking at the plan said no.

Southwood post destruction, pre construction

My middle son Leo had just finished his stint at Southampton University, having gained a Law Degree. Weary from the years of uninterrupted formal education, he decided to take a year off to work as my labourer on the mammoth project. Rosie and John Curr worked diligently with the council planners to overcome one problem after another. The planners objected only to a second storey building with a roof, and so a chalet bungalow (still with upstairs and downstairs) was allowed to be built. This was agreed, but three months had passed before we were informed that the council was still not happy. Finally a compromise was reached by introducing a barn end to the top of the gables. Why waste three months to come up with a simple solution? Simple for me I suppose. As stated elsewhere in this book, council workers are rather a law unto themselves, feeling little need to push on expeditiously with the passing of any given plan. Time is money after all, but given it wasn't theirs that was being frittered away, why should they care?

Rosie and John worked hard to get the planning passed, and late in 2005 an acceptance was gotten; during this time Leo and I spent our time and no small amount of energy removing some thirty trees from the site, some of which consisted of ash, willow, silver birch, fir, eucalyptus, hawthorn, bay, and an enormous macrocarpa tree which overshadowed the whole of the original bungalow. Only the willow was removed to pacify the council's rules and regulations, the rest as a result of over planting when the garden was initially landscaped some fifty years ago, and a serious case of negligent gardening.

In July 2005 Rosie and I got married at the local village church, and the reception was held at the not quite yet under construction Southwood. At this point we'd applied but not received planning permission; that was to take five months. A marquee was erected and many quests remarked on the size of our plot and the quality of the food. Still to this day many of the guests that day have not seen the significant changes to Southwood since.

Leo Jnr and I laying the final part of our 'M25' access to 'Gladys', the workshop

269

One guest suggested the name 'Southfork' might be more appropriate, on account of Southwood's similarity in name and size to a house called Southfork in the famous TV series called Dallas.

By December I decided to not dig footings, the rain potentially our worst enemy. Instead Leo Jr and I decided to help John Curr with an extension job he was struggling with in Surrey, thus fulfilling an obligation to him. John wanted me to oversee what was for him a large project; he was also a builder, but given his normal capacity at work was more planner and manager than actual worker, he hadn't had nearly as much experience in the doing of the job as me.

Leo and I started the work for him, staying in the soon to be extended house in Surrey during the week and coming home to Sussex at weekends. It is pertinent to note that during this period John was not at all well. He seemed to be arguing with all and sundry, which was totally out of character. One day while we were all working John collapsed on the stairs. Leo and I lifted him up on to the bed, and soon enough the ambulance arrived and took my stricken mate to hospital, leaving us rather confused. It soon became clear that John was not coming back to work, so a local builder took over the whole job and we returned to Sussex. Two months later, the shattering news came; John had a brain tumour.

When contemplating our rebuild in Sussex it became quite clear that the local sand was of too poor a quality to use in laying the significant amount of block-work. As a former Middlesex and Surrey resident I knew that gravel pits there abounded, giving one a far greater choice of bricklaying sand. Sussex sand, or at least the sand available locally, was perfect for rendering but pretty useless for laying bricks. The reason seems to be the absence of naturally occurring clay and other deposits, which given the proximity to sea have been washed out of the sand thoroughly. As a consequence water ran through the Sussex washed sand quicker than the unwashed Surrey aggregate. Laying bricks with washed sand means the sand in the mortar resembles a wet and body-less sawdust, instead of the rich and creamy workable mix I am accustomed to that holds its form when pressured. Neighbourhood tradesmen brought up on local sand did not realise the sand from Middlesex, Surrey and Kent is far superior for laying blocks and bricks. So I sent a huge empty aggregate lorry to Runfold near Guildford in Surrey to replace the local sand, enough to build the whole project. This was the best sand I have ever seen or used and this pit has now run its course.

At the beginning of April 2006 we started digging the footings. The building inspector wanted us to dig down to Australia! We settled on a depth of one point three metres. Twenty-five cubic metres of concrete later, the footings were in. Pushing the wet concrete around the right angle bends of the footings was no small task. My two eldest sons and I – ready-made tampers in hand – worked the stuff up and down, around the corners the ready-mix lorry could not get close to. By the end of the furious day our arms and shoulders were good for nothing.

As always with such operations, it was quite a relief to finally fill the trench before the rains came, and they did! We turned up one very wet morning to find two ducks swimming around our almost full trench. There was nothing fowl about these characters taking our offerings of bread, but something foul was indeed about to happen. Rosie asked me to remove a small bush, which was growing against the house wall; I swung the pick into the ground, just missing Mrs Mallard who was sitting on a previously unknown nest. She did not seem at all worried at our interest in her welfare and was soon showered with bread, grain and water and, of course, I constructed a roof over her head.

At this juncture the property was uninhabitable, and we were living in Aldwick in my wife's as yet unsold house, so first thing upon arriving at work every morning we checked her nest to see that she was okay. After about two weeks, the habitual morning inspection revealed a total of thirteen eggs! We were all thrilled. A week later we saw to our dismay that not one egg was to be found – nothing. What or who could possibly have removed all thirteen eggs without breaking any? What predator after eggs for breakfast would carry them off? Surely they'd eat them where they lay. I've asked many people more qualified than I for a possible explanation, but nothing seems to fit. For two or three days afterwards the duck came back, landed on the lawn and moved towards the still intact nest as if to remember the night's carnage, then flew away. This incident was very upsetting for us all, but much worse was to come.

Now well into the build we had the block work up to window level, the scaffold erection imminent. I should mention that prior to starting the build, a road was constructed from the front of the property down its complete right side to the back, a distance of some seventy metres. It is now fondly referred to as the M25, which would become the access to an as yet un-built workshop. A large dozen of my son's American football team turned up one Saturday to assist in the removal of all the roof tiles on the existing roof. Tiles now safely tucked away in the corners of the garden, a good deal of food ensued.

Taking the weight of the roof in the redesigned house are five RSJs (rolled steel joists), the longest at some nine metres, weighing half a ton each. We had many bonfires burning discarded timber and tree branches. On this estate a bonfire can only be lit after 4:30pm by order of the Estate Committee. Fair enough. Accordingly, our fires became a nightly affair. One memorable fire, though I wasn't present for it, involved Rosie and an overhanging tree. One night she decided to have a fire on her own. How this fire got out of control I do not know, neighbours telling me of flames thirty-feet high, scorch marks high up the adjacent macrocarpa speaking volumes. Rosie, insistent to this day that everything was under control, was threatened by the neighbours with everything from the fire brigade to the devil. Late the following day, unawares of the previous night's flameage, nor of the integrity of the proximate tree, we noticed smoke in the air. The top limb of the tree – rotten and dry as it was – had been smoking, after a damn good licking the night before, for a whole day!

From April to June, as John was ensconced in a hospice terminally ill, I'd call in on him on my way to cricket, to exchange a few good-natured insults, and to observe the passing of a friend. What has upset me most over the years is John's relationship with his brothers;

271

both selfish beyond belief. On a daily basis they'd take advantage of the lovely, kind and genuine man who'd never complain to them, because he was John. I vowed that when the time came I would let them know how badly they treated him.

Now into July and the warmest weather I have known in this country; the temperature nearly 100 degrees at one point. The chippies and we were fixing the roof trusses in place. Then it happened, an odd set of events that has taken me down a path I never could have imagined. On Tuesday lunchtime I heard a bird singing with such gusto it was difficult not to respond, but I did not. The following day at noon I heard it again, this time I investigated. After faffing about trying to find my binoculars, I located the noisy songster, and what a song it was singing! Here I was with only a passing interest in birds, looking through the lenses I'd gone and hit the jackpot; the Bee Eater. Top of most twitchers' wish list, this cracking looking bird was seemingly singing just for me, there in my own garden!

A dead looking branch at the very top of the macrocarpa was hosting one of the most beautiful birds you could ever wish to see. Its song had a quality of resonance I am fully unable to portray in word. I've read that this bird's songbook is often used by film companies to convey *the* sound of summer. There were six of us workers taking it in turn to observe the incredible looking thing, with a voice to match the amazing plumage colours. On Thursday there was no more sign of her, but on Friday she was back at the hottest part of the day. The joy!

The rather handsome Bee Eater

When I got home to relay the events, Rosie called the local RSPB and left a message. Over the weekend we heard nothing. On Monday morning, in their droves they came! Men and women twitchers alike, all experts on the bee-eater yet not one of them had ever seen our friend in England, only in the Mediterranean and North Africa. I felt very privileged indeed, particularly in the saddened light of our duck's earlier demise. That this bird came back to the very same branch three days out of four is, I was told, by the throng of twitchers, truly amazing. Of course they'd missed it, and because of this some of the subsequent visiting twitchers gave me the evil eye, as if they didn't believe my story of the viewing.

About three days later, driving along a few roads up from Southwood with the windows down, a very hot day, I thought I heard the familiar and now nostalgic birdsong. Out of the car and scanning the skies, a woman who lived two doors down from where I'd parked called to me, "What are you looking for?" I showed her a picture. She replied instantly, "That's what I saw last week." "Which day" I asked? "Come with me," she said, and I followed her to her kitchen while she consulted her calendar. "Last Tuesday. I just thought it was a Kingfisher, but seeing your picture, I now know it wasn't." I left my telephone number and said "If you see the stunning creature again, please ring me."

September now upon us; the roof on, the plasterers now in evidence, new double-glazed windows in, and front and back doors fitted. By October I was very tired, but no time to rest, we must push on. The plan was to finish and move in before Christmas. No chance. The weather though was holding up very well.

On 26th October 2006 the inevitable but no less dreadful news that John Curr was dead. Obviously, we knew he would not get better, but it still came as a shock. The funeral two weeks later was my chance to convey John's unexpressed thoughts to his family. Leo and I attended a packed church, performing as two of the six pallbearers. Upon taking the weight of the thing, I remarked, "What the hell has John put in this coffin that weighs so much?!" Digging into our shoulders the coffin could well have been full up with ready mix! One of his brothers said, "Maybe he's put on weight." We chuckled, under the duress of the dual load. I replied, "Not with you around eating him out of house and home!"

The little crematorium was packed. As one of his brothers tried to read a passage from the Bible but was overcome, unable to continue, John's wife said, "Let Leo speak now." Sent on my way by Leo with a, "Good luck," I walked down to the front, turning to face everyone. "How lovely to see the place packed full. John would be so proud." My voice breaking and tears welling up in my eyes, I began,

"I never had a brother. John was as close as I will ever come to having one… John's initials - JP - could stand for Justice of the Peace; he was that fair and just. Now he's just at peace. Because John was so kind hearted, it was easy to take advantage of him, and whilst this is not the time or the place, some close to him clearly filled their boots. If Helen or Sophie ever need a reminder of what their Dad was like, just give me a ring day or night, and I will happily relay my rich and warm experiences."

It's sad now John has gone forever
The light he turned on in me will not recover.

He leaves behind a memory so strong
Of a man with whom I could get along;
Not one to moan or whinge to me
I guess and hope that now he is free;
A man of trust and integrity

February was spent rendering and painting the outside of the house. It was at this time I had the inspired idea of using a huge pile of assorted sized logs, compiled from the entire tree cutting the previous year, to build a wooden wall-come-barrier against the fence at the back of our property. I studiously stacked the logs between the boundary fir trees using the same care and ethos as I would with bricks. Visitors to our house home in on the structure and say nice things, like, "What a wonderful idea!"; "So effective"; "Blends in so well"; and, "Looks fantastic!" My halo now resembled a hot cooking hob. Going downhill from here? Not a chance!

March was spent constructing two rather large patio areas, and a one-off barbeque made out of 252 empty wine bottles. (All consumed in this household. And yes, I am still a teetotaller.) If you are competent in laying bricks you can also lay wood and glass (and maybe even women, although not necessarily in that order!)

I spent three hours at Southwood on Boxing Day playing table tennis with my three sons and their three girlfriends. It was lovely. 2007 opened with a big push to move in; kitchen worktop delivery was put back by three weeks, Leo and the painter at full tilt, and although the kitchen floor was still to be laid, we moved in on 8th February.

From left to right: Mark, Jack, Leo Jr and Author

The first job on moving in was a dog flap for Bella, who roams the gardens day and night. She could, of course, run away since we are not yet contained all round, but she knows where her bread is buttered. By now both Leo and I were knackered, and Rosie feeling the pain in her head after a fabulous job of project managing, the organising of materials and money, she vowed never again to undertake a project so interminable.

My first grandson Eric was born nearby. Leo went off to France with his girlfriend to live in the sun and visit his grandfather, while back at Southwood I finally built my long-awaited workshop, using all left over timber from the main build and the deconstruction of the original roof. It was intended as a dual-purpose woodwork and brickwork shop; where I intend to teach brickwork and plastering for beginners.

My sixty year old left arm was by now feeling very sore. Despite resting it for many a week, my shoulder did indeed need an operation to repair its rotator cuff. It is still not right now. The plan for the property, and our old age, was to forget the building trade and try bed and breakfast. That must be an easier way to make a living, we thought.

Visitors came to our house and said, "You must be so proud to have built such a lovely house." From my perspective, used as it is to renewing houses and plots after fifty years, it is fair to report that I get more satisfaction from making bird boxes, fixing them up a tree, and then viewing the feathery creatures setting up home in my creations, than I do from any old building. The birds don't care what the houses look like, only that when in residence they feel safe, unconcerned with style of wallpaper or colour of carpet, only the presence of food and water adjacent to their homes.

I take great pleasure in being able – in both the surroundings and lifestyle I have helped create for myself and the birds – to appreciate the following. Looking out of our newly finished kitchen I was pleasantly observing a kestrel perched at the end of a bough. The next minute a crow landed on the very same branch, and then hopped along its length until it landed on top of the kestrel, who then hurried away.

I have so much admiration for birds and animals, maybe because I would like to fly. What is it that I find so much pleasure in observing? Maybe I am jealous of their ability to survive humans like me. After all they require nothing from us but our absence. My belief that they deserve to exist side by side is endorsed every single day as I feed and view them.

Another occasion I remember a large raptor depositing his or herself – seemingly for my very own rumination - outside my new study window; training my 'bins' on this welcome visitor I tried to establish its species. The first to be discounted was a sparrow hawk, which is much smaller than this specimen. A goshawk possibly, but this has the wrong colours for that. For its size and general colour it could be a buzzard, but I'm not at all convinced. Eventually after scouring through the books and the internet I settled on a juvenile goshawk, because of the spots on his back and the white strip above his eye. I tell myself I am improving! Whether indeed I am or not is, I suppose, entirely beside the point; a new, rich, exhilarating and *natural* passion has grown up from within, which at my near old age feels fantastic.

From the first Tuesday lunchtime - on that rather hot summer day when I first set my eyes on the bee-eater - until the day I die, I will remain an avid and righteous watcher of birds. As a resident at Southwood for a handful of years, I counted forty-eight species of birds. I don't know if that is a large amount or not for this country; but as I learn, wonder and appreciate further, so the list grows, as does the quiet enjoyment of observation.

My first long awaited brickwork course for beginners at Southwood came and went. The venue as planned was Gwladys, my work shop, named after a grandstand at my beloved Everton Football Club. Amongst the ten attendees included two fifteen-year old boys who phoned up of their own volition, showing real initiative; one old dear of eighty-five; and a local journalist and her newspaper's photographer. She went on to write an article about the course, inspired by the two employees' involvement and participation.

One inquisitive foreigner contacted Rosie asking lots of pertinent questions about the course, and since he showed a great deal of interest Rosie suggested he book his place and send a cheque. He replied, incredulous, "Surely you are going to pay me to attend the course." Incredible!

With an unnecessarily huge four bedroom house to keep running, the need to keep the shekels coming in was ever present. It is for this very reason that should I have been on my own I would have felt no desire to build the thing so big. Nonetheless, Rosie and I were scratching our heads as to how Southwood might help to finance itself. We tried bed and breakfast, which was not ideal but served a purpose, and was often pleasant and interesting; the having and meeting of new people in your own house. Rosie then took on teaching foreign students English, all the while I taught my brickwork class and did odd jobs around the neighbourhood.

Southwood from the back

We also investigated the possibility of fostering children, having spotted an advert in our local paper which carried the rather enticing headline, "Foster carers needed - £1,000 a week." Rosie and I enrolled with a local agency, and a visit to Southwood was arranged. Two women arrived from the agency, one very large, the other half the size. Twice they came and twice they departed enthusing over the possibilities. A course consisting of five full days was duly completed, which we thought could have been condensed into one. We were later told that I was rejected because the agency people felt I would not be able to maintain a relationship with the social workers. Having had it rammed down our throats for five weeks about the child coming first, second and third, the agency was now backtracking, saying that our rapport with the social workers was more important!

I soon realised, without the social workers' authority, that in fact the agency would not receive any placements, and therefore no money would be forthcoming. The agency acknowledged the value of my parental history to confront any difficult situation with a child, but also knew full well that if a child's well-being was at stake I would not put up with any intransigent behaviour from the social workers. On this point I bow to the agency's superior knowledge. So what about the lies, what lies?

The mantra continually repeated, "You are not doing this for the money." At £300 per week including clothes, pocket money and food, this was quite evident. If we were not to concern ourselves with money, then why did the agency print in large letters in their newspaper advert £1,000 per week? When asked about this we were informed that the £1,000 was for three children a week, though positively no mention of this was made in the advert. As such they must be guilty of breaching the Trade Description Act! Or they were just plain desperate. To sum up: do the children come first, second and third, or is the agency's monetary agenda hiding behind the children's needs? Needless to say, and sadly so at that, for I would have loved to have helped raise more children, we did not take the idea of fostering any further.

Phew! Finally finished! Enjoying the garden with my beloved Bella.

Uprooting Trees

As a builder there are times when what you know to be true is backed up in a practical and scientific demonstration of energy loss. Although, in the tenacious moments that are necessary to get a thing done, sometimes one doesn't see this fact too clearly. While my son and I were chopping up and uprooting those numerous trees at Southwood, all by hand no less, it got to the point around 11am, after a furious morning swinging axes and picks in a variety of bodily positions, that the sharpness of our tools became an apparent problem; they were blunt, our chop swings becoming more futile with each blow. Or at least that is what we thought was happening.

If anyone reading this has ever uprooted any tree of middling size by hand – a rare and mostly unnecessary thing these days with the variety of machinery available - digging down around the trunk to expose and sever its roots, they will appreciate what a beastly task it really is. The flex of the tree, with more give and moisture under the ground than above it, can seem to be a goner after just twenty concerted minutes. Hours and chopped roots later, the thing remains connected, often by one of the tap roots, so difficult to get at. And few things are more tiring to the muscles than the reciprocation of expended energy. A rooted tree, minus the fixedness of soil at its base, does this especially well.

My son recalls to me, to myself forgotten, that on this occasion, while he lay head-first in the hole, hatchet hacking away at roots, the two of us desperate to succeed before luncheon, exhausted and somewhat possessed with this need, he almost found his head squeezed between soil and root by the unexpected swinging of the trunk, a foot in diameter and six feet high. He wrestled himself out of the hole to find *me* perched atop the trunk. Like an enormous unsightly bird, to all appearances utterly mad, he swung back and forth muttering, 'Come on you bastard!" The tree gave none.

And so it was in fact our energy that had so quickly depleted after the morning's expenditure; our arms swung with such little vigour, the point of the axe and shovel and pick, the saw too, hitting the soil and roots with almost no effect. Efficacy could only be restored by fuel. Half an hour later, with a belly full of tea and sandwiches and cakes, power was switched back on; we wielded our tools with new life, and the trees then came down.

It was a stark example, within the space of an hour, how limited our bodies are when set against nature herself. And too the part of the mind in this conquesting process; had we not realised the necessity of fuel in the succeeding of our venture, we should have buried ourselves right there in that hole where we lay, fatally exhausted, precious tools at our side..... Not a bad way to go...

Problem Solving

I am convinced that we self-employed people are, by the manifold nature of our needs, above all problem solvers. Here are a few examples.

The educated man I began to employ as a more or less permanent labourer during the nineties was John Beech. The subsequent relationship made me aware for the first time of how builders in general and me in particular, have this ability of adapting to adversity in and around the job. It should be well known that self-employed builders and tradesmen in general must be mildly proficient in mathematics, geometry, geography, architecture, economics, and psychology, not to mention a weatherman's instinct, good organisational and communicative skills, plus a modicum of dexterity with weights and measures. Self-interest in physiology is paramount. I am not suggesting that we are all geniuses, just that a prolonged period of self-employed servitude will require no small amount of all the above, and much more.

A few examples of how a self-employed and practical mind is able to deliver the best possible outcome to whatever task is at hand.

While coaching my junior football team, during the winter months the lack of natural light prevented us from training mid-week, meaning all junior teams could only train on Saturday mornings. Parents did not like the team interfering with their weekend plans, and so to placate them I put myself out. I purchased two unused 1000 watt floodlights from Esher Rugby Club and fixed them on upright poles to the back of my open back transit truck. I talked our local hire shop into borrowing a generator for the evening, on the trust that we'd pay for the petrol used and returned the appliance first thing in the morning. This did not incur great cost. Some vilified me; others thought it a great idea. The reality was simply the opportunity for quality training sessions, impossible without the idea and its practical application. This meant about twenty children were being coached two evenings a week, or was it baby-sitting?

At about the age of eight my youngest son Jack had two pet rabbits called Campbell and Jeffers, named after two Everton footballers of the time. Having decided to make a rabbit hutch for them my brain kicked into overdrive. The result? Campbell and Jeffers lived like kings; a hutch standing on four legs about four feet off the ground, with two floors inside, each with an open and closed room, and a balcony at the top of the stairs their lookout post from which to view the world. At night I imagined the rabbits looking down at the foxes looking up, saying, "Do your best foxy! You can't catch me!"

Standing in my workshop minding my own business, and looking directly at our dog Bella, a thought came into my head. A dog kennel! As with the rabbit hutch, my over the top inclinations ran wild. I simply cut up a disused and damaged table tennis top to make the four sides, a ply base, and a feather-edged facing to a pitched roof. A few carpet tiles and hey presto, a kennel fit for a Queen, or the Queen's dogs. This particular female did not like her new house, and try as we might to entice her into it with bones, biscuits, and even ourselves, Madame refused point blank to enter. I feel an EBay moment approaching.

Every time I take the dog for a walk, it has to be the best dog walk ever. Finding out what she likes then expanding on that, using all local and natural habitats.

To every dog their master is a Napoleon; hence the constant popularity of dogs
- Aldous Huxley

Working at a house with the rear garden adjacent to the River Mole, waiting as I was for my newly rendered wall to dry, I found myself temporarily at a loose end. Gazing into the river I wondered whether I should try to catch something – you bet! Rummaging through the garage I found a length of very fine plastic twine, which I attached to a six-foot length of one-inch quadrant. I fashioned some sort of hook out of a safety pin, then started looking around for some fish's dinner. A freshly dug hole at the riverbank revealed worms, a perfect bait. I found a large plastic bucket in anticipation of a haul of minnows. In my hour of atrophy I caught more than I'd reckoned; two large chub each circumnavigating the bucket, head to tailing it. Not a bad hours' folly while my rendering dried!

I once had trouble with two young labourers. This is an account of how I overcame the problem without giving either of them a clout.

The job entailed knocking down a huge brick wall some fourteen feet high and sixty feet long. I hired the two young boys, one sixteen and the other nineteen years of age, to clean the old bricks and stack them up. As the two youths cleaned up the fallen bricks, they found some old lead water pipes which belonged to the owner of the wall. On my return to the site the owner asked if I had found the lead pipes. I had not seen them, and said so. Upon asking the two labourers about the said pipes, they informed me that they'd lifted and sold them to a scrap yard.

In turn I gave them each a rounded mouthful, impressing upon them the rather obvious fact that this was considered stealing. To this they looked quite blankly at me, as if it were an everyday occurrence for them, which it might well have been. I sacked them both and told them to go immediately; both asked for their wages for the day. I told them to disappear pretty sharply before I called the police. Both said they'd get me or their money eventually, or words to that effect.

At different times these two labourers called me with threats of my impending doom. After several more phone calls, Sunday lunchtime, there came a knock on my front door. I happened to be just getting in the bath, and being in the house on my own I wrapped a towel round my waist and opened the door. The two had increased to three, the third about the same size as the original two put together. He was about nineteen, six foot three inches and at least seventeen stone – a veritable beast. I stood there arguing for about two hours, and soon my entire family of four children and wife turned up and disappeared indoors. When the situation turned ugly I looked the big chap in the eye and told him to f**k off or I'd tear his arms and legs off that very moment. They backed off, leaving me exhausted, standing there semi-naked outside my house. The end of the matter, not bloody likely!

After more phone calls, more threats, I decided to take the bull by the horns. One obvious problem was that, as minors, I couldn't assault either of them. This is what I did; I went round to the younger boy's house and knocked on the door, and his mum appeared, asking, "What do you want?" Having never met her before, I told the story. The boy came to the door and his mother asked, "Is this true?" He replied that it was. With that she belted him round the head, and shut the door in my face.

I went straight round to the older boy's house and made my way to the front door. On passing the bay window I caught sight of his father on the settee, lying on top of his mother. Given they didn't see me I knocked on the front door regardless. Naturally it was some time before I got a response. The door opened, and the mother stood there and said (having never met me before either), "Who the f**k are you?" Charming! I thought.

I started to recount the story, and when the father appeared behind her I had to repeat again. He said, "My boy wouldn't do that," then proceeded to threaten me. "Do not touch my boy, or else!" I told him I wouldn't go near the boy, but if he ever came near my house again, or phoned me, or if a brick ever came through my window, I'd come back and take it out on you, the father, personally. That seemed to do the trick, as I haven't had any trouble since, a decade later. In this particular instance that was my way of dealing with troublesome youngsters, but obviously not an ideal solution for one and all.

This front-up-ness, or tendency to get a thing done if a thing is to be done, is measured more at work than in the dealing of threats. On any work that requires several tasks, where there are five things to complete and none is dependent on the other, and then I will undertake the most difficult or problematical job first. My experience is that given the choice most people will commence the easiest operation in a primordial fashion. Why this should be so I am not sure. If you decide on the principle that easy is best and first, then your list of jobs is now uphill. Could it be that I like to work downhill, finishing the hardest task first – maybe a good example of my bloody-mindedness at work.

In a newspaper recently a sad story of a young girl drug addict overdosing on heroin, her parents blaming the police and social services, indeed, everybody but themselves. Harsh, maybe! But, as a result of my collaborations with strangers all my life, I was asked by my next door neighbour what I would do if one of my children became a drug addict. This would be my response to an, as yet (thank God), hypothetical situation. Let's say for example, my daughter was living with a junkie who quite likely would have been responsible for her situation. My first thought obviously would be to remove my daughter to a safe and secure place. Then and only then would I pay this scumbag a visit. I would calmly ask him never to contact my daughter again and if, either she or I ever lay eyes on you again, I will cut your bollocks off and stuff them down your throat, good day!!!

The very same scenario is applicable if a supplier or drug pusher was another person, you see, pushers and addicts only understand two things, money and violence, so, as I would not be handing over my hard-earned cash I'm left only with savagery. I am not exactly a passive type; neither am I a thug, however, needs must. The need in this case is beyond price or deed. My children would expect of me no less than success or death, whichever came first. Having left the addict/pusher in little doubt of my intentions I would now turn mine to my daughter. From what I have learnt my daughter might not want me to remove her from the drugs or indeed this addict. No matter, at this point I would spend every minute of every day at her side. I am aware the clock would seem to have stopped when the cold turkey started, nevertheless, I would have to take what comes, after all, the prize too big, the cost of failure, extinction. Some might argue this account is lawless and violent, sure it is, but my love for my children comes way before the law of the land.

Soon after joining with my son at his junior football club, all adults were asked to come up with fund raising ideas. Our club used to play at the local school where we used two football pitches. My idea was to invite the football league's representative sides to play on our patch all on one day, possibly four or five games. I had made a portable metal barbeque that could cook twenty-five burgers at once. With a captive audience of teams and parents, money was to be made. Fifteen years later the same MO, the same income, and the same barbeque is in use.

Another problem, another brilliant idea, though this time not my idea! Architects in their wisdom sometimes come up with ridiculous new ideas, like the introduction and use of boot lintels; essentially a boot shaped lintel made of concrete. The so-called benefit was that the lintel tied the inside skin to the outside skin at the head of any window or door in one piece, but the sheer weight of the thing was no benefit to us workers! A window span of seven feet would require a lintel of eight feet six inches long, possibly weighing 450 lbs.

My mentor Bill Young would get around the problem like so. It would require four very strong men to carry/drag this abomination to the bottom of our scaffold. We would then loosen the handrail so that it revolved cleanly. Attached to this at right angles, about eight feet apart, were two small scaffold poles which rotated the handrail. A length of rope, one end around the lintel and the other end around the handrail, would serve as a hoist, gently lifting the concrete monster upwards. A perfect case of genius and idiocy, working in harmony. This became such a problem in the construction industry that eventually everyone started casting these lintels in situ, thereby saving our backs from such heavy lifting.

When my first wife and I decided to split up I didn't know whether to feel sad or relieved, let alone depressed. And so reverting to type, negativity out of the window, I phoned the Samaritans and asked the operator if they could do with some help. Very soon I found myself on a course, and spent four or five weeks in training with lots of role-play.

Eventually I was informed that my voice and quality of character were not suitable for the counselling of people in a desperate state. Clearly, my outspoken belief that everyone can and should do more with their lives, did not sit well with the powers that be, which is fair enough. The experience taught me never to take anything or anyone for granted.

One of the earliest examples I can remember of an ability to problem solve was as a teenager. As most children will do, I tried smoking at fourteen. Aged sixteen I vowed never to buy another packet whilst at work, knowing full well that even if I accepted their offered cigarettes I would not reciprocate; my co-workers soon tired of my behaviour and stopped offering me a smoke. Over a few months the habit was sunk, never to return.

Being a problem solver has its difficulties as well as its benefits. A client will invite you round to solve a perceived obstacle, unconscious and uncaring that the financial clock is ticking, while never offering money in exchange for solving their problem. Meanwhile the very same process is conducted every day in solicitor's offices, with vastly different financial consequences.

I am not quite sure if this is a problem solved or a problem aired. I leave you to make up your own mind. Walking along the road on our estate I noticed how builders had finished work at a house but not cleaned the public pathway outside. The mess they left behind, which is not obvious if you look at the photograph, is a raised blob of sand and cement some 2" or 50mm above the surface of the tarmac, just enough for some unsuspecting pedestrian to trip over. If such an accident did happen, considering the blob was in the middle of a public pathway, and then the homeowner would be liable for everything thrown at them.

The blame culture we are currently surrounded by would, I am sure, savage the people responsible. But who is? The builder must be aware of all the dangers to the public, but having left the site the blame now passes to the homeowner, who is clearly unaware of the very real physical and potentially real financial threat. If I were an opportunistic chancer how difficult would it be to fall over on a public highway and scream foul, then take a photograph of the offending obstruction and threaten a massive pay-out? Should I tell the blind and careless house owner or keep quiet? One swing with a hammer and chisel would remove the dormant threat.

I couldn't resist – a home Emergency vehicle astride this very same patch of impending danger!

The Beast

I would love to put this story in the previous chapter on problem solving, but unfortunately even if I were a brain surgeon I'd still be unable to.

Early in 2007 my middle son's best mate Mark Howe, then 24 years old, underwent brain tumour removal, completely out of nowhere; a mere few weeks from visiting the doctors due to headaches then, the dreadful diagnosis. He underwent surgery immediately. Also known as 'The Beast', named so on account of his premature height and bulk by my son, then both aged about twelve, Mark recovered well from the ten hour surgery. But after

285

only a matter of weeks he contracted meningitis in intensive care, and remained there for the best part of a year. Not only were the doctors unknowing of exactly what effecting parts of brain they had removed, or indeed what had been left after the initial surgery, the regular haemorrhaging in the weakened area as a result of the meningitis meant these questions would remain unanswered, possibly forever. Eventually The Beast left for a rehabilitation hospital, where his condition improved remarkably. He went from an uncommunicative and vegetative state to now moving and shaking his head and responsiveness in eye contact.

Mark's home is now at the rehabilitation hospital in south London; my home is on the south coast. I try to visit him once every month or so. On some occasions when I've seen a big improvement I'll drive home as if in a drug induced euphoria. Mark clearly needs stimulation, in addition to the selfless efforts of his parents and brother. With this in mind I borrowed my friends' video camera, and for about six months wherever I went the camera recorded the place, and me. Down a hole, up on a roof, at cricket matches, fishing down by the river, tours of my house and Bognor Regis in general, and then down on the pier from which I promised to throw The Beast off of when he comes down to visit our new house. We made a few discs for his entertainment, which he loved, and now mum and dad can play them back again and again if Mark so wishes. I had to return the video camera, and am still looking for new ways to stimulate him.

One stroke we pulled off was to invite West Ham United's manager at the time, Alan Curbishly, to visit with a view to giving Mark, an avid WHU fan, a moral and perhaps physical lift. Alan was fantastic with Mark, who, while the chap was in his room, kept mouthing, "Unbelievable… unbelievable!" His face was a picture unforgettable, worth the effort alone.

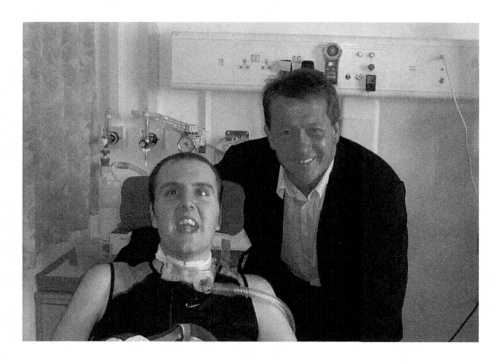

Mark used to play for my cricket club, so it was incumbent on me to invite him and his parents, and attendant nurse, to our annual cricket dinner. Mark sat there is his wheelchair loving every minute of his time with us, everyone showering him with attention. As *El Presidente* of my cricket club it was my job to make the opening speech, and my first task was to home in on The Beast, so called because when fit he weighed in at fifteen stone, with six feet and two inches in height. I regaled a story appertaining to Mark that I will relay again now.

On field late during a summer midweek game, I was bowling my slow off breaks, with Leo as wicket keeper and The Beast at slip. I walked down the wicket and motioned to The Beast that I was going to bowl a leg break. As such, "The ball will come to you, so be prepared!" Incredibly the ball pitched just in the right place, nicked the edge of the bat as planned, and went straight to him at wide slip. As the ball moved in seeming slow motion to us all, The Beast was already grinning. He took the catch yelling, wide eyed and going bonkers, then ran down the wicket laughing his head off, a picture of disbelief.

I then told the gathered throng at our dinner that that ball was not my top spinner, nor my googly; it was my crystal ball! Mark loves that story. Just as well, since I recall it every time I see him. He left the dinner to a standing ovation ringing in his ears, never to be forgotten.

Mark now has a special push button computer through which he can communicate. In truth, sadly, he has not nearly made the recovery we all hoped for him. By the standards of any young mobile individual, his is a bleak future indeed. But let it be said: the personality of this raucous, happy, mischievous and very funny lad can still be seen in the twinkling eyes, and what's left of his grin. Although irreparably changed in his ability to communicate, and what he is able to *do*, the same charming young man lives on. And it is for this, I suppose, that we can be thankful.

Several years have passed and Mark shows no sign of ever regaining more faculties. When the surgeons removed this tumour, they also extracted part of the brain responsible for his ability to swallow; consequently Mark has lost the capability of swallowing of his own volition. Because of this Mark is permanently wired up to a shunt leaving him unable to dispense with an attendant nurse or machine. In light of this it seems unclear whether Mark will ever leave the hospital to return home even in a wheelchair. It does not seem fair that for 70 years I have enjoyed rude health and poor Mark's physical life is effectively over at 25.

Sporting Achievements

What I have achieved in the sporting arena might on the one hand seem rather mundane, dig a little deeper then it becomes quite clear that with some parental help I could have been, with my extreme physicality as mentioned all over this book, somebody completely different. All sport comes naturally to me, the struggle was always never being in the right place at the right time. As you get older you realise what a helping hand this particular part of our upbringing can benefit us. My big problem as a youth growing up was having a father showing no interest in his only son, plus bringing me up as a loner. In team sports a loner is always going to struggle socially when the game is over. In the same way that work is gleaned down the pub, so it is that you will gain more favour with team management after the event or game. If a substitution is to take place, the one who does not take part socially will in all likelihood suffer. A clear indication when at school would find me not selected for the school football or cricket teams because I was not friends with the captain or schoolmaster. This has been an impediment my whole life to date, but as an unbending individual who will refuse a leg up in return for a favour, life becomes in all probabilty difficult, especially growing up.

So everything I have achieved in the sporting arena has not been without problems mentioned all over this life story. I attained a level of football excellence hardly foreseeable from humble aspirations and played for Middlesex as a senior adult. Games against current England amateur internationals showed me to not be inferior in technique, character and most definitely not fitness which was off the scale. The higher the levels I would climb the more vicious the verbals would become. Some internationals would scream "I'm going to break both your legs if you run past me again", which in truth did not bother me explicitly. The very thought of an opponent breaking my leg was laughable given the size of their legs compared to mine. I think it prudent to recall here that I never once had an injury that prevented me from playing in the next game. It is also true that I have never had a groin strain, cartilage trouble or a hamstring pull despite playing twice a week for ten years and once a week for a further ten. My problems were never the games per se, just everything on the periferi.

As a cricketer I was somewhat slow to start never having any more coaching than I had at football, nevertheless I played at a level suitable for my abilities. Being fit beyond belief I embraced all facets of cricket and after 34 consecutive years playing just Sundays I ended up scoring 12,138 runs, getting 247 outfield catches (more than anyone else I know, also a record for the team which still stands today), plus 274 bowling wickets too. I embraced the captain's role and am still president of Magdalen cricket club. I can't move on without recalling a never to be forgotten match that has never seen the like before or since or ever will be in the future…

Tomato Stopped Play

We were playing cricket against West London Deaf who were indeed deaf. We batted first and were all out for 90 runs (not good). I was eating my food between innings when the opposition captain confronted me about the lack of tea facilities and how this was disrepectable to deaf people. I asked our fixture secretary if they were told about our tea making difficulties at this time and was told he phoned them many many times but was not able to contact them, not surprising as they were all deaf! As captain I tried to placate them offering to send somebody down to McDonald's if that would help, but to no avail.

The opposition captain's language was now becoming heated going on and on about "you hate deaf people" etc etc. After about ten minutes of this, I was now ticking. Fed up with all this I jumped to my feet, at this exact moment the captain walked through the ajacient door and slammed it shut. The tomato with one bite out of it, was thrown at the back of this door in frustration, however the door had other ideas. It slammed shut then opened, just enough for the errant vegetable to squeeze through the gap hitting the departing fellow right on the back of the head! One minute later all hell broke loose! Of course it was just a freak occurrence, a million to one chance. Apoligies were useless, not suprisingly! Our dressing room now filled with both teams pushing, shoving and shouting. The person responsible (me) sitting down, my head in my hands thinking what have I done now! The opposing team refused to continue the game, hence the title 'Tomato Stopped Play'.

When time allowed me tennis, squash, snooker and all manner of sports were played where the obvious common denominator is a ball. At 70 my choice now is table tennis and for five years I have just fiddled with it but now I am going for broke. Still no coaching, what's new! There were children at my senior school who had both the time and money spent on their sports education and not one of them as far as I know has surpassed my sporting achievements, although they might tell me differently if they read this book.

The Sixties

My work and life journey started on the 7th August 1962 and I was paid the princely sum of £4.2 shillings a week. Up until Boxing Day of that year the weather was unremarkable. Then; I was playing in a charity football match on Richmond Green on Boxing Day. At half time the snow started to fall. By the end of the match the pitch was under three inches of snow. On and on it fell, one day, two days, then three. The snowflakes fell every day or part of for six weeks.

Most building workers were laid off. Luckily for us at this time we were employed at a chocolate factory refitting half a dozen washrooms. Hayes in Middlesex, the site of said factory was adjacent to a town called Southall, which I believe contains the second or third largest proliferation of Indian migrants in the country. I would say ninety per cent of workers employed here were Indians. Totally disheartening was the fact that as soon as we finished each floor of toilets and washrooms, they were wrecked wantonly. Only men were allowed to work weekends, so the women's washrooms were used for illegal smoking sessions. Not only that, excrement was found all over floors on Monday morning. Some cleaners were sacked for refusing to remove the mess. I remember watching grown men hanging onto wall mounted units pulling them clear of the wall. At sixteen years of age, I could not believe their behaviour, seeing as we had just fitted the units onto the wall. I could tell you more disgusting things going on there but I will refrain from doing so. Meanwhile, the snow was drifting four to five feet deep outside. It was quite an operation moving from outside to in and vice-versa. Changing from sweating in a t-shirt, to requiring at least two coats, when venturing outside.

There was a shop situated at the front gate where you could purchase cheap reject products. Since that time, never have I ever eaten this factory's chocolate. The contract for this job lasted well into the summer, meaning that no time or money was lost.

So there you have it, I started life in 1947, the worst winter in history, superseded by the worst winter ever, my first on the building.

As a stupid youth of fifteen my working life started on the 7 August 1962 and my apprenticeship started in August 1963, I feel well placed to recall the events of a decade beyond compare culturally, musically and spiritually.

I started work with a small building company of about thirty employees, then moved on to a brickwork sup-contractor a year later, through a lack of practical opportunity.

The next six years were to shape my whole life creating what I am today, probably as a result of bumping into Bill Young.
This man is more than worthy of the chapter afforded him. Indeed, as I will show, his words and deeds have cast a mould that will never be filled. The best I can manage was to name my middle son after him. Bill died in early 1982 and Leo William was born in the same year. One of my life's inspirations expired, another one starting.

1960 - 62 saw the end of my formal education. Aged fourteen and fifteen respectively, the big wide world beckoned. Did I know how big? Not a hope, at least not for another ten years or so. From where we lived, Richmond-upon-Thames and Kingston-upon-Thames were equidistant three miles away. Kingston now has a thriving shopping centre with a reputation as one of the best outside the West End of London. Richmond is now the most affluent borough in the suburbs of London. Back then my recollection would be somewhat different.

Growing up in an alien world called life, my first effort at hero worship was beginning to manifest itself in the shape of a handsome black boxer called Cassius Clay. Growing up without a role model was never going to be easy but I must have chosen wisely as I follow his story to this day. Walking to school, marvelling at his antics in the ring and wishing some of his confidence would rub off on me. Also yearning to borrow his left hook or over-hand right, defending myself against school bullies.

It was about this time that two adventures unfolded, that would result in a lifetime's reverence. By a strange coincidence, both would emanate from a northern town called Liverpool. Everton football club had overtaken my senses a few years earlier, now the Beatles came to prominence revolutionising music the world over. "Love Me Do" was pervading everybody's soul (although not our parents'). "She Loves you" even more so.

The late fifties and early sixties saw the demise of teddy-boys and the advent of mods and rockers. Some mods at our school rode around on scooters wearing parkers, a kind of dull green poncho. Rockers sartorial indifference required them to dress in whatever they chose to. My father's insistence that I should remain a loner compelled me to reject either camp, or gang, whatever you chose to call them. The Beatles continued to conquer the charts, whilst other music acts sprung up everywhere. For example, The Rolling Stones, The Hollies, The Kinks and many more. Richmond by this time was a very fashionable area; a now infamous pub called The Castle down by the Thames was a magnet for an assortment of colourful characters, both good and bad.

This pub used to attract two thousand customers on a Friday or Saturday night. Mind you, two hundred policemen were round the corner out of sight.

One shop I vividly remember a few years earlier was Joe Lyons Café with its art deco interior, chrome and glass everywhere. I also recall high bar stools to the front and side of this corner site meeting place. When the roller shutters went up our bar seats were open to the wind. My mother's birthday treat for each of us once a year was to plonk us down on the said high stools to partake of a Knickerbocker Glory. A glass 12 inches high was filled in layers with different colours of ice cream, and with a long spoon I shovelled it down. Across the road and facing down Richmond Bridge was the Odeon Cinema. We – being anybody we met in there -thrilled to the antics of Donald Duck during Saturday Morning Pictures. The serials running about that time included Batman and Robin, Flash Gordon, The Lone Ranger and Tonto, Roy Rogers, and Tarzan, plus others. Some serials used to scare me shitless. So where was I next week? Back for more!

As I grew out of Saturday morning pictures, the many coffee bars springing up were visited often. There were two other picture-houses in the town at this time, The Gaumont and the Ritz. As you can imagine, the rivalry was intense, especially after the morning show. Sometimes an ambush would take place, then its fight or run, whichever you were best at. I always picked the latter simply because no one had ever run past me before. The Beatles procreating influence continued apace but the next musical revolution was just around the corner. Mods and Rockers were dying out, or just killing each other. Black American music in the form of Tamla Motown and Stax records kept pace with the mop tops from Liverpool.

Listening to music was one way to enjoy yourself, the other was to listen and throw yourself in every direction. To this end, Motown was the definitive dance music, right through to the seventies. How we sang and moved to the Supremes, Four Tops, Smokey Robinson and The Temptations, Otis Redding, Sam and Dave, Jackie Wilson, all followed.

With this crazy decade only half way through, the next and – for me – most puzzling social disturbance was about to rock the whole of the western world. One song was to change all our social sensibilities and bring about, in my opinion, the breakdown of parental glue.

"Let's go to San Francisco" was the song that opened our ears to Flower Power. Whilst the effects reverberated around the world, nowhere in Europe was this scene more in evidence than Richmond in Surrey. As I have said Richmond was and is an affluent place to live, whether this was a trigger, I don't know. However, what is true was an influx of hairy kaftan wearing flower adorning, peace loving, passive creatures. Somewhat different to the gathering groups of mods and rockers travelling to most villages to beat each other senseless, usually on bank holiday weekends.

My sister was into sex, drugs and rock and roll, while my interests at this time were purely football. At fifteen I played in an adults football team so consequently missed out on all goings on. The Richmond National Jazz and Blues Festival, held annually at the Old Deer Park, home of Richmond and London Scottish Rugby Clubs, attracted music lovers in their thousands, usually over a bank holiday weekend. During this festival, the main dual-carriageway running from Twickenham to Richmond was impassable due to kaftans all over it. Adjacent to the main road were about eight football pitches covered in tents and people. Strangers informed us that they had travelled from all over Europe to be here. In trying to remember who was appearing at the athletic ground, I remember only one – Long John Baldry. I do remember my sister recalling The Rolling Stones playing The Railway Tavern opposite Richmond Station on a regular basis. The Crawdaddy Club – I think the pronunciation is right - used to be host to the Yardbirds who I believe originated locally. Whether they played the festival or not I have no idea. Huge groups of people dressed in flowery outfits would stand around very close together having a communal love-in.

You might well be accosted in the street often by a woman wanting a fag or kiss or both. The problem here might be, if you obliged everyone might join in. The whole situation was unbelievable because it seemed that you were either one of them – dressed up – or you were an alien. Surely they were from another planet, not me. Everybody jumped on the flowery bandwagon except moi, I was tempted, but putting on a dress in public would have killed my immediate ambition of becoming a bricklayer. The music charts remained full of songs about this social phenomenon but I can't quite recall them here. We know that San Francisco was the birthplace of this sixties fashion experience, nevertheless, Richmond for the duration of flower power was saturated with men dressed as girls.

As I grew into my late teens, Richmond was declared in the national press as the drug capital of Europe. My experiences at this time backed up this claim. The L'Auberge coffee bar – forerunner of today's late night wine bars – next door to the Odeon cinema was a magnet for drug pushers. One night I found myself in this establishment, heaven knows why – Girls!! – after all I was a fledgling teetotaller – Girls – most patrons bopping along to Motowns finest, when in rushed the bow street runners, "Don't move" was heard above the panic. Pure silence, all that could be heard was pills and tablets dropping like concrete confetti on highly polished timber floors. Dancers whose ankles were covered in speed and purple hearts were taken away to receive two weeks probation and a £1 fine.

Richmond became a drug riddled town with after-dark problems everywhere. However, for the visitor alternative magnets requiring little effort save walking around were on offer. Richmond Green resembles a Torremelinos beach with large numbers of office workers sitting in the sun at lunchtime. To one side, the theatre, to the other, a royal palace where Queen Elizabeth 1st died in 1603. Across the river on the far bank, another magnet for us boys, Richmond Ice Rink. Around the atmospheric green are connecting walkways exiting to the High Street, reminiscent of the Lanes in Brighton.

Small dark antique and curio shops, one after the other, interspersed with eating houses, an irresistible mix for tourists and pickpockets alike. In my opinion Richmond Park is the best and largest green space slap bang inside a major city centre. You can't visit Richmond without venturing up the hill to the top. Whereupon the view from The Lass of

Richmond Hill is famous the world over as is the Star & Garter home for disabled soldiers. Richmond back then had its fair share of moneyed patrons, but nothing resembling what it possesses today. For example, and off the top of my head, Mick Jagger, Ron Wood, Ginger Baker, John Mills, Tommy Steele, Princess Alexandra and the Goldsmith family, live on, in, or near the park.

I passed my driving test in April 1965 and nobody but nobody under 25 owned a car including me. My father owned a Cortina and I was allowed to drive it every muckspreading. As the sixties moved inexorably forward, my apprenticeship's end was in sight, compared with most students I was, shall we say, off the pace. I finished my training and put in place a ten-year timescale to become self-employed, as it was becoming obvious of my dislike for taking orders. As it turned out, I waited only about six years to join the self-employed black economy. Towards the end of the sixties, the Beatles and Tamla Motown had fractured, Cassius Clay had morphed into Mohammed Ali, and I was still an idiot.

Nevertheless my status as an employee was coming to an end. My hand was forced because of Lambeth Council's insistence that all workers on our site join their union. I left the brickwork sub-contractor for this site and rather than look for another job, decided to go it alone, aged about 28. Soon after and with one child we moved to another area where I had to start from scratch. The house we bought required rather a lot of work to become habitable, so the conundrum was thus. Work for a local builder while I put myself about or, bite the bullet, and become self-employed, the rest as they say is history.

I started the decade a boy, finished it as a dumb idiot.

My life as a kid was not good, but I survived the decade. The sixties promised much change, both political and social. In my opinion very little transformation has actually taken place. In fact we now have a situation mentioned several times earlier in this book where firstly the family unit (in my case not good) continued to self-destruct , social groups moving away from the old family unit.

Nobody of moderate awareness should fail to take heed of the implications to our conscience or indeed to our world. To me we are going backwards as we go forward. Secondly, change we were told was coming fast, so, consider this, 50 years ago the space race started, are we to accept we still send a man up into space on the back of a firework? Technological cherry picking is at work here, as is money changing hands on a colossal scale worldwide. Do some research into Nicola Tesla's life and works in the early nineteen hundreds. Now apply what he achieved then, and bring technology up to date. See a discrepancy? Go figure it.

The Modern World

If aliens came down to earth I think they'd find that our world problems have more similarities than differences. Or put another way, that we as human beings are breaking this planet apart piece by piece, fuelled in part by the financial elite pulling the strings. By that I mean the banks and financial houses worldwide with their headlong rush to profits.

Everyone knows that technology does exist to run a car on water, or to get energy from the sun, and that with sufficient investment modern technology can deliver cheap global energy for all. Why is this not happening? The oil companies and energy consortiums and their bankers would lose power overnight. In a profit driven system the world exists to suit the corporatocracy, and just like a dictator they will squeeze us all till subjugation is inevitable. America is at the very heart of this mess. The biggest industry in the States is defence manufacturing, and so without running wars America would suffer more than most. They cannot be blamed for all the world's problems, after all most technological advancements worth their salt originated from the '60s space race.

I could go on and on looking for the answers, so may I suggest you read again the newspaper column about heroes, most specifically the last line.

My ex father-in-law, the professor of entomology, once told me that most of the drug companies used to send him blank cheques to write his own salary to work for them only. He resisted to his credit. When questioning him about the absence or otherwise of boyhood diseases, for example whooping cough, polio and scarlet fever, he told me the drug companies would have us all believe they were responsible for the eradication of these and other worldwide afflictions. However, he went on to tell me that improved living and sanitary condictions plus better food played the major part in all our young lives and not vaccinations. Coming from anybody else's father-in-law this might not carry much credence, but this is coming from the number one research scientist on the planet in his chosen field of entomology i.e. leishmaniasis.

Justice will not be served until those that are unaffected are as outraged as those that are
                                                              *- **Benjamin Franklin***

New Beginnings

All I know is that I know nothing   *- **Socrates, and I***

If I haven't sent you to sleep yet, I have one more tale to tell, probably my last. Nearing seventy years of age, my last chapter has started with a bang and a new relationship; not with a woman but with a loud fast talking Indian from Robin Hood's neck of the woods. A bang, because having started playing table tennis five years ago and not progressing that much, the penny has now dropped as to how far I can advance in nationwide competitions. The reason for this 'bang' if you're wondering, having watched the world champion table tennis player on telly, I started to realise that he like me, has only two arms and two legs. Therefore there was no obvious reason why I couldn't do some of the same shots he does. As it turns out with some practice, I could do those similar shots on occasion and this changed my mind set to believe that I could develop further, my first competition coming eight days after my 70th birthday.

Back to my newest mate called Torchy, so called according to him, because he is always ready, or should that be randy (?), make of that what you will. Now, bearing in mind I don't drink , gamble, smoke, take drugs, like cars or motor bikes, my choices of male friends are somewhat limited, nevertheless my visits to his launderette became more and more frequent until he would not let me leave until we had partaken of lunch and supper. What sets this friendship apart - surely you don't think I was shagging him do you? - is the small matter of complete trust in one another, a very rare commodity in this day and age. You may recall those prophetic words from Bill Young earlier in the book, when confronted by incompetence he would proffer "he should be working in a launderette, washing out socks!!" Ha, ha. I, of course, remind him daily.

Builders and sock washers, excuse the pun, trade insults in the most affectionate way, so I wrote an expose of his shop which follows in its entirety at the end of this passage. Torch has without a doubt reaffirmed my belief that other males can also be benevolent without an ulterior motive. His family and I get on brilliantly together, making the back end of my life so enjoyable. I feel it is pertinent to say that Torch is twenty years my junior, something he never misses the opportunity to mention. As you will read shortly, four or five other assorted degenerates hang around the launderette; however, we all have skills we freely share without remuneration.

The following passage I wrote and pinned up in Torch's launderette:

Tucked away in a quiet village on the south coast is a place so funny and full of bullshit, both clean and dirty (pun intended) that I must spill all.
The owner Torchy, who thinks his battery will run forever - boy has he got a shock coming - is a Sikh from Nottingham. He used to be a cab driver. He thinks Bolivia is in Africa. How in hell did he survive all those years with his sense of direction? He can eat for England and India and is also a shrinking violet. He nearly killed himself in a car accident recently, tearing a fearful lump out of his arm. I suggested that, rather than opting for a painful skin graft, why not cut two inches off his dick and pop this in the hole. That did not go down too well with his girlfriend.

Soon after, Torch was talking to a man in the shop, who had a thalidomide wife with short arms. Now Torch was complaining about his ripped up arm when this man said: I don't know what you are moaning for, my wife would love an arm like yours When we three stopped laughing,*) I ventured "what, even a black one?"

Next up is Breeze, Torchie's brother, moody and brooding, a ticking time bomb of malevolence. A heart attack victim himself, he could induce one in anybody, just with a stare that curdles the blood. Torch and brother can recognize a car make, colour, engine size and occupant from atop the post office tower at midnight, during an eclipse. Quite a talent I suppose, but for WHAT? Seeing as one has no car and the other a Nissan Micra with an engine smaller than that of my lawnmower, neither has in fact a vehicle between them.

Dick, bless him, has trouble breathing on account of his verbal diarrhoea. He can be really funny in an anarchic way.

Russell, on first name terms with old bill and social services respectively, is an ex drug dealer and user who is slowly turning his life around with girlfriend Treacle (as in tart) and her two children who he has taken on. He likes a laugh and a drink, although not necessarily in that order and knows everybody within twenty miles of the shop.

Dan left home early to join the army which he left ten years later. He is now a self-confessed psycho with anger management issues. Funny, how I did not see the need to spend years fighting, to end up just so. Dan now wants to fight anybody, especially the army and all vicars.
Philip, an autistic antelope, who craves to live in a world full of lions and tigers, regularly gets eaten alive by all and sundry, but still maintains he is in control. He came into the shop with a two foot long plastic curved horn from which he was drinking coffee. He told Torch that it was a convenient drinking vessel. Next time Philip showed up Torch had placed a disposable cup inside an old boot he found and proceeded to drink from it. Philip enquired as to what he was doing and Torch replied "it is a convenient drinking vessel". We have heard Philip described in the shop as odd, bonkers, off his head and the often mentioned 'who the hell is that'. Any person that has eight televisions in his flat, all operating at the same time on the same program, qualifies in my eyes as being strange.

Next up is David, the oldest member of our posse. To say that David is slow moving is to say he is slower than a tortoise with piles. One day he passed Breeze in the doctor's surgery saying 'can't stop I'm in a HURRY'. Bless him he takes it all and gives it back.

Shane, another car nut, although being red haired he is now known as ginger nut. Four years in the army, he is said to have poisoned half his battalion in his guise as the army's top bottom chef.

Other regulars worthy of mention are Lisa, who likes to whine with her washing and Sara, a lesbian anarchist, who is a very good girl and the author who is often described as big headed, arrogant and a know all, particularly by Philip.

All of us, except the owner, are fools as he is the only one getting paid, while we provide all the daily entertainment free. We do receive biscuits and tea plus whatever else he put in the cups when we are not paying attention.

If I have left anybody out, you can't have been deemed worthy of a mention at the launderette of life. Go Sikh and ye shall find.

The man himself, on this day dressed curiously like a lifeguard

An old lady fell over outside his shop at about 8:45 in the morning. Onlookers carried the stricken lady into the empty shop and laid her on a bench and left, saying the laundry man will be here shortly. Unbelievable! Torch turned up 15 minutes later, dressed her bloody wound and called an ambulance, saw her off to hospital, picked up her car and deposited it back at her home. Good guy or what!

A week later old David in our posse was crossing the road in front of the shop carrying his and Torch's lunch when a stranger turned up saying "are you Torch? Here is your lunch." "Good" said Torch. "I'm starving. Where is David?" "Lying in the road" said the stranger. Torch ran out and found David prostrate on the ground, picked him up and sat a dazed

297

David in the shop. He also went to A & E where Torch found himself later that night. The staff nurse said "do you make a habit of bringing old folks here"? He replied "no I am just coming to collect the £30 he owes me for his washing!!" The lady had a broken wrist and David ten stitches in his head.

In A & E, after his van rolled over, he was lying in bed with his arm ripped open, obviously in pain; several times the nurse said she could not give him any pain killers until the doctor arrives. I remarked "if we need drugs, Russell would get here quicker than the doctor!"

Given all that you have read about me it will not come as a surprise that I'm still superbly fit. And my table tennis journey starts now at 70 - how exciting is that! Having stated many times in this book that male friends are for me at a premium, I now have three or four of the very best. How lucky am I to receive such a gift this late in life.

Epilogue

What have I learnt from putting this book together? Clearly my vocabulary has gone through the roof, as has my recall of events of a long time since past. My hopes for the future, whilst not promising are indeed much worse than I could ever state here, but I will indeed try.

Family unity seems to have been destroyed by successive government legislation, leaving insurance companies filling the fear-filled vacuum. Children grow up fearing to climb trees, new parents fearing the wrath of health and safety morons knocking on the door, wanting to know why Johnny was climbing trees and why has Johnny got a bump on his face.

What has any of this got to do with anybody else but a parent? A preponderance of single parent families clearly can't help, but surely the parent must be heard loudest, and if not, why not?

You should not bite the hand that feeds you, but maybe you should, if it prevents you from feeding yourself   *- Thomas Szasz*

Fear is all over the TV and newspapers, in our face 24/7, but, what are we in fear of? My belief that human beings are essentially benevolent has taken a real knock in the last 30 years or so is evidenced by people's headlong rush to pursue things that they do not need. Possessions are sought, egged on by marketing rhetoric telling mostly the young they will be left behind unless they have this or that. Years ago this was referred to as keeping up with the Joneses.

People were created to be loved, things were created to be used, the reason the world is in chaos is because things are being loved and people are being used. Add to the family equation the fact that we are almost taxed out of existence.

The very people who are set up to help us all, politicians and the police, exist to help themselves anyway they see fit.

When I look back, the seeds were there, but a need to work and eat took preference over critical thinking. Now the distraction is not just the former, but Ex-factor and EastEnders filling people's thought processes, depriving them of thinking for themselves. Open your mind to the real matter facing mankind; don't believe anything the government tells you unless they provide collaborative proof. You will have gathered I'm not about to roll over and accept this tripe, why should we?

Where is the world headed in 50 years or so, and should I care as I will be pushing up daisies by then. I consider that as a conscionable human being in my opinion we all must care like never before. If we don't we will end up being subservient to the state, exactly the reason so many people died in the war to save us from being so.

Another clear and obvious way - which our rulers claim is in our own interest to pursue - is the possible removal of the jury system. Juries are said to be incapable of understanding the law, so moves are afoot to replace them with a judge to adjudicate. *Resist this with all your might,* for the following reasons: Jurists whilst carrying out their task have powers beyond their normal thinking process, when finished they return to their own normality, unhindered by the consequences, gaining neither profit nor power. On the other hand a judge's power and influence will in all likelihood be enhanced greatly over time. Common law reduced further than the events at Runnymede intended. The judiciary and judges specifically in years to come will be all powerful, as would the police as a consequence also become. This is the last bastion of people power and must be retained if for no other reason than the men and women who died in the war to protect it.

Trust, what is it?

Trust to me is a beautiful thing to behold, that makes my very existence in life easier on a day to day basis.

It is painful to recall here that it soon crumbles when put to the test by ordinary things in everyday life. My experience as a self-employed man of many, many years propels me to believe that it has largely disappeared from most social positions that I have encountered throughout my life. Some members of my own family regard me as a black sheep simply because trust has broken down, with my desire to be upfront about everything.

Where has it gone?

Trust between builder and client is almost an afterthought of some forty years vintage. Looking back - not a good idea – I shudder at the past conversations that turned nasty because of breakdown of trust. If someone is aware of you being extremely trust worthy it often means they will eventually and evidently take advantage, and there are lots of advantages to be had. I suppose the question should be not, where has it gone but why has it gone? For the answer to that, look around your locality at TV cameras everywhere.

If the government doesn't trust you, why should we trust each other? If you are inconvenienced by a policeman stopping your car, why does he start the conversation believing you are automatically going to lie or mislead him? The powers that be are in my opinion institutionalised fear mongers creating mistrust among communities everywhere.

You will have read in a past chapter how a high court judge in her wisdom found against me because she did not believe one neighbour could be so kind to another, preferring to believe some other motive that she did not find, simply because it did not exist. This is very worrying for her workload moving forward. If this is an isolated incident, shame on me, if it is not, shame on everybody in positions of power and influence.

People will say to me this is just the way of the world, but not for me. Helping others is a clear theme throughout this book and my dotage will not cure me of this proclivity, nor will judge Williams. By the way I do intend to see that they get a copy of this book.

I can use a computer, but I am not an advocate of any form of control other than our own self. A policeman told me a while ago that they can check on the contents of every pc that you or I own without either having accessed your pc or having had your permission, which of course begs the question, can the police introduce something on your computer without your knowledge? Without doubt the technology does exist, can they, would they? Look around, the evidence of global control is everywhere. I am severely troubled at my children's potential future, and even more so at their children's fate.

It is regretted that the rich and powerful too often bend the acts of government to their own selfish purposes - **Andrew Jackson**

In my opinion one single statute would change every human being's life for the better, and for ever. This being, our governments around the world should be taking responsibility for printing their own money, on behalf of their people. What in effect we have is the bankers charging governments interest (government debt) that will rise and fall but can **never ever ever be paid back.** A perpetual and everlasting banker's control mechanism, that will enslave us all eventually. It would seem the only way this would change is if the Bank of England (absolutely no affiliation with England or its people) is closed down and the government governs themselves, instead of borrowing from the bank of England, what is in effect our money and making us liable for the debt. As seen recently in Ireland and Iceland (with very different results).

Debt; an ingenious substitute for the chain and whip of the slave trader - **Ambrose Bierce**

(You what?! You didn't know the Bank of England and the Federal Reserve in America are not run by government? Don't take my word for it, go check who the Bank of England's directors are, you will not find out. Somerset House in London lists all company directors but not it seems in this case – why not? Suspicious? You bet it is, no, it is pure evil.)

Weapons of Mass Deception

Television started about the same time as I was able to think cognitive thoughts, late 50s early 60s give or take a few years, this being my formative years as an apprentice and thinking adult. In the subsequent 50 years or so some thoughts on how the gogglebox had aligned with mainstream media to manipulate our lives subliminally. Today's mass media preaches on a daily basis extreme materialism, spiritual vacuosity and a self centered individualistic existence. This is the exact opposite of the attributes required to become and stay a truly free individual. Today's media propaganda almost never uses rational or logical arguments, nevertheless popular culture caters to and nurtures ignorance by continually serving up brain numbing entertainment and spotlighting degenerative celebrities to be idolised. As someone with a ruthless application of simple logic – seen throughout this book – I am unable to process such tripe in any meaningful way.

Marketing on TV now requires us to swallow downright lies and untruths in the most matter of fact way. The subliminal message clearly is preparing the masses to accept lies and decit as normal. Is there a way to stop this madness? Please bon't buy this crap!

The truth will set you free but first it will piss you off   - **Anon**

I would not like you to think that the covers of this book were too far apart

- Ambrose Bierce

Printed in Great Britain
by Amazon

22494360R00170